Decentralization, Democratic Governance, and Civil Society in Comparative Perspective

Decentralization, Democratic Governance, and Civil Society in Comparative Perspective

Africa, Asia, and Latin America

Edited by

Philip Oxhorn, Joseph S. Tulchin, and Andrew D. Selee

Woodrow Wilson Center Press
Washington, D.C.

The Johns Hopkins University Press
Baltimore and London

EDITORIAL OFFICES

Woodrow Wilson Center Press
One Woodrow Wilson Plaza
1300 Pennsylvania Avenue, N.W.
Washington, D.C. 20004-3027
www.wilsoncenter.org

Order from

The Johns Hopkins University Press
Hampden Station
P.O. Box 50370
Baltimore, Maryland 21211
Telephone 1-800-537-5487
www.press.jhu.edu

2 4 6 8 9 7 5 3 1

Library of Congress Cataloging-in-Publication Data

Decentralization, democratic governance, and civil society in comparative perspective :
  Africa, Asia, and Latin America / edited by Philip Oxhorn, Joseph S. Tulchin,
  and Andrew D. Selee.
      p.   cm.
  Includes bibliographical references and index.
  ISBN 0-8018-7919-1 (hardcover : alk. paper)
  1. Decentralization in government—Africa.   2. Decentralization in government
—Asia.   3. Decentralization in government—Latin America.   4. Local
government—Africa.   5. Local government—Asia.   6. Local government—Latin
America.   I. Oxhorn, Philip.   II. Tulchin, Joseph S, 1939–   III. Selee, Andrew D.

JQ1875.A55D423 2004
320.8–dc22   2004001537

ABOUT THE CENTER

The Center is the living memorial of the United States of America to the nation's twenty-eighth president, Woodrow Wilson. Congress established the Woodrow Wilson Center in 1968 as an international institute for advanced study, "symbolizing and strengthening the fruitful relationship between the world of learning and the world of public affairs." The Center opened in 1970 under its own board of trustees.

In all its activities the Woodrow Wilson Center is a nonprofit, nonpartisan organization, supported financially by annual appropriations from the Congress, and by the contributions of foundations, corporations, and individuals. Conclusions or opinions expressed in Center publications and programs are those of the authors and speakers and do not necessarily reflect the views of the Center staff, fellows, trustees, advisory groups, or any individuals or organizations that provide financial support to the Center.

Contents

Preface

In the last two decades, in almost every part of the world, the seeds of electoral democracy have been planted. In some countries, it has flowered; in others it has taken root. While the nature or strength of these democratic regimes has been the subject of intense and protracted debate, most analysts agree that, whatever their definition of democracy or their appraisal of the quality of existing democratic regimes, there is "more" democracy today than there was ten or twenty years ago. At the same time (and often, although not always, related to processes of democratization), most countries in the developing world have undergone processes of decentralization in which local and regional governments have been granted increasing authority and functions.

The Woodrow Wilson Center began a project to explore the effects that decentralization is having on the relationship between citizens and the state in the developing world and, more generally, on the quality of democracy. Looking cross-regionally at Africa, Asia, and Latin America, we hoped to have a better sense of the forces—both explicit and implicit—driving decentralization and the consequences these have had in the actual configurations of decentralized governance that have emerged. The approach involved looking simultaneously at both the macro-level forces driving decentralization and the micro-level responses from civil society and local governments in order to understand better the impact of decentralization on democratic governance. Further research remains to be done on the functions and performance of local government and the consequences of their increased role for citizenship and social participation.

On February 20–21, 2001, the Wilson Center hosted a meeting of eleven researchers from six countries to discuss initial findings. Subsequently, the researchers presented papers that have been revised to become part of this volume. Phil Oxhorn chaired the meeting and made formal comments on the papers.

This work has been generously supported by a grant from the Ford Foundation field offices in Santiago, Chile; Mexico City, Mexico; Johannesburg, South Africa; Nairobi, Kenya; Manila, Philippines; and Jakarta, Indonesia; and has particularly benefited throughout from the guidance of Augusto Varas, Ford Foundation representative in Santiago, Chile.

James Manor, Aprodocio Laquian, Jonathan Fox, and Gary Bland offered helpful comments that greatly improved the quality of the manuscript. Richard Stren, Joan Nelson, Gary Bland, Bob Hathaway, and Nancy Popson attended the February meeting and made helpful comments that assisted in the preparation of this volume. Andrew Stevenson, Dominic Nahas, Lia Limon, and Craig Fagan provided important research assistance to the editors.

Above all, this volume is a product of the incisive work of the researchers who have participated in the project and whose work gives substance to this book.

—Joseph S. Tulchin and Andrew D. Selee

Decentralization, Democratic Governance, and Civil Society in Comparative Perspective

Introduction

Chapter 1

Unraveling the Puzzle of Decentralization

Philip Oxhorn

One of the most striking, but probably least noticed, political trends today is that of state decentralization. Nearly every country in the world, regardless of its political system, geographical location, history, level of economic development and cultural traditions, is now experimenting with new forms of regional and local governance.[1] Only economic liberalization is perhaps more widespread among policy reforms. Significantly less widespread, but much more dramatic and with a far more uncertain future, has been the so-called "third wave" of democratic transitions.[2]

These three processes—decentralization, economic liberalization, and democratic transition—are often intimately intertwined, yet it is not always clear how. It seems that every imaginable sequence, from authoritarian imposition of, first, economic liberalization, then decentralization and, finally, democratization (Chile under Pinochet), to democratization, then economic

I would like to thank Joseph Tulchin, Andrew Selee, Augusto Varas, and Gary Bland for their helpful comments on an earlier draft.

liberalization and, as the culmination of reform processes, decentralization (Bolivia beginning in the mid-1980s) has occurred somewhere in the world. Given so much variation, one cannot discard the possibility that any relationship is merely coincidental, and that the logics driving each process are so distinct that there is no necessary or even ideal sequence.[3] Moreover, while there is a growing body of theoretical and empirical research dealing with economic liberalization and national democratic processes, the study of decentralization has lagged, and there is still much that we cannot even pretend to understand.

The present volume is an attempt to begin to address this empirical lacuna. It provides a foundation for important theoretical insights regarding both the nature and significance of decentralization, as well as its relationship to other processes of political and economic reform. In this chapter, I sketch out the broad theoretical approach taken by the authors. More specifically, I emphasize the importance of understanding decentralization as a multidimensional concept focusing on citizen participation or democratization, subnational autonomy or governance, and the importance of viewing subnational governments in relation to the central state.[4] The usefulness of this approach is underscored by a discussion of two fundamental sources of ambiguity surrounding the political and economic impact of decentralization processes: first, the ambiguous and contradictory empirical outcomes associated with decentralization processes and, second, a theoretical antinomy that is the result of often contradictory theoretical traditions that might influence the potential of decentralization policy prescriptions. Together, these ambiguities account for both the decidedly mixed outcomes of decentralization in most cases, including those studied in this volume, as well as the potential that decentralization offers for strengthening democratic regimes and civil society. As the contributors to this volume all emphasize, the challenge is to continue to take advantage of the spaces decentralization necessarily opens up, even in closed political systems, to realize decentralization's full democratizing potential. The chapter then ends with an overview of the findings from the case studies.

Decentralization as a Multidimensional Process

One of the goals of the present volume is to begin to develop a theoretical focus for understanding actual, dynamic processes of decentralization that can direct research in ways that will help fill the various empirical and theoretical lacunae. Such lacunae stem, in part, from the tendency in the vast majority of studies to characterize decentralization policies in terms of three discrete (albeit related) types that are distinguished by the degree of autonomy exercised by subnational levels of government vis-à-vis the central state apparatus. Most of these studies work with or modify the distinctions made by Rondinelli[5]: deconcentration, delegation, and devolution.[6] All three reflect varying levels of authority assigned to subnational levels of government by reforms in the central state apparatus. Deconcentration reflects the decentralization of policy administration or implementation, while policy continues to be made at the central level. Delegation includes some transfer of decision-making authority, although the central state still reserves control over key aspects of policy. Finally, devolution entails maximum decision-making authority for subnational governmental institutions. By necessity, devolution also is assumed to include a significant level of financial autonomy through guaranteed fiscal transfers from the central state and/or significant revenue-generating capacity at the level of the subnational institutions themselves.

The problem with this approach is that decentralization needs to be conceptualized along a continuum that reflects the often dynamic relations between national and subnational levels of government, and avoids oversimplifying a more complex reality. First, levels of autonomy often vary according to issue area, and some issue areas are more important than others. For example, there is undoubtedly a higher level of local autonomy concerning the issue of trash collection, even while more important policies relating to sanitation and environmental regulation are decided exclusively by national authorities. Second, even the limited spaces for autonomy associated with deconcentration can lead to demands for greater levels of autonomy as actors emerge within society to take advantage of those spaces. This is something that is emphasized in all of the case studies. Moreover, such actors may emerge because of frustrated expectations that the decentralization process itself generates, either because it falsely raised expectations for greater local control and/or because the central state is either incapable of and/or unwilling to address real problems in those areas for which it still retains significant authority. For example, central states may delegate substantial authority to local governments for the administration of national educational policies, but if those policies do not result in a greater educational performance for their children, communities may very well demand more power to determine the content of those policies.[7] For all of these reasons, even limited decentralization helps strengthen civil society.[8]

At the opposite extreme, devolution, the continued role of the central state apparatus may be lost in the analysis. "Autonomy" cannot imply that there is no relationship between different levels of government, and there is a danger of ignoring the ongoing political struggles and potential synergies involved in those relations. A high level of autonomy for local authorities, for example, does not mean that they will not continue to place demands on the central state apparatus, and vice versa. It is this continuing relationship that will define the quality of decentralized governance over time. This was clearly true in each of the case studies. Kenya stands out in this regard because of the weakness of its central state institutions. As the chapter by Mitullah and Khadiagala in this volume shows, Kenya's state has become a "lame leviathan" that is incapable of providing basic services. The void created by the virtual collapse of the state has forced Kenyan society to adopt desperate self-help measures, underscoring in a dramatic way the need for strong state institutions (democratic or otherwise) at the local level. For this reason, following Manor,[9] privatization of state-owned enterprises and services, as well as "privatization by default" resulting from the incapacity of the state to provide basic services, are not considered part of state decentralization processes. In these situations, such activities are external to the state apparatus at all levels by definition. They represent the shrinking of the state, deliberate in the case of privatization and unavoidable in the case of decentralization by default.

A similar kind of problem stems from the overwhelming tendency in the literature to equate devolution or maximum autonomy with local democracy. Normatively, this represents an ideal of democratic subnational self-government in its most inclusive sense, and this is certainly the goal shared by all of the authors in this project. The problem is that it can have the effect of conflating, both theoretically and empirically, two distinct processes. Historically, subnational autonomy has greatly outpaced the democratization of those institutions. Indeed, before the onset of the "centralizing orthodoxy" of the postwar period and the "third wave" of democratization beginning in the mid-1970s,[10] fairly autonomous subnational level governing bodies were much more the norm, and many, if not most, of these were hardly democratic in the modern sense of accountable governments selected through relatively free and competitive elections in which all adult citizens could vote. This was certainly true of New Haven until relatively recently in Dahl's classic study of local democracy,[11] and it is much more consistent with the experience of Western Europe over the centuries. Even today, when the democratic impulse behind decentralization is probably greater than ever before, subnational levels of government can be bulwarks for authoritarian practices.

From this perspective, what stands out in the six cases in this volume is a certain paradox: to a greater or lesser extent, subnational democratization has *outpaced* the level of autonomy accorded subnational governments by the central state. Rather than following an implicit teleology going from deconcentration through (democratic) devolution, the level of subnational democratization seems to vary independently of the level of decision-making authority invested by the central government in lower levels of government.

Chile illustrates this basic indeterminacy well. As Serrano and Ducci show in their respective chapters, the military government delegated increasing responsibility to subnational levels of government for administration in key policy areas, including education, health care and public investment. Regardless of this, the autonomy of subnational governments was nonexistent since all officials were also appointed by the military regime. This changed only in 1992 (two years after the transition to democracy), when constitutional amendments provided for the election of local governments, increasing their autonomy considerably. Yet key policy decisions are still made at the level of the central government, suggesting a pattern similar to other cases. At the same time, the democratization of regional governments remains limited and indirect.[12]

To address these issues, the authors in the present volume have adopted a simple, straightforward definition of decentralization that highlights what we consider to be its fundamental characteristic. For the purposes of this volume, decentralization is understood as *the transfer of power to different subnational levels of government by the central government.* As a minimum, decentralization consists of what is generally characterized as deconcentration, but beyond that, the exact characteristics of decentralization are determined by a variety of factors unique to each case. As such, decentralization is necessarily a multidimensional process. To better understand this, the authors of each of the case studies organized their research on an empirical foundation that included: (1) a general overview of the institutional setting in each case; (2) a general overview of the principal actors at the national, regional and local levels; and (3) a general overview of the critical issues in each case that decentralization might address.

In all case studies, three dimensions in particular stand out.[13] The first dimension of decentralization can be understood as the levels of autonomy subnational governments enjoy vis-à-vis the central state in terms of *governance.* By governance, I am referring to the capacity of subnational governments to control their own affairs in terms of policy design and implementation. This necessarily includes the financial resources and technical capacity available to subnational levels of government.[14] It is also independent of the level of democratization of those governments, which is the second dimension of decentralization. The idea of governance better reflects why the autonomy of subnational levels of government matters: it matters because it allows these levels of government to determine to a greater or lesser degree political processes in their respective jurisdictions. But the issue of democratization refers specifically to *who* is actually responsible for exercising such autonomy to the extent that it exists. In the six countries included in this volume, it is generally democratically elected governments, although regional governments in Chile and village heads in Indonesia are exceptions.

At the same time, such autonomy can only be understood in terms of the central state apparatus. This is the third dimension of decentralization. Again, it is important to emphasize the essential role played by the central state in conditioning the quality of local and regional governance. As the chapter on Kenya demonstrates, the central state plays a vital role in supporting subnational levels of government that cannot be easily replaced. The burden of a "lame leviathan" is as problematic for local governance and development as that of the much stronger centralizing states that decentralization was intended to alleviate in the first place. Moreover, regardless of their de facto levels of autonomy from the central state, subnational governments are often confronted by the stigma of suspicion and distrust associated with corrupt, illegitimate central states, even after transitions to democracy. This is clearest in the case studies of South Africa and Kenya, but hardly limited to them as the case studies of Mexico and the Philippines suggest.[15]

In terms of the state, one should also not underestimate the significance of the fact that most programs of decentralization were initially designed and implemented by political elites at the level of the central state, with little, if any, input from societal actors. In the case studies included in this volume, this was largely the case, with the partial exception of the Philippines (owing to the unique nature of its transition to democracy). After decentralization has been first implemented this situation frequently changes as societal actors seek to influence the continued evolution of decentralization.[16] Of the countries included in this volume, Chile is a good example of this. When the political opposition to the military regime assumed power in

1990, it championed the democratization of local governments whose role had been significantly expanded by the military regime's decentralization policies. Mexico is also a good example, where opposition parties were able to successfully use the political space opened by the regime's initial, limited decentralization efforts to eventually force a transition to democracy in the 2000 presidential elections. While the process is still in its infancy, decentralization in Indonesia appears to be following a similar course, and as the chapter by Hidayat and Antlöv suggests, local actors may even have blocked recentralizing reforms being planned at the national level. But even belated societal influence on the course of decentralization is by no means automatic, as is clear in the chapters by Serrano and Ducci when discussing regional governments in Chile, as well as in Friedman and Kihato's chapter on South Africa.

This does not mean that research should be motivated by an overly idealistic or romantic view of local actors—in effect committing the opposite error.[17] Rather, what is required is a more critical perspective that addresses the ways in which elite processes condition the institutions associated with decentralization and their impact on society and politics. This is what the authors in this volume have done in the course of their in-depth case studies.

More generally, decentralization should be viewed as part of a larger process of the *social construction of citizenship,* in which who participates and who does not matters.[18] As Charles Tilly notes, historically, it was the "struggle and bargaining between expanding states and their subjects [that] created citizenship where it had not previously existed."[19] In a similar vein, the importance of different forms of mobilization and participation by subordinate groups in transitions to democracy is often emphasized,[20] and it was certainly a decisive factor in each of the cases studied in this volume. By including societal actors in the democratization process at any level, democratic ideals are not only realized in practice, but the resulting institutional and normative results will better reflect the varied interests within society. The consensus upon which democratic institutions are consolidated will be more broadly based as well. Conversely, the problem with so-called pacted democracies from this perspective is that participation in their construction is limited to select groups within society.[21] And the principal challenge posed by pacts is to expand the participation of excluded groups, overcoming the initial limitations of the democratic process.

The same can be said of democratic decentralization, viewing it as fundamentally similar to democratization processes at the level of the political

regime or central state. While it is obvious that the ideal of democratic decentralization can be realized only by maximizing direct citizen participation once the requisite institutions are in place, it may be less obvious that
such participation is also dependent on how those institutions are designed.
For this reason, it is imperative that the institutions of decentralization be
designed with this political goal in mind.[22] Although political elites, especially democratically elected ones, in a number of countries have placed a
priority on democratic decentralization in the absence of strong citizen pressures for it, the case studies and larger literature on decentralization all suggest that democratization often is not a central concern of policymakers,
even democratically elected ones such as South Africa's African National
Congress (ANC), the Concertación governments in Chile and the first two
democratic governments in Indonesia after the fall of Suharto, when addressing the institutions of regional government. The case studies also make
clear that one reason for this is the lack of social mobilization in favor of
stronger democratic decentralization, while it is equally clear in the case of
the Philippines that social mobilization contributed to the democratization
of subnational levels of government there. In Mexico, as the chapters by
Mizrahi and Santín demonstrate, such mobilization was also critical for
overcoming the clearly undemocratic goals of Mexico's decentralizing
policymakers. Moreover, when designing the institutions for democratic decentralization, even well-intentioned elites can benefit from the input of the
societal actors who will ultimately have the largest stake in realizing successful democratic decentralization, as is underscored by the still-evolving
process of decentralization in Indonesia.

Most importantly, the concept of the social construction of citizenship
emphasizes the dynamic nature of decentralization processes and the potential for even the most limited political openings at the local level to
evolve into something approaching the ideal of democratic decentralization.
As the authors in this volume emphasize, it is this potential that offers the
most promise for addressing basic issues of socioeconomic development,
democracy, and inclusion. Yet because decentralization is a multidimensional process, it is important to constantly keep that goal in mind, both in
designing (or redesigning and improving) the institutions of subnational
government, and in trying to encourage greater citizen involvement in democratic processes at all levels of government. It is also a challenge in that
decentralization processes, both in practice and in theory, can be associated
with a variety of political and economic outcomes that reflect the fundamental ambiguity of decentralization.

The Fundamental Ambiguity of Decentralization

The six countries studied in this volume represent a wide range of outcomes associated with decentralization. This reflects not only the multidimensional, dynamic nature inherent in decentralization processes, but also two fundamental ambiguities that further complicate the challenge of achieving something approaching the ideal of democratic decentralization: first, the ambiguous and contradictory empirical outcomes associated with decentralization processes, and second, the theoretical antinomy that is the result of often contradictory theoretical traditions that might influence the potential of decentralization policy prescriptions. To understand this, it is important to first briefly recap what could be described as the almost revolutionary whirlwind of economic and political liberalization that forms the larger context within which decentralization processes have unfolded over the past two decades.

In the aftermath of the Great Depression of the 1920s and the rise of the Keynesian welfare state, it seemed as if a strong, central state could do no wrong. The success of the Marshall Plan and state planning in West European and Japanese postwar reconstruction, as well the growing economic power and political influence of the Soviet Union, meant that centralization became the guiding principle for major policy initiatives the world over. For the developing world, particularly in newly independent countries, this implied that a strong, centralized state apparatus was the key to national development and modernity. While centralized political authority had a long history throughout Latin America and much of Asia, the *developmentalist state* became the goal of even the least economically advanced countries. Surprisingly, this statist vision transcended fundamental and often polemical debates regarding "development" and the meaning of "democracy" during the sixties and much of the seventies.[23]

In a similar (albeit much less rapid and dramatic) fashion, the central state's supremacy was more or less displaced in development dogma by international economic trends and the perceived failure of the previous policy paradigm. Internationally, the economic dislocations that began with the OPEC-induced oil price increases starting in 1973 and culminated in the late 1970s/early 1980s with stagflation and recession in the developed market economies, and the debt crisis and the "lost decade" of the 1980s in the developing world, underscored the need to find alternative economic policy models, even if there was no immediate consensus on what they should be. The Keynesian welfare state in the North and the developmentalist state in the South were perceived to enter into crisis. First Margaret Thatcher, then Ronald Reagan and Helmut Kohl, ushered in a new era of the minimalist state, fiscal restraint, and economic liberalization that hit the developing world with a vengeance. In this context, the so-called Washington Consensus[24] was born and then promoted by the same institutions that would quickly jump on the decentralization bandwagon.[25] The new economic orthodoxy was even adopted (in many cases reluctantly) by political actors who until relatively recently had championed strong centralized states. Among the countries studied in this volume, this was most noticeable for the ruling parties in South Africa (ANC), Kenya (Kenya African National Union, KANU), and Mexico (Partido Revolucionario Institucional, PRI). As the respective case studies make clear, however, for the latter two, decentralization was seen as a way for the ruling parties to stay in power given the economic dislocations associated with the change in development models. The PRI ultimately failed, despite itself, and the verdict is still out on the KANU, yet their respective decentralization processes have been marked by this instrumental recourse to decentralization in an effort to block more far-reaching political change.

Parallel to these trends in economic policy–making circles, many developing countries also underwent transitions to democracy. It is important to emphasize, however, that the two processes were independent of each other chronologically and reflected very different dynamics.[26] While economic liberalization and the downsizing of the central state could reinforce what are still generally fragile democratic regimes, the ways they are pursued can also undermine democracies by augmenting people's perceptions of physical and economic insecurity, contributing to the fragmentation of civil society and increasing socioeconomic inequality.[27] While democratic regimes retain historically high levels of legitimacy in most new democracies, they are also problematic in a number of ways that threaten their quality and prospects for genuine consolidation.[28] In particular, there is the danger that democracy itself may increasingly be seen as irrelevant for finding solutions to their most pressing needs as people are forced to resort to market-based mechanisms (including buying influence through various forms of corruption), patron–client relations and, when these fail, self-help measures just to cope.[29] This is already a serious concern in Kenya, as the chapter by Mitullah and Khadiagala graphically illustrates with their discussion of the "lame leviathan."

The ambiguous relationship between the two processes of economic and political liberalization is perhaps clearest in the often contradictory consequences they have for the decentralizing reforms. While we might like to equate decentralization with greater democratization due to its common-sense association with more citizen participation, accountability, and transparency in governmental decision making, the reality is often quite different. In one of the most comprehensive reviews of the literature on decentralization in developing countries, Manor[30] identified at least seven different objectives behind decentralization reforms. While greater democratization was certainly among them, it is clear that other goals were equally important, and in many cases predominant. In particular, policymakers, donor governments, and international institutions backing decentralization often see it as a mechanism for, among other things, limiting possibilities for rent seeking by decreasing the size of the central state apparatus, decreasing governmental expenditures, increasing economic efficiency, and allowing a greater role for market forces in promoting national economic development. In many cases, decentralization seems to be promoted as much because of policy *failures* of the central state than for any clear empirical or theoretical reasons for suggesting that local and regional levels of governance are intrinsically better or less likely to fail (or at least fail in the same ways). It is as if decentralization were the default option when no other viable alternatives are apparent. There is often the implicit assumption that local leadership is somehow better than national leadership, even though in practice it might be worse[31] and is almost inevitably less capable due to lack of resources, experience, and training.

Governing elites, however, may see decentralization as a way to hold on to power. By devolving responsibilities from the central state apparatus to local and regional levels, decentralization can help political elites to diffuse demands for greater political opening at the national level (see the chapters by Mizrahi, Santín, and Mitullah and Khadiagala in this volume) and/or increase their capacity for social control by using newly decentralized institutions to further penetrate society.[32] This was clearly the strategy of the Pinochet military regime in Chile, which instituted far-ranging policies of decentralization intended to, among other things, allow for greater penetration of society in order to repress political opposition and prevent the future resurgence of the political left without opening up institutional spaces for greater citizen participation.[33] But it is not only ruling elites that can see decentralization as a way to hold on to power in a changing world. As the chapter by Friedman and Kihato suggests, ethnic and racial minorities may view different forms of decentralization as a way to insulate themselves from majority rule.

These varying and often contradictory motives behind decentralization policies raise an interesting question in trying to understand decentralization processes: how do we evaluate their "success"? Were they successful in Mexico, for example, because they contributed to democratization, or did they fail because they did not meet policymakers' expectations for retaining power by diffusing the opposition and, as Mizrahi notes in her chapter, achieving genuine economic efficiency? Similarly, should "success" in Indonesia be measured in terms of the ability of decentralizing reforms to prevent national disintegration? Or should it be measured in terms of the increase in local democratization, even if this contributes to separatist movements as was the case of East Timor when a regional plebiscite was held? Obviously, the answers to these questions depend on the perspective adopted by the analyst, which in the literature (as well as in this volume) tends to equate successful decentralization with increased participation and democratization. But the very ambiguity of motives behind decentralization in practice suggests that such a perspective may prevent a more critical understanding of the actual dynamics of decentralization. At a minimum, the objectives that policymakers have in implementing decentralization, and the obstacles this may create to more democratic forms of decentralization, must be understood. Moreover, regardless of actual practice, the relationship between decentralization and democratization may itself be ambiguous in theory, a point I shall return to below.

There is a second, more serious, ambiguity in trying to understand decentralization processes. Regardless of the intentions of policymakers, multinational development banks, and other supporters of decentralization, decentralization can increase rather than decrease waste, inefficiency, rent seeking, and corruption. Indeed, the 1998–99 Brazilian economic crisis and the current economic crisis in Argentina both had their roots in profligate regional and local governments that were more concerned with creating sources of patronage and corruption than responsible economic policies, and the inability of the central state to impose financial restraint on them.[34] In South Africa, as Friedman and Kihato note in their chapter, similar problems have led to a significant recentralization of fiscal policy. Elsewhere, as the case of Kenya demonstrates, even fiscal collapse and massive state downsizing do not by themselves end the rent-seeking behavior, and may even lead to an escalation of corruption, patronage, and ethnic violence as elites refuse to relinquish power.[35] This reflects the tendency for local, particularly rural, and even regional levels of government to be bastions of conservative, if not reactionary, politics in many developing countries.

These clearly undemocratic consequences of decentralization may also reflect the fact that it has generally been an elite-led process in the developing world, with little, if any, grassroots mobilization demanding it or input into designing it. While noting that societal pressures often become quite influential after decentralization has been implemented, Manor observes: "Has pressure from ordinary people at the grass roots persuaded central authorities in some countries to decentralize? The answer must be: hardly at all."[36] In the cases examined in this volume, this lack of popular input into decentralization programs is clear (with the exception of the Philippines), even in the Mexican case where decentralization became the springboard for the opposition movements that ultimately forced a transition to democracy through their success at the national level. Aside from the doubts this raises about elite motives for adopting decentralization, one consequence is that there may be little counterweight to the negative outcomes that decentralization can engender. Indeed, in such contexts where civil society neither demands nor expects decentralization, traditional, nondemocratic practices might be reinforced as a result of the power decentralization grants local and regional authorities.[37] Despite recent advances, this is exactly what happened in the Philippines when that country enacted its first decentralizing reforms in the early 1900s.[38] In a similar vein, Friedman and Kihato argue in their chapter on South Africa that decentralization still "has not provided a vehicle for citizens' or civil society's participation and that it cannot . . . [due to the] legacy of a political tradition in which elites were deeply suspicious of local initiative and in which political culture made it easy for them, in the main, to persuade local activists and citizens not to use decentralized governance to build alternative sites of power and initiative."

In this context, even when democratization is the explicit goal behind decentralization, there is no guarantee that it will be achieved. Despite the tendency, in practice, to assume that the problems and shortcomings of the central state apparatus can be addressed by strengthening regional and local levels of government, there are no quick fixes. Problems of corruption, rent seeking, and lack of state capacity need to be addressed directly. Ignoring these problems at the national level only invites their repetition at lower levels of government. Ironically, local and regional levels of government might even be more vulnerable to such problems in previously centralized states because of the lack of any opportunity for capacity to be built at lower levels of government. Only the central state and, in many cases, externally funded NGOs can train people and build institutions that can allow for effective governance.[39]

It is important to emphasize, however, that subnational levels of government can be the source of new political alternatives and truly innovative policies for achieving greater levels of democratic inclusion. However critical, all authors in this volume agree on both the importance of the ideal of democratic decentralization and the very real possibilities that exist for increasing the democratic qualities of even the most limited forms of decentralization found in a country such as Kenya. At worst, the case studies in this volume conclude that the success of democratic decentralization has been mixed, but none show failure. Over time, even negative authoritarian tendencies can be reversed as local groups gain experience and confidence in participating in democratic processes, and elites compete to mobilize them.[40]

More generally, at least in Latin America, a number of center-left political alternatives in Latin America first emerged at the local and regional level. These have included Causa R in Venezuela, the Frente Amplio in Uruguay, Frente del País Solidario (FREPASO) in Argentina, and the Partido Trabalhista (PT) of Brazil, among others. Probably the most famous instance of this, however, was the recent democratic transition in Mexico, where the Party of the Democratic Revolution, as well as the more traditional center-right National Action Party together were able to end the control exercised by PRI for 70 years over the central state apparatus by building on local and regional electoral strength (see the chapters by Mizrahi and Santín in this volume). Many of these parties or movements have arisen as a direct response to the economic dislocations and rising inequality that have been a consequence of both the crisis of the developmental state and, more immediately, the adoption of policies of economic liberalization that are often associated with the growing trend toward state decentralization. This might suggest that one of the unintended consequences of state decentralization guided by purely economic and/or narrow political criteria might be actually be the rise of opposition movements championing both greater concern for democratic decentralization and social equity. To a certain extent, just such a dynamic is observable in Chile's Concertación party coalition, which has governed since the transition to democracy in 1990 (regardless of its lack of support for more democratic regional governments).[41]

The Theoretical Origins of Ambiguous Outcomes

In sum, from a purely empirical perspective, the outcomes and goals of decentralization are both ambiguous and contradictory. This is the first source of fundamental ambiguity in decentralization. Ironically, increased democratization and greater levels of citizen participation seem to be among the least common goals and even when they are high on policymakers' agendas, there is no guarantee that this will be the actual outcome.

What is perhaps even more surprising is that there are important theoretical debates that might explain why so many contradictory goals and outcomes are associated with decentralization. For example, in terms of economic theory, it is easy to forget that for most of the postwar period, economic "orthodoxy" was in many ways the mirror image of today's so-called Washington Consensus: high levels of central planning, economic strategies emphasizing protectionism in order to stimulate industrial production for national consumption, and inflexible labor markets reflecting a more pronounced political as well as economic role of organized labor throughout the world. Even profligate government spending or "economic populism" seemed justified, if not rational, given the spectacular success of the developmentalist state until severe economic crisis started to intervene in the 1970s and 1980s.[42] This suggests that a theoretical antinomy is the second fundamental source of ambiguity surrounding the decentralization puzzle: quite simply, competing theoretical perspectives predict very different, even contradictory, outcomes from state decentralization.

Turning specifically to democratic theory, the theoretical antinomy has at least two sources. On the one hand, the pluralist view of liberal democracy often idealizes local politics as a seedbed of democracy. At least since De Tocqueville, local politics have held a privileged space for educating citizens in democratic norms, organizing them in the pursuit of their interests through electoral politics, and more generally checking the centralizing, authoritarian tendencies of the central state apparatus. Significantly, one of the most influential and definitive theoretical elaborations of pluralist democracy was Robert Dahl's seminal study of city politics in New Haven, Connecticut.[43] Even Joseph Schumpeter recognized that only local politics could allow for greater levels of citizen participation beyond voting for candidates (as opposed to choosing among policy alternatives), because it fell into "the little field which the individual citizen's mind encompasses with a full sense of its reality."[44] The problem, of course, is projecting such democratic impulses toward the national level (something that Schumpeter himself adamantly opposed) and preventing less-democratic dynamics from national-level politics from completely overwhelming these local dynamics— regardless of the level of state centralization.[45] In many developing countries, this tendency has only been exacerbated by the social and economic consequences of the way that the currently dominant neoliberal development model has been implemented.[46]

The liberal/pluralist view of democratic politics, however, is not the only one. The communitarian alternative places community interests above those of the individual voters so important to the liberal/pluralist view. While arguably still "democratic," it entails a very distinct conception of democracy.[47] Like the foundational work on liberal/pluralist democracy, communitarian theories of democracy are also based on what is essentially local politics. The work of Jean-Jacques Rousseau stands out here, including its tendencies to at least implicitly endorse a "tyranny of the majority" that marginalizes (or worse) minorities and makes active citizen participation redundant by stressing the objective nature of the "common interest." Applied to the national level, such theories can support extremes of centralization.[48] While contemporary communitarian theory deliberately attempts to moderate, if not completely avoid, such tendencies, it has not been immune from influential criticisms along these same lines, again underscoring the fundamental ambiguity of the meaning of local democracy.[49]

To a certain extent, this theoretical antinomy reflects irreconcilable normative positions. It only highlights both the need to understand most decentralization processes as being elite led with little input from society, as well as the importance of examining the various motives that such elites have in designing decentralization programs.

Going beyond normative differences, however, part of the theoretical antinomy may be a consequence of the different models of democracy that subnational[50] and national politics necessarily encompass. As Jane Mansbridge notes, local government historically has been characterized in terms of a *unitary* model of democracy and is, in fact, the oldest form of government.[51] Its origins, she argues, can be traced back to hunter–gatherer societies and it is based on concepts of common interest and common respect. At the national level, this model cannot be applied. This is because, among other things, the face-to-face interactions associated with the unitary model are impossible to achieve and, in place of the common interest of the single community, there are the conflicting interests of multiple communities. An *adversarial* model of democracy thus began to emerge in the seventeenth century, based on elections and representatives that could reconcile these differences and provide an alternative to the kinds of personal interactions characteristic of grassroots politics.

In terms of decentralization, the contrast between these two models of democracy highlights the very problematic (from a democratic perspective at least) relationship between subnational and national levels of government. There is no clear and obvious way to reconcile these two models of democracy, and much will depend on the relative influence of societal or elite actors in designing the political institutions located at the national and subnational levels—suggesting a real problem in today's context, where societal-level influence has been most noticeably lacking in the design of decentralization policies.

In Western Europe, as well as Canada and the United States in North America, this problem was more or less resolved in ways that provided the basis for increasing levels of democracy because of the dominant role that city governments had come to play in defining national politics long before centralizing tendencies at the level of the nation-state became predominant.[52] This had the effect of ensuring greater societal input in the creation of state institutions, forming part of the process of political struggle that defined the institutional structure of today's nation-states in those regions. In all of these cases, to a greater or lesser extent, the national state structures that were created retained important spaces for local and regional autonomy, which eventually would allow for increasing levels of democratic participation. In the United States, for example, the fact that the country was founded by the original thirteen colonies should not be underestimated in this respect. As Dahl[53] discovered in his study of New Haven's politics, the advent of pluralist (as opposed to oligarchic) politics was due more to socioeconomic change in the community, and no institutional changes were even required because local government already enjoyed a significant degree of autonomy from higher levels of government. More recently, in these same countries the emergence of "new social movements" has influenced the devolution of state prerogatives to increasingly democratic local levels of government.[54]

In most developing countries, including the countries studied in this volume, colonialism often had the opposite impact in terms of reinforcing centralist tendencies.[55] This, in turn, helps explain the noticeable lack of effective demand from society for decentralization today. While recent transitions to democracy have been effected by a variety of new social movements, these have not had the same impact on decentralization as the new social movements in older democracies. The primacy of the demand for disposing of the existing authoritarian regimes is one reason, but such movements in developing countries also had very different characteristics than their West European and North American counterparts.[56] Not surprisingly, the tensions between local and national level democracy often tend to be reconciled in favor of the latter. If spaces for local participation and democracy are even on the agenda, they may be easily sidestepped by other concerns and interests.

In seeming to stress the contradictions and limits, both in theory and in practice, of decentralization, my goal is to highlight its indeterminate, multidimensional nature. It is influenced by a variety of factors, including the competing objectives of its proponents (both apparent and real), as well as the complex interplay of other processes of economic and political change that also affect the goals and outcomes of decentralization processes. In this way, all of the contributors to this volume, myself included, seek to discover or uncover the secrets to successful democratic decentralization. Admittedly, progress toward achieving that goal has not always as great as we would wish, but progress has been made. Such success reflects the efforts of political elites who have taken up the cause of democratic participation at all levels of government, as well as important social actors in civil society who have challenged political elites to open up closed political systems. Democratic regimes in general and even limited state decentralization open up space for more concerted efforts at democratic decentralization. The continued challenge is to build on democratic advances, even limited ones, which have already taken place as part of a dynamic, multidimensional process of decentralization that cannot ignore the economic and political obstacles that may arise. In this sense, the Mexican case is perhaps most inspiring because it demonstrates how even the limited spaces opened up by decentralization policies intended to block democratic change can be pried open through concerted citizen mobilization.

Ultimately, it is impossible to escape the conclusion that processes of economic liberalization, democratic transition, and state decentralization are intimately interrelated. But in stating the obvious, it is important not to draw the wrong conclusion. While the three processes are perhaps inseparable in today's world, they can and often do pull polities (and politicians) in different directions. Economic liberalization can certainly spill over into political liberalization and definitely has inspired much of the state decentralization that has taken place to date. Yet high levels of inequality and economic dislocations have associated been associated with it,[57] and these trends do little to strengthen the new democratic regimes that have emerged often in parallel with changing economic policies. Decentralization frequently gets caught in the middle. Economically driven programs of state structuring that may or may not result in democratic decentralization are often used by various political elites to further economic liberalization by shrinking the size of the central state, mitigate the social impact of the economic dislocations associated with economic liberalization, hold on to political power, and/or promote a genuine deepening of democratic participation. As a result, there are both unprecedented opportunities for achieving democratic decentralization, while there are undeniable obstacles. In exploring both, we hope to begin to unravel the puzzle of decentralization.

This Volume

The following eight case studies represent an effort to explore the issues relating to decentralization in six countries located in three distinct parts of the globe. The focus is on what has been achieved, what remains to be done, and the identification of the principal actors and issues involved in decentralization. It is admittedly a preliminary effort, given the dearth of research directed at the central issues involved. The individual chapters provide an empirically rich overview to the context of decentralization in each country. Because the project began with a clear set of research questions, there is an important degree of coherence among the case studies, despite the very different dynamics found in each country. Indeed, the *heterogeneity* of experiences is one of the clearest conclusions that all of the researchers shared.

The volume is organized as follows. In Chapter 2, Yemile Mizrahi argues that Mexico presents the irony of being both a federal system and one of the most centralized states in Latin America. Nonetheless, the state's needs to shore up its legitimacy and to seek new, efficient methods for delivering services have led to several cycles of decentralization since 1970, with the most important occurring after 1982. Opposition gains in local and state elections during the 1990s in particular forced the federal authorities to negotiate with subnational governments. Many aspects of health care and education were decentralized in this period. However, since the country's leaders were primarily concerned with perpetuating the rule of the official party, decentralization projects generally sought to devolve services to local and state governments without substantial decision-making authority or fiscal powers. The new climate of democratic competition since 2000 may open opportunities to develop a better set of institutional arrangements that empower subnational governments.

Despite the efforts of Mexico's ruling party to the contrary, Leticia Santín del Río (Chapter 3) demonstrates how the processes of decentralization and democratization are closely linked in Mexico and that municipalities have become a locus for democratic experimentation. In the 1990s, civil society organizations grew in numbers and strength and began to form wide-ranging coalitions that pressed for greater political openness and economic reform. These organizations increasingly discovered that the municipal arena presented significant opportunities for citizen participation and joined opposition political parties in demanding greater municipal autonomy. At the same time, mayors from diverse municipalities across the country joined together to push for increased municipal autonomy. Together, these efforts have helped make municipalities a flourishing space for citizen participation. However, much remains to be done to establish adequate normative and legal instruments to ensure that municipalities can operate effectively and with well-defined responsibilities.

In Chile, decentralization has involved devolving authority to administer important policies to regional and municipal governments. The main purpose behind decentralization, according to Claudia Serrano (Chapter 4), is to improve democratic governance by facilitating citizen participation. However, she notes that these objectives have only been partially achieved. The historical centralism of Chile's political system, and the especially strong authoritarian imprint of the Pinochet regime when the decentralization process began, have helped undermine some of the democratic potential of the process. Moreover, decentralization to the regional level has primarily meant the transfer of administrative functions to governments that are indirectly elected and that operate within regions that have little historical cohesion. The regions, which are identified by number rather than by name, were created even though they lacked strong regional identities. Regional managers are appointed by the president and the regional councils are elected by the municipal councils, so that they have no direct electoral link to the citizenry. In addition, the regions depend entirely on national government transfers for their operations. As a result of these factors, the regions are more implementing agencies of the central government than decentralized authorities in their own right.

María Elena Ducci (Chapter 5) looks at this problem through the eyes of one of Chile's southern regions, Region IX, popularly known as La Araucanía. She notes that despite the democratic rhetoric that central government authorities use in describing Chile's decentralization process, those in the regions farthest from the capital feel that they have very little autonomy or input. Different sectors have different degrees of autonomy from central government control; however, public works and health care are extremely centralized and urban development is quite decentralized. In addition, there is a growing movement in some of the regions for greater autonomy and the construction of an elected regional government. While these demands are still weakly organized, they find a great deal of resonance among citizens who feel that decisions about their region's development should be taken closer to home.

In South Africa, on the other hand, the decentralization process has been uniquely shaped by the transition from apartheid and by the suspicions that national elites harbor toward local initiatives. Steven Friedman and Caroline Kihato (Chapter 6) argue that South Africa's decentralization was driven largely by negotiations among domestic political elites, although they borrowed ideas suggested by international actors. The legal basis for increased local governance, contained in the postapartheid constitution, extends certain authorities to nine provinces and 284 municipalities. However, the structure of provincial and municipal government has greatly constrained their margin of subnational authority. Provinces rely on the national government for 90 percent of their revenues and most of their areas of authority are shared with the national government through an arrangement known as concurrency. Municipal governments have greater autonomy, in theory, since they raise most of their own revenues, but resource differences among municipal governments have prevented them from becoming an effective arena for citizen participation. Moreover, the ANC's centralist party organization, which demands party discipline from provincial and municipal officials, has further limited the independence of subnational authorities and promotes the tendency of elected officials to be more responsive to the party hierarchy than to their own constituents.

Friedman and Kihato suggest that decentralization could eventually serve to open up new spaces for civic participation in South Africa; however, it will require a new commitment from elites that local participation and contention is worthwhile. The unique dynamic of the anti-apartheid struggle may serve as the foundation for creating such participation. The fight against apartheid had strong local roots, especially in the urban townships. Although this was always subject to central authority and ultimately local struggles were seen within the context of the national struggle for liberation, this process has left an ethos of resistance and local networks of grassroots organization. These civil structures could become the building blocks for further social participation in local governance in the future.

In contrast, Kenya has undergone relatively little decentralization in recent years. Gilbert Khadiagala and Winnie Mitullah (Chapter 7) argue that Kenya, like many African countries, faces serious problems that prevent effective decentralization, including a legacy of political authoritarianism and the inability of the state to address basic needs. Under colonialism, the power of tribal authorities was circumscribed within a strongly centralist colonial regime. Although Kenya's independence constitution prescribed a return to strong regional and local governments, this fell apart within a year after independence as a single party consolidated its control over the national government and began to exercise tremendous supervisory authority over subnational governments. Several attempts to generate local spaces of citizen participation from the 1960s through the 1980s fell prey to clientelistic politics and central government oversight. National leaders substituted patron–client relations in the place of open participation as a system for managing ethnic cleavages among Kenya's population.

In the 1990s, however, economic crisis brought about increased demands for democratic opening. This led to the creation of a somewhat more competitive political system and some additional devolution of authority to local governments. In addition, the state's inability to provide basic services led to "decentralization by default," as nongovernmental organizations and community groups developed practices of service provision in the absence of state services. Nonetheless, Khadiagala and Mitullah note that real decentralization is unlikely to proceed further in Kenya without greater democratization, since current elites are suspicious of local bases of power that could challenge their authority. Moreover, the inability of the central government to perform its basic functions raises questions about how relevant decentralization is in the context where the state is a "lame leviathan."

In the Philippines, decentralization has proceeded quickly, driven by the process of democratization and the burgeoning of citizens' organizations demanding open and accountable government, according to Leonora Angeles and Francisco Magno (Chapter 8). Of all the cases studied, the Philippines presents the most extensive devolution of responsibilities to subnational authorities and the clearest example of a decentralization process driven by citizens' demands to participate in local governance. Historically the Philippine state was highly centralized and based on elaborate patronage-based interactions. The fall of the authoritarian Marcos regime led to the 1987 constitution that created elected subnational governments and to the 1991 Local Government Code that created a set of mechanisms for popular participation in decision making at a local level. Today, subnational governments account for approximately 40 percent of state revenues and have wide-ranging taxation authority, in addition to receiving national government transfers fixed by pre-established formulas.

Subnational governments in the Philippines—including provinces, municipalities, towns, and *barangays* (neighborhoods)—have primary responsibility for a range of state functions, including health care, welfare, infrastructure, agricultural policy, and housing. In many of these sectors, commissions made up of representatives from civil society, government, and business have oversight responsibility for state investments. Angeles and Magno argue that local governments have become the locus of innovation and citizen participation. Participatory bodies have given citizens an important say in their government's functioning and helped break down patronage networks. At the same time, they note that participatory instruments often benefit larger organizations that know how to influence policy, and that civil society organizations are often too weak to take advantage of opportunities for participation. Moreover, some local governments lack the necessary knowledge, resources, and transparency to carry out their functions effectively. They conclude that more research is necessary to understand why some subnational governments perform better than others, how civil society organizations can play an effective role in local governance, and how social learning can be reinforced.

Indonesia was a highly centralized state until a series of laws in 1999 that led to a rapid and very dramatic decentralization process that took effect 1 January 2001. Syarif Hidayat and Hans Antlöv (Chapter 9) argue that during President Suharto's thirty-two-year rule the relationship between the state and civil society "was characterized by paternalism, rent-seeking and a centralization of power." In 1995 the central government collected 95 percent of taxes and spent 90 percent of state revenues. The resignation of Suharto in the midst of a profound financial crisis, growing demands for democracy, and fears of ethnic separatism, led the interim Habibe administration to pursue two laws that granted vastly increased authorities and resources to Indonesia's 380 districts and municipalities beginning in 2001. The national government is now responsible only for religious affairs and "the federal four" (finances, foreign affairs, defense, and justice).

While Hidayat and Antlöv note that it is too early to evaluate the decentralization reforms fully, they find that local elites have largely captured the local governments, the quality of government services has fallen, and disparities among localities have increased. The rapid and largely undemocratic way in which the reforms were implemented left little opportunity for citizen input or careful planning, sequencing, and implementation of the decentralization process. Nonetheless, they point to several positive developments that may bode well for decentralized governance in the future. Citizens generally feel that their local governments are responsive to them, and there are important opportunities to develop local solutions to local problems, instead of waiting for decisions from the capital. At the same time, legal provisions giving greater authority (although not resources) to villages have initiated an important process of village-level democracy. The authors worry, however, that without a strong commitment from the national government to decentralization, opportunities may be lost to achieve an integrated system of decentralized governance with both devolution and accountability.

Notes

1. James Manor, *The Political Economy of Democratic Decentralization* (Oxford: Clarendon Press, 1999).

2. Samuel Huntington, *The Third Wave: Democratization in the Late Twentieth Century* (New Haven, Conn.: Yale University Press, 1991).

3. For a similar argument dealing specifically with the relationship between economic and political liberalization, see Philip Oxhorn and Pamela Starr, *Markets and Democracy in Latin America: Conflict or Convergence?* (Boulder, Colo.: Lynne Rienner, 1999).

4. By subnational government, I refer to all levels of government below the level of the central state. This includes local as well as regional levels of government.

5. Dennis Rondinelli, "Government Decentralization in Comparative Perspective: Theory and Practice in Developing Countries," *International Review of Administrative Science* 47, no. 2 (1981): 133–45. See also Rondinelli, "What Is Decentralization?" in *Decentralization Briefing Notes,* edited by Jennie Litback and Jessica Seddon, 2–8, WBI Working Papers (Washington, D.C.: World Bank Institute/Poverty Reduction and Economic Management Network, n.d.).

6. Manor, *Political Economy of Democratic Decentralization;* and Eduardo Canel, "Municipal Decentralization and Participatory Democracy: Building a New Mode of Urban Politics in Montevideo City," *European Review of Latin American and Caribbean Studies* 71 (October 2001): 57–78.

7. Such demands may not emerge, however, as discussed in the case studies on South Africa, Kenya, and Chile. I will return to this point in what follows.

8. I would like to thank James Manor for reminding me of this important point.

9. Manor, *Political Economy of Democratic Decentralization.*

10. Huntington, *Third Wave.* I will return to a discussion of these issues in the following section.

11. Robert Dahl, *Who Governs: Democracy and Power in an American City* (New Haven, Conn.: Yale University Press, 1961).

12. See also Dagmar Raczynski and Claudia Serrano, eds., *Descentralización: Nudos Críticos* (Santiago: Corporación de Investigaciones Económicas para Latinoamérica, 2001).

13. A fourth dimension is external influences, including multinational development banks and donor countries. While important, it is not a defining characteristic of decentralization per se. External pressures have been instrumental in the adoption and design of decentralization programs, but the nature of decentralization needs to be understood in terms of the three other dimensions that will be discussed in what follows.

14. Financial resources can be self-generated, provided through central government transfers, or both. While the government transfers can create dependence, such dependence becomes a serious threat to subnational autonomy only to the extent that the level of transfers can be easily manipulated for political reasons. Such transfers may also play an important redistributive role in many countries where regional inequalities favor some provinces or cities over others in terms of their relative ability to generate revenue that can be spent on economic development and social services, for example.

15. Chile is also interesting in this regard. Prior to the 1992 municipal elections, mistrust of local governments was not unusual given the lack of turnover in local government personnel after the transition to democracy. The elections contributed greatly to changing this, giving local governments a renewed legitimacy that benefited even those municipal governments in which supporters of the former military regime won. Conversely, as the chapters by Serrano and Ducci show, the lack of similar democratizing reforms at the regional level has denied them the same level of legitimacy and popular support, even though this level of government is now led by appointees of popularly elected presidents who therefore are unlikely to have been supporters of the former military regime.

16. Manor, *Political Economy of Democratic Decentralization.*

17. Kenneth Roberts, "Beyond Romanticism: Social Movements and the Study of Political Change in Latin America," *Latin American Research Review* 32, no. 2 (1997): 137–51. Cf. John Gaventa and Camilo Valderrama, "Participation, Citizenship and Local Governance," Background note prepared for workshop on "Strengthening Participation in Local Governance" (Institute of Development Studies, University of Sussex, 21–23 June 1999), and subsequent report of the workshop.

18. Philip Oxhorn, "Social Inequality, Civil Society and the Limits of Citizenship in Latin America," in *The Politics of Injustice in Latin America,* edited by Susan Eckstein and Timothy Wickham-Crowley, eds. (Berkeley: University of California Press, forthcoming).

19. Charles Tilly, "Citizenship, Identity and Social History," in *Citizenship, Identity and Social History, International Review of Social History Supplement 3,* edited by Charles Tilly, 1–17 (Cambridge: Press Syndicate of the University of Cambridge, 1996).

20. See Dietrich Rueschemeyer, Evelyn Stephens, and John Stephens, *Capitalist Development and Democracy* (Chicago: University of Chicago Press, 1992); Guillermo O'Donnell and Philippe Schmitter, *Transitions from Authoritarian Rule: Tentative Conclusions about Uncertain Democracies* (Baltimore: Johns Hopkins University Press, 1986).

21. Terry Lynn Karl, "Dilemmas of Democratization in Latin America," in *Comparative Political Dynamics: Global Research Perspectives,* edited by Dankwart A. Rustow and Kenneth Paul Erickson, 163–91 (New York: Harper Collins Publishers, 1991).

22. Rondinelli, "What Is Decentralization?"

23. The state's role in promoting development was so ingrained in policymakers' thinking that policies were endorsed in the defense of capitalism that today would loosely be labeled as antimarket, if not anticapitalist. For example, see the classic work

of modernizationist economics by Walter Rostow, "Take-off into Self-Sustained Growth," in *The Economics of Underdevelopment*, edited by A. Agarwala and S. Singh, 154–88 (New York: Oxford University Press, 1963).

24. John Williamson, "The Progress of Policy Reform in Latin America," in *Latin American Adjustment: How Much Has Happened?* edited by J. Williamson, chapter 9 (Washington, D.C.: Institute for International Economics, 1990).

25. The collapse of the Soviet Union and market reforms in China further cemented what is arguably an antistate (read anti–central state) bias among mainstream policy-makers. While important debates continue on the role of the state in promoting economic development—for example, Economic Commission for Latin America and the Caribbean, *Changing Production Patterns with Social Equity: The Prime Task of Latin America and the Caribbean Development in the 1990s* (Santiago: United Nations, 1990); Peter Evans, *Embedded Autonomy: States and Industrial Transformation* (Princeton, N.J.: Princeton University Press, 1995); A. Amsden, "Editorial: Bringing Production Back in Understanding Government's Economic Role in Late Industrialization," *World Development* 25, no. 4 (1997): 469–80; and Nancy Birdsall and Augusto de la Torre, with R. Menezes, *Washington Contentious: Economic Policies for Social Equity in Latin America* (Washington, D.C.: Carnegie Endowment for International Peace and the Inter-American Dialogue, 2001)—and major international lending organizations such as the World Bank are beginning to focus more on the importance of strong state institutions, as seen in Shahid Burki and Guillermo Perry, *Beyond the Washington Consensus: Institutions Matter* (Washington, D.C.: The World Bank, 1998), it is hard to imagine that strong centralized states will have the same dominant role that they enjoyed during much of the postwar period, at least for the foreseeable future.

26. Oxhorn and Starr, *Markets and Democracy in Latin America;* see also Philip Oxhorn and Graciela Ducatenzeiler, eds., *What Kind of Market? What Kind of Democracy? Latin America in the Age of Neoliberalism* (University Park: Pennsylvania State University Press, 1998).

27. Philip Oxhorn, *When Democracy Isn't All That Democratic: Social Exclusion and the Limits of the Public Sphere in Latin America* (Coral Gables, Fla.: North-South Center at the University of Miami, 2001). See also Oxhorn, "Social Inequality, Civil Society and the Limits of Citizenship in Latin America," in *The Politics of Injustice in Latin America,* edited by Susan Eckstein and Timothy Wickham-Crowley (Berkeley: University of California Press, forthcoming).

28. Douglas Chalmers, Carlos Vilas, Katherine Hite, Scott Martin, Kerianne Piester, and Monique Manuel Segarra, eds., *The New Politics of Inequality in Latin America: Rethinking Participation and Representation* (Oxford: Oxford University Press, 1997); and Felipe Agüero and Jeffrey Stark, eds., *Fault Lines of Democracy in Post-Transition Latin America* (Miami: North-South Center Press, University of Miami, 1998).

29. Manuel Antonio Garretón, "Social and Economic Transformations in Latin America: The Emergence of a New Political Matrix?" in *Markets and Democracy In Latin America: Conflict or Convergence?* edited by Philip Oxhorn and Pamela K. Starr, 61–78 (Boulder, Colo.: Lynne Rienner, 1999).

30. Manor, *Political Economy of Democratic Decentralization.*

31. Mexico is perhaps the best example of this. While local government and regional governments were central to the success of its recent transition to democracy, these same governments can also be seedbeds of reaction, corruption, rent seeking, and authoritarianism. See the chapters by Mizrahi and Santín in this volume; and Wayne A.

Cornelius, Todd A. Eisenstadt, and Jane Hindley, eds., *Subnational Politics and Democratization in Mexico* (La Jolla: Center for U.S.–Mexican Studies, University of California, 1999).

32. Manor, *Political Economy of Democratic Decentralization.*

33. Philip Oxhorn, *Organizing Civil Society: The Popular Sectors ánd the Struggle for Democracy in Chile* (University Park: Pennsylvania State University Press, 1995).

34. The complexity of decentralization is only underscored by the now obviously mistaken conclusion of an important World Bank study of decentralization that Argentina represented an example of "successful institutionalization of hard budget constraint" on lower levels of government. The same study did conclude, however, that no one could have predicted that the decentralizing reforms institutionalized in the 1988 Constitution would be a principal cause of the 1998–1999 economic crisis in Brazil. See Shahid J. Burki, Guillermo Perry, and William Dillinger, *Beyond the Center: Decentralizing the State* (Washington, D.C.: World Bank, 1999), 41–44.

35. Mitullah and Khadiagala in this volume; Jacqueline M. Klopp, "Pilfering the Public: the Problem of Land Grabbing in Contemporary Kenya," *Africa Today* 47 (Winter 2000): 6–26.

36. Manor, *Political Economy of Democratic Decentralization,* 31.

37. Frances Hagopian, "Democracy by Undemocratic Means: Elites, Political Pacts, and Regime Transition in Brazil," *Comparative Political Studies* 23 (July 1990): 147–70.

38. Manor, *Political Economy of Democratic Decentralization,* 35.

39. There are important exceptions, such as the state of Kerala in India and the city of Porto Alegre in Brazil. But even here, capacity was built up at the regional and local levels over a period of years. Moreover, the dynamic that generated successful subnational governance in both cases began at the local level through political struggles, not at the national level in a top-down process of imposition. For discussions of the Kerala and Porto Alegre experiences, see Patrick Heller, *The Labor of Development: Workers and the Transformation of Capitalism in Kerala, India* (Ithaca: Cornell University Press, 1999); and Leonardo Avritzer, "Democratization and Changes in the Pattern of Association," *Journal of Interamerican Studies and World Affairs* 42 (Fall 2000): 59–76. I will return to the issue of elite imposition versus social struggle in the development of local governance below.

40. I would like to thank James Manor for reminding me of this point.

41. The rise of the Chilean opposition was not directly based on a call for local democratization. This was subsumed in the demand for a transition at the national level to replace the military regime. Once this had taken place, however, local democratization became a more prominent component of the Concertación reform platform, and resulted in constitutional changes in 1992.

42. Even corruption, the quintessential form of rent-seeking behavior within the state apparatus, was seen as positive from a development perspective, at least in "moderate" doses. See Huntington, *Political Order in Changing Societies* (New Haven, Conn.: Yale University Press, 1968). See also Albert Hirschman, "The Turn to Authoritarianism in Latin America and the Search for Its Economic Determinants," in *The New Authoritarianism in Latin America,* edited by David Collier, 61–98 (Princeton, N.J.: Princeton University Press, 1968).

43. Dahl, *Who Governs.*

44. Joseph Schumpeter, *Capitalism, Socialism and Democracy* (New York: Harper and Row, 1950), 258.

45. P. Bachrach, *The Theory of Democratic Elitism: A Critique* (Boston: Little, Brown and Co., 1967).

46. Oxhorn, *When Democracy Isn't All That Democratic;* Oxhorn, "Is the Century of Corporatism Over? Neoliberalism and the Rise of Neopluralism," in Oxhorn and Ducatenzeiler, eds., *What Kind of Democracy?*

47. B. Parekh, "The Culture of Peculiarity of Liberal Democracy," *Political Studies* 40 (1992): 160–75.

48. C. B. Macpherson, *Democratic Theory: Essays in Retrieval* (Oxford: Clarendon Press, 1973).

49. See Stephen Holmes, *Passions and Constraint: On the Theory of Liberal Democracy* (Chicago: University of Chicago Press, 1995). The perspective adopted in this volume actually tends more toward a communitarian position than a strictly liberal one. For example, see Michael Walzer, "The Civil Society Argument," in Chantal Mouffe, ed., *Dimensions of Radical Democracy* (London: Verso, 1992): 89–107, and "Rescuing Civil Society," *Dissent* (Winter 1999): 62–67. In this regard, it is also worth pointing out that Walzer stresses the importance of the central state in reining in the potential abuses of civil society (and, by implication at least, local government).

50. I use the term "subnational" to refer to both local and regional levels of government within the same state.

51. Jane Mansbridge, *Beyond Adversary Democracy* (New York: Basic Books, 1980).

52. Some have even argued that this historical level of societal pluralism associated with Western Europe's feudal past distinguishes it from other regions of the world and explains why democratic institutions have been much more stable there. See Louis Hartz, *The Founding of New Societies: Studies in the History of the United States, Latin America, South America, South Africa, Canada, and Australia* (New York: Harcourt, Brace & World, 1964).

53. Dahl, *Who Governs.*

54. Jean Cohen, "Strategy or Identity: New Theoretical Paradigms and Contemporary Social Movements," *Social Research* 52 (Winter 1985): 663–716.

55. Claudio Véliz, *The Centralist Tradition of Latin America* (Princeton, N.J.: Princeton University Press, 1980); and Macpherson, *Democratic Theory.*

56. Diane E. Davis, "The Power of Distance: Re-Theorizing Social Movements in Latin America," *Theory & Society* 28 (August 1999): 585–638.

57. Roberto Koreniewicz and William Smith, "Poverty, Inequality, and Growth in Latin America: Searching for the High Road to Globalization," *Latin American Research Review* 35, no. 3 (2000): 7–54.

Part I

Latin America

Chapter 2

Twenty Years of Decentralization in Mexico: A Top-Down Process

Yemile Mizrahi

One of the most peculiar features characteristic of the Mexican political system throughout its history has been excessive political and economic centralization. Although according to its Constitution, Mexico officially has a federal system of government, in practice power has remained firmly concentrated in the central government.

Centralism in Mexico has deep historical roots. Since Aztec times and later during the colonial period, the center has dominated the periphery. During the nineteenth century, the conflict between the liberals with their federalist ideas and the conservatives who were defenders of centralism ended with the construction of a state that was officially federal but strongly centralized. As Mauricio Merino has affirmed, "[T]he synthesis between the liberal ideas of the times and the rural reality of the country was what was established in daily practice."[1]

The centralist tradition dominated again after the Revolution of 1910. Although the Revolution began in the periphery as a rebellion against the centralist and dictatorial regime of Porfirio Díaz, it ended by consolidating an extremely centralized and authoritarian government. Compared to other countries, Mexico has one of the most centralized governments in the world, even when compared to countries with unitary systems of government.[2]

The results of centralization in modern Mexico have been excessively negative: a serious regional imbalance (relatively rich states in the north of the country and excessively poor states in the south), a very unequal distribution of wealth (one of the most unequal in Latin America), enormous bottlenecks impeding efforts to guarantee sustained economic development in the country, and low levels of efficiency and efficacy in public services provided by the government.

Given the government's deteriorating capacity to respond to the population's growing needs and demands, and given the resulting erosion of political legitimacy at all levels of government, the federal government was motivated to introduce administrative reforms aimed at decentralizing functions, powers, and resources to state and municipal governments. Although the government promoted decentralization as a "democratic" measure, in reality the federal government's objectives were neither to increase political participation nor to introduce democratic reforms, but to increase government efficiency and maintain hegemony of the Partido Revolucionario Institucional (PRI). Paradoxically, as we will see further on, these reforms did not substantially increase the government's efficiency, and yet, they did successfully contribute to erosion of the PRI's hegemony.

Following the recommendations of international institutions such as the World Bank and the Inter-American Development Bank, since 1970, and especially since 1982, the government has promoted a series of decentralization policies aimed at imprinting improved efficiency and agility on the state apparatus and thus legitimizing the state in the eyes of society.[3] The central idea behind these policies is that state and municipal governments can be more efficacious in the provision of public goods and services because they are closer than the federal government to the users of these services and, therefore, can be more sensitive to the needs and preferences of the populations in each region.[4]

Approximately twenty years after the introduction of these reforms, it is worth asking about the results of decentralization in Mexico. What forms have these decentralization policies taken? And what challenges still lie ahead?

Without a doubt, compared to 1982, today states and municipalities possess greater functions, powers, and resources to help them carry out their governmental tasks. Nonetheless, Mexico continues to be very centralized.

Compared to other Latin American countries, both public expenditures and revenues continue to be very concentrated at the federal level. Even though today states and municipalities have greater economic resources, they continue to depend financially on the federal government and, perhaps more importantly, lack the autonomy necessary to manage those resources. The states and municipalities do not have sufficient maneuvering room to make their own decisions, design their programs, and introduce innovative solutions to resolve their problems. In fact, state and local governments in Mexico continue to play a marginal role in the promotion of economic development. Maybe that explains why twenty years after the introduction of decentralization policies, serious regional imbalances and profound social inequalities continue in Mexico.

To a large extent, the forms that these policies took and their results can be explained by the weight of the centralist tradition in Mexico. Decentralization was a process induced from above and aimed at decongesting the load of responsibilities of the federal government. Decentralization in this sense follows a centralist logic. The forms taken by the decentralization policies in Mexico are best explained by their political purpose: continued hegemony of the Partido Revolucionario Institucional (PRI).

Decentralization did not promote nor did it have the intention of promoting a new political equilibrium among the federal, state, and municipal governments. Nor was it destined to foster increased democratization in the country's political life. Decentralization was conceived as an administrative rather than a political reform. As discussed below, the governments of Miguel de la Madrid (1982–1988), Carlos Salinas de Gortari (1988–1994), and Ernesto Zedillo (1994–2000) tried to achieve increased levels of efficiency and efficacy in the provision of public services, but without losing the reins of political control for the PRI.

The long-lived hegemony of the PRI left a unique imprint on the decentralization process in Mexico. Thus, it was no surprise that as a result of the strengthening of the opposition since the mid–1980s, the drive for decentralization acquired increased dynamism. In effect, once the opposition parties controlled various state governments,[5] the theme of federalism was converted into one of the most important political issues in the country. As discussed below, both opposition political parties and diverse nongovernmental organizations strongly pressured the federal government to redefine intergovernmental relations in Mexico and revise the old subordination of states and municipalities to the central government, most of all in the area of fiscal activities.

The decentralization process that began top–down and with the intention of increasing the capabilities of the government and maintaining, at the same time, political control, ended without achieving its objectives. In spite of the introduction of decentralization policies, during the last twenty years the quality of life for most Mexicans has deteriorated significantly, the number of poor people has risen,[6] regional inequalities have continued and in some cases worsened, and the PRI finally failed to maintain its political control. In the year 2000 for the first time in history, the PRI lost the presidential elections.

In the following sections, I describe the principal characteristics of intergovernmental relations in Mexico, analyze various decentralization policies that have been introduced in the country, particularly since 1982, and evaluate their results.

Centralizing Federalism in Mexico

Mexico's political Constitution establishes in Article 40 that "the United States of Mexico is a federal, representative and democratic Republic." In practice, the political system has been centralized, authoritarian, and not very representative. To a large degree, the contradiction between the official federalism and the actual centralization is captured in the same constitutional text, since at the same time that the Constitution recognizes the federal pact, it grants to the executive power broad discretionary powers to intervene in diverse public matters. According to Marván, the concentrations of power and centralism "are not foreign to the design of federal institutions established in the Constitution. . . . Rather they result from the implementation of a combination of constitutional provisions that permit the centralization and concentration of power."[7] According to the Constitution, the federal government has the power to intervene in matters of commerce (domestic and international), education, health, work, agriculture, energy, natural resources, and nutrition. Over the years, the federation has concentrated powers that originally were held jointly with or reserved for the states.[8] From an economic perspective, the federal government has also centralized fiscal powers: the central government has the exclusive power to collect income taxes, and, since 1980, sales taxes as well.

In addition to its powers to intervene in these areas of public policy, the executive has the power to introduce legislative proposals in Congress and possesses enormous influence in the definition of the federal budget. The Constitution does not authorize the Senate to participate in the approval of the federal budget. The budget is discussed and approved only by the Chamber of Deputies, which prevents the states of the republic from participating through their representatives in the Senate in the decision of how much and how resources are spent within their state boundaries.[9]

Strictly local responsibilities are defined by exclusion: according to Article 124, all powers that are not expressly granted to the federation are understood to be reserved for the states.[10] However, almost all constitutional articles contain restrictions that limit state authority. In fact, as Courchene and Cayeros affirm, "the Federal Pact of Mexico, mentioned in various articles of the Constitution, reflects certain distrust in the states." And, they add, the references to federalism in the Constitution are more related to the division of power, and not, as in other federations, to the way that federalism improves the living conditions of citizens.[11]

Political centralization, nonetheless, also is explained to a large degree by political reasons: the prolonged hegemony of the PRI. Since its birth in 1929 and until the year 2000, the "official party" controlled the federal executive power without interruption. Until the middle of the 1980s, the PRI controlled the majority of municipalities in the country and governed in all the states of the republic. And until 1997, the PRI maintained an absolute majority in the Congress. As C.F. Friedrich suggests, given the absence of an operating political opposition, "federalism is condemned to remain on paper." Federalism needs political plurality to be able to function. If the same political party controls all levels of government, and opposition political parties do not have real opportunities to "oppose," the counterweights officially established in a federal system become inactive.[12]

The hegemony of the PRI permitted the federal executive to control and subordinate other levels of government, in both the political and the economic realms. The president of the republic, who was the natural leader of the party, not only possessed the power to decide who ought to be the candidates to fill different offices in the popular election, but also had discretionary power to transfer resources to the states and municipalities. In spite of the existence of well-established formulas for transferring economic resources to the states and municipalities, the federal government concentrates the largest part of public revenue and expenditures in its own hands and possesses a great amount of autonomy in spending and investing resources throughout the national territory.

The lack of political opportunities outside of the PRI gave rise to an important discipline within the party. Insubordination of the governors or municipal presidents to the executive had serious consequences, from financial strangulation to the removal of their public duties.[13]

Since the government of President Lázaro Cárdenas (1934–1940), Mexican federalism has taken on a "centralist" character.[14] By expelling Plutarco Elías Calles from the country,[15] Cárdenas was able to consolidate presidential power and subordinate the Congress and the Supreme Court of Justice to the executive. Using the broad discretionary powers granted by the Constitution, Cárdenas expropriated enormous tracts of land and carried out the greatest redistribution of agricultural land since the Revolution. Faced with the fear of fomenting local despotism, and starting with the assumption that state and municipal governments lacked the capability necessary to organize and promote development, the federal government centralized the definition and implementation of social and economic policies in the country. Since then, power concentrated in the country's capital and specifically in the presidency remained key to the stability of the country.[16]

Until the 1970s, the excessive economic and political centralization did not seem to overly concern the government. The economy had grown at sustained annual rates of 6 percent and maintained low levels of inflation. In addition, the PRI maintained an almost absolute hegemony of power and until 1968,[17] political stability did not seem to be threatened.

The central idea driving economic policies since the 1940s was import substitution industrialization. Although industrialization became the principal motor of the economy, it also was one of the factors that most contributed to the deepening of regional imbalances. Industrial activities were principally concentrated in central Mexico (Mexico City and environs) and some states in the north.[18]

Toward the beginning of the 1970s, the Mexican "economic miracle" began to show signs of exhaustion. The economic deceleration on one hand, and the excessive economic concentration in central Mexico on the other, motivated the government to seek solutions to reverse these tendencies. It is in this context that decentralization began to be considered for the first time as a public policy tool to relieve the federal government of its excessive responsibilities and functions and achieve, in this manner, increased levels of efficacy and efficiency in public services and greater equity among regions.

Decentralization Policies

The Rhetoric of Decentralization (1970–1982)

The government of Luis Echeverría (1970–1976) was the first to become interested in decentralization as a strategy to promote economic development in other regions of the country. Although the government promoted plans and programs that incorporated the idea of "regional planning" and carried out studies about the country's various regions,[19] its impact was minimal. However, since then, decentralization has remained a fundamental part of government rhetoric.

In its first years, the government of José López Portillo (1976–1982) confronted the worst economic crisis that the country had experienced in decades. With the goal of encouraging economic growth, the government took a greater interest in promoting public policies that fostered regional decentralization. During this administration, various incentives were used such as credits and subsidies to establish manufacturing plants in other regions of the country. State planning committees (Comités de Planeación para el Desarrollo del Estado; COPLADE) were created at the state level throughout the country. These committees, presided over by respective state governors and composed of all municipal mayors, became official entities for planning public expenditures. For the first time, the state and municipal governments were taken into consideration in the planning and definition of public expenditures. Decision-making powers, however, remained concentrated in the federal government.[20]

With the petroleum boom, however, the priorities of the López Portillo administration changed. Instead of rationalizing expenditures and seeking greater efficiency and efficacy in the deliverance of public services, the government defined as the principal task the "administration of abundance." The introduction of structural economic and administrative reforms, including decentralization, was postponed.

Normative Decentralization: The Administration of Miguel de la Madrid (1982–1988)

Declining oil prices and the debt crisis plunged the country into the worst economic crisis in its history. The government of Miguel de la Madrid therefore considered the introduction of structural economic and administrative reforms to be urgent. In addition to reducing the participation of the state in the economy and promoting the opening of trade and direct foreign investment, the government deemed the decentralization of national life as fundamental. In effect, De la Madrid promoted the broadest decentralization policies that had been introduced up to that point. Three measures in particular were emphasized: reforms in planning processes, municipal reform, and financial reforms. Nonetheless, these policies had a normative official character and in most cases were not adopted in practice.

According to the National Development Plan of 1982–1988, regional policies proposed to "decentralize and redistribute responsibilities among the three levels of government; relocate productive activities in the national territory; steer economic activity toward middle-sized cities; and form a transversal network of communications and transportation to reverse the imbalanced regional development."[21] The decentralization and redesigning of responsibilities among the three levels of government rested in two entities: the COPLADE, which had been created by the previous government and were responsible for establishing the criteria and priorities of the states and municipalities, and the "development agreement" (Convenio Unico de Desarrollo, CUD), a new legal instrument established to coordinate the three levels of government. In the CUD, the amount of public resources that the states and municipalities received from the federal government and the conditions for using these resources were established.

Although officially the states and municipalities acquired a greater level of participation in the planning process, the CUD became a new control mechanism. The federal government continued retaining control over the amount, destination, and conditions of the resources distributed to the states and municipalities. In addition, the federal government retained the capacity to transfer additional resources in a unilateral manner, without consulting the COPLADE or the CUD. As Merino has affirmed, coordination among different levels of government is not synonymous with agreement: "Coordination assumes the definition of objectives on the part of the federal government, which local entities [then] join [adhere to]."[22]

One of the most important administrative reforms carried out by the De la Madrid government was modifying Article 115 of the Constitution. This reform tried to strengthen the legal base of municipalities to clarify and make explicit their functions and responsibilities. The reform, introduced in 1983, gave municipalities a fundamental tool necessary to carry out their functions. However, many of the functions and powers established in the new Article 115 were irrelevant for the majority of municipalities in the country. As Merino affirms, the reform was formulated using the criteria of an urban municipality as a starting point.[23] The reform authorized the municipal governments to charge a property tax, and specified in a detailed manner the public services for which they were responsible, but did not give municipalities greater margins of autonomy to promote social development and counter the burdensome weight of the state government in the decision-making process.

In spite of the introduction of these important reforms in the legal and normative field, the traditional pattern of intergovernmental relations was not substantially altered: the states and municipalities continued to be very much subordinated to the federal government. This was particularly evident in the financial area. In effect, in spite of decentralization reforms introduced by the De la Madrid government, the federal government continued concentrating public expenditures and revenue in its own hands. From a financial perspective, decentralization did not advance much.

State and municipal governments' financial dependence on the federation has been traditional in Mexico. Nonetheless, this dependency increased considerably after 1980 with the introduction of a fiscal reform known as the National System of Fiscal Coordination. With the objectives of making revenue collection more efficient and achieving a better nationwide distribution of resources, the sales tax was joined with the creation of the value-added tax (IVA), and the federal government was granted the exclusive power to collect this tax. Until then, the states had the power to charge a so-called "tax on commercial income." Instead of renouncing their collection power, the states would receive transfers (shares) of the taxes collected based on pre-established formulas. Since 1980, state and municipal governments' revenues have depended almost exclusively on the transfer of resources that they receive from the federal government.[24]

In 1988, at the end of De la Madrid's six-year term, state revenues depended on average on 61 percent of the resource transfers that they received from the federal government.[25] For municipalities, this proportion was 58 percent.[26] Financial centralization was also evident from the perspective of managing total expenditures and generation of total revenue by the various levels of government. In 1988, the federal government was responsible for 88.4 percent of all expenditures, compared to 9.8 percent by the states and 1.8 percent by municipalities.[27] In the same year, the federal government generated 84.1 percent of total revenue, the states, 13.3 percent, and the municipalities, only 2.6 percent.

Despite reform of Article 115 of the Constitution toward the end of De la Madrid's administration, few municipalities had a real ability to increase their own revenues, and therefore, continued to be heavily dependent on the transfers they received from Mexico City. The states continued to lack the ability to generate their own revenues, given that since 1980, they only had the power to collect the so-called "payroll tax" (a tax that was a disincentive to job creation, and that some states could not even levy because they lacked the ability to collect it) and charge for some public services such as issuing driver licenses, automobile ownership titles, and birth certificates.[28]

Finally, many of the economic resources transferred to the states and municipalities, such as the Inversión Pública Federal (IPF) and expenditures in regional development, continued being allocated discretionally by the federation. Frequently, the amount of these resources depended strictly on the personal relationship between a state governor and the president of the republic. In addition, most of these resources came with a series of restrictions that left state and municipal governments with little maneuvering room to define their own priorities and attend to local needs.

During the De la Madrid administration, the most important legacy in the area of decentralization was the establishment of legal foundations to lay down the rules for intergovernmental relations. But the balance among the various levels of government did not change. Perhaps the aspect that best reflects the persistent effort of the central government to maintain the reins of political control is its intervention in electoral processes throughout the country. Although De la Madrid promised to respect the popular vote when he came to power, during his term various "electoral abuses" were committed that culminated with the now famous "fall of the system" in the presidential elections of 1988. Although opposition parties' electoral victories were recognized in some isolated municipalities in the country, the government did not recognize a single opposition victory in state elections. Without a doubt, the most controversial case was the election of the governor of Chihuahua in 1986 in which the PRI proclaimed victory of its own candidate after a clearly fraudulent electoral process.

The uninterrupted control of the PRI over all state governments in the country explains much of the lack of dynamism in the decentralization process. The governors, being in fact representatives of the federation, had few incentives to advocate for increased powers, resources, and functions, and to confront the federal government. This situation changed radically during the next presidential administration when the opposition for the first time succeeded in governing on the state level.

"Centralizing" Decentralization: The Administration of Carlos Salinas de Gortari (1988–1994)

In the presidential elections of 1988, the PRI faced a serious threat from the opposition. On one side, Cuauhtémoc Cárdenas and a group of PRI dissidents organized a front on the left with great public appeal. On the other side, Manuel Clouthier with the Partido de Acción Nacional (National Action Party; PAN), organized the most aggressive political campaign that the PAN had organized up to that time. The elections were distinguished by a series of irregularities that ended with the "fall of the system": computers turned themselves off and stopped transmitting electoral information flowing in from all corners of the country.

Although the PRI officially won the presidential elections, for the first time it lost its absolute majority in the Congress. The PRI was weaker than ever before and needed support by the opposition to be able to govern. The lack of legitimacy with which President Salinas de Gortari arrived in office left an important imprint in the design, formulation, and implementation of the government's public policies, including of course, decentralization efforts.

The principal political objectives of President Salinas were to recover his government's legitimacy, retake political control within the PRI, and ensure PRI hegemony to the point that it was possible.[29] Although the president was forced to recognize some opposition victories at the state level,[30] during his period in office, intergovernmental relations were characterized by strong political and economic centralism.

Salinas de Gortari was the president who most abused "metaconstitutional" powers by removing an unprecedented number of governors from their posts.[31] But perhaps the strengthening of centralism was most evident in his spending policies, and in particular, in his social spending policies framed within the Programa Nacional de Solidaridad (PRONASOL), the most important program of his government.

During the Salinas de Gortari administration, the amounts transferred to states and municipalities grew significantly, which contributed to decentralizing the management of public expenditures. While in 1988 the federal government managed 88.4 percent of total expenditures, in 1993 this percentage dropped to 64.5 percent. The states, which only managed 9.8 percent of all expenditures in 1988, went on to manage 30.5 percent of total expenditures in 1993. In spite of this redistribution of expenditure management in favor of states and municipalities, the most important decisions regarding how the transferred resources would be managed remained under the control of the federal government. Moreover, outside of government transfers that continued to be allocated based on a pre-established formula, many transfers to the states and municipalities were allocated discretionally and based on political–electoral criteria.[32]

In the following section, I analyze the most important policies related to decentralization during the Salinas de Gortari's term: policies aimed at community development and combating poverty, and the decentralization of health care and education services.

Given the neoliberal economic reforms introduced by the government during the previous period, PRONASOL was designed to restore the social fabric and respond efficiently and efficaciously to a multitude of unsatisfied social demands. As Cornelius, Craig, and Fox state, PRONASOL "was designed to remind the population, and world governments, multilateral financing agencies and potential investors, that the technocrats that were leading the neoliberal economic revolution were not insensitive or irresponsible when faced with the social costs that were being incurred as a result of the introduction of these reforms."[33]

During the Salinas de Gortari administration, decentralization disappeared from government discourse as an important theme on the public agenda.[34] In its place, PRONASOL was announced as the government policy aimed at promoting regional development, decentralizing functions to the states and municipalities, reducing poverty, and strengthening citizen participation. In effect, the most important innovation of this program was precisely that it required societal participation to carry out a wide range of social projects: schools, electricity, roads, hospitals, potable water, and so on. The central idea behind this project was that traditional social programs introduced by the federal government to diminish poverty and promote regional development were inefficient because they lacked community support. Therefore, it was essential to promote the creation of new social leaders who would emerge from the communities and could serve as interlocutors between the government and society. Through the organization of so-called "solidarity committees," PRONASOL was aimed at fostering a new form of citizen participation that would channel resources to communities.

Although undoubtedly PRONASOL brought economic resources to thousands of communities that had previously been ignored, this program to a large degree bypassed municipal and state authorities and ended up centralizing both decisions on how resources would be allocated and project definition in the federal government, particularly the Treasury Ministry and Social Development Ministry (SEDESOL).

In principle, the activities of PRONASOL were stipulated in a Convenio de Desarrollo Social (CDS) that the federal executive signed with the governor of each state. In these agreements, joint investment commitments were formulated. These accords should have originated in the COPLADES, the planning entities established by the previous government. In practice, PRONASOL operated directly through SEDESOL delegates who received proposals and petitions directly from the communities organized in the solidarity committees. Many resources transferred to states did not pass through the CDSs, but were allocated in a parallel manner and managed by delegates of the federal offices in each state. Moreover, the SEDESOL delegate reached the point of having more power than mayors or the governor both in reference to the amount of resources allocated and project approval. As Cabrero affirms, PRONASOL weakened the state and local levels of government by trying to establish direct contact with communities.[35] Finally, the distribution of PRONASOL resources by federal entities was erratic and obeyed political criteria to a great extent. PRONASOL allocated important resources to areas in which the political opposition had become strong.[36]

In spite of PRONASOL's good intentions to foster citizen participation and to alter, in this manner, the traditional and paternalistic development model, it did not achieve its objectives. In the first place, the citizen participation fostered by this program was not channeled through institutions. The community participated in the startup of particular projects, but when the project ended, this citizen participation evaporated. Citizen participation through the solidarity committees did not contribute to the fostering of greater responsibility among municipal and state authorities vis-à-vis the citizenry. Second, poor people, for whom this program was destined, generally had few organizational skills. Many poor communities that were not able to organize themselves did not obtain resources. Third, if PRONASOL managed to bring resources to communities that had never before been so privileged, in many cases it did so by bypassing local authorities who had insufficient incentives or means to apply pressure necessary to respond to the needs and demands of their citizens. In other words, although PRONASOL served as an arm of the federal government to "bypass" local bosses, it ended up weakening municipal and state authorities in general and taking away from the most professional, responsible, and democratic governments the ability to participate in the regional planning process and develop a long-term vision. It is no surprise that in many poor states in the country, PRONASOL's resources were used to construct basketball courts in place of hospitals and schools. Although those projects reflect what the community "decided" to build, they also reflect the lack of planning and a more rational allocation of resources. Finally, after six years of operation, PRONASOL did not contribute to the reduction of regional imbalances nor to the alleviation of poverty. The clearest example is Chiapas, a state that received very considerable quantities of resources during the entire six years and which remained submerged in absolute poverty.

Since the 1980s, the federal government has manifested its intention to decentralize healthcare and education services in favor of the states. How-

ever, during the 1980s, it made few advances on this front. Although some
legal modifications were made to facilitate the transfer of these services to
the states, the operation of these services remained in the hands of the federal government.

Education

In 1992, the federal government signed with the state governments and the
National Union of Educational Workers the National Accord for the Modernization of Basic Education. This accord established that the federal government would transfer to the states the responsibility of operating the educational system, the financial resources necessary to operate the system,
active students, and labor relations with the teachers.[37] A large part of the
decision to decentralize the educational system was motivated by an intent
to break up and thus limit the power of the union, the largest and most powerful in Mexico.[38] The decision was also undoubtedly motivated by a need
to relieve the federal government of its excessive responsibilities and improve the quality of educational services.

Critics argue that the process reflects a decentralization of functions
rather than the system as a whole, since the most important decisions, such
as the allocation of resources for education, teacher salaries, curricula design, teacher training, and student performance evaluation, remained in the
hands of the federal government.[39] Many governors, above all from the opposition, complained openly, stating that in reality the problems were decentralized, without giving state governments the autonomy and sufficient
incentives to resolve them. By conditioning the transfers destined for educational services without giving the state governments the power to reward
or punish teachers for their performance, the governors were converted into
simple administrators and were capable of promoting better educational
services in their states.

The accord also created confusion regarding specific responsibilities of
the three levels of government in the area of education. School construction,
for example, is a joint responsibility of the federal and state governments,
while school maintenance is the responsibility of the municipality. Municipalities insist that more schools be constructed, while the state and federal
governments demand improvements in maintenance by municipalities. The
result, frequently, is that neither the construction of new schools nor the
maintenance of existing schools takes place.

Finally, the distribution of educational transfers across the country has been unequal, since resources have been allocated for education without taking into account expenditures that some states make out of their own budgets. In some states, such as Chihuahua, Baja California, Nuevo León, Coahuila, and the Estado de México, the governments earmark a large part of their revenues for education, while in other states, such as Oaxaca, the Federal District, Quintana Roo, Guanajuato, among many others, education is covered entirely by federal government transfers. In brief, the federal government does not adequately take into account the effort that some states make to pay for and improve the educational services.

Health Care

As in education, since the 1980s the government has manifested its decision to decentralize healthcare services to the states. Up to 1987, some responsibilities had been decentralized in fourteen states. Similar to what was taking place in the area of education, the decentralization of healthcare services during the 1980s was more a decentralization of functions, since the fourteen states were under the firm control and supervision of the Public Health Ministry.[40] However, in the 1990s (and during the administration of President Ernesto Zedillo), the decentralization of healthcare services made significant advances that were actually more positive than those made in education. In 1995, the National Health Council was created, in which all states and the federal government were represented. This council served as an entity for coordination, negotiation, and the resolution of conflicts between different levels of government. On the other hand, the states had more autonomy to decide how to allocate resources destined for healthcare services than for education.[41] However, the federal government continued having significant discretionary powers to allocate healthcare resources to the states, establish doctors' salaries, and establish quality standards. Finally, according to some studies, healthcare services have not experienced a significant improvement as a result of decentralization. The quality of healthcare services continues to be deficient, the number of physicians per capita in many areas of the country continues to be insufficient, and regional disparities persist. Moreover, as Cardozo Brum argues, in states that have still not decentralized their healthcare services, such as Zacatecas, important advances have been observed in performance indicators, which indicates that there are alternatives to decentralization to improve healthcare services.[42]

The "New Federalism": The Administration of
Ernesto Zedillo (1994–2000)

The guerrilla uprising in Chiapas in 1994, the assassination of the PRI candidate for president, Luis Donaldo Colosio, the strengthening of the political opposition in many states, and the brutal economic crisis unleashed in 1995, severely restricted the maneuvering room of the federal government to resolve multiple social, political, and economic problems.[43] Although the federal government and in particular, the president, continued concentrating enormous discretionary powers at the top, for President Zedillo it was clear that excessive political and economic centralism constituted one of the most serious obstacles to reversing socioeconomic inequities, regional imbalances, and deterioration in the quality of life for the majority of the population. It was no surprise, therefore, that a few days after coming to power, the president had announced the "New Federalism" as a political priority of his government, and that decentralization had been converted into a core idea of this project.

The New Federalism intended to reform financial relations among the various levels of government; reduce the discretionary power of the president; strengthen state and municipal governments; encourage an effective separation among the executive, legislative, and judicial powers; promote increased transparency in electoral processes; and contribute to the democratization of public life.[44] During the Zedillo administration, there actually were important advances in decentralization: the amount of resources transferred to the states and municipalities increased significantly, most of all after 1997 when the mid-term elections took place and the PRI lost its majority in Congress. Given opposition party pressure, particularly from the PAN, the PRI accepted an increase in the amount of resources transferred to states and municipalities. Up until this date, 80 percent of all resources collected by the federation remained in the center, while 17 percent went to the states and 3 percent went to the municipalities. In 1998, the federal government reduced its share by almost ten percentage points, reserving 70.9 percent of all resources for itself, and allocating 24.4 percent to the states and 4.7 percent to the municipalities.[45] In addition, the federal government introduced a series of rules that reduced the discretionary power of the federal government and made more transparent the process of distributing these resources. Other advances during Zedillo's term included training programs for municipal authorities were financed; functions of sectors such as agriculture, environment, road construction and maintenance, and public security were decentralized to the states; and the new Article 115 of the Constitution was reformed to grant increased powers to municipalities.[46]

However, much of the inertia of the past has continued. First, the majority of total expenditures continues to be managed by the federal government, although the participation of states and municipalities has increased.[47] Second, states and municipalities have returned to being even more dependent on transferred resources (shares, transfers, and allocations) from Mexico City since they continue to lack the power to increase their own revenues through increased tax levies. In 1996, transfers were almost six times greater than states' own revenues.[48] According to a study carried out by the government of Nuevo León, in 2000, an average 91.4 percent of state revenues derived from federal transfers; the same figure for municipalities was 70.6 percent.[49]

Third, the majority of allocations and transfers that the states and municipalities receive come earmarked for specific projects, reducing considerably the autonomy of state and municipal governments to decide how to spend their resources. In the words of Giugale et al., "[I]t seems that the states receive more orders than funds."[50] The imposition of conditions on the transfer of resources reflects the distrust that the federal government continues to have in the states and municipalities.

Fourth, the majority of "unconditioned" resources (transfers) are used to pay current expenditures, which leaves few resources available for investment. For the states that pay for educational services out of their own budgets, educational expenditures represent an enormous budget obligation. States such as Chihuahua, Baja California, and Nuevo León earmark around 90 percent of their transfers to cover educational expenditures.[51]

Fifth, although the legal framework has advanced in the area of decentralization, ambiguities in the allocation of responsibilities among the three levels of government persist. This has a negative effect since each level of government can blame one or both of the other levels for not carrying out its responsibilities, and may hope, in this manner, that the others will grant more resources or resolve existing problems.

Sixth, although transfers to the states and municipalities increased substantially, most of all since 1997, many of these transfers are allocated directly to the municipalities and not to the states. Since 1998, with the creation of the so-called Section 33 (substituting for Section 26 under which PRONASOL was established), many of the resources dedicated to regional development and combating poverty have been transferred directly to the municipalities.[52] This has weakened the ability of the states to plan and make decisions regarding expenditures.[53]

Finally, resource transfers do not take into account the abilities and past performance of municipal and state administrators. While officials in many municipalities do not know how to manage the resources that have been transferred to them, others believe that their efforts have not been rewarded with increased resources. Effective mechanisms do not exist to ensure that the transfer of resources is carried out according to performance indicators and that, in this manner, incentives are generated to encourage states and municipalities to become more responsible in managing expenditures.

Decentralization, Democracy, and Regional Development: An Evaluation

Since the 1980s, the Mexican government has implemented decentralization policies that have significantly increased both the resources available to states and municipalities and their power and responsibilities to provide public services. The final evaluation of the impact of these policies, however, should be measured with respect to their ability to respond to and resolve the problems that encouraged their creation in the first place: promoting more balanced regional development, reducing poverty levels, increasing the quality of public services—that is, raising the quality of life of the population.[54] In the case of Mexico, it is precisely here that the evaluation is not completely positive. In effect, in twenty years, the economic and social reality of Mexico has not changed significantly, and in some regards, we could say that living conditions have worsened. Today there are more poor people in the country than there were in 1980,[55] inequalities between the north and south persist, and public services continue to be inadequate. Of course, a large part of the situation can be attributed to the various economic crises that the country has suffered in the last twenty years. Nevertheless, asking whether decentralization has contributed to reducing the gap between rich and poor and between prosperous states and states submerged in poverty is worthwhile. The principal problem has not been a lack of economic resources. In the last twenty years, the government has promoted various programs and channeled large quantities of financial resources to promote regional development and combat poverty. How can we explain, then, the negative results?

Although decentralization can have important economic impacts, it is not a panacea. If decentralization offers the possibility of achieving better concordance between public goods provided by the government and preferences by the population in order to achieve positive results, this policy ought to be accompanied by democratic institutions and mechanisms that permit citizen participation.[56] Moreover as World Bank analysts state, "decentralization well done can have many economic benefits: producing increased efficiency, [and] responding better to the population in the provision of public services. But poorly done, decentralization can have undesirable consequences: macroeconomic imbalance, the exacerbation of regional imbalances, and the reduction in the quality of public services."[57] The success of decentralization depends, therefore, on the political institutions in which it is framed and the particular ways in which decentralization is introduced in each country.

In the case of Mexico, the precariousness of democratic institutions and the fundamental objective of the federal government to ensure the hegemony of the PRI explain to a large degree the forms that decentralization has taken and the results of decentralization policies. Since the 1980s, decentralization was introduced by the federal government with the firm objective of *not* losing the reins of political control. If particular decentralization policies sought to relieve the federal government of responsibilities that it could not carry out efficaciously, they were not conceived as instruments designed to change the balance of power among the three levels of government nor to increase the accountability of state and local authorities to their citizens. Decentralization was conceived of as an administrative policy aimed at maintaining the PRI in power.

Many of the "errors" that supposedly could be avoided in the adoption of decentralization policies were committed in Mexico. According to World Bank analysts, although a uniform way of implementing decentralization in all countries in the world does not exist, there are certain errors that ought to be avoided: (1) decentralizing resources without decentralizing responsibilities; (2) allocating resources in a uniform manner without considering the diversity of size, population, and above all abilities that exist among distinct states and municipalities; (3) not relying on normative and legal frameworks and organizations that are in charge of coordinating, negotiating, and resolving conflicts among various levels of government; (4) not preparing and disseminating reliable and exact information about all aspects of decentralization; and (5) decentralizing abruptly and uniformly.[58]

From this long list of errors, we could say that in the case of Mexico, the first error is the most evident: decentralization of resources without corresponding decentralization of responsibilities. The principal problem—with all of its variations—of decentralization in Mexico is that until 2000, state and municipal governments continued to lack the autonomy necessary (and thus, the responsibility) to make their own decisions and foster economic development. The balance of power among the three levels of government has continued to favor the center. Although resources have been decentralized, state and municipal governments do not have sufficient maneuvering room to manage these resources nor do they have adequate incentives to be accountable for expenditure management. By placing conditions on a large portion of the resources transferred to the states and municipalities, the federal government assumes that these levels of government are not sufficiently responsible nor capable of managing expenditures more autonomously. But without possessing more freedom to manage their resources, state and municipal governments can neither develop their abilities nor become more responsible. It becomes, in effect, a vicious circle. In addition, by conditioning and earmarking resources transferred to states and municipalities, the federal government privileges control ex-ante and not ex-post over the transfer of resources. Consequently, performance indicators that could serve as more efficacious instruments in controlling the management of the expenditure of resources transferred by the federal government have not been developed. States and municipalities that are more responsible and capable in expenditure management could be rewarded with more resources when their indicators are positive. The federal government could continue to have more direct control over resources in those states and municipalities with less capacity or responsibility to manage them. Moreover, efficiency and performance indicators could encourage states and municipalities to become more accountable and increase their governance capabilities since this would bring them not only more resources but also more autonomy from the central government.

The remaining errors pointed out by the World Bank analysts also resonate in the case of Mexico. Decentralization has proceeded in effect by following uniform criteria. The great diversity of the population, abilities, and resources that exist among municipalities and states has not been taken into account. The reform of Article 115 of the Constitution, for example, assumes that all municipalities can levy taxes and provide services such as paving roads, installing and maintaining street lighting, and so on. However, for rural municipalities, these reforms continue to be practically irrelevant. Moreover, the allocation of resources to states and municipalities in the country has also followed uniform patterns. Consequently, richer states feel that resource transfers are not just, since they do not take sufficiently into account their share of the gross national product and their ability to levy and collect taxes. Poor states, on the other hand, feel that the transfers allocated by the federation are not sufficiently compensatory. Under the current system of economic transfers to the states, richer states continue to be favored by the federal government.[59]

In the legal and normative realm, decentralization has made great advances. However, some problems still exist. In various public policy areas, such as education, environment, and highway construction and maintenance, confusion continues regarding the responsibility and powers that correspond to each level of government. In addition, although an institute that provides financial consulting to states and municipalities exists,[60] an intergovernmental relations office that coordinates, negotiates, and resolves conflicts among the three levels of government and that has the capacity to respond to all matters relevant to intergovernmental relations (health care, education, environment, regional development, etc.) does not exist.

Finally, regarding the production and dissemination of information, the balance in Mexico has been negative. A great vacuum in the production of information, most of all financial, exists. The National Institute of Geography and Statistics (INEGI) disseminates information that analysts and even government officials consider unreliable. States have very different abilities to produce financial and economic data. And until recently, the federal government had not made a sufficient effort to publicly disseminate information produced by various government ministries.

Once the PRI was defeated, the search for a new (less centralized) balance of power among federal, state, and municipal governments is without doubt one of the biggest challenges that the government of President Vicente Fox faces. And this challenge is complicated enormously because the democratization of political life in Mexico has not advanced uniformly throughout the country. In the Mexican "sea of democracy," authoritarian islands continue to exist.[61] Giving greater levels of autonomy to governors or mayors who govern in an authoritarian manner would contribute to fostering local bosses, the same problem that created the excessive centralization of power after the Revolution. The challenge of decentralization in Mexico implies, therefore, not only the recognition of economic, social, and political diversity, but also deepening and consolidating democracy.

Notes

1. Mauricio Merino, *Fuera del Centro* (Veracruz: Universidad Veracruzana, 1992), 12.

2. Alberto Díaz Cayeros, "Diez Mitos Sobre el Federalismo Mexicano," in *La Ciencia Política en México,* edited by Mauricio Merino (Mexico City: FCE-CONAC-ULTA, 1999).

3. Enrique Cabrero, "La Ola Descentralizadora: Un Análisis de Tendencias y Obstáculos de las Políticas Descentralizadoras en el Ámbito Internacional," in *Las Políticas Descentralizadoras en México (1983–1993): Logros y Desencantos,* edited by Enrique Cabrero, 104–31 (Mexico City: Miguel Angel Porrúa-Centro de Investigación y Docencia Económicas, 1998).

4. Banco Interamericano de Desarrollo, *America Latina Tras una Década de Reformas* (Washington, D.C.: Banco Interamericano de Desarrollo, 1997), chapter 3.

5. Around the beginning of the 1980s, the Partido de Acción Nacional (PAN) began mobilizing numbers of people during its campaigns. However, for years the PRI and the federal government resisted recognizing opposition electoral victories. The pressure continued to grow until the end of the 1980s when opportunities began to appear for the opposition. The PAN candidate won the gubernatorial race in 1989 for the first time in the history of Baja California state. Two years later, the PAN also controlled the state of Guanajuato. In 1992, the PAN won the elections in Chihuahua state. The Partido de la Revolución Democrática (PRD) obtained its first victory in the Federal District in 1997. In 2000, the PAN controlled the governments in the states of Querétaro, Guanajuato, Baja California, Jalisco, Aguascalientes, Morelos, and Nuevo León. The PRD controlled the governments in Zacatecas, the Federal District, Tlaxcala, and Baja California Sur. In Chiapas and Nayarit the PRD and the PAN govern in coalitions with other parties not related to the PRI.

6. According to a study carried out by Nora Lustig for the Inter-American Development Bank in 1999, the proportion of the population living in absolute poverty in Mexico increased from 28.5 percent of the population in 1984 to 42.5 percent in 1996. Lustig, *La Superación de la Pobreza: Diálogos Nacionales* (Washington, D.C.: Banco Interamericano de Desarrollo, February 1999).

7. Ignacio Marván, "Reflexiones Sobre Federalismo y Sistema Político en México," *Política y Gobierno* 1 (1997).

8. Alberto Díaz Cayeros, *Desarrollo Económico e Inequidad Regional: Hacia un Nuevo Pacto Federal en México* (Mexico City: Miguel Angel Porrúa, 1995), 11.

9. Marván, "Reflexiones."

10. Merino, *Fuera del Centro,* 60.

11. Thomas Courchene and Alberto Díaz Cayeros, "Transfers and the Nature of the Mexican Federation," in *Achievements and Challenges of Fiscal Decentralization. Lessons from Mexico,* edited by Marcelo Giugale and Steven B. Webb (Washington, D.C.: World Bank, 2000), 203.

12. C.J. Friedrich, "Federalism and Opposition," in *Government and Opposition* 1, no. 3 (1996): 286. Federalism, on the other hand, also generated conditions favorable to the development of opposition parties, most of all in undemocratic regimes. A political party can organize itself more easily on a local level than on a federal level, where it needs the support of a much greater quantity of resources and sympathizers. Likewise, for an authoritarian political regime, recognizing an opposition victory on a local level can be more tolerable than recognizing one at a national level. This point is further described below.

13. Party discipline was also strengthened by the introduction in 1933 of the clause prohibiting reelection to positions filled by public elections. Mayors and local and federal deputies have a mandate to serve for three years and cannot seek reelection for consecutive terms. Governors, senators, and the president of the republic have a mandate to serve for six years and cannot be reelected.

14. Alicia Hernández Chávez, "Federalismo y gobernabilidad en México," in Marcello Carmagnani, *Federalismos Latinoamerianos: México, Brasil, Argentina* (Mexico City: FCE-El Colegio de México, 1993).

15. Plutarco Elías Calles made himself the "supreme leader" of the Revolution in the 1920s. After founding the Partido Nacional Revolucionario (PNR), the "grandfather" of the PRI, Calles became the revolutionary leader who governed behind the scenes. Once Cárdenas had him expelled from the country, the president of the republic became the natural leader of the official party during his six years in office.

16. Merino, *Fuera del Centro*, 23.

17. In 1968 the student movement was harshly repressed by the government. The famous "massacre of Tlatelolco" inaugurated a new, slow, and very gradual period of transition in Mexico.

18. Cabrero, "La Ola Descentralizadora," 104; Victoria Rodríguez, *Decentralization in Mexico: From Reforma Municipal to Solidaridad to Nuevo Federalismo* (Boulder, Colo.: Westview Press, 1997), 62.

19. Cabrero, "La Ola Descentralizadora," 105.

20. Merino, *Fuera del Centro*.

21. Cabrero, "La Ola Descentralizadora," 106.

22. Merino, *Fuera del Centro*, 57.

23. Ibid., 116.

24. Courchene and Díaz Cayeros, "Transfers and the Nature of the Mexican Federation," 126.

25. The resources that the federation transfers to the states and municipalities are apportioned according to various criteria. "Shares" of fiscal resources are allocated according to a formula that takes into account the amount collected in each state, total population, and poverty level. Conditions regarding use are not placed on these resources. In contrast, "transfers" (and since 1997, "contributions") are earmarked as compensation for regional imbalances, and in most cases are distributed with more discretion. These resources must be used for specific projects. In addition to these resources, the federation invests in the states and municipalities. The distribution of federal public investment is also discretionary. Until 1999, the federal government had an additional fund (called Section 23) for contingencies, which was also distributed on a discretionary basis. This fund was eliminated in 1999. For a description of intergovernmental transfers, see Cayeros, *Desarrollo Económico e Inequidad Regional,* 1995; and Courchene and Díaz Cayeros, "Transfers and the Nature of the Mexican Federation."

26. Cabrero, "La Ola Descentralizadora," 131.

27. Ibid., 126.

28. The states have the power to request credit from the national private banks; they cannot request credit from foreign banks. The loans are guaranteed based on federal shares, and can only be used to cover investment costs and not operating costs. Although some states such as the Estado de México, Nuevo León, and Jalisco acquired large debts during the 1980s and 1990s, the total debt of state and municipal governments is still equivalent to a small proportion of the gross national product. In comparison with other countries in Latin America, the state governments' combined debt does not represent a threat to macroeconomic stability. See Marcelo Giugale, Fausto Hernández Trillo, and Joao C. Oliveira, "Subnational Borrowing and Debt Management," in *Achievements and Challenges of Fiscal Descentralization. Lessons from Mexico,* edited by Marcelo Giugale and Steven Webb (Washington, D.C.: World Bank, 2000), 239. During the 1990s,

the federal government rescued various state governments, since with the increase in interest rates in 1995 and 1996, the states could not pay their debts. Since 1997, the states have also acquired the power to collect a gasoline tax, but many states have decided not to collect this tax either because they do not have the ability to collect it or to avoid public discontent.

29. Salinas faced serious opposition within his own party, given that since the government of Miguel de la Madrid, antagonism between technocrats and the political elite increased. This antagonism was the origin of the split in 1987, when Cárdenas and a sizeable group of PRI supporters left the party.

30. The PAN's first electoral victory was recognized in 1989 in the state of Baja California. In 1991, the PAN rose to power in Guanajuato, albeit after a large postelectoral confrontation. Given the evidence of fraud, the PAN organized a mass mobilization that forced the Salinas government to cancel the elections that the PRI had officially won. Although an interim governor from the PAN was named, Vicente Fox, who was candidate for governor in 1991 and one of the strongest critics of the Salinas government, could not take power until after the next election in 1995. Finally, in Chihuahua, the PAN won the gubernatorial election in 1992. No state-level electoral victories by the PRD were recognized during the Salinas government.

31. Salinas dismissed ten governors and removed an additional five governors to serve in federal government posts.

32. Juan Molinar and Jeffrey A. Weldon, "Electoral Determinants and Consequences of National Solidarity," in *Transforming State–Society Relations in Mexico: The National Solidarity Strategy,* edited by Wayne A. Cornelius, Ann L. Craig, and Jonathan Fox, 123–41 (La Jolla: Center for U.S.–Mexican Studies, University of California-San Diego, 1994); John Bailey, "Centralism and Political Change in Mexico: The Case of National Solidarity," in *Transforming State–Society Relations in Mexico: The National Solidarity Strategy.*

33. Cornelius et al., *Transforming State–Society Relations in Mexico.*

34. Cabrero, "La Ola Descentralizadora," 111.

35. Ibid., 114.

36. Cornelius et al., *Transforming State-Society Relations in Mexico.*

37. Carlos Ornelas, "El Ámbito Sectorial: La Descentralización de la Educación en México. El Federalismo Difícil," in *Las Políticas Descentralizadoras en México (1983–1993): Logros y Desencantos,* edited by Enrique Cabrero (Mexico City: Miguel Angel Porrúa-Centro de Investigación y Docencia Económicas, 1998).

38. Rodríguez, *Decentralization in México,* 70.

39. Enrique Cabrero and Jorge Martínez-Vázquez, "Assignment of Spending Responsibilities and Service Delivery," in *Achievements and Challenges of Fiscal Decentralizations. Lessons from Mexico,* edited by Marcelo Giugale and Steven Webb (Washington, D.C.: World Bank, 2000), 153.

40. Ibid., 160.

41. Ibid., 162.

42. Myriam Cardozo Brum, "El Ámbito Sectorial: Análisis de la Descentralización en el Sector Salud (1983–1993)," in *Las Políticas Descentralizadoras en México (1983–1993). Logros y Desencantos,* edited by Enrique Cabrero (Mexico City: Miguel Angel Porrúa-Centro de Investigación y Docencia Económicas, 1998), 258–59.

43. Perhaps the episode that most clearly reveals the limitations of presidential power is the difficulty that President Zedillo had dismissing (following the traditional

scheme) the PRI governor of Tabasco. The gubernatorial election in this state was egregiously fraudulent, and the PRD, the principal opposition party in the state, had documented proof of the fraud. Although President Zedillo "negotiated" the resignation of the governor with the PRI in exchange for which the party would support the electoral reforms proposed by the government, the governor of Tabasco rebelled against the federal government and refused to resign. Until the last day of his government, Roberto Madrazo represented one of the strongest opposition forces to the president within his own party. The case of Tabasco has been splendidly analyzed in Todd A. Eisenstadt, "Electoral Federalism or Abdication of Presidential Authority? Gubernatorial Elections in Tabasco," in *Subnational Politics and Democratization in Mexico,* edited by Wayne A. Cornelius, Todd A. Eisenstadt, and Jane Hindley (La Jolla: Center for U.S.–Mexican Studies, University of California-San Diego, 2000).

44. Rodríguez, *Decentralization in México.*

45. Carlos Martínez Assad and Alicia Ziccardi, "Límites y Posibilidades para la Descentralización de las Políticas Sociales," in *Las Políticas Sociales de México al Fin del Milenio: Descentralización, Diseño y Gestión,* edited by Rolando Cordera and Alicia Ziccardi (Mexico City: Instituto de Investigaciones Sociales, Universidad Nacional Autónoma de México, and Miguel Angel Porrúa, 2000), 721.

46. Some of the most important points of this reform were the municipality's power to govern and not just to administer through the municipal council was recognized; powers exclusive to the municipality that before were held concurrently with the state, such as public works, police, and potable water, were recognized; limitations were eliminated so that the municipalities of different states could work together in the provision of services; and the municipality was guaranteed the right of initiative vis-à-vis tax base. Juan Pablo Guerrero y Tonatiuh Guillén, eds., *Reflexiones en Torno a la Reforma Municipal del Artículo 115* (Mexico City: Miguel Angel Porrúa-Centro de Investigación y Docencia Económicas, 2000).

47. There are no figures available after 1996. In addition, there are inconsistencies among available databases. But according to Cabrero and Martínez-Vázquez ("Assignment of Spending Responsibilities and Service Delivery," 143), from 1994 to 1996, the share of the federal government in the management of total expenditures was reduced by two percentage points.

48. Giugale et al., "Subnational Borrowing and Debt Management," 60.

49. This information was given to me directly by the treasurer of the Nuevo León government, who designed a study and proposal about the new national system of governmental transfers. The dependence of the states on the central government is greater than that of the municipalities because municipalities have greater powers to generate their own revenues by charging property taxes. This is the most important independent revenue source for municipalities.

50. Giugale et al., "Subnational Borrowing and Debt Management," 62.

51. Yemile Mizrahi, "¿Administrar o Gobernar? El Reto del Gobierno Panista en Chihuahua," *Frontera Norte* 16 (1996); Ornelas, "El Ámbito Sectorial: La Descentralización de la Educación en México."

52. Juan Pablo Guerrero, "Algunas Lecciones de la Descentralización del Gasto Social," in *Las Políticas Sociales de México al Fin del Milenio: Descentralización, Diseño y Gestión,* edited by Rolando Cordera and Alicia Ziccardi (Mexico City: Instituto de Investigaciones Sociales, Universidad Nacional Autónoma de México, and Miguel Angel Porrúa, 2000); Assad and Ziccardi, "Límites y Posibilidades para la Descentralización

de las Políticas Sociales," 729. Together with the dismantling of PRONASOL, the government of Zedillo introduced a new program to combat poverty that was much more focused on individuals who ranked among the poorest of the poor. PROGRESA was the most important program aimed at combating poverty of his six-year term and its operation remained in the hands of the federal government. Although these resources were spent in the municipalities, contrary to other earmarked programs, PROGRESA was a completely centralized operation. For a description of PROGRESA, see Assad and Ziccardi, "Límites y Posibilidades para la Descentralización de las Políticas Sociales."

53. The reaction of the PRI governor of Puebla, Manuel Bartlett, against the central government is symptomatic of this situation. Bartlett promoted state legislation which established that projects financed by resources transferred to the states and municipalities ought to be approved by the Municipal Planning Committees, in which mayors and nongovernmental organizations participated. Given that the PAN controlled the majority of urban municipalities in Puebla, Bartlett opposed letting the municipalities receive the resources without first having the resources pass through state government controls. Although Bartlett's rebellion against Mexico City was announced as a rebellion of the traditional "political elite" of the PRI against the "technocrats" led by President Zedillo, many PAN governors (silently) supported the stance of the PRI governor. For them as well, the allocation of resources earmarked for municipalities reduced their maneuvering power in planning and deciding how to spend resources in their states.

54. Olivier Lafourcade, "Preface," in *Achievements and Challenges of Fiscal Decentralization. Lessons from Mexico,* edited by Marcelo Giugale and Steven B. Webb (Washington, D.C.: World Bank, 2000), xv.

55. Lustig, *La Superación de la Pobreza: Diálogos Nacionales.*

56. Banco Interamericano del Desarrollo, *America Latina Tras una Década de Reformas,* 176.

57. Giugale et al., "Subnational Borrowing and Debt Management," 4.

58. Ibid.

59. Cayeros, *Desarrollo Económico e Inequidad Regional;* Cabrero, "La Ola Descentralizadora."

60. The Institute for the Technical Development of the Public Treasury (INDETEC) depends on the Treasury and Public Credit Ministry. In 2000, the federal government created a Decentralization Committee within the Treasury Ministry to coordinate intergovernmental fiscal relations. Beyond the fiscal realm, however, there is no authority/ office that can respond to issues such as education, environment, highways, and so on.

61. One example is undoubtedly Víctor Cervera Pacheco, governor of Yucatán state, who relied on traditional patronage practices.

Chapter 3

Decentralization and Civil Society in Mexico

Leticia Santín del Río

Current politics in Mexico are characterized by expressions of plurality, competition, and political competition for the integration of powers and the representation of authorities in the three levels of government: federal, state, and municipal. This new map is an expression of a long process of democratization that has manifested in diverse areas while modifying the relationship between society and government. This relationship has changed rapidly and substantially in the last few years. This is particularly notable when living conditions of many groups of Mexicans have deteriorated. Over the last three decades, numerous policy reorientations have taken the form of decentralization processes. In a parallel manner, civil society groups demanding economic improvements and the opening of social, legal, and political spaces have increased their activities and found new forms of participation.

Since the administration of Miguel de la Madrid (1982–1988), the country has begun to put into practice decentralization policies. This has resulted from the pressure of the foreign debt and the drastic reduction in public

59

spending destined, among other line items, to welfare assistance, poverty alleviation, health care, and social security. These line items were inherited from the long period of stabilizing development (1934–1981) that modified the supposed social justice pact that had existed since the revolution of 1910. Mexican government officials felt obligated to define a new development model characterized by domestic market openness, control of the deficit and fiscal moderation, and privatization of the economy. The government was forced to transfer its role as motor of growth to other agents: international capital, private domestic businesses, and civil society. This effort, initiated in the context of a de jure federal system, but a de facto centralized one, did not combine economic transition with a clear political transition favoring a political party system and, consequently, a broader distribution of power outside the center. The adjustment process mandated by the economic reforms had a high social cost—millions of people in both urban and rural areas experienced declining standards of living. The inertia of the authoritarian political system limited institutional and administrative reforms in state and municipal governments, even as it operationalized decentralization policies. But decentralization of the national government was also limited by the traditional rigid control of municipalities exercised by state governments; this situation militated against incorporating *bottom-up* efforts to establish democratic governance.

The top-down decentralization promoted by the federal government could not alone resolve the problems inherited from a centralized *presidencialista* (presidential) system and corporatist political pacts orchestrated by a small group of leaders in the Partido Institucional Revolucionario (PRI). Nevertheless, in recent years this process has required the building of a democratic relationship between government and society. This transformation has been manifesting itself at the municipal level and through various forms of civil society participation that have influenced change at the national and state levels of government.

Decentralization and democratization in Mexico have taken parallel paths. Many scholars argue that in countries with centralized authoritarian regimes, decentralization has had (or will have) a positive and direct impact on democratization processes, as seen in the construction of electoral coalitions at the national level or in the impulse to create institutional structures that promote citizen participation. However, the relationship between the two phenomena in Mexico is generally in the opposite direction. In brief, the strengthening of opposition political parties, and the activism of social movements, nongovernmental organizations, civil society groups and networks, as well as the pressure of principally urban municipal governments on higher-level government entities, have pressured the federal government to carry out more extensive reforms not only as part of the decentralization process, but also in response to demands for the deepening of democratization. Among the latter are demands for legal and political recognition of numerous social and political organizations.

Even though the Constitution has conferred upon municipalities the right to play a role in national government since the early twentieth century, municipalities did not have the authority, resources, or political wherewithal to convert themselves into autonomous decision makers and managers.[1] Civil society organizations that emerged in the 1960s through the late 1980s took upon themselves a variety of service-delivery functions at the local level. In the early years, they began with a series of short-term efforts demanding high levels of technical competence that were focused on serving the urban poor, workers, and rural populations and relied on European financing. This dynamic changed somewhat during the economic crises of the 1980s. It reoriented itself toward the establishment of better articulated projects through the formation of networks of civic organizations committed to social development (Organizaciones Civiles para la Promoción del Desarrollo; OCPDs) or related nongovernmental organizations (NGOs).[2]

Social Initiatives, Citizen Participation, and Democracy

As suggested above, civil society organizations were heavily involved in diverse social and economic projects during the 1960s, 1970s, and most of the 1980s. Most of the work of these organizations was aimed at benefiting marginalized populations on a small-scale basis, which meant that these were isolated and fragmented efforts. These organizations did not establish among the diverse movements and organizations many collaborative networks. Their political/ideological grounding was generally either Christian or leftist allied with development self-help efforts. These social action frameworks of assistance and promotion can be understood as "two paradigms of intervention in society to attend to social demands."[3] Even when these expressions of citizen responsibility and participation were isolated, they engendered positive outcomes, accumulating experience related to marginalized social sectors among Christian base groups and groups representing the political left. These latter groups were calling on existing civic organizations to discover more advanced ways to join forces in networks of social activism.

Over the course of thirty years, the diverse social and popular movements achieved a higher level of maturity in the face of the authoritarian inertia of the national regime, while channels of pluralist expression were opened with great difficulty. Starting with one of the most important social movements of this period, the student movement of 1968, a parting of the waters was achieved. This was a social movement comprised mainly of the urban middle classes, a product of the efficacy of revolutionary politics. It was also the result of a growing consciousness among these social groups of political and human rights and a commitment to promoting modernization. Participants in this movement were critical of the country's economic policies, even when they were the beneficiaries, and oriented their struggle toward opening new spaces for economic and political participation. As we know, the Mexican political system responded to the demands of the movement with direct physical repression, but also with a typical populist "opening" characterized by cooptation of the dissidents within the political networks that supported the PRI, and open hostility against those who stayed outside the limits of the system. Nevertheless, after this political event, the concept of civil society began to be used in Mexico as a consequence of what had been put into play by organized civil society groups demanding space for independent and socially and politically free decision making.

By the end of the 1980s, the logic of the system in place reached its limits (increased public spending, rising indebtedness, and protectionist policies). Under these circumstances, it was difficult to sustain the political pact and traditional control imposed by the regime. The authoritarian and exclusionary practices of the government and the politics of harassing civil society organizations caused the latter to search for a way to construct and strengthen a distinct civic identity. From there arose *networks* of civil society organizations, along with a critique of the dominant mechanisms of corporatism, cooptation, and authoritarian *presidencialismo*. The government manifested an open and progressive discourse toward civil society organizations and the citizenry in general, convoking in practice consultations with the citizenry and specific social projects. Yet, at the same time, it regularly harassed organizations and individuals through fiscal control mechanisms imposed to force their submission to the corporatist system, or publicly ignored social groups and civil society organizations beyond its control. In the face of this ambiguous dynamic, initiatives to construct networks of citizen organizations for promoting social development were concentrated on bringing together the efforts, experiences, and interests of numerous men and women committed to the idea that "democracy, dignity, peace and the public recognition that not all social life needed to pass through the spheres of government, political parties and for-profit businesses."[4]

Phases of Citizen Organization

There are two significant awakening periods of civil society organization networks and alliances committed to building democratic governance. During the first period, 1988 to 1994, various groups demanded solutions to fraud and corruption and declining living standards among the majority of the population, as well as citizen input into the design of public policies. This period was characterized by the emergence of large numbers of civic action groups and networks. A second phase, from 1994 to 2000, was marked by networks joining together to demand and support the deepening of electoral reforms to guarantee truly free, autonomous, and fair elections. In addition, civil society organizations wished to influence decision making at the municipal level, since in many areas the municipality became fertile ground for exercising grassroots power in improving and maintaining public sector goods and services at the community level.

Faced with government control mechanisms beginning in the 1990s, both civil society organizations and diverse political and social actors at the local level began to join forces to demand the transfer of federal resources and transparency in their allocation. In brief, NGOs adopted a public position calling for deepening the weak processes of decentralization that had been put in motion since 1982, and presented themselves to the national government as responsible and capable. Both phases were important for the process of bringing together actors and interests with national influence.

Civil society organizations often carry out both defensive and offensive functions. For instance, such groups may defend individuals or specific groups seeking legitimate access to spaces for social participation. They also serve as offensive instruments that seek to broaden access and participation of the citizenry at various levels of government and to establish mechanisms of control over the same system in the form of accountability. Civil society organizations struggled for basic civil and political rights in the 1980s and 1990s, within both the private and public sector spheres. However, at the same time, it must be emphasized that this development of civic organizations and nongovernmental organizations through networks and alliances did not, in all cases, turn out to be congruent with a spirit of democratic participation. There were tendencies and temptations to retain the interests of dominant groups or authoritarian practices, thereby maintaining exclusionary practices. Therefore, some of these organizations distanced themselves from broad-based and inclusive political projects.

Between 1983 and 1996, approximately twenty-four networks of OCPDs emerged at state and national levels to confront the serious problems caused by the economic and political deterioration of Mexican society. One element in this emergence of flourishing civil society organizations was the experience of mobilization efforts throughout the country from 1988 to 1994 to contend with seismic disturbances (in the wake of the earthquake disaster of 1985 and the government's response). In 1991, the struggle for free and fair elections and citizen dignity took the form of the so-called Navista citizen movement (from Dr. Luís Nava, an opposition party candidate) in the state of San Luís Potosí. This movement emerged in response to electoral fraud. Shortly thereafter, the Movimiento Ciudadano por la Democracia (Citizen Movement for Democracy) was formed, a network made up of citizens, journalists, intellectuals, civil society groups and NGOs from twenty states. Then in 1994, the Alianza Cívica/Observación Electoral (Civic Alliance/Electoral Observation) was established. According to Jorge Alonso,

> Civic culture promotes the accountability of those who govern and the defense of the governed. One recognizes the necessity to expand the public sphere with broad-based controls [exercised by] . . . civil society. Only a strong civil society is capable of unleashing processes of democratization. . . . The new civil society is weaving together articulations that are more horizontal, and is promoting the emergence of a new type of citizen consciousness.[5]

In 1991, Rafael Reygadas commented that social and civic organizations dedicated to the promotion of development and experience with Centros Populares de Desarrollo de la Niñez (Popular Centers of Child Development), street children, and defense of children's rights, began to professionalize their work, and set up the Colectivo Mexicano de Apoyo a la Niñez (Mexican Collective in Support of Children; COMEXANI), which, like the movement for democracy, brought together a large number of organizations from the entire country. Also in 1991, in the same manner NGOs from

Jalisco, Mexico City, and Morelos established the Red Interinstitucional de Iniciativas Civiles por la Desarrollo y Democracia (Interinstitutional Network of Civil Initiatives for Development and Democracy; Red INCIDE).

More and more issue-based networks, as well as networks with broader sociopolitical aims emerged to confront the crisis caused by government socioeconomic policies in the 1990s. Thus, after the U.N. Conference on the Environment and Development, or the Earth Summit in 1992 in Brazil, various groups whose work had been focused on housing joined forces to form the Mexican Section of the Habitat International Coalition (HIC-Mexico). Member organizations include the Centro Operacional de Vivienda y Poblamiento, A.C. (Operational Center for Housing and Settlement, A.C.; COPEVI), Fondo Social de la Vivienda, A.C. (Housing Social Fund, A.C.; FOSOVI), Centro de Vivienda (Housing Center; CENVI), Casa y Ciudad, A.C., (House and City), all of which have a great deal of experience in popular housing, environment, and ecology.[6]

In response to the rising incidence of malnutrition, some fifty organizations united to obtain food at low cost and to organize coalitions around the idea that adequate nutrition as a human right should become part of Mexican Constitution. Thus, the Frente por el Derecho a la Alimentación (Front for the Right to Food) arose in 1997, gaining recognition even outside of Mexico. Also in 1997, a broad-based forum was established around the theme of children, the elderly, work, rural areas, and the role of women, creating a common project under the name Foro de Apoyo Mutuo (Forum for Mutual Aid; FAM).

In 1994, an important civic participation event took place. Within the framework of an open electoral campaign and faced with the emergence of the Ejército Zapatista de Liberación Nacional (Zapatista Army for National Liberation; EZLN) in Chiapas on January 1, two significant civil society networks were established. The fundamental objectives of Alianza Cívica/ Observación 94 were to seek electoral reform and unprecedented election monitoring by citizens. A total of 20,000 citizens in the thirty-two states monitored the 1994 elections. At the same time, faced with the conflict in Chiapas and to support the indigenous communities of Chiapas, two networks were formed to promote peace: the Coordinación de ONGs por la Paz (Coordination of Nongovernmental Organizations for Peace; CONPAZ) and the Espacio Civil por la Paz (Civil Space for Peace; ESPAZ), which organized citizens to provide security for participants in San Cristóbal de Las Casas during the dialogue between the federal government and the EZLN.

In the process of forming these networks and coalitions, a pluralist participatory construction of society was created, leaving behind the model of isolated and focused work with which the social intervention had begun. Moreover, the networks succeeded in breaking away from the old corporatist models of organization and participation of national government administration, which had monopolized national representation and even international representation of civil society organizations in Mexico.

The Search for Identity and Legal Recognition by Civil Society Organizations

The possibility of counting on legitimacy in the form of legal recognition by the state was one of the primary tasks that the networks of civil society organizations undertook in the interest of promoting various social policies, especially those concerned with environment, housing, education, health care, child advocacy, and nutrition.[7] "The processes connected to the discussion and development of legislative proposals in this period were a strongly disputed area that put into contention the identity and political future of the OCPDs." The networks sought to incorporate a series of social practices in legislation that would in turn change public policies as well as make them viable. In sum, what was in play was "the place, the tasks, the identity of specific subjects and the recognition of the intervention of Mexican society."[8] Thus, in these essential aspects of social policy, the government was willing to set the practical limits of NGOs and define their work as legal or illegal, thereby complicating the element of recognition regarding their public interventions.

In this respect, it is worth mentioning that Mexican law imposed a series of limitations on most civil society organizations. In particular, the government achieved this through the Fiscal Miscellany law imposed in 1989. Elements and limitations related to carrying out nonprofit work were also established in the Civil Code. Moreover, the Chamber of Deputies approved income tax legislation that transformed the legal status of NGOs. They became legal organizations and were required to pay taxes and adhere to the same legal guidelines applied to large for-profit corporations, both domestic and foreign. This legislation inevitably made evident a series of issues that the civil associations and organizations needed to confront. However, they did not yield when faced with legal constrictions to their ability to establish themselves, since they sought ways to increase recognition, articulation, and broader organization. Paradoxically, these fiscal laws ultimately caused the OCPDs to find points of convergence around their principal task of social development, despite the fact that such laws represented legal pressures aimed at the control and taxation of civic associations.

NGO networks soon emerged. Faced with the authoritarianism of the Fiscal Miscellany law, civil society organizations found new ways to respond, including mechanisms for dialogue with government authorities and other entities of civil society. They succeeded in establishing the Convergencia de Organismos Civiles por la Democracia (Convergence of Civic Organisms for Democracy) in August 1990. The Convergencia was made up of more than 120 OCPDs and had a presence in eighteen states; FAM joined the Convergencia in 1992. The direct consequence of this great mobilization of civil society networks was the establishment of an inclusive and pluralistic vision of mutual cooperation.

The Convergencia devoted itself to the task of seeking diverse legal forms of association, in addition to mechanisms for suggesting fiscal reforms in response to the government's 1989 legislation. In this way, the affiliates hoped to constitute themselves as true nonprofit organizations of social interest and benefiting third parties. Their principal area of work was essentially oriented toward groups that did not have access to the minimum goods, services, and opportunities necessary for individual and/or social well-being. In this way, NGOs defended their role as organizations dedicated to meeting the most vital and urgent demands of the most needy popular sectors. At the same time, they defended human rights and the environment, and tried to achieve constitutional recognition of adequate nutrition as a right. In addition, these civil society organizations were committed to influencing the planning, follow-up, and evaluation of public policies, in the capacity of an organized citizen counterweight to government power for the promotion of development.

For its part, the FAM was successor to the Fundación por el Apoyo a la Comunidad (Community Support Foundation; FAC), which had been set up by the Archdiocese of Mexico to respond to the thousands of people affected by the earthquakes of 1985. FAC relied on national and international financing and resources. The links established through these actions served over time as mechanisms that brought together private financial institutions and foundations and civic organizations for promoting socioeconomic development to support diverse sectors of the population.[9] The FAM was formed in 1992 with the clear mandate of articulating new social policies on behalf of civic groups and associations. Organizations such as Fundación DEMOS, which was created to attract foreign resources, joined the FAM.[10]

It is interesting that by 1995 FAM was already comprised of 250 member organizations in various states. FAM was responding to multiple social issues, as well as initiating its own specific project of systematizing information about Mexico's external debt. Through a strategy of demanding responses from the government, FAM was requesting that the government negotiate agreements with foreign creditors that would permit the channeling of resources destined to pay the debt to go to regional development projects. At the same time, both Convergencia and this organization created novel pluralist and decentralized strategies for influencing policies in diverse states and for scrutinizing the national government's social and economic policies.

These networked organizations were not the only ones that established spaces for democratic action in tasks that benefited the population. However, they represent the best-organized and well-defined examples in Mexican society that have opened spaces for responsible participation of the citizenry. Their contribution is significant for the new ideas that they developed to scrutinize public policies, which made evident the need to redefine the responsibility shared between government and the citizenry in a more democratic fashion. In addition to successfully maintaining a certain autonomy, the networks defended their right to exist as nonprofit civic associations whose legal recognition was established many years ago in Article 9 of the Constitution. However, because they were critical of the prevailing political system, they had to contend with a series of obstacles created by the Fiscal Miscellany law. To the extent that diverse civil society organizations joined together in networks and coalitions and established policies that defended popular causes, they achieved legitimacy as spaces for citizen action. At the same time, the networks demonstrated that if all that is governmental is public, not all public fora are part of governmental action. Thus, the networks acquired legal identity and social recognition for the well-being of the collective.

The networks demonstrated that their projects and actions could not be generated from the center. Thus, civic responsibility and new forms of citizen participation and decision making extended to citizen education activities. Their goal was to make the population more conscious of their ability to defend their rights in the areas of gender equality, health care, adequate nutrition, housing, health and welfare of children, youth, and indigenous peoples, as well as their ability to defend legislation for professional support in the face of traditional corporatist inertia.

Citizen Initiatives to Guarantee
Basic Conditions for Democracy

In 1988, the political situation was tension ridden; economic crisis prevented the government from taking clear steps toward a political transition, that is, a multiparty system, impartial democracy, and broader distribution of power outside the center. A major source of tension was generated by the left when Cuauhtémoc Cárdenas abandoned the PRI, united numerous political forces and parties in the Frente Nacional Democratica (National Democratic Front), and ran as the Frente's presidential candidate in the 6 June 1988 elections. Denouncements of electoral fraud sparked a period of ongoing political crisis.

The demand for a strong multiparty system implied that political groups with different platforms recognized that they represented only selected groups in society, not everyone. Because of the PRI's prolonged hegemony, a political culture existed that confused the domination of one party with the dominion of the totality. In brief, the core party-state tended to avoid definitively recognizing political forces beyond its frontiers and systems of control. Meanwhile, the political opposition forces were either not open to dialogue, as was the case of the Partido de la Revolución Democratica (Democratic Revolutionary Party; PRD) during the government of Carlos Salinas de Gortari (1988–1994), or engaged in achieving specific negotiations, such as those between the PRI and the Partido Nacional de Acción (National Action Party; PAN) in the framework of economic adjustments. In the first years of this government, times were still difficult enough to preclude imagining a stable government regime sustained by a peaceful presidential succession every six years.

The Navista movement of San Luís Potosí in 1991 opened up new possibilities for citizen participation in politics. Diverse organizations joined forces with Convergencia's electoral oversight network, including the Red Mexicana de Acción Frente al Libre Comercio (Mexican Action Network Against Free Trade), Academia Mexicana de Derechos Humanos (Mexican Academy of Human Rights), Centro Potosino de Derechos Humanos (Potosino Human Rights Center), and Servicio, Desarrollo y Paz (Service, Development and Peace). Thousands in San Luís Potosí took to the streets in support of fair elections and again when electoral fraud became apparent. Citizen groups later became involved in electoral oversight elsewhere, such as Tabasco, Chihuahua, and Michoacán states between 1991 and 1993.

The Convergencia concluded that establishing the minimum conditions for democracy was urgent. Networks of civic organizations at both state and national levels developed and improved their oversight methods, carried out studies on voter preferences, media behavior, and means of buying and co-ercing votes, and created reliable and impartial voter registration systems. From this accumulation of coordinated efforts, the pluralist, nationwide coalition, Alianza Cívica/Observación 94, was born.

All of the organizations mentioned thus far joined together to optimize their work and capabilities. A new electoral reform resulted in the ability to democratically name citizen advisors as members of the Instituto Federal Electoral (Federal Electoral Institute; IFE), effectively limiting the previous role of the Interior Ministry as an oversight institution. At this juncture, it be-came possible to begin changing electoral practices and structures that con-tinued to be subordinated to the PRI and the government. In this manner, an opening was created in 1994 to begin reforming the Federal Code of Elec-toral Institutions and Processes. For the first time, the government and the PRI no longer had a majority in the IFE. The *ciudadanización* (citineniza-tion) of the most important electoral decision-making organization expanded in such a manner that the same civil organizations, and particularly the Alianza Cívica, successfully proposed to numerous citizens that they be-come part of the 300 district councils and 32 local electoral councils in the country, that is, 3,000 nonpartisan citizens for the 1997 elections. This ciu-dadanización of the IFE constituted one of the most important democratic victories toward achieving democratic legislative and bureaucratic represen-tation, even when multiple mechanisms still needed to be defined. In brief, nonpartisan citizens (who were chosen on the basis of rotation or lottery prior to each election) assumed responsibility for ballot counting and validation.

Despite great enthusiasm and many opportunities to develop dissemina-tion and education campaigns in favor of a "clean game," the civic networks were harassed by numerous governmental and bureaucratic demands in their attempts to carry out these tasks. They also suffered police infiltrations to obtain "inside information."

At present, NGOs in Mexico form an integral part of all spheres of pub-lic and private life (Tables 3.1 and 3.2). They coordinate participation in ar-eas such as social assistance, social promotion, squatters' rights, human rights and democracy, legal advice, women, indigenous peoples, migrants and refugees, ecology, popular fronts, culture, civic education, and research and education institutes, among others. In the last ten years, they have mul-tiplied and are typically recognized as nonprofit groups independent of the

Table 3.1

NGOs by State, 1995–2000

State	1995–2000	2000	Increase (%)
Aguascalientes	27	91	237.04
Baja California	66	304	360.61
Baja California Sur	12	56	366.67
Campeche	7	119	1,600
Coahuila	39	418	971.79
Colima	23	47	104.35
Chiapas	42	148	252.38
Chihuahua	44	231	425
Distrito Federal	1,182	1,930	63.28
Durango	20	56	409.09
Guanajuato	97	235	142.27
Guerrero	11	56	409.09
Hidalgo	25	63	152
Jalisco	229	491	114.41
Estado de México	81	309	281.48
Michoacán	65	156	140
Morelos	32	171	434.38
Nayarit	5	21	320
Nuevo León	27	538	1,892.59
Oaxaca	37	192	418.92
Puebla	55	150	172.73
Querétaro	25	135	440
Quintana Roo	4	59	1,375
San Luis Potosí	24	103	329.17
Sinaloa	24	103	240
Sonora	53	146	175.47
Tabasco	12	40	233.33
Tamaulipas	19	102	436.84
Tlaxcala	7	25	257.14
Veracruz	45	203	351.11
Yucatán	6	28	366.67
Total	2,364	6,887	191.33

Sources: Centro Mexicano para la Filantropía, A.C., data for 1995–1996 and 2000; Sergio Aguayo, ed., *Almanaque Mexicano* (Mexico City: Grijalbo/Hechos Confiables, 2000), 311.

state and political parties. They are fundamental actors in an evolving democratic system.

Although NGOs have a strong presence, there still are tasks pending to continue facilitating their work, such as the creation of a series of rules and laws more suitable to their existence. Nonetheless, there also exist perversities in the creation of civil organizations that feign to be civil organizations

Table 3.2

Number of NGOs Registered with Ministry of Treasury and Public Credit by State, 1999

State	Number of NGOs	State	Number of NGOs
Aguascalientes	45	Nayarit	12
Baja California	115	Nuevo León	268
Baja California Sur	23	Oaxaca	77
Campeche	11	Puebla	129
Coahuila	125	Querétaro	95
Colima	29	Quintana Roo	33
Chiapas	169	San Luis Potosí	91
Chihuahua	169	Sinaloa	61
Distrito Federal	1,352	Sonora	87
Durango	19	Tabasco	24
Guanajuato	158	Tamaulipas	89
Guerrero	30	Tlaxcala	19
Hidalgo	55	Veracruz	105
Estado de México	222	Zacatecas	17
Michoacán	159	Total	4,162
Morelos	65		

Source: Data from *Diario Oficial,* 1999 in Sergio Aguayo, ed., *Almanaque Mexicano* (Mexico City: Grijalbo/Hechos Confiables, 2000), 310.

but in reality are a pretext for the government and political parties. Facing this possibility, true civil organizations lack mechanisms and well-defined legal frameworks to detect this type of case, since in reality they continue the struggle or serve other interests. At the same time, more systematized information about civil organizations is still required. Given their impressive growth on the national level within their short lives, a current map of their work needs to be maintained to take advantage of potentialities in organization, proposals, fieldwork and their experience to promote the practices of democratic governance, which ought to be institutionalized.

National Political Associations

National political associations, a new form of civic association, participate in the development of democracy throughout the country. They receive financing from the federal government to carry out their activities, which include publication of educational materials, and education and training in public policy development and research techniques.

These organizations "fit" between political parties and NGOs, and their work is directly related to promoting democracy. These associations are informal in the political sense, as members support particular causes or policies rather than political party platforms. Associations can provide support for political candidates and even reach accommodations with local party organizations. In 1999, forty-one national political associations were registered, compared to nine in 1997.

Promoting Citizen Participation at the Municipal Level

In the process of top-down decentralization, one of the most important administrative reforms of the De la Madrid government was revision of Article 115 of the Constitution. (See Mizrahi, Chapter 2, for additional commentary on the De la Madrid administration.) This reform tried to strengthen the legal base of the municipality, by clarifying and making explicit its functions and responsibilities. Introduced in 1983, the reform gave municipalities a fundamental tool for carrying out their functions. However, many of the functions and capabilities established in the new Article 115 were irrelevant for the majority of municipalities in the country. As Merino states, the reform was created based on urban criteria.[11] The reform authorized the municipal governments to collect a property tax and specified in a detailed manner the public services for which they were responsible, but did not extend municipalities' autonomy to promote social development and counter the burdensome weight of the state government in the decision-making process.

Although the municipality was a key entity in the promotion of social and political organization, the reform of 1983 tried to grant it only a role as provider of urban services with relative autonomy. Because of the limited functions granted, many civil society organizations dedicated themselves to the task of gradually converting the municipality into an entity able to attack major problems in two ways. First, the municipality could constitute itself as an entity promoting the creation of conditions that would help the nation transition toward a true multiple-party system, and thus, strengthen democracy. Second, municipalities could become essential agents of social development, on the one hand, by alleviating poverty through implementing social welfare policies, and thereby strengthen their capacity to design government plans and programs. On the other hand, they could modify the relationship between the government and local society, by providing advice on federal government tasks, as well as supporting the local citizenry through education programs designed to prepare them to request accountability on municipal management. Municipalities could also create educational and training programs for their functionaries, as well as develop new relationships and instruments of democratic government to be able to redefine relationships between local government and civil society, thus strengthening participatory democracy.

Before 1988, OCPDs served to educate popular leaders. Opposition parties began to establish their own strategies to compete politically and win spaces of power at the municipal level. On the one hand, once the PRD was established, it organized a strategy to win municipal offices and increase its political presence, principally in the south of the country. On the other hand, the PAN carried out a much more aggressive strategy to win local elections and position itself, particularly in semirural and urban municipalities in the north of the country.

In this manner, by the end of the 1980s, the OCPDs operating at the municipal level planned to work directly with local governments captured by opposition parties. Initially they worked with rural municipalities, but rapidly extended their work to municipalities containing small cities.

In 1989, ten civil society organizations formed the Red INCIDE. Among other things, the Red functioned as a pedagogical source for strengthening the political education of local populations and for training functionaries in local public sector management. The Centro de Servicios Municipales "Heriberto Jara," A.C. (CESEM), established in 1990, has provided technical information and comparative studies on numerous municipal services. The CESEM has also become a spokesperson for diverse civic groups, academics, and politicians on issues concerning municipalities.

CESEM and other civil society organizations are committed to municipal management within a democratic logic, and thus to reducing the temptation of presidencialismo and corporatism at the local level. The Centro increased its advisory tasks in order to clearly define their municipalista project. Centro researchers extended their reach to become familiar with other Latin American governance experiences, while also designing projects in support of indigenous autonomy. In the context of the quincentennial of the Conquest in 1992 and preparations for commemorating 500 years of indigenous, black, and popular resistance, the OCPDs were invited to present workshops to members of indigenous communities about the role of the municipality and its importance as a major institution in developing relationships between citizens and government in a democratic society.

Numerous NGOs came to specialize in municipalista work. Included here are the Red de Autoridades Democráticas (Network of Democratic Authorities), comprised mainly of politicians; Equipo Pueblo, with a presence in the states of Veracruz and Chihuahua; Acción Cuidadana para la Educación, Desarrollo y Democracia (Citizen Action for Education, Development and Democracy, A.C.) in Jalisco; and the Instituto Mexicano de Desarrollo de la Comunidad, A.C. (Mexican Institute of Community Development; IMDEC).[12]

The municipalista movement was consolidated in response to increased demands on the OCPDs for education and training to the extent that state and federal governments provide inadequate support or that they did so through excessively bureaucratic means. Today OCPD participation and intervention in the municipal arena continue to be essential.

Municipalista Associations

Given the lack of effective training and education for municipal civil servants and the difficulties of coping with the clientelistic and authoritarian political system of many local governments, the climate was favorable for the exchange of experiences among municipalities that were receiving training from the OCPDs. In this sense, municipalista associations were able to develop beyond citizen networks and strategically position themselves vis-à-vis political parties.

In 1994 the Asociación de Municipios de México, A.C. (Mexican Municipality Association; AMMAC) was established. This association is comprised mainly of PAN municipal governments, although it is pluralistic and includes municipal governments headed by other parties. The AMMAC's fundamental objectives consist of strengthening municipalities and the municipal policy, encouraging democratic practices at the municipal level, and establishing solidarity as a guiding principle of municipal government.

From nineteen founding members (mayors), today the AMMAC has more than 200 members who collectively govern 35 percent of the national population. It is the first municipalista organization in Mexican history. Among other contributions, AMMAC members have

- Assisted in obtaining reform of Article 115 in 1999
- Urged the creation of a new framework for distributing financial resources through the Law of Fiscal Coordination, in collaboration with

the Commission for Municipal Strengthening in the Chamber of
Deputies
- Struggled for a productive and respectful relationship with other government entities
- Developed links with international municipalista organizations to exchange innovative experiences
- Organized fora, workshops, congresses, and courses to support professionalization in the municipal arena and to increase the efficiency and efficacy of local public administration aimed at simplifying administrative processes

AMMAC has had an active and proactive position in the municipalista debate. In addition to developing research on municipal issues, its principal areas of interest today are decentralization and deconcentration, organizational reengineering, strategic planning, transparency and accountability, total quality management and human resources, professionalization of civil servants, intergovernmental relations, and modernization.

Given the AMMAC's affiliation with the PAN, most of the members preside over large cities, although rural municipalities are also represented. Thus, the AMMAC's vision of government has been called "enterprise municipality." Given that the PAN has continued to govern in the state of Guanajuato and in half of its municipalities, there are two principal tasks: understanding the diversity of municipalities in the state, and accepting that there are multiple rhythms in the process of devolution and/or transfer of functions, given that each municipality has its own modalities and timing. For the AMMAC, the decentralization of resources, functions, and responsibilities is not feasible without establishing a permanent dialogue with the municipal entities that receive resources, functions, and responsibilities, and the state government that provides them.[13]

Local governments run by the PRD created the Association of Local Authorities of Mexico (AALMAC) in October 1997. Association members are committed to municipal development and democracy, and create programs based on the following normative principles: honesty, solidarity, respect, mutual support, and social justice. In 1997, AALMAC municipalities numbered eighty-one in the states of Morelos, Hidalgo, San Luis Potosí, Michoacán, Veracruz, Tamaulipas, Oaxaca, Chiapas, Guerrero, México, Hidalgo, and Nayarit.

AALMAC's principal objectives include the promotion of exchanges among mayors from diverse Mexican and foreign municipalities to improve the function and exercise of municipal management; strengthening democratic political culture at the municipal level; promotion of legislative initiatives in local and national congresses to encourage the development of municipalities; and negotiation with fiscal authorities at higher levels of government and the private sector for the investment of resources.

To strengthen the federalist system, AALMAC has proposed seeking solutions that improve the distribution of public powers and functions. It has also sought solutions regarding the redefinition of intergovernmental relations, so as to achieve the separation and appropriate balance of powers. AALMAC members are committed to the inclusion of indigenous peoples through a new relationship with government, and support the reevaluation of economic activities to obtain a more equitable distribution of revenues to correct social inequalities.

The AAMLAC has also encouraged the reform of Article 115 in the Constitution in order to recognize the municipality's character as a government more than as an entity that administrates services. This effort was successful in 1999. In addition, the association successfully achieved a multiple collaboration agreement with AMMAC in February 1999, a relationship that has been fluid and enriched by the exchange of experiences and the joint tasks of encouraging municipal development.

The association of PRI-governed municipalities, the National Federation of Municipalities of Mexico (FENAMM), was created in 1997. The goal of this association is to work for municipalismo throughout the country by encouraging institutional, juridical, treasury, and administrative modernization in the municipalities. Comprised of 1,788 municipalities (of a total 2,443), FENAMM is the largest organization municipality association in the country. FENAMM has encouraged the organizational consolidation process and has reached consensus on a reform platform for municipalities that is considered urgent. The FENAMM has created its own municipal training school to achieve those ends.

Dilemmas and Challenges of "Bottom-Up" Democracy in Mexico

Although great progress in creating and expanding democratic processes has resulted from changes introduced by the center, many changes began outside the center. The society as a whole, with civil society mobilization and local government modernization, has been instrumental in the transition to democracy. They have also applied pressure to speed up the decentralization process.

In the early stages, administrative decentralization deconcentrated and decentralized the problems, but not decision making, spending, and revenue-collection authority. Meanwhile, the profile and characteristics of Mexican democracy were being transformed via citizen mass mobilization, networking among civil society organizations dedicated to various issues of local and broader scale socioeconomic development, opposition party participation in elections, and the municipalista movement.

In the 1990s, structural limits prevented local governments from making more qualitative leaps. These limits resulted from the political inertia that authoritarian local bosses and presidencialista preferences reproduced within local governments, as well as legal and administrative difficulties. Democratization and decentralization strategies at the national and state levels eventually led to the recognition that reforms were also necessary at the municipal level. Partly in response to municipal government inertia, civil society organizations multiplied and formed networks, which in turn increased their influence to pressure for democratic solutions in various arenas. In this manner, the organizations were also strengthened in their struggle for social legitimacy and legal recognition.

The municipalista movement and mobilization of NGO networks have focused on the following general areas: democracy and economic rights (poverty alleviation and implementation of social welfare policies; decentralization of decision-making, resource allocation, and external financing authority); democracy and political rights (at federal, state, and municipal levels); democracy and legitimacy (legal reforms to obtain recognition and social legitimacy, central government follow-up of municipal reforms and legislative proposals from the local arena to encourage citizen participation at local and national levels); democracy, municipalismo, and local authority (involving municipal associations, networks of researchers, municipal governments, citizen participation, and dialogue with state assemblies).

Dilemmas and challenges in the context of deepening the development of political democracy are summarized below. First, at the municipal level, reforms with a greater reach are needed. Attaining municipal autonomy requires decentralization and economic development policies originating from the grassroots level. Political reforms must be expanded to include municipalities and how they interact with local civil society. Finally, municipal administration must be strengthened through strategies aimed at encouraging transparency, increased local participation, and greater political accountability.

Currently, the debate between states and the national government on municipal autonomy and the states' relationship to the federation has begun to address issues of organizational capacity and the possibilities of local governance with citizen participation. Substantive advances have concentrated on extending the autonomy of urban municipal governments to facilitate their public service delivery mandate, and interacting with state governments in an atmosphere of greater respect and intergovernmental collaboration. Still pending is the extension of greater autonomy for the majority of semi-urban and rural municipalities, as well as the tasks of redesigning the political and economic structure of municipalities and defining their relationship with civil society.

To understand the reforms under Article 115, it is important to consider how they fit within Mexico's "old" political system. While the contents of some reforms are clearly progressive, traditional forms of authoritarian power at the state and municipal level still exist, which can slow the pace of structural change. At the same time, municipal reform is not only a concept, but is fundamentally a process that should be institutionalized through each state's legislative body. This national constitutional reform will take form according to the political realities of each state. Each state will assimilate the reform to a greater or lesser degree, depending on whether traditional corporatist customs or interests persist that do not allow the reform to rapidly advance in a de jure or de facto sense (or both).

Now that an opposition party president has taken office without massive electoral fraud and social upheaval, the sociopolitical environment is more favorable to new normative and legal instruments and designs for institutions and intergovernmental relationships in state constitutions. Existing problems, however, may continue if centralist inertia is reproduced. The municipalista movement should include, therefore, community actors and elected bodies such as the Chamber of Senators, Chamber of Deputies, and local assemblies to discuss legislative and constitutional reforms.

NGOs and their networks, academic institutions, municipalista associations, and national political associations are fundamental counterparts to legal reforms and the democratization process, since they represent the connection between citizen initiatives and those of local, state, and federal governments. Organized civic action matures through experience in conflict and negotiation, which serves as a core arena of democratic political processes. Future challenges ought to be addressed through short- and medium-term efforts to institutionalize participative dynamics, thereby allowing citizens and their organizations to develop with political support.

Municipalities are capable of limited self-reform; they can sustain themselves with citizen participation in order to achieve integral social development at the local level. Both civil society groups and municipalities must continue to develop and sustain relationships with legislatures at all levels in this process of democratization and institutionalization of participatory dynamics. In a similar fashion, designers of local organizations should consider institutionalizing the relationship between civil society and local government by taking advantage of the experience of local NGOs and respective networks. In this way, both the risks and successes of social development projects can be shared by civil society and government.

Notes

1. Enrique Cabrero, "La Municipalización, un Proceso Necesario ante un Federalismo que se Renueva," in *Municipalización en Guanajuato: Una Estrategia para el Fortalecimiento Municipal* (Mexico City: UAM/Codereg/Gobierno del Estado de Guanajuato/Dirección General de Fortalecimiento Municipal, 2000).

2. The concept of nongovernmental organizations was established at an international level, created in the United Nations a few years after World War II. These organizations were considered independent of governments and permanent international associations dedicated to promoting cooperation mechanisms for development between Western European countries and the countries of the so-called Third World. In Mexico, thanks to Rafael Reygadas (*Abriendo Veredas: Iniciativas Públicas y Sociales de las Redes de Organizaciones Civiles* [Mexico City: Convergencia de Organismos Civiles para la Democracia, 1998], 619), we have a serious work that systematizes the history of civil society organizations. Reygadas prefers that, in the Mexican context, they be called "civil organizations for the promotion of social development" (OCPDs), to give them greater concordance with their origin, context, and fundamental identity in the country, in place of a generic reference established at the international level. In this chapter, I use the terms "nongovernmental organizations" (NGOs), "OCPDs," and "civil society organizations" interchangeably.

3. Reygadas, *Abriendo Veredas,* viii.

4. Ibid., xiii.

5. Jorge Alonso and Juan Manuel Ramírez Sáiz, eds., *La Democracia de los de Abajo en México* (Mexico City: La Jornada Ediciones/Consejo Electoral del Estado de Jalisco/Centro de Investigaciones Interdisciplinarias en Humanidades, Universidad Nacional Autónoma de México, 1997), 28.

6. See Reygadas, "Génesis Social del Proyecto de las Redes de OCPD's: Neoliberalismo y Promoción," in *Abriendo Veredas,* 41–56.

7. Among the most notable literature that collects these experiences of social pol-

icy and the civil society entities involved, we can cite: Convergencia de Organismos Civiles por la Democracia, A.C., "Elementos para una Política Social Alternativa: Presentación Sinóptica de Algunas Propuestas" (Mexico City: Convergencia de Organismos Civiles por la Democracia, A.C., Comisión de Política Social, July 1994); Joy L. Peebles, "Las Organizaciones No Gubernamentales de Derechos Humanos en México" (Ph.D. diss., Facultad Latinoamericana de Ciencias Sociales, Mexico City, 1993); and Alberto Arroyo and Mario Monroy, *Red Mexicana de Acción Frente al Libre Comercio: 5 Años de Lucha (1991–1996)* (Mexico City: Red Mexicana de Acción Frente al Libre Comercio, 1996).

8. Reygadas, *Abriendo Veredas,* 155.

9. Ibid., 173.

10. Foro de Apoyo Mutuo, cited in Reygadas, *Abriendo Veredas,* 175.

11. Mauricio Merino, *Fuera del Centro* (Veracruz: Universidad Veracruzana, 1992), 116.

12. IMDEC is a civil association founded in 1963. It offers professional services in communications and organization. Currently, it is a member of the Forum of Civil Organizations (FOCIV), which comprises over thirty collectives in the metropolitan area of Guadalajara, Jalisco.

13. Cabrero, "La Municipalización," 16.

Chapter 4

State Decentralization and Regional Actors in Chile

Claudia Serrano

Studies addressing the decentralization process underway in Chile are few. In general, they have focused on institutional aspects and fiscal decentralization, with special emphasis on the trajectory and evaluation of public investment decisions at the regional level, a subject of particular interest to the Subsecretaría de Desarrollo Regional y Administrativo (Undersecretariat for Regional Development; SUBDERE). Another group of papers includes the essays of Sergio Boisier of the Instituto Latinoamericano y del Caribe de Planificación Económica y Social (ILPES), which are focused on regional development issues. Another line of work has focused on regional competitiveness associated with decentralization.[1]

A lack of research has been apparent in the area of popular participation, which is not accidental, given that this is a particularly weak component of the process. There are a few theoretical reflections about the benefits of de-

I am grateful to Philip Oxhorn for his helpful comments on a previous version of this chapter.

centralization for civil society,[2] but no one has undertaken research on the subject. Lira and Marinovic[3] have studied the institutionalized mechanisms of social representation through diverse regional councils. However, researchers have not yet developed studies focused on the strengths and weaknesses of regional civil society and regional actors from the perspective of their contribution to a transformed and enriched democracy.

The primary argument of those who are committed to decentralization in Chile concerns its relationship to the strengthening of democracy: it promotes the creation of democratically elected regional and community authorities who represent a subnational community that has its own characteristics, potentials, and limitations, and its particular development options. They state that decentralization permits greater expression of regional and local identities, allows the coordination of actors in common projects, and creates a public administration that is closer to the people. Public opinion, political and social leaders, and government officials declare deep commitments to decentralization. They say that they value and take into consideration the contribution of the regions, understanding that there is no single homogenous group of people who are subjects of the national government, but rather that there are groups of citizens with contributions they wish to offer.

However, when examining the Chilean decentralization model, one observes a half-completed decentralization, whose completion is difficult because of traditions of centralism with little focus on citizenship and with local civil society as a weak protagonist. The reasons for this contradiction are various. Perhaps the most important reason is related to the origin of the process, which was initiated within the framework of an authoritarian context devoid of consideration for citizen concerns. It is sufficient to remember that the expression of the popular will in any area of national responsibility did not have a place during the 1970s when military leaders governed the country.

Within the context of a democracy, other factors are relevant, such as the centralist tradition of the Chilean state and the fears on the part of national authorities that the process could generate a lack of fiscal discipline. During the entire democratic period, the latter has been a structural factor that has limited the range of possibilities available to managers and public policymakers.

Thus, decentralization continues to appear as a promise, although it has generated what in the beginning did not exist: regional actors' demands for increased autonomy and a faster decentralization process. However, a dilemma remains. To the present, the government has taken steps in administrative areas and in public investment. How does it advance the decentralization process in a way that creates a governing system that is more democratic, participatory, and truly regional, given that regional actors and civil society have been largely absent up to this point? How can a process be regionalized that has the mark of being decided upon and negotiated at the national level (where empowered and active citizens have not been present)? How could social actors become vested and active in the decentralization process rather than exclusive reliance on changes in institutional arrangements? These are the questions that I discuss in this chapter.

Elements of Institutional Decentralization Process

Decentralization is understood as the transfer of powers and responsibilities from the central level of the state to the subnational levels. Although it has an important expression within the administration of the public apparatus, this is a process with a fundamentally political character, that is, the redistribution of power. At the same time, decentralization demands significant changes in organizational culture and models of public sector management associated with new tasks and responsibilities that decentralized administrations ought to address.

For (political) decentralization to take place, the government level to which the center transfers powers must be legally independent, and have democratically elected authorities. Without a political dimension (transfer of power), "deconcentration" is an apt description of administrative decentralization. Deconcentration refers to transferring to subnational levels specific functions, without the decision-making authority and autonomy needed to make public policy decisions.[4]

Benefits of decentralization described by some theorists include contributions to modernization and the increased agility of management by bringing government administration closer to the citizenry. This allows the government apparatus to connect more directly with citizen priorities and concerns. At the same time, decentralization reduces the size of the state apparatus, the number of transactions and procedures, and the speed of responses. Decentralization is also considered useful in the context of market globalization: decentralized decision-making structures can operate more quickly and more flexibly, thus benefiting both private and public sectors.

Economic Efficiency Perspective

It is generally assumed that decentralization favors a more efficient allocation of public resources, because the decentralized allocation of resources reflects to a greater degree the demands of local citizens, which also improves social well-being. Subnational governments could create greater well-being in the diverse communities throughout the country, adjusting the collection and allocation of public resources to equally diverse preferences. It is assumed that people's preferences vary among regions, and that authorities in each region will be in a better position than outsiders to perceive and satisfy the needs and demands of those jurisdictions. In this manner, efficiency will increase when local taxes and fees finance subnational governments' actions, thus helping the community confront the economic costs of said actions.

Some researchers assert that the efficiency of government decentralization is directly related to the exercise of "good government." To the extent that public policy options are expressed in terms of costs (taxes) for citizens, through voting citizens will support or not support these policies and the authorities that implement them. The citizen-taxpayer will directly express his/her preferences regarding policy options, or in other words, options related to the desired combination of public goods.

These arguments are related to citizen control of public sector management. The quality of government improves when it becomes closer to the citizenry it ought to serve, because it increases the likelihood that the public sector will have to be accountable for its acts.[5] Local revenues (taxes) are situated at the foundation of the argument regarding the efficiency of fiscal decentralization, which directly establishes a link between taxes and benefits that emphasizes efficiency and fosters local responsibility.

Fiscal decentralization alternatives differentiate themselves according to the degree of autonomy that the central government grants to the subnational governments, and the ability to establish compensation or redistribution mechanisms among regions or localities with different economic capacities. At one extreme is a decentralization model in which the subnational level acts autonomously, both with regard to revenues (taxes) and public expenditures. This is the public choice model. At the other extreme is the principal/agent model, or the "deconcentration" of responsibilities, in which transfers from the center finance the tasks that the principal wants the agent to undertake.[6]

The principal/agent model, which is the most common model in Latin America, opens up a series of questions regarding the most adequate way to ensure that the principal guides and controls the agent so that the agent acts in a defined manner. On the other hand, it also asks how to fulfill the spirit of decentralization and guarantee that the agent has maneuvering room to allow him/her to satisfy local preferences.

In the Chilean case, the central government establishes the financial/fiscal limits among the different levels of government (central, regional, and local) and allows these jurisdictions to act autonomously, as long as they do not cross those limits. The central level defines financial discipline at the macroeconomic level, which orients public spending and investment. At the same time, it tends toward microeconomic fiscal autonomy, allowing the regions to make their own decisions regarding public sector investments according to norms and procedures that the central level establishes.

There are differences in fiscal management between regions and municipalities. Regions allocate public investment resources according to certain criteria that the central level has defined. Although they rely on their own management budget, they do not have direct access to tax revenues. Municipalities have the capacity to generate their own resources, but do not actually set tax rates. Rather, local governments receive resources through the redistributive mechanism of the Municipal Common Fund and the central government transfers associated with the delivery of social services.[7]

The Chilean model of decentralization is characterized by large transfers from the central level in the financing of subnational governments. Of these transfers, most correspond to education and healthcare spending, which are "extrabudgetary," meaning that they are not accounted for in current municipal budgets.[8]

Political Perspective

At present, a principal concern in many countries vis-à-vis democracy is to extend it beyond the formal institution of suffrage. This concern is generally focused on building community, understood as the area of ownership where links among people and trust in healthy civic debate and sharing of responsibility are renewed. This renewal is related to the extension of the notion of citizen rights and the broadening of the public arena as a space for debate regarding the construction of shared social norms.

Some of the primary arguments in favor of government decentralization are related to the same themes that come up when discussing issues related to citizen control of public sector management. According to these arguments; decentralization strengthens democracy, brings decision making closer to the citizenry; facilitates and promotes greater citizen participation and involvement in politics and programs that affect them; and leads decision makers to make decisions that are more closely connected to people's real needs, thereby increasing the programs' relevance. All of this is within a context of the democratic election of authorities who, after gaining the support of voters, should give an account of their activities/accomplishments on behalf of the voters. Within this framework, the local level is a privileged arena for developing participatory processes that involve people through policymakers' actions. Citizens feel that these processes address subjects that affect the quality of their lives. They also believe that each of them has the responsibility to participate, as well as the right to demand and oversee the execution of the processes and their results.

Decentralization and local development form a strong base for identity, community construction, and citizen legitimacy to encourage processes and experiences of local social control. At the foundation of local development, the construction of a "feeling of community" occurs that creates identity and relevance and makes way for a vision of a shared future that inspires local actors to take part in actions of public interest within the local arena. "Depending on its development, local civic culture encourages the creation of a new citizen pact, expressed in the assumption of a local identity, a future project and citizen co-responsibility."[9] Recently in Chile, policymakers are taking steps in this sense, but it has been difficult to bring together decentralization, democracy, and citizenship at the regional level.

Decentralization Process in Chile

A strong central state played a decisive role in the formation of the Chilean nation. Ministries were established to oversee diverse areas of social life (e.g., education, health care, and housing), and administration was designed to operate at the direction of the central government. Regional and local governments became dependent on and subordinate to the central government. Similarly, the head offices of private companies and nongovernmental organizations are traditionally located in the capital.

The military government initiated the decentralization process in 1974, which was an entirely top-down process. At the end of the 1990s, debate emerged about the need for delineating regional economic and sociopolitical differences (by regional actors themselves) that should in turn direct decision making toward achieving the self-sustainable development of large territorial areas.[10] In contrast, the foundations of local government prerogatives are associated with liberal principles underlying the "municipalization" of education and health services in the 1980s.

In Chile, regional and municipal governments are mainly subnational administrative services for ministries and departments in Santiago. Subnational governments have little power or authority to raise and spend money, on the one hand, or to make decisions on how public monies are spent on the other. Principal responsibilities of regional and municipal governments are concentrated in public investment (infrastructure, economic development) and in primary and secondary education and primary health care, respectively. The Treasury Ministry is responsible for nearly all aspects of public spending at all levels of government. In practice, this means that regional and municipal governments have little decision-making power over the annual budgeting process, and in some cases, control over the distribution of program resources at the local level is already approved and defined in Santiago.

Finally, another factor that complicates effective decentralization is a long history of national government involvement and specified responsibility for services that regional and municipal governments deliver (e.g., primary education, public health) at least in part. In other words, in contrast to other countries, in Chile there is no clear-cut or "natural" division of responsibilities between the central and subnational governments that might be refined or expanded upon.

Three periods can be identified in the trajectory of the decentralization process in Chile. The first concerns administrative reorganization efforts, and the second, functional decentralization (greater functions turned over to municipalities). The third period is characterized by democratization at the municipal (or communal) level and the encouragement of decentralization at the regional level.

1974 to 1976

In 1974, the government enacted Law No. 573, reorganized the country into thirteen regions and fifty-one provinces. According to this decree, municipalities were considered territorially decentralized units in the formal sense, although still influenced strongly from the center. Two years later, Law No. 1289 went into effect, which redefined the role of municipalities as functionally decentralized units responsible for service delivery. This law granted municipalities the role of "agents of economic and social development" at the local communal level.

In this period, the government also initiated the "deconcentration" of central government administration, which was expressed in the creation of Secretarias Regionales Ministeriales (Regional Ministerial Secretariats; SEREMIs). In addition, some administrative instruments or roles were created that later became key decentralization elements at the regional level, such as the Fondo Nacional de Desarrollo Regional (National Fund for Regional Development; FNDR), and the SUBDERE, both created in 1975.

1976 to 1989

This period is known for the "municipalization of services." Reforms implemented between 1976 and 1989 were aimed at broadening municipalities' range of authority, multiplying the responsibilities and resources of the same. These reforms institutionalized certain functions that allowed municipalities to share responsibilities with the central government in the provision of educational and health services. The municipality was converted into an instrument/executor of social policy.

In the 1980s, the transfer of public education and primary health clinic administration was expanded. A financing system was developed consisting of transfers from the central government based on subsidies granted for these establishments. During the 1980s, the real value of these subsidies fell because they were not adjusted for inflation, creating substantial budget deficits.

The government began to decentralize education in 1980. This process consisted of the following steps: (1) the government transferred public schools to municipal administration, (2) the government modified the financing system for education from a historic practice of paying for expenses to providing enrollment subsidies at the local level per student for daily attendance at school, and (3) the government created a new system of offering free educational services, as the State financed selected establishments through direct subsidies from the center. The central government continued to be responsible for curricula requirements, as well as financing.

Phases in health sector reform are summarized below. First, the government created the Instituciones de Salud Previsional (Preventive Healthcare

Institutions; ISAPREs), which are private institutions authorized to collect obligatory health insurance contribution from their affiliates (6 percent of taxable income starting in 1984, and 7 percent from 1986 to the present) in exchange for directly or indirectly providing healthcare services. Second, the government reorganized the Health Ministry, allowing the ministry to define the functions of distinct public entities within the sector and increase their degree of decision-making autonomy. The ministry remained in charge of normative functions of planning and control and created twenty-six health services, which became decentralized autonomous units. In addition, it created an entity in charge of administering and channeling financial resources to public and private healthcare services, including the Fondo Nacional de Salud (National Health Fund),[11] Central de Abastecimiento (Supply Central), and Instituto Nacional de Salud Pública (National Public Health Institute).

The most important reform was the municipalization of primary healthcare facilities, which began in 1981. This process culminated at the end of 1989 with more than 90 percent of the establishments transferred to municipal administration. The changes in the ways in which these facilities were financed deserve emphasis: invoicing systems were set up at the subnational level, which succeeded in encouraging efficiency at the level of public healthcare providers. With this, the government tried to end the historic central government stranglehold on public health sector administration and operations.[12]

1990 to Present

The current period began in 1990 with the resurgence of democracy, and is characterized by a new impulse to strengthen decentralization at the local and regional levels. At the local level, officials are democratizing the municipalities and electing mayors and council members through arrangements set out in the Supreme Decree of the Organic Law of Municipalities of 1992.[13]

At the regional level, officials are undertaking the most innovative changes vis-à-vis the administrative political tradition in Chile through the Constitutional Organic Law on Government and the Internal Administration of the State. This law defines the roles of the Regional Council and regional government. At the same time, it establishes the regions as geopolitical entities, having gained legal status and relative autonomy in 1993.

They are to assume increasing responsibilities in the allocation of public resources associated with regional development.

The regional government system is somewhat complicated. It is based on presidential structure, as seen in the power held by the regional manager (the *intendente*), who is appointed by the president of the Republic, but also quasi-democratic in that Regional Council members are elected by local communal councils but not by the citizenry. Thus, they are not known by the citizenry, in spite of the power that they wield allocating public investment resources. Finally, the regional system includes a commitment to technical efficiency and management, expressed in the tasks entrusted to the regional government's technical team, which effectively implements the investment decisions that the council makes.[14]

Under the Law on Regional Government and Administration, the regional governments are agents of harmonious and equitable development of their territories. This legislation assigns to them the design and approval of policies, plans and programs related to regional development, functions pertinent to territorial order, and functions related to fostering economic activity. However, regional governments' exclusive tasks in the area of public investment demand most of their attention.

Public investment is the instrument available to regional authorities to guide respective development processes. The four instruments of decentralized public investment include the FNDR, Inversión Sectoral para Asignación Regional (Sectoral Investment for Regional Allocation; ISAR), Inversión Regional para Asignación Local (Regional Investment for Local Allocation; IRAL), and Programming Agreements. A summary of the principal characteristics of these public investment funds appears in the Appendix.

The FNDR is the oldest, dating back to 1975, and the most regional of the funds. It is defined as a territorial compensation fund for financing social and economic infrastructure in the regions. Its objective is to promote harmonic and equitable territorial development, while safeguarding the preservation and improvement of the environment (Law on Regional Government and Administration). FNDR resources do not derive from a specific public ministerial sector nor are they preassigned, except according to how the fund must meet its operating costs and normative functions. This fund has been growing significantly since 1990.[15]

The SUBDERE is in charge of the interregional distribution of resources according to a formula that considers criteria of territorial equity in assigning 90 percent of the resources).[16] The remaining 10 percent of the resources are distributed according to specific emergency criteria (5 percent) and efficiency criteria (5 percent). FNDR funds allocated according to efficiency criteria are distributed according to a formula comprising a minimum of the following indicators: portfolio of regional projects and level of expenditures of the region. Emergency funds, on the other hand, are allocated based SUBDERE-defined criteria, which are used by regional managers in projects submitted to the Subsecretariat.

Another three instruments of fiscal decentralization constitute an innovation in the transfer of investment resources from the central and ministerial sector levels to the regional level. These resources, unlike those of the FNDR, require a kind of agreement or negotiation with the sector level. Two of them, the ISAR and the Programming Agreements, constitute agreements between the ministries and regional governments. The IRALs deepen the decentralization process, bringing to the municipal level decisions regarding highly localized social investment projects. The IRAL funds allow regional governments to carry out small-scale projects associated with social development and overcome community shortages. As a result, FNDR resources do not have to be designated for specific maintenance projects and can be earmarked for more general development projects.

Regional decision making in designing and executing public sector investment is a central element in the decentralization process. It is understood as an excellent indicator of the powers effectively transferred and a signal of regional government capacity to direct its own regional development. It is expressed, for example, in the commitment that the president made in 1994 to double public investment in at the regional level from 24 percent to 42 percent of all public investment. This has positive and negative aspects. Among the positive aspects, it is worth mentioning that the Regional Council makes decisions about important investment projects, and afterward the regional government carries these out, giving support and life to these authorities. However, the investment process consumes and annuls other concerns. Strengthening local capabilities, endogenous development, development planning, promoting productivity, local economic development, and the role of civil society are all secondary in the Chilean decentralization process.

Another element to consider is that around 1995, all regions relied on a regional development strategy that, although it has been criticized for its level of generality, operated as a navigational map. Indeed, it functioned much like a common reference point during the financing of investment projects. These strategies were reformulated and brought up to date in 2000. It is worth emphasizing that a positive outcome of the strategies is that their formulation contributed to the creation of a participatory dialogue about regional development.

The existence of these funds constitutes, in practice, the regional authorities' power. The discussion about alternatives for investment, projects, territorial areas on which to focus, and so on, could easily open a fruitful and participatory debate about regional development. However, as discussed in the following sections, it is clear that regional governments duplicate in their relationships with municipalities and local organizations the centralist scheme that they themselves criticize with regard to the national government.

A synthesis of developments since 1990 indicates that regional governments have gradually obtained necessary technical instruments in a very brief time period. The chronology is as follows:

1993   Proclamation of the Constitutional Organic Law on Regional Government and Administration.

Installation of regional governments.

Beginning of ISAR operations and functioning of the FNDR.

The president announces the national government's commitment to double public investment under control of regional governments from 24 percent to 42 percent of all public investment.

1995   The first programming agreements enter into operation.

A formal regional development strategy is agreed on in all regions.

Installation of administrative plans to support and further develop regional management.

1996   IRAL begins to operate.

First terms of first regional councils end; new councillors installed.

1999   The government surpasses its goal of doubling investment under control of regional governments. The Law on the National Budget for 2000 assigns 45 percent of public investment to regional governments.

2000   The government designs regional development strategies for the 2000–2006.

2001   End of second term of regional councils and installation of new councillors.

Decentralization and Regional Development

In this section, I identify the actors in the decentralization process, and with this, the social construction of the regions. The actors discussed here include the national government, expressly regional public authorities, intermediate regional authorities, private sector enterprises, universities, and civil society in general.

As noted previously, the Chilean decentralization process has been focused largely on institutional and administrative revisions and reforms; interaction and debate within the public sector have been minimal, and concerns about citizen participation of extremely low priority. Regional actors influence and are relevant in regional development inasmuch as they form a part of the social construction of a geopolitical entity within which they build links of identity and meaning. A managerial presence with characteristics of an enclave in the region does not form part of the local system of actors, a situation apparent in all regions of the country. Using the distinction that Arocena made, these actors with identity, influence, and capacity as interlocutors are distinct from regional agents, who do not have those attributes.[17]

Three factors are decisive for the potential of local actors. First is the presence of regional actors with a high degree of diversity and complexity. Second is the existence of an accumulation of social capital and capacity to build and develop trusting and cooperative relationships that make it possible to undertake common initiatives. Third is that the actors have agreed on a political project to occur within a specific geopolitical area ("territorial political project").

The territorial political project is related, in the first place, to a regional identity that allows regional actors to share a vision for the future. It is a shared vision, an ideal that they hope to attain that contains and expresses a vocation of the regional actors and thus expresses itself as a political project with commitment to ensure that it is carried out, a mobilizing force, and participatory. This is a political instrument more than a technical one. In this sense, who ought to take it on as his/her own is the group of regional actors: the public sector, which will translate it into programs and projects; the private sector, which will express it in investments, innovations, and productivity; and the community sector or civil society, which will experience it as its own area of action or context, where they will encounter elements of identity, sociability, and influence for the development of citizen initiatives.

In order for this territorial political project to be expressed and expanded with real mobilizing capacity, it is necessary to collect and express the desires, potentials, and flaws of the territory. A distinct regional identity that enables one to define shared purposes and goals is also necessary.

Looking at the situation of the regional governments in Chile from the starting point of these definitions, it is clear that they are not bearers of a regional political project, which is associated with other weaknesses of the regional development process. The territorial division presents the first stumbling block, because the actual regions are not depositories of a common trajectory or identity. To this, add the weakness of the system of local actors, the scarce or nonexistent participation of the private sector in the regional debate, the weakness of small and microenterprises to identify themselves as actors in the development process, the difficulties of coordinating the regional public sector, the lack of protagonists and leadership within these themes on the part of regional universities, and so on.

Role of Central Government

Authorities at the central level conceived of the idea and carried out decentralization with SUBDERE clearly acting as protagonist in the design and concept promoted. Over time it has constructed a corporatist identity among the regional councilors that make up a national association and the National Consejo Nacional por la Regionalización y la Decentralización de Chile (Council for the Regionalization and Decentralization of Chile; ONAREDE). However, these councillors have never successfully presented an authentically regionalist proposal or complaint. They do not introduce themes for debate, nor do they speak out at the level of public opinion or of the political players involved in decision making. The SUBDERE, in agreement with the Treasury Ministry, drives the regional development agenda, which leaves little maneuvering room in which regional societal energies could be unleashed, given the marked centralist tradition of Chilean society.

The model remains trapped in an institutional perspective and a stringent fiscal discipline that prevent the regions from establishing financial autonomy; consequently, the regions cannot become responsible to the citizenry for their decisions. At the same time, because they are not administered at the regional level, functional issues, except those that refer to public investment, also do not foster a citizen-focused perspective that allows people to clearly visualize the importance that the regional authority has or the sense it makes to, in the end, support regional strengthening beyond issues of a strictly economic nature. In other words, the subjects that hold the most interest for the citizenry are related to health care, education, crime prevention and law enforcement, and employment. These are not areas within which the regional government participates directly, except through investment.

Regional Authorities

Effective decentralization and regional development depend on the democratic system, that is, the representative election of local authorities. These authorities, as political heads of the region, play a substantial role in the construction of the system of local actors to the extent that they can rely on having the necessary authority, legitimacy, and resources to carry forward the regional development project and to the extent that they are able to strengthen sociocultural aspects rooted in the region, thereby creating or strengthening feelings of pride and regional autonomy. To these representative and democratically elected authorities are added the functionaries of the decentralized public administration, giving form to a legitimate regional institutional structure as related to the citizenry.[18]

The manner of electing the authorities, the spaces in which they act, the ability to effectively represent the community and govern with order according to a mandate that emanates from the citizenry are fundamental aspects affecting development opportunities. The role of regional authorities is understood with regard to three tasks. The first of a technical-political nature is related to their role in the investment process, both at the moment of selecting projects and defining strategic lines of regional development. The second is related to their representative role insofar as they are democratically elected authorities. The third and very important task refers to articulating various initiatives, ideas, actors, and opportunities. In this area, these authorities have the capacity to generate local synergy, operating as channels of communication among different spheres related to development and carrying out the role of articulator and coordinator from within public administration. At the same time, they operate as facilitators in the creation of spaces for work, agreements, consensus, and negotiation with civil society, private sector enterprises, nongovernmental organizations, and so on.

In the following sections, I review the roles carried out by the regional manager and the Regional Council, and regional government.

Regional Manager

The regional manager, appointed by the president, is the principal figure of the regional public apparatus, which to a certain degree is paradoxical, since he is the president's representative in the region and thus of the national government. One of the criticisms of the institutional model of decentralization is the questioning that is done of the role of regional manager in relation to his/her double role as representative of the region and of the central government. This implies contradictory mandates, given that the region, as a decentralized subnational entity, is situated on occasion in a position of conflict with the executive.

With regard to this concern, proposals have been made to democratically elect regional managers or to eliminate the regional manager's responsibility to preside over the Regional Council. In the latter proposal, an elected representative of the Regional Council would preside over the same, while the regional manager would coordinate SEREMIs and service directors in the regional cabinet.

The regional manager has enormous influence in setting the style of regional management, which is expressed in his/her capacity to build working teams, instances of coordination, and cross linkages. The regional manager's role in the construction of the local system of regional actors is key because she or he can establish channels and spaces with a regional perspective and identity. If the regional manager generates a work dynamic that makes various actors talk with one another, thereby promoting a constructive debate about regional themes, the regional manager generates a management style under which the plans of the region may begin to advance little by little. In contrast, if the regional manager has the tendency to approach problems in a segmented manner, it becomes more difficult to move from the primacy of sector or local criteria to more regional criteria.[19]

Regional Government

The regional government strictly speaking is composed of two entities, the Regional Council, which brings together the councilors, and the regional government, understood as a team of professionals and technical experts. Both have responsibility for the investment process, the first to allocate investments, and the second to carry out the management tasks associated with said processes. Both have, in addition, responsibilities in the areas of maintaining administrative order and promoting economic development.

The Regional Council has assumed a leadership role in the regional development process and has acquired, with the passage of time, increased managerial functions and experience in the decision-making process with regard to public investment. However, this body of representative authorities faces difficulties positioning itself within the system of regional action because its members are not directly elected, which reduces its legitimacy and its ability to identify with the citizenry. To this it is worth adding its limited experience in governance (two terms).

At the same time, the Regional Council has defined its role as concentrated in the technical strategic area (investment projects) more than the political representative area or channel of citizen participation, all of which limit its maneuvering room within the regional system.[20] Other problems associated with the management of the council are related to the lack of technical elements with which to discuss investment projects (e.g., regional development planning), the difficulty of dedicating itself to other tasks that transcend the theme of public investment, and the role of reconciling various political views in decision making.

The principal problem of the Regional Council is one of legitimacy, given that councilors are chosen through indirect elections, which does not help reduce the distance between citizens and their representatives. In other words, the councilors, although they have been legitimized as regional authorities and are respected simply because they allocate investment resources, do not represent the regional community, and are not financed by its citizens, nor do they feel that they ought to be publicly accountable for their undertakings, thus being weakened as regional actors.

The regional government itself, leaving aside the Council, is the professional and administrative team on which the regional manager relies. In contrast to other authorities, such as the SEREMIs and the heads of services, this is a regional team. It is organized around the Division of Administration and Finance, which has as its responsibilities the administration and transfer of the resources that the central level provides, and the Division of Analysis and Management Control, which has as its responsibilities the tasks of regional planning. The regional government networks with provincial governors, universities, and municipalities.

Being a relatively new institution, the space that this entity has attained in the regional dynamic is notable, probably because it is the only entity whose purpose is of an exclusively regional character. The regional government frequently interacts with SEREMIs and heads of services, placing emphasis on a regional perspective. This daily participation in conversations and agreements related to investment projects has generated for the professionals of the regional government a legitimate space within the group charged with regional action. Nonetheless, problems of capacity in certain areas of responsibility and the lack of specialists and technical equipment exist.

Intermediate Regional Authorities

In this section, I discuss the roles that the SEREMIs, Secretarias Regional Ministerial de Planificación y Coordinación (Regional Ministerial Secretariats for Planning and Coordination; SERPLACs), and the directors of regional services—all key figures in the regional development process—are carrying out.

The SEREMIs answer to the regional manager and to their respective ministries. They have a double mandate, to be representatives of the ministry in the region and to be members of the regional manager's team in the areas of their expertise. This ambiguity makes difficult the possibility of operating in accordance with regional criteria, and so they intersect sector priorities and goals with those that do not necessarily coincide.

If these individuals are not emotionally tied to the region, it will be difficult for them to develop an identity as regional development actors. Instead, they will remain tied to their sector mandate, which does not grant them the ability to commit themselves to or to speak as equals with other relevant regional actors. This is a complicating factor for these actors, because they have power delegated from the central level, but at the same time, will not succeed in making themselves into important regional development actors.

Regarding the SERERMIs, two positions circulate: on one hand to strengthen their role as links between the sector and decentralized levels, and on the other hand to clearly transfer the sector-related public services to the regional level, which would make this institutional role unnecessary.[21] Perhaps the main difference between the two positions is principally a problem of time or the gradual nature of the process, which makes clear that a strengthened region ought to assume increasing responsibilities that are still in the hands of central government ministry authorities.

In any case, the SEREMIs could play a much more relevant role than that which is apparent at first glance. They are called on to reconcile the sector logic with that of the region. In order to achieve that goal, they ought to be suitable authorities that have legitimacy to carry out their responsibilities, with the strong backing of the regional manager and with the ability to present strictly regional themes to their respective ministries. They ought to be respected in the region and in their sectors. As the regional institutional system is currently operating, the aforementioned does not occur, because the SEREMIs do not successfully place themselves in the intermediate sector–regional locus, they have difficulty bringing together the various public services, or because their own sectors do not value them.

Strictly speaking, the SERPLAC is the regional secretariat of the Ministerio de Planificación y Cooperación (Planning and Cooperation Ministry), which is to say it is a SEREMI, much like the other regional ministerial secretariats. However, this secretariat does not experience the sector–regional duality, but rather is, since its inception, an exclusively regional entity tied to the investment process: it is a support office for regional management and the work of the regional manager.[22]

The SERPLAC plays an important role in the regional public investment process that is made evident in two instances. First, during the planning and pre-investment process, it supports the development of ideas and project profiles, interacting actively with municipalities and the public services. Afterward, it participates in the evaluation of projects and collaborates with the regional manager in structuring the portfolio of projects to present to the Regional Council for its approval.

Regional planning consists of generating ideas and project profiles that are appropriate to the regional development strategy. It has a component of foresight that tries to stimulate the process and not only react to problems and deficiencies. However, in practice, the SERPLAC is consumed by short-term urgent actions tied to the investment process, thus debilitating its more proactive role. Although SERPLAC falls short from the perspective of integral regional development, its administrative development allows the definition of investment criteria and development of investment plans with the private sector.[23]

In a country with a long centralist tradition like Chile, institutional decentralization alone does not generate processes and stimuli that trigger regional energies, if in a parallel manner a significant quantity of state action that the sector ministries carry out operates under centralized management criteria. A process of sector deconcentration must accompany decentralization.

This subject has been of concern to the government. Under the coordination of the SUBDERE, a deconcentration program for the 1998–2000 period specified specific goals in the areas of administration, budget, personnel, and programs. Examples of key services for regional development are the Dirección de Arquitectura y de Vialidad, Ministerio de Obras Públicas (Administration of Architecture and Roads, Public Works Ministry), the Servicio Regional de Vivienda y Urbanismo (Regional Housing and Urban Development Service; SERVIU), and the Instituto Nacional de Desarrollo Agrícola (National Institute of Agricultural Development), to name only the most important from the perspective of public investment. To the extent that these services and departments have a view toward intervention that looks toward the territory and the region, opportunities for dialogue, communication, and articulation with other regional authorities and actors are made easier.

The differential logic of sectoral and regional behavior definitely creates a power struggle that can only be resolved if the various ministry teams have a common purpose, that is, if the central government accepts losing some control over decision making in the regions.[24]

The sector authorities present in the region (directors of regional public services) are complex actors in the system of regional actors, since their principal mandate is the institutional one defined at the national level of respective ministerial offices or departments. Additionally, they are called on to develop a regional/territorial perspective that accents the development imperatives of the region. This call comes daily from the professionals in the regional government and other services with the objective of developing projects for which coherence with the regional development strategy, coordination among sectors, and perspectives of interdisciplinary work are required. In other words, the course of events within the regional dynamic acts as a pole of attraction to which the services ought to react and respond, opening themselves gradually to a regional than a sector-centered style of work.

Overcoming this tension between the central level of government and the dynamic of sectoral authorities within the process that the regions experience demands an active commitment on the part of the center to favor and stimulate deconcentration. At the same time it requires in the same region an environment (level of debate, areas of interest, participant actors, scope of the projects in play, quality of the plans, etc.) that favors identification with the regional dynamic.

Regional Universities

In the social construction process of the regions, universities can nurture economic development through scientific research and applied technologies. In addition, through highly trained professionals, they can contribute to the construction and design of regional projects, and at the same time contribute to reinforcing social capital and cultural identity.

Adequate identification of the problems in each region and the areas of potential development allows the universities to orient part of their research work to these themes, identifying opportunities to put vanguard concepts, services, and technologies into practice for the benefit of enterprises and institutions that require them. In this manner, in the view of universities and regional governments, focusing research work on concrete problems and knowledge that would be useful to regional development objectives occurs.

The president articulates the national government's position regarding the role of universities in the process of decentralization and regional development. In the second meeting of universities and regional governments that took place in Concepción in December 1995, he pointed out that "the universities ought to be the soul of the decentralizing process." In effect, since 1995 the "Universities and Regional Governments" program has been underway, which brings together the thirteen regional governments and the regional universities. Since its beginning, this program has successfully carried out relevant projects for strengthening university institutions, but has not advanced in exploring cooperative initiatives in the area of technological innovation and support of new productive processes.

Expectations regarding university contributions to regional development are greater in regions where universities with recognized institutional prestige exist and are capable of strengthening regional identity and generating greater cultural depth. In turn, such capacity can facilitate the accumulation of regional social capital. Examples of the symbolic role that such a university could play are the Universidad de Concepción and Universidad Austral (Valdivia), both of which are nationally known. However, in neither of these cases are the universities carrying out their expected role.

The area that offers greater promise from the perspective of regional development is research and development in science and technology, hence linking the university task with economic development. However, the possibility of reconciling the interests of the private sector with those of academic university sector has not been made concrete except in a few limited situations.

The relationship of the universities with the public sector is different from that with the private sector. In the former, universities' role is limited to carrying out research financed through the FNDR or as candidates for institutional development projects via the same fund. Also, they network with entities such as the Corporación de Fomento de la Producción (Corporation for Production Support; CORFO) and Servicio de Cooperación Técnica (Technical Cooperation Service) in programs for the formation and support of small- and medium-sized enterprises. In contrast, with the private sector, some attempts at coordination in economic development areas have occurred. The most substantive attempts thus far are related to carrying out joint programs for training professionals and technical specialists in areas that are regional priorities.

Roles of Private Sector, Political Parties, and Civil Society in Decentralization and Regionalization

Private-sector executives do not have a global vision for regional development. Their vision is generally limited to opportunities and problems encountered in respective markets. They are typically convinced that they are responsible for development advances through their investments, and that the public sector is falling behind, supporting private enterprises through some investments in infrastructure, but maintaining an unfriendly policy that lacks clear rules and is bureaucratic.

Nor is the position of the public sector vis-à-vis the private sector positive with respect to those who assume that it is only motivated by its economic interest, relying on the government to remove obstacles without contributing anything in return. Even if functionaries and business executives coincide in the need to establish a strategic agreement, there is great incapacity to achieve one. The public and private sectors appear cut off from one another, and mutual distrust appears to have worsened in recent years. Efforts have been made to overcome this barrier and find a common language, but results have been meager. An example is the Foros de Desarrollo Productivo (Productive Development Forums) carried out in the regions in 1997, which lacked a clear mission and received negative evaluations from participants. The economy-related SEREMIs with active participation of regional managers and regional governments were responsible for driving them on. A consensus has been reached that the forum did not generate strategic debate, open channels of communication, nor bring about concrete, positive results for the participants.

The public sector has two channels to the private sector, without mutual coordination. One is through the regional institutional structure that principally addresses large enterprises and managerial organizations, and the second is through financing and support instruments that are attractive to medium and small enterprises.

Through the channel of the regional institutional structure, without continuity, business executives are brought together to encourage them to dialogue and participate in conversations or debates about regional development, which tend to successfully generate strategic agreements for cooperation. This takes place through different means: the regional productive forum, settings for discussing the budget, seminars, and direct dialogue with the regional manager. Another aspect of the relationship that the regional government opens up refers to conversations and even the possible agreements about projects and investments, especially on subjects such as roads and ports, which are of interest to the business managers. All of these initiatives refer to large enterprise executives.

The public sector gains access to small- and medium-scale enterprise executives through the instruments of productive support and conversion plans associated with CORFO mechanisms, which follow a distinct line in the regional discussion about development mentioned above. In other words, they neither touch nor cross paths with the regional institutional structures, nor with the instruments of public investment in regional decisions. In effect, the CORFO, one of the principal mechanisms to stimulate small- and medium-scale enterprises, never tried to strengthen regional identities or regional government.

Within the private sector, there are substantive differences between large-scale enterprise managers linked to international capital who, although they have access to the regional manager and regional government, definitively resolve their problems and concerns directly in Santiago, and the small- and medium-scale local enterprise managers.

The large-scale enterprise executives, organized in powerful industrial associations, have little interest in discussions about regional development and have logged a long list of complaints and/or requests presented to the public sector to facilitate their productive role. However, they are not willing to attend meetings or participate in debates about the challenges of regional development, nor are they willing to reconcile common work strategies. They are only interested in agreements that show concrete results in the short term, have a limited and specific reach, and do not involve economic and social regional development projects. For these executives, the fact of being located in a particular region does not make them actors with regional links. For them, geopolitical location is a contextual factor related to production, rather than as multifaceted beneficial interactions for their corporate development.

Small and medium-sized enterprises, except for a few exceptions, are not significant actors, nor do they participate in conversations about the meaning of regional development. Here there is a link to be made. These enterprises are much more carriers of regional identity and development projects anchored to the region than large multinational enterprises, and it is more possible to establish with them a joint work project. They are not focused on Santiago, and they find more opportunities in the institutional and geopolitical regional context. However, they have not developed a vision that identifies and decidedly links them to regional development. They do not form powerful industrial associations, as in the case of the large enterprises, and their internal coherence as a group is much weaker.

An important piece of information relevant to the discussion about the role of the private sector in regional development is the strictly regional profile that national development has. One talks about forestry, fisheries, mining, or manufacturing regions, but this reality does not constitute identity in the sociocultural and sociopolitical sense, but only a characteristic or pattern of the region.

Political parties have played a decidedly contradictory role in the decentralization process. They are very centralized structures in which decisions are not only made in the center, but also by a small group that controls the party without opening it to a democratic process. The parties are responsible for presenting candidates to regional councilors. Being regional structures that lack dynamism, opening themselves up with difficulty to new topics and leaders, they do not successfully accept decentralization or regionalism as part of their own agendas, and are even less likely to open space and raise local figures that can respond to these demands. The political parties are trapped in the electoral calculus. The party in Santiago decides the nomination of candidates to local councils, following a negotiation process within the alliances of the government and the opposition. Afterward, it is again the party in Santiago that decides the candidates for councillors who will be voted for by the councils.

A major challenge for the decentralization process is successfully creating a representative system that overcomes the logic of party quotas, and at the same time, puts the parties in tune with decentralization. This happens because they themselves initiate a decentralization and democratization process of their internal structures, making way for dynamic leadership and wholly regional processes, which implies that they lose some of their political control.

The success of decentralization depends on understanding it and assuming that it is a democratizing process of public life that empowers citizen participation and consolidates mechanisms of social control of government management, both in its national and decentralized expressions. Decentralization will be successful to the extent that civil society acquires an important role. Thus, citizen participation is fundamental to granting legitimacy to the process. Decentralization is transferring power from the central level to the decentralized levels, reaching the citizenry and not only the decentralized structures of government. Decentralization is important to democracy. It grants the broadening of the body of rights and liberties, the gradual incorporation of excluded and marginalized sectors of representative institutions, and more control and citizen participation in the performance of public administration.

The idea of participation associated with decentralization refers to decentralized authorities, councils, and councillors being bearers of popular interests. The regional government represents the political space of articulation of regional and local will and ought not to be a transmission belt of national government decisions. It also allows the strengthening of civil society and the creation of public policy in harmony with the citizenry.

Subnational Spaces for Popular Representation

Regional Councils will not be discussed at length here. It is sufficient to recall that one of their stated goals is to make participation of the regional community effective, and that the Councils are vested with normative, decision-making, and enforcement powers to realize such participation. However, the Regional Councils have thus far focused on technical-political activities in regional development, especially the design and execution of public investments, rather than popular participation.

Under existing legislation, each province should have a Consejo Económico y Social Provincial (Provincial Economic and Social Council; CESPRO), an advisory entity. The CESPRO should be comprised of the governor, twenty-four elected members (eight each from labor groups and economic enterprises; three each from cultural and professional organizations; and two from private foundations and corporations that foster development), and several appointed members (one each for each branch of the armed forces and a maximum of four representatives of higher education institutions) Principal functions of CESPROs are to present proposals for the regional development plan and the regional government budget, and carry out studies and give opinions on subjects related to provincial development.

CESPROs have been legally constituted in about half of the provinces; some Councils are inactive.[25] Reasons for failure to legally constitute these entities are many, but the most common are lack of interest among local organizations in participating (80 percent) and the lack of adequate legal personnel and resources. Provincial governments have been losing importance as territorial, institutional, functional, financial, normative, and participatory entities vis-à-vis regions and municipalities.

Governance at the municipality level consists of the democratically elected District Council, and the Consejo Económico Social Comunal (District Socio-economic Council; CESCO), an advisory entity composed of the mayor and representatives of the local community. The objective of the CESCO is to ensure the participation of community organizations that are defined/recognized by their place of origin and function-based characteristics in activities relevant to the economic, social, and cultural progress of the district.

The CESCOs are composed of a variable number of representatives according to the size of the population of the district or the group of districts as follows: 40 percent elected by legally constituted neighborhood committees; 30 percent elected by community organizations, including labor unions; and 30 percent chosen by the representatives of local economic activities.[26] Thus far, the CESCOs have been described as ineffective; leaders do not appear to represent the organizations that created them. Their roles as advisors to the municipality and as channels for local demands are minimal.

The democratizing promise of decentralization will not be realized if local capacities to fully exercise citizen rights and to occupy spaces opened by public policies are not effectively supported. In this particular niche where the citizenry and the state meet, civil society and in particular, nongovernmental organizations have an important role to play.

Civil society can be construed in a broad as well as a narrow sense. In the broad sense, it includes all citizens, associations, and institutions that may be considered autonomous agents vis-à-vis the state and the market. In a narrow sense, it refers to private nonprofit organizations and associations whose purpose is to promote the public interest or community well-being. Civil society in its narrow expression (nongovernmental organizations, private development organisms, or civil society organizations) has increasingly collaborated with governments in the social policy realm. The complexity and heterogeneity of social problems militate against the likelihood that any government has an arsenal of all possible responses or even the best responses to the same. Consequently, governments at all levels turn to civil society organizations to participate in joint projects of social and economic development. These organizations are slowly emerging as regional actors in sociopolitical matters.

However, the role played by civil society organizations in the construction of regional identity and how they have advanced their contributions to local debates about development are still unknown. In addition, these entities have a clear community profile, since they are identified with the locales in which they work. It is difficult for them to make the symbolic and political jump to the regional level. In the context of the social construction of culture and identity then, the region is occupied mainly by public authorities with little or no participation by civil society in the narrow sense discussed here.

Principal Criticisms of Decentralization

Although the decentralization process to regions has advanced significantly since enactment of the Law on Regional Government and Administration in 1993, much remains to be done. The regions continue to depend on the center, regional authorities lack autonomy and legitimacy in their own right, regional actors are weak, and the citizenry participation factor is the weakest link in the process.

The principal problems are related to restrictions that prevent the regions from obtaining their own revenues through taxation. At the same time, the regions do not have functional powers in the administration of public goods and services with direct impact on the citizenry's quality of life. Citizen participation in regional democracy, on the other hand, is weak. Chilean decentralization has a markedly institutional and administrative character, but even the institutional mechanisms that have been installed are insufficient and create their own difficulties because the power transfer is only partial.

Major criticisms are related to the establishment and authority of regional councils; the double role of the regional manager; investment funds based on regional decisions connected to ministerial responsibilities (ISARs) that leave little maneuvering room for the region; insufficient resources (although they are constantly increasing), the slow pace of the deconcentration process; the inadequate authority of the SEREMIs; the lack of administrative authority; and questions related to the rationales of existing geopolitical boundaries.

One example of the snail's pace of moving from norms to implementation regulations in is that although under the law the regions may request the transfer of responsibilities from any department of the central government, this power has never been used. Paradoxically, a consensus exists among government and nongovernment actors regarding the stalled process as well as general ideas of what should be done; however, this does not translate to action. It seems that no one knows how to overcome problems of political will. Official and nongovernmental sources assume that in the near future democratically elected institutional structures in the regions will have received functional responsibilities from the central government for designing and providing public services. It is also assumed that the SEREMIs disappear at this juncture, since ministerial representation in the region will no longer be necessary. Similarly, the SERPLACs would disappear, and regional governments would directly assume their tasks.[27]

However, clear and positive signals of movement in this direction are not apparent. Moreover, even within the regions numerous obstacles retard the development of regional leadership, such as the lack of definition and ambiguities in the institutional model of decentralization. Much authority remains in the hands of the central government because administrative support is inadequate. In particular, regional governments lack sufficient authority over personnel administration. To continue the process of decentralization, the following actions are necessary: transfer new and greater powers to the regions, modify the system of electing authorities, and advance the process of fiscal decentralization.

Effective management by subnational governments of their own development depends on the institutional design of decentralization and a wide spectrum of normative issues. However, there are other factors that influence the process in ways we are just beginning to recognize, including the innovative capacity, prestige, and autonomy of local leaders, the character of public sector professionals and technical experts, the legitimacy of authorities, the negotiation capacity and coordination of local actors, networks of relationships based on trust, and the capacity for economic development and technological innovation, among others. Briefly, these intangible factors refer to a type of intelligence and social energy that are put into motion at the service of a collective project, which only social actors from the region can construct.

While improving the institutional design is crucial, another equally important issue is developing and strengthening a shared regional identity in which civil society has a significant role, universities exercise roles of technological and cultural leadership, and regional actors impose the rhythm and characteristics of regional development. Recognizing and stimulating the roots of identity and specificity of these actors according to their own interests are necessary.

Notes

1. See, for instance, José Espinoza and M. Marcel, "Descentralización Fiscal en Chile" (Santiago: Comisión Económica para América Latina e el Caribe/Gesellschaft für Technische Zusammenarbeit, 1994); G. Aghón, "El Financiamiento Municipal: Principales Desafíos y Algunas Opciones," in *Desafíos para el Fortalecimiento Municipal,* Working Paper 34, edited by Abalos J. et al. (Santiago: Corporación de Promoción Universitaria, October 1994); Ahgón and C. Casa, "Descentralización en América Latina, Seminario Internacional Quito, Ecuador," *Desafíos para el Fortalecimiento Municipal;* Aghón and Letelier, "Local Urban Government Financing: A Comparison Between Countries," *Estudios de Economía* (University of Chile, Department of Economic and Administrative Sciences) 23 (August 1996); Claudia Serrano, "Gobierno Regional e Inversión Pública Descentralizada," *Colección de Estudios CIEPLAN* 42 (June 1996); Serrano and Jorge Rodríguez, "Cómo Va el Proceso de Descentralización del Estado en Chile," in *Construyendo Opciones. Propuestas Económicas y Sociales para el Cambio de Siglo,* edited by R. Cortázar and J. Vial (Santiago: Corporación de Investigaciones Económicas para Latinoamérica, 1998); Gabriel Salazar, *Inversiones Sectoriales de Asignación Regional: ¿Inversiones Sectoriales de Decisión Regional?* (Santiago: Subsecretaría de Desarrollo Regional y Administrativo, Departamento de Estudios, 1995); Consultadora Focus, "Evaluación Ex post Fondo Nacional de Desarrollo Regional 1990–1994" (Santiago: Subsecretaría de Desarrollo Regional y Administrativo, 1995); and various documents prepared for Undersecretary for Regional Development (SUBDERE).

2. R. Borges Mendez and V. Vergara, "The Participation-Accountability Nexus and Decentralization in Latin America" (paper presented at "Decentralization and Accountability of the Public Sector," Annual World Bank Conference on Development in Latin America and the Caribbean, Valdivia, Chile, 21–23 June 1999; I. Finot, *Descentralización del Estado y Participación Ciuadana en América Latina: Un Enfoque Crítico,* Documento CEPAL LC/IP/R.206 (Santiago: Comisión Económica para América Latina e el Caribe, 1998).

3. Luís Lira and Fernando Marinovic, *Estructuras Participativas y Descentralización: El Caso de los Consejos Regionales en Chile* (Santiago: Comisión Económica para América Latina e el Caribe/Instituto Latinoamericano y del Caribe de Planificación Económica y Social, 1999).

4. To establish the "best combination" of decentralization and "deconcentration" in a unitary state, issues of intraterritorial equity and redistributive mechanisms among regions with different levels of resources must be considered.

5. D. Artana and R. López Murphy, "Descentralización Fiscal y Aspectos Macro-económicos: Una Perspectiva Latinoamericana," in *Descentralización Fiscal en América Latina: Nuevos Desafíos y Agenda de Trabajo* (Santiago: Comisión Económica para América Latina e el Caribe/Gesellschaft für Technische Zusammenarbeit, August 1997); A. Shah and J. Huther, "Una Medición Sencilla de la Calidad del Buen Gobierno y su Aplicación al Debate sobre el Nivel Apropiado de Descentralización Fiscal," in *Descentralización Fiscal en América Latina: Nuevos Desafíos y Agenda de Trabajo* (Santiago: Comisión Económica para América Latina e el Caribe/Gesellschaft für Technische Zusammenarbeit, August 1997).

6. E. Di Gropello, *Descentralización de la Educación en América Latina,* Serie Reforma de Política Pública 57 (Santiago: Comisión Económica para América Latina e el Caribe, 1997); Eduardo Weisner, *Descentralización Fiscal: La Búsqueda de Equidad y Eficiencia,* Informe de Progreso Económico y Social en América Latina (Washington, D.C.: Banco Interamericano de Desarrollo, 1994).

7. Municipal revenues are divided among municipalities' own revenues and transfers. Municipalities' revenues form part of the current municipal budget and come from tax revenues, fees, concessions, and other revenues, such as a redistributive fund consisting of contributions from all municipalities in the country. This latter is called the Municipal Common Fund, whose objective is to resolve problems related to budget shortfalls and differences in fiscal revenue levels among districts.

8. Juan Pablo Valenzuela, *Descentralización Fiscal: Los Ingresos Municipales y Regionales en Chile,* Serie Política Fiscal 101, Proyecto Regional de Descentralización Fiscal (Santiago: Comisión Económica para América Latina e el Caribe/Gesellschaft für Technische Zusammenarbeit, 1997).

9. Luis Verdesoto, *El Control Social de la Gestión Pública: Lineamientos de una Política de Participación Social* (Quito: Ediciones Abya-Yala, 2000).

10. José María Saavedra, "Origen de la Reforma Administrativa," in *Proyecto Evaluación Histórica de la Regionalización en Chile* (Santiago: Corporación Tiempo 2000, 1996).

11. Under this modality, paying beneficiaries of the public health insurance system, which consists of a network of private service providers assigned to the system with preestablished prices for services, provide a co-payment for the health care they receive.

12. S. Galleguillos, "Descentralización Financiera en el Sector Salud Chileno," in *Descentralización, Nudos Críticos,* edited by Dagmar Raczynski and Claudia Serrano (Santiago: Corporación de Investigaciones Económicas para Latinoamérica, Asesorías para el Desarrollo/Ediciones Andros, 2001).

13. Two years later in 1994, the government amended the Law on Municipal Revenues and the territorial tax on real estate. Regarding education, the government readjusted the value of the academic subsidy for students. In the area of health care, the government substituted subsidies for a type of loan delivered through a training system.

14. In the following section, I develop in detail the role of these and other regional actors.

15. The only exception corresponds to the case of the FNDR provisions, which are additional resources incorporated into the fund with a specific orientation and that arise with the objective of allowing some investments in sectors that are seen as national level

priorities to be approved by regions. The central government bureaucracy determines the area of action for which the resources are designated, but the Regional Councils decides which concrete projects they will carry out.

16. The SUBDERE considers socioeconomic and territorial indicators. Socioeconomic indicators include rate of infant mortality, percentage of the regional population in extreme poverty, average regional unemployment rate, inverse of regional product per capita, health sector indicators (number of patients per hospital bed, thousands of beneficiaries per doctor in the region, rate of live births without medical attention, rate of infant malnutrition), indicators for the education sector (illiteracy rate, inverse of educational coverage), indicators of the sanitation sector (percentage of the urban population with access to potable water, percentage of the urban population with access to sewer system), indicators related to the territorial conditions of each region (inverse of population density [number of inhabitants per square kilometer raised to the negative one power], percentage of the population living in rural areas, index of ecological deterioration, and paving and construction costs).

17. José Arocena, *El Desarrollo Local: Un Desafío Contemporáneo* (Montevideo: Editorial Nueva Sociedad, 1995).

18. Claudia Serrano, "Inversión Pública y Gestión Regional, Nudos Críticos," in *Descentralización, Nudos Críticos,* edited by Dagmar Raczynski and Serrano (Santiago: Corporación de Investigaciones Económicas para Latinoamérica, Asesorías para el Desarrollo/Ediciones Andros, 2001).

19. In Serrano, "Inversión Pública y Gestión Regional," I discuss the themes of regional authorities, universities, and enterprises.

20. Luis Lira and Fernando Marinovic, *Estructuras Participativas y Descentralización. El Caso de los Consejos Regionales en Chile* (Santiago: Comisión Económica para América Latina e el Caribe/Instituto Latinoamericano y del Caribe de Planificación Económica y Social, 1999).

21. Subsecretaría de Desarrollo Regional y Administrativo (SUBDERE), *Bases para una Política de Descentralización,* Working Document (Santiago: SUBDERE, 2000); E. Valenzuela and G. Martelli, *Regionalismo en Chile: La Reforma Pendiente para el Desarrollo* (Santiago: Fundación Ebert, 2000).

22. During 1998 the Ministerio de Planificación y Cooperación (Planning and Cooperation Ministry) presented a proposal to transfer the Secretarias Regional Ministerial de Planificación y Coordinación (Regional Ministerial Secretariats for Planning and Coordination (SERPLACs) to be subordinate to the regional government. This initiative did not move forward because of objections by the Controller General of the Republic.

23. Regarding this point, the FNDR provision for fostering production represents progress by including economic development criteria in regional management, but this mechanism does not successfully overcome the gap between actions and policies in the area of public investment in regional decisions.

24. Examples of such processes include SERVIU, which allocates annual resources to regions before allocations for each program are defined in Santiago, and the regionalized budget design process of the Ministerio de Obras Públicas in 1999.

25. Luís Lira and Fernando Marinovic, *Estructuras Participativas y Descentralización: El Caso de los Consejos Regionales en Chile* (Santiago: Comisión Económica para América Latina e el Caribe/Instituto Latinoamericano y del Caribe de Planificación Económica y Social, 1999).

26. Law 1,695 describes functional district organizations as nonprofit legal entities whose objectives are to promote and represent specific values of the community within

the territory of the district or group of districts, including private education institutions, parents' and proxies' centers, cultural and artistic centers, mothers' centers, and environmental groups, professional organizations, private volunteer organizations, sports and recreation clubs, youth organizations, and others that promote participation of residents in community social and cultural development.

27. Valenzuela and Martelli, *Regionalismo en Chile.*

Appendix

Fondo Nacional de Desarrollo Regional (National Fund for Regional Development; FNDR)

Description	Fund for financing of actions in the distinct spheres of regional social and economic infrastructure, with the objective of creating harmonious and equitable territorial development, while safeguarding the preservation and improvement of the environment (Law on Regional Government and Administration).
Origin	Created in 1975. Until 1992, it was the only instrument for decentralized investment.
Allocation of resources	Subsecretaría de Desarrollo Regional y Administrativo (Undersecretary of Regional Development; SUBDERE) carries out interregional distribution of resources according to a formula that takes into account criteria of territorial efficiency and equity (90 percent of all resources). The process is summarized below:

- The Ministry of the Interior requests resources for the FNDR for the following year from the Treasury Ministry.

- The Treasury Ministry defines a budget framework for each region. With regard to socioeconomic compensation, the idea is that the lower the level of development of a region, the greater its allocation of the total amount of the FNDR. With regard to territorial compensation, the FNDR's allocation criteria favor regions farthest away from the capital.

- The mayor, with the technical support of the regional planning secretary, creates a regional investment budget and presents it to the regional government.

- The regional government approves the investment budget.

The remaining 10 percent of resources is divided according to criteria of emergency (5 percent) and efficiency (5 percent). Resources proportions are allocated according to efficiency criteria and then distributed according to a formula that takes into account as minimums the following indicators: (1) portfolio of regional projects and (2) level of expenditures of the region. Mayors present requests for emergency resources to the SUBDERE, which defines the projects to be approved.

(continued)

Fondo Nacional de Desarrollo Regional (Continued)

Sectors that are financed	Forestry, farming, fisheries, mining, industry, retail and wholesale trade, finance and tourism, energy, transportation, communication, potable water and drainage, housing, health, education and culture, sports and recreation, justice, defense and security, and multisectoral projects. Each category includes projects financed through Inter-American Development Bank credit, or with resources that correspond to the traditional FNDR.
Financing	FNDR projects are financed with national government resources. Inter-American Development Bank resources are accessed through a loan agreement with matching national resources.

Inversión Sectoral para Asignación Regional (Sectoral Investment for Regional Allocation; ISAR)

Description	Corresponding to preinvestment and program and project studies, ISARs are the responsibility of a ministry or its regional services, and destined for a particular region.
Origin	1992
Allocation of resources	These "ISARizado" programs operate through the allocation of resources to the regions by a ministry or service so that the Regional Council can distribute them among projects under consideration by the Regional Manager. Such projects should be adjusted to principles and criteria of the ministry or service on which the program depends.
	The ministries on which each "ISARizado" program depends are responsible for the definition contents and technical procedures for the interregional distribution of resources. The ministries or services also define the norms of eligibility and technical evaluation of the projects.
Sectors that are financed	The programs that operate in this way are: Neighborhood Improvement Program, Subsecretaría de Desarrollo Regional y Administrativo (Undersecretary of Regional Development (SUBDERE); Sports and Recreational Infrastructure, Dirección General de Deportes y Recreación (General Sports and Recreation Administration; DIGEDER); Secondary Roads Program, Ministerio de Obras Públicas (Public Works Ministry; MOP); Rural Potable Water Program, MOP; Urban Paving Program, Ministerio de Vivienda y Urbanismo (Ministry of Housing and Urban Development; MINVU)
Relative participation in Inversión de Decisión Regional (region-oriented investment) (1999)	21.91 percent

(continued)

Inversión Sectoral para Asignación Regional (Continued)

Programs Included	Ministry/Service	Description
Neighborhood Improvement Program	Ministerio del Interior (Interior Ministry)/ SUBDERE	Offers access to sanitation resources and solutions for low-income urban and rural households who live in marginal sanitation conditions through the financing of two types of projects: (1) construction of sanitation infrastructure with associated public works of urbanization, and (2) actions concurrent to the financing of studies, acquisition of lands, technical inspections, agreement orders, and guarantee of titles, among others.
Sports and Recreation Infrastructure	DEFENSA/Dirección General de Deportes y Recreación (General Sports and Recreation Administration; DIGEDER)	This is a subsidy of the DIGEDER that allows the creation, modification, or replacement of sites for sports and recreation activities. It finances priority district projects according to the District Plan for Sports and Recreation, which has the double purpose of identifying needs and achieving an adequate district coordination between the sports sector and the sectors of education, health, housing, and community organization, among others.
Secondary Roads Program	Ministerio de Obras Públicas (Public Works Ministry; MOP)	This program finances road conservation works, that is, maintenance and repairs to retain quality and benefits that the original design offers or offered. This MOP program can also finance structural modifications, such as a change in the standard from earth to stones and very rarely from stones to asphalt, or modification in road geometry.
Urban Paving Program	Ministerio de Vivienda y Urbanismo (Ministry of Housing and Urban Development)	This program is destined for paving and repair of streets, alleyways, sidewalks, and supports, with the objective of creating more and better public roads. It finances the following projects: public road maintenance, pavement projects, major roadway improvements, and construction of feeder roads.
Rural Potable Water Program	MOP	Designed to provide potable water to rural communities, this program finances preinvestment projects such as hydroelectric assessment and viability reports, water source studies, drilling or digging wells, design of service installation, expansion and/or rehabilitation of existing works, and projects needed to supplement existing works.

Programming Agreements

Description	Formal accords between one or more regional governments and one or more ministries in which they define actions related to investment projects that they agree to jointly carry out in a given timeframe. These agreements articulate sectoral and regional objectives, bringing together resources from both levels to carry out projects of mutual interest. They permit the undertaking of large investment projects of one to five years duration.
Origin	The first agreements were signed in 1994 and began to operate in 1995.
Allocation of resources	Financing of agreements goes through the following phases: • Formulation of ideas: Identification of principal projects that solve regional problems according to the regional development strategy • Protocol of intent: Parties to the agreement sign protocol of intent that begins negotiations with the ministries • Definition of Program or Project: Specification of projects, design of preinvestment studies if they do not already exist, creation of commitments of technical units that will be responsible for study results and follow-up • Writing of programming agreement: Allocation of responsibilities and obligations of parties to the agreement • Presentation to Regional Council: Approval and signing of agreement
Sectors that are financed	There are no restrictions. However, large investment projects in the areas of infrastructure and housing are preferred.
Financing	Projects are financed with sectoral resources (average 70 percent of total), and regional resources of the Fondo Nacional de Desarrollo Regional (National Fund for Regional Development).
Number of agreements signed as of December 1998	33

Inversión Regional para Asignación Local (Regional Investment for Local Allocation; IRAL)

Description	These are clearly local investment projects that are distributed to the districts.
Origin	1996
Allocation of resources	At the sectoral level, the Fondo de Solidaridad e Inversión Social (Solidarity and Social Investment Fund; FOSIS) and Subsecretaría de Desarrollo Regional y Administrativo (Undersecretary of Regional Development; SUBDERE) determine the amounts of investment for each region. The regional government distributes these resources among districts. In prioritized districts, the municipal council determines projects to be funded.

(continued)

Inversión Regional para Asignación Local (Continued)

Sectors that are financed	Programs that participate in financing offered by IRAL offers and the ministries or services to which they belong follow: Urban Improvement Program, SUBDERE; Local Development Program, FOSIS; Youth Development Program, FOSIS; Rural Productive Support Program, FOSIS; and Support Service for Territorial Management, FOSIS.
Financing	Programs are financed with central government resources allocated in the Law on National Budgets.

Programs Included	Ministry/Service	Description
Urban Improvement Program	Ministerio del Interior (Interior Ministry)/ Subsecretaría de Desarrollo y Administrativo (Undersecretary of Regional Development)	Finances investment projects that generate employment and improve quality of life of the poorest segments of the population, such as construction, repair, improvement, conservation, expansion, or replacement of potable water, sewer, rainwater drainage systems; street surfaces, passageways, and sidewalks; household electrification; cleaning and normalization of canals, footbridges, bridges, and paths; and topographical surveys.
Local Development Program	Ministerio de Planificación y Cooperación (Planning and Cooperation Ministry; MIDEPLAN/Fondo de Solidaridad e Inversión Social (Solidarity and Social Investment Fund; FOSIS)	Seeks to improve material and nonmaterial living conditions of inhabitants in low-income areas through implementation of action plans.
Local Program for Youth Development	MIDEPLAN/FOSIS	Oriented to empower young people who live in poor areas, improving their quality of life, developing their individual and collective identity, and fostering their integration into local activities and interaction with adults in the community.
Rural Productive Support Program	MIDEPLAN/FOSIS	Seeks to develop capacities (organizational, technical, and management) and create income-generating opportunities and/or employment, broadening opportunities for participation in goods and services markets. Supports entrepreneurial groups or organizations, stimulating the creation, formation, and participatory execution of innovative economic projects or that add value to existing products/services, generate

(continued)

Inversión Regional para Asignación Local (Continued)

		additional sustainable income, and take into account for their execution the coordination of a group's own actions and resources, those of FOSIS, and where possible, those of other institutions.
Support Service for Territorial Management	MIDEPLAN/FOSIS	Tries to empower groups and organizations in places and sectors selected by Municipal Councils to execute Local Development Programs, Rural Productive Support Programs, and Urban Improvement Programs in the generation of local development initiatives pertinent to their needs and concurrent with district and regional development strategies within poverty alleviation framework.

Chapter 5

Local Governance and Democratization: The View from the Chilean Border

María Elena Ducci

The analysis of decentralization in Chile can be approached from distinct perspectives, and the ways of understanding it and evaluating advances in the process can be very different. One perspective is that of the capital, the administrative, economic, and political center of the country. Another perspective is that of the regions (or periphery, or subnational units), which maintain an openly critical position regarding the way decision-making powers are distributed in Chile today.

Therefore, we find, on the one hand, a beautiful discourse on decentralization coming from the central government, according to which decentralization is necessary in order to achieve a greater degree of democratization. For the same reason, it is presented as a state priority. On the other, from regional and municipal governments, and especially from civil society, there are constant complaints about the lack of freedom to make decisions regarding local development and the apparent incapacity of the central government to hand over some of the power that it holds. This chapter focuses on the vision from the periphery.

First, I present the fundamental arguments with which the push for de-centralization has been justified, and then I analyze the official discourse currently used in Chile in relation to those arguments. Second, I describe historical events that explain the pure centralism of the Chilean state as the result of a series of actions legitimated socially and culturally until they seemed "natural, inevitable and immutable."[1] Next, I show how government officials and inhabitants of Region IX, La Araucanía, which is far from the capital, perceive what is happening. At present in Region IX, there exists a serious conflict among the Mapuche, who are the original inhabitants of the area, timber company managers, and the government. Finally, I present the plan of a civil society group that is openly struggling to accelerate the process of decentralization and ensure that the process is effective. This group, Los Federales (The Federals), has gained great visibility in recent years.

The Underlying Logic and the Official Discourse

The need to decentralize seems a constant today in the discourse of Latin American governments. It is not a random event, which leads researchers to examine the underlying causes of this push toward decentralization unleashed in the 1980s that "is being proclaimed as a new panacea to confront the problems that affect certain local groups."[2]

But something like this "trend" also occurred in the countries of the North. The discourse of decentralization was developed in Europe in the 1960s and 1970s, when the cycle of postwar economic growth was exhausted, and economic restructuring became necessary.[3] Strong and centralized states had until that time promoted accelerated and successful growth. With the postwar industrial growth strategy no longer useful, strong, centralized states ceased to be thought of as necessary, and centralization was then considered to be excessive.[4]

Whatever the reasoning used today in Latin American countries to justify the need to decentralize, behind it lies the economic crisis of the 1980s. At that time, the welfare state became exhausted as a means of addressing social problems. With its exhaustion arose pressures from multilateral and bilateral financial agencies to restructure the local economy and decrease the size of the state in order to increase efficiency.

The arguments that developing countries use vary, but one can synthesize the following. First, they identify with the neoliberal ideology that demands modernization of the state to adapt it to new worldwide conditions of globalization and open economies. In this context, decentralization allows improvement of the efficiency and effectiveness of the state apparatus, in that decentralized services can be better administered and controlled by subnational governments. In addition, it fosters the participation of private entities whose superior efficiency, according to the neoliberal discourse, ensures the provision of better public services to all citizens.

Another justification, not always clearly explicit, is the desire to increase the legitimacy of the political regime. This is achieved by promoting a reform that tries to reinforce the weight of subnational government levels in the national political game, giving them greater autonomy to make decisions regarding their own development and to control their resources by broadening the responsibilities and abilities of local actors.[5]

However, as Von Haldenwang observes, reforms that intend to generate new models of administration and government do not always have the ability to increase the legitimacy of the state. This risk exists because these changes generate expectations that can result in disillusionment, because the state inevitably fails to fulfill expectations, which in turn leads "dangerous losses of legitimacy."[6] As articulated by regional government representatives below, the veracity of Von Haldenwang's observation is proven. Some mayors state this clearly:

> Are we communal government or municipal administration? Do we only administer or do we govern? They are two very distinct realities and the answer and its consequences are not at all innocent.[7]

The third argument most used in the decentralization discourse is that of the potential of this process to accelerate local development, deepen democracy, and decrease inequality among regions and local communities. At the end of the 1980s, Borja suggested that decentralization "seems integral to democracy" because it broadens the area of rights and liberties, allows the incorporation of the most excluded sectors, and increases the population's control over public administration.[8] Not all of these positive outcomes seem to be operative for the regional actor who observes and experiences the changes from his or her location far from the center, as seen in Chile today.

The official discourse is summarized in the following statement by Vice President Carlos S. Figueroa, which is representative of the seductive panorama that the central government has proposed as a goal:

The country needs and requires [region-based government and non-government actors] who are their own bosses, self-sustainable, self-sufficient, with the capacity to develop their own dreams . . . , [who are] enterprising, free of pretexts that inhibit them in mind and spirit to take on their development, intellectually capable, educated, imaginative, healthily ambitious.[9]

The official discourse places the emphasis on the initiative that the regions should take to increase their weight in the national dynamic. However, it says nothing about the delegation of power and decision making that the central state needs to make so that the regions can in turn become independent and take responsibility for their own development.

In the official discourse, the theme of increased equity, granting increasingly greater capacity to "the people" to decide the way they want to address their future, is also found. Further on, I discuss whether this gradual advance is taking place and, if so, at what pace. According to central government official Eduardo Dockendorff, "[T]he key is in gradual but steadfast advancement in the process of transferring power to the people, and with it, making the people the principal protagonists in their own development."[10]

When the deepening of democracy becomes explicit as a national objective, the generality of the suggestion makes it difficult to understand how it can be turned into practice, without first making concrete what it means for citizens to actively participate in the country's political life. According to Dockendorff, "An absolute democracy is that in which power is widely distributed in the society, making all citizens able to participate actively in the construction of the personal and country project[s]."[11]

With all of this, it ought to be recognized, that pro–central government supporters understand the problems that prevent advancement of the decentralization process, at least at the theoretical level. Dockendorff, the current undersecretary of the General Secretariat of the Presidency, emphasizes that, among the largest current obstacles in the way of perfecting democracy and improving equity, are political-administrative centralism and economic and territorial concentration. He also notes that the limited autonomy and weakness of civic organizations, and the lack of resources for regional and local management of social programs are obstacles to the progress of decentralization.[12]

The Constitution of the Republic defines Chile as a unitary state, a fact that is accepted even by the most radical social actors in the push for decentralization; until now, no one has suggested the possibility of federalism or anything similar. Thus, the process of decentralization has been coming about and will continue to come about within the existing institutional framework.[13] According to the central government, decentralization is being carried out at a slow but positive pace.[14]

Regional and municipal government actors, however, do not have such a positive perspective, and feel that the central level is impeding a more decided advance. They believe that their perspective is captured by the skepticism that Urzúa and García were already showing in the 1960s with respect to the decentralization promoted by the central government's bureaucratic apparatus:

> By its own measure, the bureaucracy is a sociologically conservative group that is inclined toward the status quo, and that, by its rigorous formalism, does not tend toward any dynamic action. Very much on the contrary, it tends to direct it.[15]

The Historical Origins of Chilean Centralism

According to Valenzuela, "Centralism, like fate, has tried to become common sense in Chile."[16] This author based his writing on his experience as mayor of a medium-sized city and how he experienced the force of centralist pressures. In an attempt to rewrite the national history, he states that centralism is a historical construction that has been validated as the most ideal for national development, without respecting the feelings or the abilities of the populations outside the center.

The centralist legacy that Chile received from the colonial period, when the center of the world was in Spain and all instructions regarding what to do and how to do it came from the Crown, cannot be ignored. However, extreme difficulties of communication characterized this epoch. The territories were isolated for months or even years, and local authorities were forced to make medium-term and immediate decisions according to their own criteria. The transformation process of the newly independent nation into an autonomous entity was not simple. In the beginning, the nation-state was very tumultuous and unstable, as leaders with very different visions regarding the degree of autonomy that the regions ought to maintain relative to the central government confronted each other.

Chile's "federalist experiment" was carried out between 1823 (when the "Act of Union of the People of Chile" was signed) and 1829, a chaotic epoch during which several presidents and "supreme directors" came and went. A national congress was formed in this period and members wrote a federalist constitution that was approved in 1826, but the constitution was never put into practice. The congress dissolved itself in 1827, although this failure did not imply the disappearance of the federalist group. The attempts to function as a federated union produced constant conflicts and struggles among groups led by members of the central and regional oligarchies. In the end, with the ascent of José Joaquín Prieto Vial (1831–1841),[17] who was allied to the conservatives, to the presidency, the "mythical decades of stability began and what the federalists view as an 'authoritarian and centralized state that has lasted until today'"[18] triumphed. The foundations of the centralist system are found in the constitution of 1833 (which was in effect with modifications until 1925). Its principal ideologue was Diego Portales,[19] who thought that the necessary republican virtues did not exist in Chile for the adequate functioning of the democratic system, and therefore, it was necessary to create an authoritarian state "with the zeal of the public good, through men capable of understanding it and carrying it out."[20]

This put an end to decades of struggle between civil and military leaders and is, in the official history, the cornerstone that allowed Chile, unlike many of its neighbors, to enter into a prolonged period of peace and development. Portales "built the Administration morally and materially, reestablished order, work, morality and the spirit of duty. . . . The strict and efficient administrative structure created by Portales was maintained until 1891 and even afterward."[21]

Portales's conservative and hegemonic system prevailed for about sixty years. Although the liberals—linked to the mining and guano-producing bourgeois of the North and the financial bourgeois of Valparaíso—thereafter participated in governance, the state continued to represent the interests of the oligarchy without opening itself to a representative democracy. The installation of the parliamentary system, which at the end of the nineteenth century displaced the presidential system, did not produce major changes, since the parliamentarians represented the oligarchs, who at that time were not only landowners but also included mine owners and financiers.[22]

The "oligarchic" regimes were replaced in the 1920s by governments that sought to industrialize the country, but always through the centralized state and with a strong paternalistic bent. In the words of Martínez Keim, "Chile is definitely a country constructed on the institutional nature of government, [that is, built up] from the State."[23] Consequently, the issue of decentralization today is managed by the state as a matter of institutional change; addressing it does not begin with local needs, potentials, and aspirations.

Another fundamental element for explaining national centralism is the concentration of investment and institutions in Santiago since the nation's beginnings. "The history of Chile is told as a history of Santiago, because there politics occurred and works were undertaken."[24] The debate about how much the national government should spend in the capital city is chronic, given that, according to the defenders of decentralization, each peso invested in the center is subtracted from investments elsewhere. For example, today Santiago is the only city in Chile that has a subway and a major international airport, and has the greatest concentration of universities and museums. Table 5.1 shows some other indicators of the gap in services and resources that characterizes the capital city as compared to Region VIII, Bío-Bío, the second best-equipped region of the country, and Region IX, La Araucanía.

Without attempting to provide a detailed account of the historical evolution of the system of government and its relationship to decentralization, the preceding points are useful in understanding that centralism has been imbued in the spirit of the country since its beginnings as a nation, and that paternalism, which exists at all levels, is not rooted in recent history, but rather extends far into the distant past.[25]

Perceptions at the Regional Level

To better understand how the decentralization process is taking shape on an everyday basis in the regions, I proceed with a description of Temuco, the capital of Region IX, La Araucanía. Temuco, a city of approximately 250,000[26] people, of which around 30 percent are indigenous, is located 620

Table 5.1
Social Indicators by Region

Region	Movie Theaters	Newspapers	Hospital Beds	Doctors
Metropolitan area of Santiago	158	417	9,651	3,758
Bío-Bío	17	81	4,330	946
La Araucanía	2	12	2,303	372

Source: Instituto Nacional de Estadísticas, 2000 (www.ine.cl).

kilometers south of Santiago. Compared to other medium-sized cities in the country, Temuco is experiencing exceptionally rapid growth. Development in Temuco is based on commercial and service activities for the surrounding region. In 2000, the population of the La Araucanía region was 874,000, of which 62 percent resided in rural areas and 27 percent were Mapuche (18 percent in urban areas and 81 percent in rural areas). (See also Table 5.2.)

With the goal of understanding the perspective of this region, I carried out a series of interviews of government officials responsible for planning and service delivery in the areas of health, education, and housing and urban development in Region IX and representatives of civic organizations. These interviews revealed the gigantic gap between perceptions of region inhabitants and those of central government representatives regarding advancement of the decentralization process.[27]

The first conclusion I reached is that levels of decentralization are very diverse, depending on the sector. Thus, at one extreme, such as public works, all decisions regarding large-scale infrastructure, such as size, location, and route in the case of highways are made in the country's capital. Of the sectors studied in more detail (health, education, and housing and urban development), health seems to be the sector most dependent on the center, and the area with the most autonomy in decision making is urban development.

The interviewees' opinions are summarized below. Naturally, they necessarily show the bias of groups who have traditionally felt themselves to be peripheral to the centers of decision making; their appraisals are not likely to be shared by many central functionaries and actors.

In the area of health care, the process is defined by a local official as "stuck, in spite of much discussion," because of the lack of competence of regional functionaries.[28] The healthcare sector is especially complicated in the context of the Chilean state, since the healthcare system has two branches, theoretically complementary, that experience difficulty in coordinating themselves in everyday activities. On the one hand, there is the Servicio Regional del Ministerio de Salud (Health Ministry Regional Service;

Table 5.2
Social Indicators of La Araucanía

	Percent of Population Living in Poverty	Unemployment Rate	20% Richest/ 20% Poorest	Percent of Population in Two Largest Cities
1990	45.1	4.1	14.6	32.0
1998	34.3	8.7	12.7	

SEREMI de Salud, or SEREMI) that represents the Ministry of Health. It is responsible for oversight, as it carries out national policies and programs in the region, in addition to being responsible for preparing annual budgets and disbursing central government funds for specific activities and programs. On the other hand, there is the Servicio Regional del Salud (known as the Servicio), which is responsible for standards of care and other technical matters, and is in charge of healthcare establishments (hospitals, public health offices, clinics). The responsibilities of both entities (SEREMI and Servicio) are not, however, clearly defined. In practice, at the national level, the Servicio has higher prestige and visibility, while the SEREMI has a secondary role limited to the administrative functions assigned to it by the national Ministry of Health.[29]

Add to this complicated panorama the requirement that many decisions must be confirmed by the central government. It is understandable that local functionaries feel that the decentralization policy in their area is at a standstill. From their perspective, a clear intent on the part of the central government to transfer responsibilities to the region is lacking. A concrete example, which for the SEREMI in La Araucanía is a source of constant problems, is its inability to sign agreements with the Servicio on specific issues. Given that the SEREMI also lacks the authority to manage resources, it winds up acting as an administrative entity that transfers resources to the Servicio for programs and actions defined between the Servicio and the central government.[30]

The SEREMI de Salud in La Araucanía is composed of five people, including the regional secretary. These administrators are often dismissed by their superiors in the Ministry of Health in Santiago when they attempt to perform their mandated tasks, such as defining the health sector's annual budget for the region. For instance, from October to November 2000, the SEREMI developed a regional ISAR (basically capital investment, such as purchase of equipment, construction of healthcare facilities, etc.) for the health sector of 198 million pesos for 2001.[31] In mid-January 2001, Ministry officials in Santiago informed the SEREMI that the ISAR had been reduced to 138 million pesos. SEREMI officials were not consulted about the budget cut decision, nor were they informed before the budgetary year began. After receiving notification of the central government decision, SEREMI and Servicio officials were forced to decide on which programs and activities to suspend for lack of resources.

Also in 2000, central government officials decided—again, without taking regional actors' opinions into account—to invest 240 million pesos in

healthcare services for the Mapuche people. Since the Mapuche have become a pressing political problem, this decision by Santiago followed a national strategy of improving the living conditions of this ethnic group, but
it was not the result of demands from the region. In the central government's
Ministry of Health, officials created a "Mapuche Health Program" that
works independently of regional health services. This program consists of
an interesting experiment that integrates the traditional medicine of the Mapuches with Western medicine. Based in a regional hospital, the Maquehue
Hospital in Padre Las Casas, program administrators are trying to manage
both visions of health in a complementary manner.

The following anecdote demonstrates the way in which the government's
"opening for decentralization" reaches regional functionaries. One of the
five officials in Region IX's SEREMI de Salud was invited (an unprecedented move) to participate in a budgetary meeting of the Ministry of Treasury in Santiago, where officials discussed the budgets to be assigned to
each region. At the meeting, the SEREMI official was informed that the
amount earmarked for Region IX had previously been defined by central
government officials.

All of these situations produce a sensation of "immense frustration"
among regional government personnel: "We wear ourselves out producing
projects for each budgetary exercise, attending meetings . . . with minimal
results."[32] Health sector budgets that are defined in the region must be negotiated afterward with MINSAL (Ministerio de Salud) officials, who ultimately decide how much each region will receive. The weight of the Ministry is so great in these decisions that, according to the opinion of local
functionaries, the principal reason that the region has obtained 5 billion pesos to resolve bottlenecks in emergency services was a visit to the region by
the previous administration's minister of health, Alex Figueroa (1994–
1996). This occasion gave the Regional Medical College, high-level functionaries, and regional politicians the opportunity to personally lobby the
ministry, and the result was the allocation of 5 billion pesos.

Regarding housing and urban development, regional functionaries believe that the Ministerio de Vivienda y Urbanismo (Ministry of Housing and
Urban Development; MINVU) is one of the most decentralized components
of the state apparatus. This appears quite evident in Temuco with respect to
urban development, but it is not so obvious in relation to housing. Urban development plans for Temuco and other cities of the region are subject to a
bidding process, and winners are selected and contracted by the SEREMI
for MINVU. The contracts are carried out by local contractors and consult-

ants (all of whom have received university degrees in Santiago and/or abroad).

The functionaries recognize that a strong dependence on the center (MINVU) exists in terms of defining the amounts invested awarded to the region, but once the funds are received, regional functionaries decide how to distribute them in the region: "Once [the funding is] assigned, we decide here" what to spend where and how to spend it."[33] However, "sometimes an order assigning the funds to a project that we have not requested arrives. . . . That makes us very angry . . ." "Because one mayor overspent his funds, . . . we have to take the money out of the global fund" (the amount directly assigned by MINVU to a project for a specific district). "There we feel passed over . . . not always, but sometimes that happens."[34]

The SEREMI in Region IX for MINVU is composed of two architects and a civil engineer, who carried out eight regulatory plans in early 2001. They contracted out the cartography and later bid the plans. The funds for carrying out the plans were obtained by means of a programming agreement between the municipal government and the Association of Municipalities to administer a program of five to six years. The municipality and SEREMI have yet to approve the plans, as the latter must give its report to the Regional Council,[35] where a planning commission must approve it. Given that CORE members generally do not have technical skills, it has become a bottleneck, causing delays in plan approval times.[36]

With regard to housing programs, activities and programs defined by the central government are applied in the region. In recent years, however, some changes that adapt the housing to climatic conditions and local cultures have been introduced, and the Housing Department is developing unprecedented pilot programs with characteristics specific to each region. Another recent and important change for the autonomy of this sector is that now it is possible, through an official government order, to reassign funds to different programs, if regional officials believe that such is necessary. Until very recently, funding amounts assigned for the program were fixed; thus if all of the anticipated, basic housing was not built, for example, the amount not used was lost to the region and returned to Santiago.[37]

The Mapuches have also had an impact in the design of plans and programs. Mapuche territory cannot be incorporated into the scope of local regulatory plans; consequently, MINVU funds cannot be assigned to the development of existing settlements. Given that the Mapuches are reclaiming land in many areas, the SEREMI's plans for MINVU funding are sometimes stalled for months or years. For example, the regulatory plan of the city of

Imperial was delayed because local Mapuches did not accept the proposed city limits. For some Mapuches, giving up their land is unthinkable, while others are interested in selling or exchanging their land (which is permitted by law). This has been the cause of many conflicts and has created "islands" of usable lands surrounded by Mapuche land, thereby hindering use of the land in urban planning objectives.

According to a Region IX official, the Ministry of Education (MINEDUC) is among the most centralized state bureaucracies, particularly in terms of budgetary decision making: "We have little or nothing to say [about budgets] as a region."[38] An educational reform, which was initiated in the 1980s "without any previous consultation," sought to improve administration of the educational system and to foster private sector participation as a provider of resources for education. According to some mayors, it has not functioned in that manner: "The functions of the municipality became essentially administrative . . . with the role of paying salaries and processing medical licenses to teachers, transforming municipalities into simple employers."[39]

MINEDUC defines annual operating budgets through the Fondo de Inversión en Educación (Education Investment Fund) for each region, based on population. In addition, an emergency fund exists that can be used for urgent projects that are approved by the Ministry. For capital expenditures, the Fondo Nacional de Desarrollo Regional (National Fund for Regional Development; FNDR)[40] is used, which also must be approved at the central level.

Decentralization of the education sector has given increased autonomy to educational establishments, since now each school can design its own curriculum, plans, and program of study, with the only condition being that they respect the minimum curriculum content demanded by MINEDUC. In 1996, the ministry designed model programs, allowing local educators to adapt them to their own realities. The problem that has arisen in the public sector regarding this opportunity is the lack of ability of school personnel to make these adaptations, while undertaking the excessive work loads that are typical for these functionaries. However, private schools, which attract the most capable educators and offer broader curricula, are making these adaptations.

In spite of the fact that MINEDUC has not defined a special increase in financing for the poorest areas of the country, changes are observed in this region related to the situation of the Mapuches. Starting with the Indigenous Law approved in 1992–1993, MINEDUC and the Corporación Nacional de Desarrollo Indígena (National Council of Indigenous Development;

CONADI) must create opportunities for intercultural bilingual education. In Region IX, this means that functionaries must organize schools in which studies are carried out both in Spanish and in Mapudungún. Only when this law was passed did Chilean central government officials stop thinking that the country was monocultural, and began to officially recognize the existence of other cultures that are also integral parts of the nation. Of course, MINEDUC was not prepared for changes of these dimensions, and the transition process has in turn been slow.

The Universidad de Temuco has opened an area of studies in multicultural, bilingual education. However, few students have enrolled in it, and as of this writing, there is no a great interest among practicing teachers to enroll. This disinterest can be explained in part because competency in the language of the other culture is still not a requirement to work in an indigenous community. However, both the Universidad de Temuco and the Universidad Católica have been carrying out important work to help advance acceptance of the Mapuches in mainstream culture.

In 1996, the Multicultural, Bilingual Education Program was initiated, and in 2000 the first pilot programs in schools were launched. In Region IX, programs were organized in three schools in the Lumaco district, one of the zones with the highest concentration of indigenous people. A major objective of the program is to establish/promote a bicultural coexistence in which each culture maintains respect for the other.[41]

The program includes teacher training, but this is voluntary. On the other hand, many Mapuche children have been persecuted in public schools because of their linguistic and cultural differences. Even Mapuche teachers who have had this sort of experience are not always willing to collaborate in the new program. Some members of the Mapuche communities express the following attitude: "I do not want my children to speak a language that today is not useful."[42]

This program also includes cultural agents, community residents who act as mediators between public school teachers and the community. Since many dialects exist among the Mapuches, it is essential that the agents belong to the same community where they work and are elected by their fellow community members. It is hoped that these cultural agents will create a peer relationship between the teacher and the community, since the Mapuches do not accept the idea that a teacher "tells them what to do." In cases in which good coordination has been achieved between the agent and the professor, the results have been excellent, but this does not always happen easily.[43]

The issue of the dialect diversity, together with the lack of a formal written language accepted by all, has caused MINEDUC to propose that each community define its written language as it sees fit. Of course, this aspect makes creating a general bilingual program even more difficult.

In summary, a review of what is happing at the level of regional functionaries reveals very diverse situations. These range from complaints about being ignored or dismissed and feeling hopeless about improvements to much more pragmatic and positive positions that things are improving at the regional level, albeit slowly.

However, a contradiction arises when one walks around the central streets of the prosperous and growing city of Temuco, and inhabitants proudly show off recently opened shops, so modern "that they seem to be from Santiago." The yearning to look like the capital is revealed everywhere. In fact, the new housing development constructed in recent years in the northern zone of the city, designed to house the growing middle class, resembles a Santiago suburb. Perhaps the most impressive sign of the strength of centralism in Chile is the desire among people in the regions to be like the capital.[44] However, some of the inhabitants are not in agreement with this, and they are struggling hard to oppose what they consider the oppression of the center. We will talk about them in the following section.

Los Federales: An Anti-Center Movement

Temuco, capital of La Araucanía, is home to two members of Los Federales, the group whose opposition to centralism is the strongest in the country. "The men dressed in black" are openly engaged in a fight against centralized power.

> Our current challenge as a nation is to overcome centralism because it is unsustainable and does not have a future. This system generates high costs and provokes a growing deterioration in the quality of life of Chileans and of their natural and cultural environment. (From "Manifiesto de los Federales," March 2000.)

One of the central objectives of Los Federales is election of regional managers (who are currently appointed by the president); this demand has been completely ignored since 1998. Another goal is to foster the creation of local political parties in the regions. In La Araucanía, the Agrarian Party and

Media coverage of Los Federales in Chilean press. (From Diario El Mostrado, 7 March 2000, available at: www.elmostrador.cl.)

the "Center Center" quickly transcended a regional character to attain influence at the national level.

Diego Benavente is a regionalist leader from La Araucanía who has gained national visibility because of his participation in this movement. He is openly critical of the way that the country's system of government is managed, as well as certain specific policies. For example, he states that the multifamily housing that MINVU is constructing resembles "confinement cells" more than homes, and that trying to develop culture in the regions is almost impossible because of the inequities that have concentrated resources in the center. He also believes that the historic roots of Chilean centralism are found in the colonial past: "In North America, people were taught to work and govern. . . . Here in Latin America, we were taught to pray and obey . . ."[45]

For the past fifteen years, he has participated in the "Regionalization Working Day," the first of which he helped organize in 1984. In his opinion, these exercises have achieved very little, an opinion that is shared by the mayor of Temuco: "To this . . . is added the lack of political will to continue advancing in the country's decentralization process . . ."[46]

Benavente states that one of the bases of national centralism can be found in the career of Portales, who to avoid bossism suggested that state functionaries should travel the country, thereby allowing national "unification."

Apparently, the application of Portales's ideas had the expected results, making Chile a basically centralist country.

Benavente has been developing this and many other ideas through a column in the newspaper *Austral,* published every Tuesday since April 2000. The impact that his column has had on the local population has surprised him in a positive sense: "Before the column, I thought that I was an idealist. . . . Now they support me . . . , they give me information, even people of other political persuasions . . ."[47]

For Benavente, strengthening regional leaders is fundamental, and a sufficient critical mass of regionalists ought to be at least two or three per region. In addition, he believes that the development of local means of communication is essential:

> To decentralize it is necessary to have one's own means of communication that gives creativity a free rein, channels our concerns and gives space for the generation of necessary leaders to create and construct opinions different from official opinions or those of the center.[48]

With respect to members of the national congress who represent the region, some of whom participate in Los Federales, Benavente states that the strength of the centralist system is such that "the machine absorbs and overrides them." This opinion is notable, upon consideration of the fact that although the current president of the Chamber of Deputies belongs to Los Federales,[49] the process of giving more power to the regions does not seem to be advancing.

Jorge Bravo, another adherent of Los Federales who lives in Temuco, believes that the regionalist discourse is gaining acceptance in the country, according to what was observed in the last regionalist meeting that took place in late 2000 in Pucón (Region IX). But he also states that while this theme continues to be of secondary importance in the country, the process will not advance. Recognizing that since the government of Frei Ruiztagle (1994–2000), only 42 percent of total investment has been in the regions, "the people continue to feel that the decisions are made in the center."[50]

Although there are several local regionalist movements, the majority continue in their endeavors with "much discussion and few concrete actions."[51] To change this, public opinion must be influenced, and an atmosphere more favorable to change must be generated. Los Federales are attempting to foster alliances among regions in order to increase pressure on the central government. According to Bravo, the region of Tarapacá is advancing the most rapidly in creating its own identity. A group of intellectuals are working on the recovery of local history; and the region has its own newspaper and local television channel.

Los Federales declared themselves to be a movement in September 1999, and in spite of their small numbers (eight in the beginning and eleven two years later), the outstanding nature of their members and their unusual and theatrical way of demonstrating have granted them national visibility. They have succeeded in getting the attention of the press and other media every time they demonstrate.

> Confronted with groups that have strategic importance and the ability to articulate themselves politically, the State has much more limited space for repression. When these groups are affected by decentralization, they can exercise significant pressure on the regime and in this manner influence the pace of reform.[52]

On 7 March 2000, the newspaper *El Mostrador* (electronic edition) reported:

> Los Federales have arrived!

> A curious manifestation, between protest and declaration of principles, was carried out yesterday by the self-named Federales, a regionalist movement that brings together people of distinct political colors, characterized by the wearing of black clothes and dark glasses. They say that they have chosen their clothing as a sign of mourning due to the democratic vacuum in the regions that inhibits the election of their authorities. More than creating a simple exhibition of appearance and dress, in the best Hollywood style, Los Federales are determined to advance the process of regionalization.[53]

The black clothing tries "to give the understanding, with a bit of humor, that in the regions [i.e., outside the center] we do not have our own color, nor our own identity; in addition we identify ourselves with Roman numerals."[54] In a manifesto published by Los Federales on the Internet, they present a series of statements that reflect their position on decentralization. Two of those statements are reproduced below.

> Without a large consensus and commitment in pursuit of decentralization, justice and territorial economic and social equity will never exist in our country.

. . . [W]e note a serious weakness of the political system, in its proposals and in our society in general, with respect to the limited [credence given to] . . . the urgency and necessity to advance in pursuit of a more decentralized Chile.[55]

In contrast to the sometimes rancorous and negative tone of regional officials and other stakeholders, Benavente's vision is redemptive: "It is important to advance a few steps more for our children. . . . Today it is utopian, but it is [eventually] attainable."[56]

Notes

1. Esteban Valenzuela, *Alegato Histórico Regionalista* (Santiago: Ediciones SUR, 1999).
2. Carlos De Mattos, "La Descentralización, ¿Una Nueva Panacea para Enfrentar el Desarrollo Local?" *Revista Economía y Sociedad* 3 (March 1990): 165–78.
3. José Luis Curbelo, "Economía Política de la Descentralización y Planificación del Desarrollo Regional," *Pensamiento Iberoamericano* 10 (July–December 1986).
4. Ibid.
5. For more discussion about the significance and real possibilities that decentralization offers, see Carlos De Mattos, "La Descentralización," and Curbelo, "Economía Política de la Descentralización."
6. Christian Von Haldenwang, "Hacia un Concepto Politológico de la Descentralización del Estado en América Latina," *Revista EURE* 16, no. 50 (1990): 61–77.
7. Sady Melo, "El Inconcluso Proceso de Municipalización," in *Municipios y Desarrollo, Balances y Desafíos,* edited by Carlos F. Pressacco (Santiago: Instituto Latinoamericano de Doctrina y Estudios Sociales, 1994), 104.
8. Jordi Borja, "Dimensiones Teóricas, Problemas y Perspectivas de la Descentralización del Estado," in *Descentralización del Estado, Movimiento Social y Gestión Local,* edited by Jordi Borja (Santiago: Facultad Latinoamericana de Ciencias Sociales, 1987), 166–67.
9. Carlos S. Figueroa, "Universidades y Gobiernos Regionales: Planificación, Estrategias y Desarrollos Coordinados" (presentation at Actas del Tercer Encuentro, La Serena, Chile, 10–11 April 1997).
10. Eduardo Dockendorff, "Los Desafíos de la Política Social del 2000" (Santiago: Ministerio Secretaría General de la Presidencia, 1999), 24.
11. Ibid.
12. Ibid.
13. See chapter 4 of this volume.
14. *El Mercurio,* 2 August 2001.
15. Germán Urzúa Valenzuela and Anamaría García Barcelato, *Diagnóstico de la burocracia chilena (1918–1968)* (Santiago: Editorial Jurídica de Chile, 1971), 13.
16. Esteban Valenzuela, *Alegato Histórico Regionalista* (Santiago: Ediciones SUR, 1999), 17.

17. Who, parodoxically, arose as regional leader in Concepción (Region VIII).

18. Valenzuela, *Alegato Histórico Regionalista*, 51.

19. Diego Portales (1793–1837) led a conservative group called the "Estanqueros," opponents of Chile's liberal government. When the conservatives rose to power, he served in various ministries (Interior, Foreign Relations, War and Sea). He remained in the government of Joaquín Prieto and was named vice president (1830–1833), but refused the presidency. He was governor of Valparaíso between 1832 and 1833.

20. Valenzuela, *Alegato Histórico Regionalista*, 51.

21. Germán Urzúa Valenzuela and Anamaría García Barcelato, *Diagnóstico de la Burocracia Chilena* (Santiago: Editorial Jurídica de Chile, 1971), 24.

22. Marcelo Martínez Keim, "Comprensión del Déficit de Ciudadanía en Chile: La Paradoja de su Desarrollo," *Revista Paraguaya de Sociología* 104 (January/April 1999).

23. Ibid., 19.

24. Valenzuela, *Alegato Histórico Regionalista*, 54.

25. For more discussion of this theme, see G. Salazar, "Descentralización y Sinergía Histórica Local: Fracasos y Desafíos," 1997 (available at: www.uchile.cl); Alan Angell, "La Descentralización en Chile," *Revista Instituciones y Desarrollo* 3 (1999); José A. Mariman, *Reflexión y Análisis Sobre el Proceso de Descentralización en Chile* (Santiago: Subsecretaría de Desarrollo Regional y Administrativo/U.N. Development Programme, 1998).

26. Instituto Nacional de Estadísticas, Santiago, Chile, 2000. The exact number of inhabitants reported is 248,594.

27. I did not try to generate a representative sample of interviews, but rather selected key people in the management of priority sectors of development, in addition to opinion leaders with high local visibility and national-level recognition. I carried out a total of eight interviews.

28. The point of view of the healthcare sector was obtained from an interview with the person in charge of health investments in the region, who was immediately under the regional secretary in the hierarchy.

29. This is the case except when they are led by personalities capable of great political management. M.E. Ducci, ed., "Contexto de la Salud en Chile," Documento de Trabajo (Santiago: Instituto de Postgrado e Investigación, Facultad de Arquitectura, Pontifica Universidad Católica, 2000).

30. Jaime Neira, regional manager of health investments, SEREMI de Salud, Region IX, La Araucanía, interview by author (Temuco, La Araucanía, 2001).

31. For a definition of the ISAR, see Chapter 4, this volume.

32. Neira interview.

33. María Elena Harcha, architect, director of urban development, SEREMI/MINVU, interview by author (Temuco, La Araucanía, 2001).

34. Ibid.

35. The Regional Council is composed of advisors elected by the municipal councils.

36. Harcha interview.

37. Patricio Vargas, architect, director of Housing Department, SEREMI/MINVU, interview by author (Temuco, La Araucanía, 2001).

38. Carlos Moraga, regional ministerial secretary of education of Region IX, interview by author (January 2001).

39. Rene Saffirio, mayor of Temuco municipality, said, "Desde las comunas, la necesidad de articulación interinstitucional . . . impone para su éxito la reforma educacional." (Actas del Tercer Encuentro, La Serena, Chile, 10–11 April 1997, 244.)

40. The FNDR, according to the Organic Constitutional Law on Regional Governments and Administration, in Article 73, "will be an investment program aimed at overcoming the territorial inequities through social and economic infrastructure with the final goal of establishing a harmonious and equitable territory. . . . In practice, FNDR's resources have constituted the principal financing instrument for the management of territorial development, [with the] understanding that funds are disbursed according to regional decisions, invested in critical places and according to territorial priorities, and are not like the sectoral funds that grant financing for the development of the regions from the national and unitary republic perspective. From there the importance of this fund is found in the depth of decentralization processes and financing of democratic culture" (pp. 86–87). Subsecretaría de Desarrollo Regional y Administrativo, Interior Ministry, "Orientaciones Generales para el Uso del Fondo Nacional de Desarrollo Regional (FNDR) en Fomento Productivo," Seminario Taller "Desarrollo y Gestión Local" (Santiago: Friedrich Ebert Stiftung, October 1997). Also, see Chapter 4, this volume.

41. The theme of mutual respect is a very complicated issue in Chile, where traditionally the Mapuches have been considered lazy, not very evolved and without value recoverable for the "official" culture. Discrimination has been and is strong also in Region IX. On the other hand, Mapuche communities considered public schools to be interference in their cultureon the part of the white man; Mapuches who are most adapted are considered "white men." This has changed in some zones, but an undercurrent of discrimination and rancor continues to exist.

42. Moraga interview.

43. Ibid.

44. A dream that in a parallel manner is replicated in Latin American capital cities, which are trying to make themselves into the great cities of the North and especially of the United States.

45. Diego Benavente, director of Araucanía Corporation, representative of Movimiento de Acción Regional (MAR) in Temuco, founding member of Los Federales, interview by author (Temuco, La Araucanía, January 2001).

46. Saffirio, "Desde las Comunas," 246.

47. Ibid.

48. Benavente, weekly column, *Diario Austral* (Temuco).

49. The deputy Víctor Barrueto (PPD), president of the Chamber of Deputies, is one of the founders of Los Federales.

50. Jorge Bravo, regionalist of La Araucanía, member of MAR, interviewed by author (Temuco, Temuco, La Araucanía, January 2001).

51. Ibid.

52. Haldenwang, "Hacia un Concepto Politológico," 76.

53. *El Mostrador,* 7 March 2000 (available at: www.elmostrador.cl).

54. Anton/io Horvath, senator for Region XI, founding member of Los Federales, in *El Mostrador,* March 2000.

55. Manifesto published by Los Federales on the Internet (available at: www. geocities.com).

56. Benavente interview.

Part II

Africa

Chapter 6

South Africa's Double Reform: Decentralization and the Transition from Apartheid

Steven Friedman and Caroline Kihato

Postapartheid South Africa has developed a curious propensity for adopting internationally fashionable remedies for purely endogenous reasons. There are many examples, but none is perhaps as striking as the society's current tentative experiment in decentralization.

The enhanced role of subnational government appears to stem entirely from the specificities of recent political history, that is, the nature of the fight against apartheid and of the negotiated settlement which ended it. There is a certain irony here, too, since domestic politics has not, until relatively recently, seemed particularly hospitable to the decentralization of power. Nevertheless, a set of very particular circumstances steered elites toward at least formal recognition of a need for decentralized governance.

How, then, do we explain that very particular local circumstances produced an outcome so consistent with current world trends? At least part of the answer owes less to coincidence or osmosis as it does to direct influence: international actors who enjoyed credibility among local parties presented decentralization to them as a possible answer to some of the problems with which they grappled. After inspecting the product on offer, local elites more often than not decided that it addressed a problem that troubled them and adopted it. And this may suggest that South Africa's experience is not unique at all—that here, as in many other societies, fashionable governance ideas were accepted not because gullible locals were talked into adopting the latest snake oil remedy from the disingenuous North, but because the fashion seemed to local elites to offer a way out of real dilemmas and to provide solutions to real problems.

In South Africa—as, no doubt, in many other countries—this begs questions. The most obvious is the degree to which decentralization indeed possesses the properties attributed to it by its purveyors. Less obvious but equally important is whether local elites are adopting this strategy for the stated reasons—which tend to stress the intrinsic beneficial properties of decentralization—or because they see them as means to ends that could easily be jettisoned if more effective remedies present themselves, and are implemented with less than complete enthusiasm because they really are being adopted for reasons other than their innate merits. Circumstantial evidence for skepticism on both fronts is plentiful in the South African case.

In this chapter we readily concede that decentralization in post-1994 South Africa is far more substantial than during the apartheid period—and that subnational government plays a more prominent role in governance here than it does in most of Africa. But we will also suggest that it has not provided a vehicle for citizens' or civil society's participation and that it cannot, therefore, yet be seen as an instrument to deepen and thus strengthen democracy. This, we suggest, is a legacy of a political tradition in which elites were deeply suspicious of local initiative and in which political culture made it easy for them, in the main, to persuade local activists and citizens not to use decentralized governance to build alternative sites of power and initiative.

The Institutional Setting

The nine provinces are established by Chapter 6 of the Constitution, which endows them with elected legislatures. They are also constitutionally obliged to "facilitate public involvement in the legislative . . . [process]," and to "conduct [their] business in an open manner."[1] Proclamations, regulations and other (legislative) instruments "must be accessible to the public."[2] The way in which they channel public participation is, however, not mandated.

But provinces have extremely limited legislative opportunities. The constitution lists areas in which they have sole legislative competence, but these are fairly narrow, including abattoirs, ambulance services, certain archives and libraries, liquor licenses, provincial sports, roads and traffic, and veterinary services, "excluding regulation of the profession." They may also legislate on a range of municipal matters.[3] The significant functions assumed by the provinces are subjects of concurrent legislative competence, including agriculture, gambling, consumer protection, disaster management, primary and secondary education, environment, health services, housing, language policy, police, public transport, urban and rural development, and welfare services.[4]

"Concurrency," a concept especially salient in Germany (which was particularly influential for reasons to be explained later) was first introduced in the 1993 Interim Constitution. It means that the legislative authority is held jointly by national and provincial government, but that the former is entitled to set "norms and standards"[5] within which the latter is obliged to operate. No limit is placed on the definition of this term; thus, in principle, the national government could override any provincial legislation on a concurrent function by setting very detailed "norms." Similarly, provinces are entitled to pass their own constitutions within parameters set by the national constitution, including the stipulation that they could provide for "the institution, role, authority and status of a traditional monarch."[6] Beyond this concession to supporters of African tradition, it sought to ensure that the constitutions remained tightly within parameters limiting their capacity to express diversity. For example, they must not only be consistent with the national constitution but "must comply with the values" expressed by it.[7]

That provinces are largely subordinate to the center—the Constitution also allows the national government to take over provincial powers or functions if a province "cannot or does not fulfill an executive obligation in terms of legislation or the Constitution" or action is needed to prevent a province "from taking unreasonable action that is prejudicial to the interests of another province or to the country as a whole"[8]—was recognized by the constitution drafters who sought to compensate them, again in the German fashion, by creating a National Council of Provinces (NCOP), composed of representatives chosen by provincial legislatures, with the power to deliberate on legislation passed by the directly elected legislature, the National Assembly. In theory, this meant that, while uniform national "norms and standards" would be imposed, the provinces could, through the NCOP, play a key role in determining them. (Where the National Assembly and NCOP deadlock on a bill affecting the interests of provinces, the former's will can ultimately prevail, but only by two-thirds vote and then after a complex mediation process.[9]) A further significant feature is that, where bills directly affected provincial legislation, each province casts a single vote, implying that delegates were voting the interests of their province rather than their party (similarly, constitutional changes require the support of six of the nine provinces).[10] This provides, in principle, for the Council to become a forum for the expression of subsidiary regional identities and interests within particular parties. But, in practice, this possibility has not been realized.

Another severe limitation on the power of provinces is that they have very limited revenue-raising powers: besides the right to raise funds from gambling, for example, they are dependent on block grants from the central government. In contrast to similar arrangements elsewhere in the world, this does not give the center the power arbitrarily to withhold funding for provinces or to manipulate it to reward compliance and punish independence. The Constitution establishes a Fiscal and Financial Commission, one of whose tasks is to arrive at a formula determining the "equitable share" of national revenues that accrue to provincial and local governments. But, while in theory provinces are free to allocate their block grants in any way they please, they are constrained by concurrency, which can allow national government to determine spending patterns by decreeing norms and standards (by, for example, mandating particular teacher/pupil ratios in schools). In some cases, the center does this in practice by determining social pensions in the national budget and requiring provincial welfare departments to pay these or by negotiating public service workers' wages in national bargaining (the agreed wage rates are binding on provinces). While further taxation powers for provinces remain, in principle, on the agenda, the trend has been toward greater fiscal control by the center in response to overspending in the provinces.[11]

In principle, the Constitution is more enthusiastic about local than provincial government. Chapter 3, which deals with "co-operative governance," makes a symbolic point by referring to "spheres" rather than "tiers" of government in an explicit attempt to avoid the notion of hierarchy. It stipulates that all "spheres" must "respect the constitutional status, institutions, powers and functions of government in the other(s)'" exercise their powers and functions in a manner that does not encroach on the "integrity of government in another sphere" and "co-operate with one another in mutual trust and good faith."[12] Chapter 7 declares that: "A municipality has the right to govern, on its own initiative, the local . . . affairs of its community, subject to national and provincial legislation, as provided for in the Constitution," and that national or provincial government may not compromise or impede a municipality's ability or right to exercise its powers or perform its functions.[13] It charges local government with, among other goals, providing democratic and accountable government for local communities (but, as with the provinces, does not mandate a particular way of doing this); promoting social and economic development; and encouraging the involvement of communities and community organizations in local government. It also assigns local governments "developmental duties," in particular to "participate in national and provincial development programmes."[14] They are also assigned a role in "co-operative government": the national and provincial governments must support and strengthen their capacity "to manage their own affairs, to exercise their powers and to perform their functions," while draft national or provincial laws that affect their "status, institutions, powers or functions must be published for public comment in a manner that allows organized local government, municipalities and other interested persons an opportunity to make representations."[15] "Organized local government" is specifically recognized, and parliament is instructed to pass a law providing for "the recognition of national and provincial organisations representing municipalities."[16] At present, they are represented in the NCOP (but without voting rights) and on the Financial and Fiscal Commission. Local democracy is endorsed by, for example, a stipulation that local councils "must conduct their business in an open manner."[17]

But this serves merely to mask the extent to which municipalities are formally subordinate to the other "spheres." The status and powers of each municipality are determined by national and provincial legislation[18]; provinces must "provide for the monitoring and support of local government in the province" and the other two spheres have "the legislative and executive authority to see to the effective performance by municipalities of their functions."[19] And, even within these, the issues on which municipalities may legislate are even more limited than those assigned to the provinces. A sample includes billboards and the display of advertisements in public places; control of public nuisances; facilities for the accommodation, care, and burial of animals; and licensing of dogs. While some are a little more substantial, such as trading regulations, air pollution, building regulations, childcare facilities, electricity and gas regulation, municipal planning, municipal healthcare services and public transport, and some water and sanitation services,[20] these are, as noted above, subject to higher "spheres" and must be assigned to municipalities by them. Legislation passed in 2000 also allows provinces to determine the institutional structure of councils. Provincial premiers are empowered to instruct municipalities to meet an "executive obligation" imposed by law—or simply to take action when this is considered necessary "to maintain economic unity."[21]

In contrast to provinces, local governments enjoy formal revenue-raising powers. Local governments raise 90 percent of their budgets from their own sources, compared to 10 percent or less at the province level. Their most important source of revenue is surpluses accrued on "trading services," that is, the sale of electricity and water to businesses and households. They are also empowered to levy municipal fees on property owners, a form of local property tax that is intended to pay for the provision of other services. While the ability to raise its own funds means that local government has significant opportunities for financial independence, it does not necessarily guarantee it. The ability to raise funding from fees and taxes is constrained by what is commonly referred to as a culture of nonpayment, and what commentators argue is a hangover from the fees and service boycotts of the 1980s. In reality, nonpayment is a result of various factors including poor billing systems and the inability to pay. The impact of nonpayment is felt particularly acutely by rural municipalities and municipalities without a significant industrial base. So that while nonpayment has the potential to cripple some municipalities, urban councils with larger resource bases are able to survive its impact because receipts from manufacturing and industry cushion the effects of the shortfall. The budget of Johannesburg, the largest city, for example, exceeds that of Gauteng province in which it is located.

In order to ensure the financial viability of council's that have a weak ability to recover service charges, local governments are entitled to transfers from the central government, although these are merely "add-ons" to their budgets, while for provinces they form the core. Local governments' "equitable" share is, in fact, limited to an amount meant to subsidize the cost of services for indigent people. It is calculated on the basis of poverty levels in each municipality; in Johannesburg, it pays for R90.56 worth of services for each indigent person (about US$11.50). In a more sustained attempt to address the problem, a Demarcation Board established by legislation and appointed by the national government has reduced the 800-plus municipalities to just over 250. Among other things, the Board's mandate was to enhance the ability of local governments to meet their constitutional obligations, including service provision to its constituencies, and more significantly, to ensure the financial viability of municipalities.[22] Some of the criteria for establishing municipal boundaries included integration, redistribution of finances, administrative efficiency and effectiveness, cost effectiveness, and financial sustainability.

Although redrawing municipal boundaries is essential given the historical inequalities and racial nature of the pre-1994 system, the process gave so much focus on technocratic objectives, whose bottom line is a positive balance sheet, that "soft" governance issues such as enhancing democracy were overshadowed. Some commentators argue that reducing the number of municipalities has increased the distance between local government representatives and their constituencies, and that this will have negative consequences for local democracy. But the African National Congress (ANC) argument is that the problem in local government lies less in its democratic structure and function than in its inability to deliver services to citizens. Consequently, it is the financial administrative and management structure that needs to improve, not its level of democracy. This is further reinforced by the fact that municipalities and civil society organizations had little influence over the demarcation process. Despite claims by the demarcation board that it had widely consulted municipalities, several complained that they had not been adequately involved in the demarcation process and were unhappy with its outcome.[23] Opposition emerged from residents' associations and councilors over the board's decision to include Midrand into Johannesburg, yet despite these protests and accusations that the board's decision did not make economic sense, the board's decision was retained. While the board was well within its mandate to make the final decision, there is a growing sense in South Africa, as will be illustrated later in the chapter, that local decisions are taken at higher levels of government with local government and civil society organizations (CSOs) having little influence over their outcome.

Following publication of its White Paper for Local Government in 1998, the central government has introduced legislation that provides the legal framework within which the third sphere operates. It consists of three major pieces of legislation that are said to help transform local government structures, create efficient municipal units of optimal size, and transform the way in which municipalities carry out their functions: the Municipal Structures Act, the Municipal Demarcation Act, and the Municipal Systems bill (at the time of this writing, the last-named bill had not been passed by parliament). On the one hand, this legislation creates a unified system that is also more equitable than any other in the country's history. It also widens the scope of local government activities, making it an important player in development and economic growth. But a closer look at the legislation reveals that although it confers numerous functions on local government,[24] there is a limited commitment to decentralizing authority to it to make its own decisions.

The Municipal Structures Act establishes the different types of municipalities as well as their operational structures and functions. The original Act[25] perhaps illustrates the attitudes of policymakers on the question of decentralization. It gives the national minister powers to determine municipal types across the country. Section 4 states that "the Minister must . . . determine whether an area in terms of the criteria must have a single category A municipality or whether it must have municipalities of both category C and category B."[26] A subsequent amendment transfers these powers to the Demarcation Board. The Act also provides that members of the executive council (MECs), (the council being the provincial equivalent of a ministry, have the powers to establish and disestablish a municipality if, among other things, it is unable to fulfill its constitutional obligations. To some extent, the move toward centralizing the decision-making process on the structure, form, and functions of local government is understandable—there is a need to ensure uniformity and coordination in a system that was fragmented by apartheid. Also, there is need for a structure with oversight and that is distant enough to see the "big picture" in local government. Yet whether these objectives are accomplished by provinces which themselves have capacity problems is questionable. In addition, the degree to which municipalities and civil society are involved in making decisions on the form and structure of their own municipalities is limited. Although the Act stipulates that the MEC should consult organized local governments, it gives scant attention to participation and appears to impose the will of higher spheres on local government. First, the extent to which organized national local government—the South African Local Government Association—is representative of local governments is questionable. Second, participation of the citizenry in the decision-making process is not considered or actively provided for in the Act.

Broadly, the Municipal Systems Bill sets up various administrative mechanisms such as credit control, performance management, and delegation systems that assist local government in carrying out its functions. Perhaps the more interesting aspects are its attempt to legislate local government's relationship with citizens. The Bill stipulates that local governments must develop a culture of participation, and suggests mechanisms for citizen cooperation and participation in decision making. Section 7, for instance, states that "a municipality must seek to develop a culture of municipal governance that complements formal representative government with a system of participatory governance and for this purpose encourage, and create conditions for communities, residents and ratepayers in the municipality to participate in local affairs."[27] To some extent, this reflects South Africa's tendency to legislate on virtually all aspects of governance, but it also illustrates the limited space that municipalities have to maneuver because they are constrained by legislation that is designed elsewhere.

This is perhaps most notable in the policy on integrated development planning (IDP). Planning in South Africa is currently governed by two laws, the Development Facilitation (DFA) and Local Government Transitional Act (LGTA). Both feature a deliberate attempt to change the nature of planning as well as to decentralize it by locating functions and responsibilities in local governments. The LGTA, enacted in 1993 (see below), states that an integrated development plan is aimed at the integrated development and management of the area of jurisdiction of the municipality concerned in terms of its powers and duties, and which has been compiled having regard to the general principles contained in Chapter 1 of the Development Facilitation Act, 1995, and, where applicable, having regard to the subject matter of a land development objective contemplated in Chapter 4 of that Act.

This definition gives the value context, or underpinning principles, within which IDPs are to be formulated. As provided for in the DFA, these principles provide substantive guidelines to land development, including principles related to the following:

- Spatial integration of geographical areas, such as compact cities and mixed land use planning[28]
- Integrating sectoral plans, such as transport and water, into a single planning process
- Sustainable, efficient, and effective planning by, for example, ensuring that the projects identified by the IDPs are affordable to the municipal council and communities and by linking municipal budgets to identified projects
- Ensuring political accountability in the decision-making process by, for example, involving stakeholders in the monitoring and review process, and
- Capacity building and institutional development

According to the definition in the LGTA, municipal plans are to adhere to "good practice" codes—stipulated in the DFA—that provide guidance for the formulation of IDPs and a criteria against which existing and new plans are to be judged. Although the principles listed in the DFA are intended to give municipalities the necessary guidelines for planning within their jurisdiction, a closer look reveals that they, in many ways, prescribe the content of municipal plans. Effectively, where applicable, these should contain compact cities, mixed land use development, integrated rural and urban areas, and so on. Thus, in addition to providing a planning ethic that includes principles such as sustainability, efficiency, effectiveness, accountability, integration, and "community" participation, DFA principles also stipulate the end product of a municipal development plan.

While the LGTA stipulates *what* municipal plans should look like, the White Paper focuses on describing *how* IDP should proceed. It describes it as a "planning process" that will enable municipalities to identify short-, medium-, and long-term strategies to fulfill their developmental mandates.[29] It outlines nine phases integral to formulating IDPs:

- An assessment of the current situation
- A determination of community needs through consultation
- Developing a vision for development in the area
- An audit of available resources, skills, and capacities
- A prioritization of needs
- Development of integrated frameworks and goals
- Formulation of strategies to achieve the goals
- Implementation of projects and programs
- Monitoring to measure impact and performance

Thus, law prescribes the process and product of IDPs. It defines not only the parameters within which they are to be framed but provides rigid guidelines on *how* and *what* their outcome will be in every municipality. It is easy to understand the attention to detail. Given the lack of capacity in most municipalities and the fact that the nature of planning has changed—providing the need to ensure that municipal officials understand the essence of the new planning requirements—it is necessary to provide the requisite guidelines. But when does national government become too prescriptive? When do its "guidelines" and "codes" begin to affect local government autonomy and its ability to develop creative flexible plans that respond to changing local conditions? There is a perception that IDPs are too rigid.[30] Policy that is too prescriptive could have adverse effects on the third sphere's ability to respond efficiently to local needs. Planning also becomes a top-down rather than a bottom-up activity.

> [T]he system of inter-governmental relations in which local government is located is centralized. . . . This . . . is evident in the policy framework, not only in the directive for municipalities to be "developmental" but also in the different avenues through which national and provincial governments have trespassed on municipal planning autonomy. . . . With both inputs and outputs pre-specified, municipalities have little discretion to behave "strategically" in responding to need. Indeed, it is the more powerful or independent municipalities (who can afford to challenge or ignore the policy framework) that have behaved more strategically in the planning process.[31]

But national policy is faced with two opposing needs: to regulate municipal planning in order to provide clear guidelines for local governments that are attempting this kind of planning for the first time and, conversely, to give municipalities a free rein when developing plans to guarantee their autonomy and to place trust in their ability to respond to local needs. Finding middle ground is difficult, as local autonomy is dependent largely on how municipalities perform in the new planning paradigm and, depending on their performance, how effectively they challenge national policy.

A significant difference between local government and the other "spheres" is that it is the only one which partly provides for direct election of representatives by constituents. While both national and provincial elections are conducted using the closed-list proportional representation system,[32] municipal elections use a mix between this system and direct election of constituency (or "ward") candidates. Until 2000, 40 percent of municipal councilors were elected on party lists through the proportional system, and 60 percent were "ward" councilors. In the 2000 election, the ratio was changed to 50:50 in urban areas.

It is also worth noting that the formal democratic content of local government in rural and peri-urban areas is compromised by the ANC's concern to accord a degree of recognition to traditional or chiefly authority; chiefs are not only a key component of the support base of the Inkatha Freedom Party (IFP), whose cooperation the ANC wishes to retain, but of the ANC itself in the Eastern Cape, which is its traditional stronghold. The Constitution allows national legislation to "provide for a role for traditional leadership . . . at [the] local level on matters affecting local communities,"[33] and the result has been a stipulation guaranteeing representation in local government to traditional authorities as well as some other interest groups. Potential conflicts between local government and traditional authorities were originally averted because rural local governments lacked executive powers and chiefs remained in control of the areas under their jurisdiction. The demarcation completed in 2000 has, however, altered this balance, and tribal areas are now under the (at least, de jure) control of elected local governments. Prior to the second local elections in December 2000, traditional leaders resisted the change, prompting a delay in the elections. Traditional leaders are now entitled to 20 percent of local government seats in their areas (although they may not vote). The issue, however, remains unresolved. In 2000, the government published a bill proposing to retain many of the chiefs' powers while mandating that traditional authorities and municipal councils must "co-operate with one another in areas of common interest: and endeavor to resolve any dispute amicably."[34] But there are legal complications surrounding the bill. It confers power to traditional leaders that constitutionally belong to local governments, and therefore to meet the demands of chiefs a change in the constitution is required.[35] Now that the elections are over with without disruption by chiefs and supporters, it is unclear whether there is enough political will to meet traditional leaders' demands.

Finally, an aspect of the system relevant to this volume is decentralization to citizens or interest groups rather than local levels of government. Perhaps the key example is the creation, by the South African Schools Act, of school governing bodies (SGBs) composed of parent, teacher, and pupil representatives, which are, at least formally, permitted to make policy decisions.[36] Since this mode of school governance implies a devolution of national government authority to local interest groups, it is arguably of relevance to our theme.

Origins of the System

As implied earlier, the system originates directly from the nature of the political compromise negotiated in the early 1990 and less directly, in the case of local government, to the nature of the last decade of "struggle" against apartheid. On the first score, neither of the key parties to the negotiations—the National Party, which presided over apartheid, and the African National

Congress, which led the fight against it—were "natural" recruits to the notion that subnational government should enjoy substantial powers. Admittedly, apartheid, in its desire to segregate blacks politically and geographically, created regional political units that had substantial formal powers. But they were not regarded by ideology or law as instruments of decentralization in a common polity; instead, they were meant to be entirely separate political units that, in some cases, evolved into putative "independent states." The dominant white polity was strongly centralized, as the NP sought to extend and strengthen control over provinces and local governments controlled by the white opposition; attempts to reform apartheid in the face of black resistance during the 1980s further strengthened national executive control as elected provincial administrations were replaced by nominated authorities and local governments were, formally at least, partly subject to Regional Services Council, which brought together members of racially segregated municipalities in each area and which, therefore, formally distanced decision makers from their constituencies.

The ANC, for its part, saw decentralization as a means of diluting majority rule and retaining important vestiges of apartheid. The system's attempt to create an equivalence between race and geography and the explicit interest shown by both the NP and IFP in creating enclaves shielded from majority rule explained this view. It insisted that devolution to regional governments would allow minorities to maintain privileges and prerogatives that apartheid had bestowed on them, that is, it would enable whites to escape the consequences of majority rule or black elites who had presided over the apartheid system's ethnic "homelands" to retain their hold on parts of the country or both. While, during the negotiation period, this appeared to be an irrational fear, since whites do not form a majority in any of the country's more than 250 magisterial districts, the elections have since indicated that this concern was more than merely symbolic since, in the Western Cape province, one of only two in which black Africans were not in the majority,[37] a coalition between white and "colored" (mixed race) voters has twice deprived the ANC of an electoral majority. Whether the nonblack African Western Cape government would have used strong regional powers to install a form of neoapartheid will always remain moot. But the result, and the explicitly racial tone of much of the campaign that produced it (which strengthened fears that the opposition vote was based largely on antipathy to the majority), certainly convinced many in the ANC that its opposition to strong regions had been vindicated.

Less credible was repeated ANC insistence that only a strong unitary state would ensure effective action against poverty and inequality. This view is commonly expressed by postindependence African elites but, in societies as different as India and the United Kingdom, the most effective redistributive experiments have been conducted at the subnational level—in the former by regional governments controlled by the Communist Party, and in the latter by the Labour-controlled Greater London council. The South African response may have owed more to a knee-jerk response to apartheid's attempt to balkanize the country than to reality. Finally, these considerations reinforced a centralizing impulse in a movement that saw itself not as one party among many but as the authentic representative of the nation.[38]

That the negotiations produced elected subnational government bodies despite this context was the result of the balance of forces, a strategic calculation by the NP that was assiduously promoted by pivotal Northern states, and the fact that a key black party with a strong interest in subnational government, the IFP, would not participate in a settlement that established an entirely unitary state. While the Interim Constitution of 1993 was the outcome of a compromise, an examination of the text—and an analysis of the politics of the negotiations—suggests that the ANC largely won the argument (a view confirmed by the propensity of academic opponents of majority rule to spend the next few years in agonized debate on why the NP's negotiators "gave it all away").[39] This judgment applies even more strongly to the current constitution, adopted in 1996 by the first universally elected parliament. Because the opposition parties were unable on any issue (because of divisions within their own ranks) to muster the one-third of the vote necessary to block ANC preferences, it was a Constitution that largely reflected the ANC's will.

Nevertheless, ANC dominance of negotiations was relative, as it was obliged to offer some inducements to the white minority to surrender power. Regional government ultimately came to be seen as a concession worth making. Second, as noted earlier, the white government was not the only actor that the ANC was obliged to take into account: the negotiations also included a substantial international dimension and were strongly influenced by the major Western powers.[40] This helped shape the accommodation on regional government.

The demand for federalism—or at least a very strong form of regionalism—was led not by the NP but by the IFP, which governed the ethnic "homeland" of KwaZulu. It insisted that it would participate in a democratic order only if a very strong form of federalism was included in the constitution. The ethnic dimensions of this demand were clear since even a cursory glance at stated IFP positions made it clear that its concern was to ensure autonomy for one region in particular—its own—and that it saw federalism as a vehicle for Zulu ethnicity (as well as for its own right to govern a province in which it confidently expected a majority). One of its principal demands was, therefore, constitutional recognition of the Zulu monarchy. The NP was more concerned to secure its and its constituency's continued access to power through power sharing in the national executive. But it too endorsed a (watered-down) version of the federal option in the hope that this would dilute majority party power.

Whatever the rationale, the ANC retreated from an attempt to avoid elected regional governments. This owed something to the domestic balance of negotiating power, but as much, if not more, to an assiduous attempt by the Western powers, in particular the United States, Canada, and Germany, to "sell," to both sides of the negotiating table, federalism as an alternative to enforced minority participation in central government. The U.S. position was explicitly articulated in mid-1992 by then assistant secretary of state for Africa Herman Cohen who, at a crucial juncture in the negotiations, declared that his government was opposed to minority vetoes, but that it saw federalism as an appropriate guarantee for minorities.[41] German political foundations, in particular the ANC's partner, the Friedrich Ebert Stiftung, were also influential in persuading ANC leaders that the German brand of "cooperative federalism" could allow them to accommodate elected regional government in a manner that would prevent rather than reinforce balkanization.[42] But it also remained resolutely opposed to federalism, understood as a system which bestows significant exclusive powers on provinces. The 1993 settlement, therefore, provided for elected provincial government with some exclusive, but mostly concurrent powers, but left much of the detail for later negotiation. The NP's negotiation strategist, Roelf Meyer, insisted that this was deliberate, since it believed that the tide would turn toward strong regional government as regional ANC elites governed provinces and developed power bases in the provincial system.[43]

Meyer was half right: ANC-governed provinces did, in the main, quickly conclude that subnational governments needed real powers and, in the two years after 1994, provinces, particularly at times those governed by the ANC, repeatedly demanded more powers. But he erred in assuming that the inevitable debate between ANC regional elites and the center would be resolved in their favor—or in that of more exclusively provincial powers. The ANC leadership saw the provincial demands as a threat: then deputy president (now president) Thabo Mbeki warned at a 1995 ANC meeting that they were a disguised form of "tribalism,"[44] and ANC constitutional specialists soon began to argue that granting provinces exclusive powers created incentives for conflict. Exclusive powers for provinces, it was argued, created a "competitive" or "conflictual" federalism—Canada and Australia were cited as examples. What South Africa needed was "cooperative federalism" in which the incentives in the intergovernmental relations system rewarded cooperation rather than competition or conflict. The result, after further study tours to Germany, was the 1996 Constitution discussed earlier.

Local government played a very different role. First, it was not seen by the ANC's negotiating partners as a means of checking majority rule. The IFP had little enthusiasm for strong local government—ironically, its federalist position led it in the opposite direction. Because local government is an area of provincial jurisdiction, the IFP argued against entrenched powers for it because this would dilute provincial prerogatives.[45] The NP was more concerned about proposing a devolution of local government powers to "neighborhood committees"—because cities remained largely segregated and neighborhoods therefore racially homogenous, this would indeed have allowed the affluent to escape democracy's consequences—than in attempting to enhance the autonomy of local governments.[46] Similarly, white right-wingers, who had won some sixty municipalities in white local elections in the early 1990s, were, as we shall see, more concerned about ensuring minority prerogatives in local government than in advocating enhanced powers.

In contrast, the ANC had reason to see local government as a source of power rather than constraint. To a significant degree, the domestic resistance to apartheid during the 1980s had been mobilized at the local level, in opposition to segregated local government. Urban resistance to apartheid began in the mid-1970s; the ideology that underpinned the system insisted that blacks were "temporary sojourners" in the "white" urban areas,[47] there only to sell their labor, and so black "townships" in the urban areas were starved for resources and denied local government rights. Beginning in 1960, they were served by councils that had no decision-making powers and were widely seen as collaborators with white domination. The celebrated Soweto protests of 1976 soon led to demands for black local government rights and the formation of rudimentary civic associations that sought to challenge urban apartheid.

This form of resistance gathered momentum dramatically in 1984 in response to one of the apartheid state's most conspicuous blunders, the exclusion of the black African majority from a new constitutional arrangement and the establishment of segregated local governments in the black townships. These racially exclusive municipalities were portrayed by some in the government as substitutes for rights in the national legislature. They were also expected to act as autonomous municipalities in the absence of a viable revenue base. Apartheid had ensured that there was little business activity in black townships and so the burden of paying for urban services in these areas fell exclusively on their residents who, even if they were content with this form of representation, could not afford to pay for it. As a result, much of the fight against apartheid within the country in the 1980s was waged by urban civic associations against the system's urban manifestations. Inevitably, the battle proceeded amid much rhetoric about the importance of local grassroots power and was presented as an attempt for local residents to win the right to determine their own local destinies. As a result, the ANC's reservations about provinces did not extend to local governments, whose potential to contribute to democracy and development was often extolled by the movement's representatives.

As in many parts of the South, however, enthusiasm for local government was more rhetorical than real. While the stalemate between white local government and black resistance did produce a 1993 agreement that provided for a transition from racial to nonracial local governments and which was translated into a law—the Local Government Transition Act (see above)—the constitutional negotiations ignored local government and the section of the 1993 interim constitution that made provision for it was the result of belated negotiations (after the constitutional bargaining had ended), between an ANC negotiator, Thozamile Botha, and the white local government, in which, as noted above, conservative white municipalities (which favored continued racial segregation) played a significant role. The result was a series of "minority protections" or concessions to white fears of local majority rule.[48] The stipulations mentioned above, which currently define the constitutional status of local government, were added only during the later constitutional assembly process.

To understand why local government was largely ignored despite the context mentioned above, it is important to note that, while the civic associations' fight against urban apartheid was waged with great vigor by many township residents—and did much to strengthen at least the rhetorical commitment of many activists to democratic accountability at the grassroots—it was, at all times, an integral part of the broader anti-apartheid struggle. The activists who engaged in it were loyal members of the resistance movement and, in most cases, supporters of its chief organizational expression, the African National Congress. This meant, first, that the fight for local de-

cision-making power was always a means to an end—the defeat of apartheid
—and that, as the achievement of that goal neared, the expression of local
power receded into the background, dwarfed by the far more pressing goal.
Second, despite its effect on the political culture of the resistance movement—which is, of course, now the government—the civic movement was
never a source of alternative power to that of the national movement. It was
always its loyal servant and so was disinclined to challenge national leaders when local prerogatives were threatened. The result, arguably, was to
produce a local government system whose autonomy is honored in theory
but subjected to a host of pressures in practice.

In sum, South Africa's decentralization experiment was not the outcome
of a neoliberal reform project, nor was it an attempt to reduce public attention to specific issues or problems or an effort to respond to demands for
greater accountability to citizens, although these factors have played a role
in the way in which it has worked in practice. It was a response to specific
local political exigencies. And, while this origin may have ensured the creation of a decentralized system, it is also responsible for the lack of elite enthusiasm for decentralization as a means of public participation rather than
political and administrative necessity.

Decentralization in Practice

For many scholars and analysts—and, perhaps, some politicians—an important rationale for decentralization is the devolution of decisions to regions and localities. It is, therefore, regularly seen as a means to make government more accessible and participatory, a way of democratizing. Similar,
decentralization can be portrayed—and in South Africa has been[49]—as a
way of recognizing difference by allowing identities that are in the national
minority, but the regional or local majority, to find expression in the political order. It seems fair to conclude, however, that in postapartheid South
Africa, decentralization has been viewed primarily as an administrative device, that is, a means of transferring government functions, and, equally or
more importantly, financial responsibilities, to a more "appropriate" level,
and has been judged largely as an instrumental means to the effective delivery of services.

This is particularly true of the provinces. The first few years of the provincial system were characterized by substantial administrative incompetence.
This was hardly surprising, given both the dearth of governance skills in a

society where most citizens were excluded from government until seven years ago and the fact that the new provincial governments were responsible for entirely new geographic units, some of which composed several racially or ethnically distinct administrations created by apartheid. Media commentators, businesspeople (indeed, a large swathe of the elite regardless of party loyalty) responded by questioning the value of the provincial system and suggesting that government "delivery" would be much enhanced if the system was jettisoned.

The response is significant. While citizens are clearly entitled to demand administrative competence from government, they do not necessarily respond to its lack by questioning whether that level of government ought to exist at all; no commentators or politicians have responded to national or local governance inadequacies by suggesting that either "sphere" of government be abolished. The implication is that provincial government is seen not as a sphere of representation, but as an administrative instrument to ensure efficient delivery and that it is by this standard, not its ability to provide citizens with access to decisions, that it is judged and found wanting.

This must be qualified: the provincial system remains in place, at least in part because the government believes that there would be significant opposition to its abolition.[50] But it has responded to the problem of managerial weakness by extending administrative control over them. This is most noteworthy in the fiscal arena. Provincial overspending prompted direct management of provincial budgeting by the national Department of Finance, particularly in provinces whose capacity was considered weak. The intervention has prompted a marked improvement in the ability of provinces to balance their budgets, although critics insist that this gain has been achieved at the expense of curtailing their delivery capacity.[51] Provinces who lack the funds to perform their functions—a common problem in a period of national fiscal stringency as the government pursues deficit reduction—can apply for funds from the national government. But these are tied to specific purposes and their management and spending are tightly monitored. The central government has also sought to enhance provincial capacity by playing a greater role managing their administrations.

Important as this trend is, however, it would be misleading to portray it as a substantial setback for a provincial autonomy that was beginning to flower. While the immediate post-1994 period did, as noted above, see provinces, particularly those governed by the ANC, demanding enhanced powers, the constraints on provincial decision making remained significant. Provincial legislatures rarely made laws, with the exception of some administrative instruments. Capacity problems probably played the major role here, but concurrency may also have been influential since its effect was to establish the primacy of national legislation. Another factor that may have contributed is party discipline (a factor to which we will return). This problem became substantially more acute after 1996 and the establishment of the NCOP, which placed demands on the legislatures, which even assemblies with considerable capacity would have struggled to meet. The effect of the change was to ensure that legislative action moved firmly to the national level. If provinces wished to influence national laws, they would need to analyze, research, and debate them—and mandate a provincial delegate—in a matter of weeks. Chambers that had struggled to pass laws under far less demanding circumstances were clearly not going to rise to the challenge.

The administrative effects of concurrency were striking. To ensure coordination and cooperation between the center and provinces in concurrent functions such as education, health, and welfare, the national minister meets regularly with the provincial MECs in councils knows as MINMECS.[52] While this was a necessary device to ensure the sorts of cooperation envisaged by the Constitution, the effect was to ensure that MECs and their senior civil servants became part of the national department's implementation team. The effect was, at the very least, to create an identity crisis, as MECs sought to balance their provincial loyalties with those to the minister, at worst to ensure that they became implementing arms of national decision making.

Finally, provincial decision making has been profoundly affected, as implied above, by the effect of party discipline,[53] particularly in the governing ANC, not because it is more inclined to impose discipline than any other party but because it alone controls more than one province and can therefore decide whether to allow its provinces to adopt differing positions on issues. The NCOP model stands or falls by whether parties—and in this case the ANC—insist on enforcing a party line on decisions. If they do, the council simply duplicates the voting patterns in the National Assembly (elected by popular vote) and the promise of a provincial say in national decisions remains illusory. It is difficult to understand what contribution to governance is made by two houses reaching identical decisions. If it does not, the council has the potential to become a vibrant forum as different ANC provinces adopt differing positions depending on their understanding of their regional interests. Since the ANC is a broad "liberation movement" rather than a programmatic party, bringing together a diverse range of interests and values, the latter would not threaten its hold on power and might conceivably strengthen it.[54] However, the ANC has chosen to impose party discipline and NCOP votes mirror those in the other house, turning the council into a rubber stamp: on no issue has it divided on provincial rather than party lines. Besides removing an opportunity for democratic vigor, the effect is to ensure that provinces' "say in decisions" really amounts to little more than the right to vote a party line decided in the national cabinet.

The ANC national leadership's insistence on imposing uniformity on provincial decision making has increased apace over the last few years. By far its most important manifestation is a decision that the ANC candidate for premier—head of the provincial government—would be chosen not by provincial branches but by a national committee. The system was first used in 1999 and, in three provinces, the premier is not the candidate chosen to lead by the provincial ANC at its previous congress.[55] The center has also intervened to replace provincial ANC leaders who were considered to be more concerned with internecine squabbling than with governance. The premiership change followed a period in which the national ANC leadership had suffered defeat in every internal party election, including those for provincial leaders, which were contested. The move's defenders said the leadership had been forced to act because provinces were electing "populist" candidates whose command of heated rhetoric far outweighed their ability to govern. In some cases, this claim conformed to widespread perceptions among the society's elite, regardless of party or perspective. But the effect has been to ensure a uniformity that is remarkable—all ANC premiers' inaugural addresses to their legislatures after the 1999 election broadly mirrored the themes struck by the state president in his opening address to the national parliament.[56]

In sum, provinces have very limited decision-making powers. There are examples of provincial legislation that display a province-specific approach to a public policy question. One example is Gauteng's residential landlord and tenant act that allows tenants of apartment blocks who feel aggrieved at landlords' decisions to seek mediation. In the main, however, the provinces function primarily as implementers of national decisions. With very few exceptions, their legislatures are reduced to overseeing the administrative performance of provincial executives, a task that is performed with varying degrees of vigor but rarely if ever to the degree envisaged by democratic theory.

This may help explain why public confidence in provincial government is lower than that in its national equivalent,[57] and why participation by civil society—and by citizens generally—in its decisions is limited and weak.

Certainly, the provinces do little to encourage participation. While there was some initial enthusiasm in some provinces' Reconstruction and Development Programme (RDP) offices, which were meant to implement the RDP, the post-1994 government's agenda for reengineering government into a vehicle for development and democracy) for the establishment of multi-interest forums, this dissipated, to the relief not only of government officials who preferred to be insulated from the public but from critics who felt that the forums, like their equivalent during the negotiation period of the 1990s, risked providing guaranteed access to decisions to unelected extraparliamentary elites whose representativeness was not proven.[58] The only attempt to provide citizens with access to public representatives was the establishment by Gauteng's legislature, after a Canadian-funded study into public participation mechanisms, of the Petitions and Public Participation Committee, which heard petitions from members of the public. Important as this mechanism was, however, the evidence suggests that it has been used more by affluent suburban residents with the means to organize and circulate petitions than by grassroots citizens who most need mechanisms to enhance their access to government.[59]

As suggested above, local government is, at first glance, far better equipped to offer grassroots citizens a say in decisions. This impression is strengthened by the government's major policy statement on this level of government, its White Paper for Local Government,[60] which repeatedly stresses the importance of local democracy as well as development. Local government is not, of course, uniform and we should expect differences among municipalities. However, there clearly are local governments that do offer their citizens routes to participation, as well as seeking to represent the interests of local citizens.[61] In the main, however, local governments are not the autonomous vehicles for participation suggested by policy documents.

The second local elections held in 2002 launched the "final" form of the democratic local government system (until then, local government arrangements had, officially, been interim mechanisms). The third sphere is, as a result, said to be gearing up to carry out functions and to some extent make policy decisions that are required by its new status. But the level of government that is "closest to the people" is perceived as least responsive to them, when compared to other levels of government. A study carried out by the Institute for Democracy in South Africa shows that only 36 percent of South Africans perceived local government as responsive.[62] By contrast, 63 percent felt that national government was responsive to their needs. Moreover, because of their proximity to citizens, it is presumed that CSOs would engage most with local government on policy issues. But research shows that civil society engages less with local than with provincial and national governments.[63] There are various reasons for this that include the extent to which local government is perceived as a legitimate sphere, that is, as one that listens and responds to citizens' needs. The fact that resistance during the 1980s systematically undermined the credibility of apartheid local governments might also have contributed toward lowering public esteem for the institution itself.[64] And negative sentiment may be enhanced by local governments' limited capacity to deliver basic services.

A key constraint, however, is a variant of that which obstructs attempts to build strong provincial governments—the assumption that local governments are primarily instruments of government development goals rather than a sphere of representation. This strain of thinking was first expressed by then minister responsible for the RDP, Jay Naidoo, who, early in the first postapartheid administration, declared that local government was the "arms and legs of the RDP." While the comment was cited by many in government as evidence of the seriousness with which it treated local government, scholars and analysts noted quickly that limbs—the role reserved for local government—did not think; this activity is left to the brain. Naidoo's remark seemed to suggest that his national ministry would do the thinking and then convey the appropriate messages to municipalities who would act to implement the will of the brain.

Government actions also tended to confirm the view of those who fear that it afforded greater priority to development "efficiency" than to the need for local governments to express local preferences. While the principle of local democracy was never questioned, in reality local choice was subordinate to development. Thus, the DFA, designed to speed the release of land for development in general and the delivery of low-cost housing in particular, allowed government tribunals to override local governments, provided that they received the approval of the relevant provincial MEC.[65] More subtly, government development plans tended to determine roles and priorities for local governments rather than allowing them to make their own choices. Thus, a 1995 Municipal Infrastructure Investment Framework (MIIF) assigned them functions in the development of infrastructure. This alone would sharply constrain local governments' options, given the time and effort required to discharge its MIIF obligations. However, the pattern has been repeated often, prompting repeated complaints by municipal officials that they are required to fulfill "unfunded mandates" in areas such as housing. We have already noted that IDPs are ostensibly avenues for local choice of development priorities but that, in practice, the legislation that mandates them constrains municipal options. Thus, the expectation that municipalities become agents of development and "delivery" tends to steer them toward particular tasks and to narrow the zone of choice available to municipalities. Even where local governments do attempt innovative approaches, these usually seek to apply different methods of reaching objectives set nationally, not differing policy approaches.

Second, capacity difficulties in local government have, as in the provinces, forced direct intervention in their management by the center. For a variety of reasons—resource constraints, apartheid-induced education backlogs, lack of governing experience by the majority and, in the view of some, the continued predominance of administrators who are survivors of, and steeped in the culture of, apartheid local government—severe skills deficits have ensured that revenue raising and financial management are key constraints for many local governments. In response, central government has intervened to "strengthen their capacity" to manage their finances.[66] The national department of constitutional development (whose local government functions are now performed by the department of provincial affairs) has attempted to manage the "transformation" of local government into effective, service-oriented, administration from the center. As noted above, recent legislation which resulted from the White Paper mandates a particular form of administration and representation in metropolitan areas—the "unicity" that provides for only one metropolis-wide form of representation—despite the reservations of critics who fear that the effect will be to distance local councils even further from their electorate, thus eroding their effectiveness even more. The gap between electors and elected is particularly wide[67] and, in this view, is a more important cause of municipal governance weakness than technical constraints. So the "unicity's" merits are hardly self-evident and different metropoles might well reach different conclusions on whether to adopt it. They have, however, all been compelled to take on a uniform system of representation and administration.

Finally, within the ANC, local government is subject to similar influence or control from the national leadership as the choice of provincial leadership. The first round of local elections, in 1995 and 1996 saw many local activists who had distinguished themselves as civic or shack community leaders denied an ANC nomination. It was widely assumed that the reasons for this were that the movement needed the seats for people owed a favor who, in many cases, did not live in the area they were to represent and had been imposed on the local area by the provincial or national leadership. The strength of party loyalties,[68] however, ensured that all were defeated when they contested the election as independents against the ANC candidate. The effect was to confound a postapartheid conventional wisdom which suggested that a constituency system would be more likely to produce accountable representation than closed-list proportional representation because representatives would be directly responsible to voters. Local government, the only "sphere" with this form of representation, is also the one that enjoys the least trust among the electorate.[69]

The trend toward centralization deepened in the second round of local elections as a national committee selected ANC candidates for key local government posts. Most notable of these is that of executive mayor, introduced for the first time in 2000. The implications were noted by the then city manager of Johannesburg who observed that it would ensure that mayors were accountable to the national ANC which, he added, would ensure their efficiency since they could be fired by the movement if they did not perform.[70] The notion that accountability to local voters might create avenues for sanctions to be imposed on nonperformers did not appear to occur to him.

Local governments' leeway to adopt independent approaches may, therefore, be slightly greater than the provinces'. But both their room for maneuver and their willingness to take policy approaches that differ significantly from those at national and provincial levels is weak, if it exists at all. Despite mobilization for local decision-making power during the 1980s and an official rhetoric that supports local democracy, local governments are constrained by capacity limits (which also ensure central intervention), expectations that they will implement national development priorities, and enhanced control of candidate selection by the ANC. The effect is to ensure that, despite some important local experimentation on administrative issues and on public participation, local governments essentially implement the priorities of national government and of the national leadership of the governing party.

Channels for Citizen Participation

One of the most significant strides made by local government legislation is to create channels for citizen and CSO participation in prioritizing needs and budgets, and planning living and working spaces. For the first time in South Africa, there is legislation that mandates local governments to ensure citizen participation in decision making. But, as argued earlier, the law limits local flexibility and bridles local government, and by extension citizens and "communities," into ensuring specific development outcomes. The space within which citizens and CSOs have to maneuver is further limited by the process of implementation.

Research in various municipalities shows that the approach to the IDP process is very "mechanical." Both the broader purpose of carrying out the participatory process and the purpose of the process itself lose meaning when attention is paid to the exercise of defining, performing, and completing each phase in sequence. Initial observations of the processes in various municipalities show that there is an overemphasis on "sticking" to the phases which, in many cases, deters the process from achieving its broader goals. "As a result the process becomes an exercise in following procedure rather than a strategic exercise to determine and implement a developmental agenda."[71]

The causes for this could be rooted in the policy itself, and in the lack of capacity among local government employees, consultants, and facilitators of the participatory process. By prescribing the process, the policy leaves little room for implementers to create flexible, innovative ways of tapping into local knowledge. It also redirects the focus to completing each step in the process rather than achieving development goals. In essence, prescribing the IDP process provides local government with a list of "tasks" to perform. The advantage is that, apart from providing a guideline for municipalities, it also makes it easier to evaluate what phases have been carried out and which are still outstanding. But the problem with processes that lend themselves to "task-oriented" evaluation is that they become more focused on defining what is required and completing the tasks than on *how* the tasks are performed. This may affect the outcome, and hence the achievement of the broader goals of the process.[72]

> The instrumental aspect of management needs to be complemented with a realization of the importance of the expressive aspect . . . , in which values and ideas are promoted . . .[73]

The inexperience of implementers also plays a part in the emphasis on the planning procedure at the expense of its product. Firstly, given that IDPs diverge considerably from traditional planning, local authorities, consultants, or facilitators are still trying to grapple with the new planning principles and feeling their way through the process.

Consultants spend too much time explaining concepts that they themselves do not understand. What is a strategy, a project, or a priority? In addition, they are too linear and technical and, in the process, fail to capture essential information in the participatory process.[74]

IDP practitioners also try to mold an inherently interactive and dynamic process into a linear format. Although policy typically describes the IDP planning process as a linear step-by-step procedure, in practice, planning is "typically interactive where steps are often leapt over and missed; earlier decisions are constantly revisited and changed."[75] This is the essence of good planning practice where there is a constant reformulation of goals and strategies as priorities and their cost implications become clearer. When practitioners try to fit a dynamic process within a static framework, it reduces the opportunity for actors to explore issues and create a more participatory process. Moreover, participants who do not understand the concepts used, and whose thoughts are not structured in the way that the process is, find it very difficult to engage. When they do, it requires an experienced facilitator to capture the principles behind the "stories" and place these in the correct phase in the process. More often than not, the capacity and experience required are lacking. Thus, because implementers are consumed with the structure of the participation process and the sequence of the phases, they inevitably fail to capture information essential for the generation of a "good" end product. Perhaps most importantly, experiences across the country show that IDPs are not "bottom-up" processes; instead, they are consultant driven,[76] limiting the decentralization of decision making to citizens.

Given South Africa's history, IDPs are a bold attempt to establish an inclusive decision-making process that involves the direct participation of citizens. But do citizens really have the power to influence planning and budgetary decisions? Not only are the values of decentralizing decision making—such as creativity, flexibility, tapping into local knowledge and experience—lost when the spontaneity and adaptability of the process is limited by rigid requirements and the dominance of "experts," so, too, is the sphere of influence of people on the ground.

Attempts at Decentralization in Schools

Decentralization attempts in the schools reveal mixed outcomes. The South African Schools Act mandates the creation of SGBs, which consist of teachers, parents, the principal as an ex officio member, and pupils in the case of high schools. SGBs are allocated a variety of functions. The Act distinguishes between two sets:

- Functions conferred to all governing bodies, which include developing the school's mission statement, adopting a code of conduct, supporting educators and staff, determining school times, administering and controlling school property, recommending the appointment of educators and nonteaching staff to the head of department.
- Functions that are allocated to governing bodies by the MEC upon proof that they have the capacity to carry them out. SGBs are required to apply for these, which include maintenance of school buildings and grounds, purchase of textbooks and educational materials, development of extramural activities, and paying of services to the school.[77]

While the Act has provided a voice for stakeholders who previously had none, there is evidence, particularly in underfunded schools, that SGBs have limited decision-making powers. First, the distinction made in legislation between the two categories of functions clearly shows a reluctance to devolve funding to SGBs that lack the "requisite capacity." Evidence from recent research shows that capacity is often measured by the availability of "hard" resources in the SGB such as professional skills and sound budgeting and managerial systems in the school. Not surprisingly, schools that have historically been advantaged—those in relatively well-off communities able to raise extra funds, which also have infrastructure and access to professional skills at low cost—have the power to determine their own budgets. Historically disadvantaged schools without access to professional skills and infrastructure have less of a say on how budgets are drawn up or even on deciding procurement procedures for their schools. These matters are all decided at the provincial level. As a result, decentralization seems to favor well-resourced schools, limiting the extent to which poorly resourced ones can make critical financial decisions. Well-resourced SGBs, for instance, are able to raise more funds through fees and employ extra teachers and improve their school facilities. Poorer SGBs do not have this luxury. The unintended consequences of this have been the widening of the gap between poor and well-resourced schools and the replication of a skewed school system that is not unlike the apartheid system. Some commentators have argued that some previously disadvantaged schools are worse off than they were under apartheid.[78]

Perhaps the biggest problem is that there is no real effort to establish a capacity-building program which ensures that the playing fields are leveled for SGBs in previously disadvantaged schools. According to research, current SGB training offered in various provinces is far from sufficient and has not been provided to all SGBs.[79] SGBs also have the power to raise their own funds, which they can use as they please. Those that can afford it appoint extra teachers or improve school infrastructure and learning materials. Schools that are unable to raise extra money rely on provincial government funds which, after paying for services and salaries, are barely sufficient to provide enough textbooks. This is despite the implementation of funding norms and standards which ensure that a greater proportion of funds are allocated to poorer schools. Decentralization in this instance is widening the gap between well-resourced and poor schools, and undermining policy imperatives to facilitate equality in the school system. But it is also limiting the extent to which stakeholders—particularly those who are socially and economically disadvantaged—can make decisions.

Civil Society Involvement in Public Policymaking Processes

The postapartheid government has also created formal avenues through which civil society can participate in the policymaking process. Formally, all citizens can engage with the government on policy issues at various points in the policymaking process by, for example, submitting comments on green or white papers or making written or oral submissions to parliamentary committees. While these avenues do provide civil society the space to influence public policy, a variety of reasons suggest that the influence is fairly limited. First, the post-1994 era has seen a decline in funding for CSOs. Consequently, their impact or ability to participate in policymaking is limited by their lack of funds or administrative capacity. Second, the formal process tends to be dominated by large NGOs with the skills and financial capacity to articulate policy positions and publish reports. A rural CSO without the skills or with little access and knowledge of the process is less able to participate in the formal process. Yet even when CSOs participate, there is a perception that government does not listen or is "impervious" to policy suggestions from groups in civil society and that it uses participation to legitimate decisions that have already been taken.[80]

But influence in public policy is not only limited to formal avenues of participation. CSOs also use informal mechanisms to engage government—

behind-the-scenes negotiations, petitions, lobbying and mobilizing interest groups. The government's tolerance of these forms of public engagement implies that it allows freedom and, by extension, autonomy in civil society, particularly when compared with other African states. Research shows that even those CSOs with links to the government use informal mechanisms of influence as much as they do formal ones.[81] To some extent, this illustrates that even those organizations with good or working relations with government perceive that they have the space to express themselves in more radical ways. However, whether these forms of interaction really influence policy decision making is unclear and difficult to gauge. Survey results, however, show that CSOs perceived that they had a far better chance (albeit limited) of influencing policy when both informal and formal mechanisms were used than when they restricted themselves to just one method of engagement with government.[82]

Overview of Principal Actors

It should be clear by now that the society's history has been one in which authority has emanated from the top; this obviously militates against local independence and initiative. We would, therefore, expect to find a clear "top-down" hierarchy within the government system.

There are, however, countertrends. First, while, as noted earlier, domestic resistance to apartheid proceeded within a context of loyalty to national political movements and their leadership, it also produced stress on grassroots initiatives. While this was often more rhetorical than real, it did introduce a new ethos and set of values into resistance politics that, at least in principle, countered the norm of influence exerted from the top. More important, perhaps, was the influence of the trade union movement that took shape in the 1970s,[83] and whose emphasis on grassroots initiative and organization had a significant influence on resistance strategies during the 1980s. This may partly explain why the early post-1994 period offered some important exceptions to an expected trend. Examples include some displays of independence by the ANC parliamentary caucus, calls by ANC provincial premiers for more powers, and the tendency of ANC provincial branches—and, in 1997, its annual conference—to almost invariably elect candidates who opposed the national leadership's nominee.[84]

But the recent trend has been sharply toward greater national control. Besides the examples mentioned earlier, such as national control over the choice of provincial premiers and executive mayors, the independence of the caucus has largely evaporated and, at the time of this writing, the senior ANC member on the national assembly's key financial oversight committee had been replaced because, most analysts agree, he was considered too independent by the party leadership.[85] There is, generally, a marked trend toward conformity within the governing party. In fairness, it is worth mentioning here that much the same could be said, for example, of the official opposition, the Democratic Alliance, whose leadership has similarly extended its control over the party. Since significant differences in approach exist within the major parties, it is too early to tell whether this trend is, for the moment, irreversible. There is still, however, significant variation of approach within government. Civil society, including groups who are sympathetic to the ruling party—most notably the union movement, which has campaigned against the government's macroeconomic policy—continues to provide a source of opposition on policy issues (although far less so on monitoring the probity and competence of government office bearers).

This background helps explain the identity of the principal actors at the three levels (or "spheres") of government. Given the background sketched here, the national cabinet and the ANC's national executive committee are dominant actors, a trend that is increasing not only as a result of the centralization described above but as the governing party "deploys"[86] more of its activists to key civil service posts.[87] The IFP continues to serve in the government and is an influence on policy in some areas; it is, for example, possible that the national government's distinctly nonliberal immigration policy is largely a result of the influence of IFP leader Mangosuthu Buthelezi, who is also the minister responsible for immigration control.[88] But it has not been sufficient to, for example, secure concessions to traditional leaders' demands sought by the IFP.[89] Relations between government and opposition are adversarial, ensuring that the latter has no direct influence on decisions.

The influence of national civil service departments is less easy to gauge. The postapartheid order has been marked by some significant conflicts between ministers and senior civil servants, in particular the directors-general who are administrative heads of departments—so much so that the government has introduced legislation to address this.[90] And this is in turn the result of a strong ministerial preference for appointing to senior posts people who are politically close to them, which can ensure that a change of minister also brings with it a change in senior public service personnel. Postapartheid governance has, therefore, taken precisely the opposite trajectory to that of Britain, where civil service continuity in the context of turnovers in ministerial personnel makes it difficult for political heads of department to establish their authority. Here the problem is whether there is sufficient continuity to ensure a familiarity with administrative routine and institutional history adequate to allow a minimum level of governance, and whether there are sufficient checks on ministerial control to ensure that procedures are respected. That said, senior civil servants inevitably retain significant influence on policy, although given the background sketched here, key influences are likely to be those at the apex of the system who are as likely as not to owe their position to the minister.

The trend toward centralization in the ANC is also mirrored by one within the national government, which has seen an increasing trend to concentrate powers and functions in the office of the president,[91] which inevitably reduces, at least relatively, the influence of individual ministers and directors-general. Similarly, a concern for coordination in government has led, since 1999, to the formation of ministerial "clusters" in which ministers whose portfolios deal with a common theme such as public order or economic growth, cooperate closely. The effect here is to, at least in principle, reduce the latitude of individual departments and enhance the weight of collective decision making.

Political influence over administration does not, however, mean that decisions are taken solely by national ANC leaders. Certainly, a tendency during the first postapartheid administration to draw CSOs into decisions has declined (but has not disappeared entirely). But inevitably, as in any reasonably complex government system, a significant role is played by technical specialists, most of whom do not serve in government but are drawn in to decision making when required. Thus, in the first administration, it was not uncommon to encounter policy processes, including a wide range of interest groups. In addition, "green papers" (which express proposed government policy and invite comment on it) and "discussion documents" would circulate widely as the government sought to ensure that policy was the outcome of wide consultation (albeit only among organized interests rather than grassroots citizens).[92] The current style is far more likely to rely on contributions from technical specialists. And it is perhaps of some interest that while the inner circle of government would tend to be composed of people close to the ANC national leadership politically, this is not necessarily the case when technical teams are chosen. Thus, the government's current macroeconomic strategy (which, while it was drafted during the first administration, was a process assiduously promoted by the current president) was framed by a group that included a University of Cape Town professor with no links to the governing party and a scholar from the University of Stellenbosch, which under apartheid served as the "Oxbridge" of the apartheid state's elite. But, consistent with the drift toward reliance on technicians, the document was not canvassed with interests affected by it: the labor movement was ignored even though the largest union federation is an ally of the governing party.[93] A current investigation into the desirability of a basic income grant is the responsibility of a white Afrikaner male, the group whose claimed monopoly over positions is the first target of current affirmative action policies. And there are examples of government departments commissioning research from scholars known to be hostile to the current government. Technical assistance is, therefore, welcome irrespective of its source, on the obvious assumption that the core political decisions are taken by people in the inner circle and that, given the skills deficit discussed elsewhere, the government cannot afford the luxury of heeding its inner circle only. Clearly, however, the ability to frame "technicalities" also translates into influence over policy.

It is also worth noting that, for a variety of reasons too complex to discuss here,[94] the elite, whether in government or not, is particularly sensitive to foreign opinion. One consequence is to give donor governments significant influence despite the fact that foreign aid makes up a minuscule 5 percent of the national budget. This ensures that the influence is not imposed; it stems neither from aid dependence nor from the superior power of Northern countries. Rather, the desire of the domestic elite to achieve "world class" standards reinforces the concerns of donors in proposing strategies designed to achieve that status. There is also a community of interest in which both government and donors are, for different reasons, eager to emphasize the technical over the political, that is, the need to enhance government technical efficiency over the need to strengthening democratic participation.[95]

One further aspect of national governance is worth noting here. The 1996 Constitution established a set of independent institutions that are meant to protect the public interest by playing a watchdog role. They include the public protector (who plays a Scandinavian-style *ombuds* role) and auditor-general (who monitors public accounts), as well as the human rights and gender equality commissions (which are meant to operate in the wider society as well as in government). These institutions do not have formal powers to enforce decisions, but do play significant roles within the government system. But, while the public protector and auditor-general have played the independent role envisaged, the Human Rights Commission has mixed independence on some issues with, in its critics' view, a role as an agent of government strategy, as, for example, when it held hearings into racism in the media which, while the government remained studiously aloof from the process, were seen by some as an expression of some of its concerns. It has been argued, however, that they do play a significant role in entrenching the idea that institutions independent of the governing party are essential to a democratic system.[96]

Civil Society Autonomy?

The extent to which civil society provides—or perhaps more to the point, can provide—an independent voice in South Africa has been subject of much debate. Despite the government's tolerance of CSO activities, there are arguments that the postapartheid state has attempted to co-opt civil society groups by drawing them into state-led decision-making structures such as the National Economic Development and Labour Council, which aims to promote dialog among business, government, labor, and communities on issues of social and economic policy,[97] and policy implementation structures such as local development forums (LDFs).[98] CSO–government relations are complicated in part by the dependence of some CSOs on government funding and contracts. After the first democratic elections in 1994, donors began to redirect funding to the government, preferring to establish bilateral agreements with it. Consequently, CSOs that had received foreign funding prior to 1994, because they were considered more legitimate than the government, lost most of their income, which resulted in the collapse of many. The funding crisis in the sector prompted the government to intervene to create the Transitional National Development Trust, which was designed to provide temporary funding solutions for CSOs faced with financial collapse.[99] Following this, a more permanent structure—the National Development Agency (NDA)—a statutory body mandated to "be a conduit for funding from the government of the republic, foreign governments, and other national and international donors for development work to be carried out by civil society organizations"[100] was established.

The involvement of government in funding civil society has raised questions about civil society autonomy. Some commentators argue that the independence of civil society is compromised. Should the government become a major source of CSO funding, then it is likely to impact negatively on the sector's autonomy. But it is unclear what impact the NDA will have on the survival of the sector as it has only recently been established. Political commentators argue that although the Transnational National Development Trust made some contributions toward the ailing sector, its impact was negligible given its limited budget of R120 million (about US$15 million). Nevertheless, government's involvement in the funding of civil society, particularly in the context of dwindling and unreliable donor funding, is worrying because it provides government leverage over civil society and interferes with civil society's watchdog role.

Provincial Dynamics

Some of the provincial dynamics have been noted above. It should be noted initially that party politics at the provincial level creates the potential for greater pluralism and diversity. In the Western Cape, an opposition party (the Democratic Alliance) governs, and in KwaZulu Natal another (the IFP) rules in coalition with the ANC. The range of parties represented is broader than that in the national assembly, and in some provinces such as Eastern Cape and North West, regional opposition parties have a significant presence in the legislature. At least in theory, ANC regional leaderships chosen by provincial branches might forge relationships with other parties in their province.

But in the seven provinces governed solely by the ANC, the centralized appointment of premiers has inevitably created the (justifiable) assumption that provincial executives are largely the creatures of central government. In these provinces, it is also worth remembering that the leaders elected by provincial branches before the national leadership intervened have not ceased to exist and in some cases remain leaders of the provincial party. While they have ostensibly accepted the decision of the national leadership replacing them with nationally selected leaders, it is not automatic that this will endure forever; tension between premiers and provincial ANC rivals is constantly rumored and might impact on provincial governance in ways not currently visible to the public.[101]

The role of provincial executives is, as noted above, also complicated by concurrency, whose effect is to make national ministers in the relevant government departments significant actors in the provinces. The same, of course, can be said of their senior public servants. And the oversight function performed by the independent institutions created by the constitution also extends to the provincial sphere—provinces do not have their own oversight institutions. Thus, for example, the Human Rights Commission has taken legal action against the Eastern Cape government for its failure to pay social pensions.

Traditional leadership, discussed earlier, plays a far more significant role in those provinces with large rural areas than it does at the national level. At the formal level, a provincial house of traditional leaders in these areas offers chiefs a platform, albeit one with advisory powers only. More significantly, chiefs play important roles in politics and development in four provinces. These vary greatly. In KwaZulu Natal, traditional leaders are, in the main, a key source of support for the IFP; in exchange, the IFP zealously defends their authority and capacity to dispense patronage. In North West province, chiefs are far less influential but are, in the main, said to support the United Christian Democratic Party led by the former "president" of the area's apartheid-era ethnic "independent homeland" Lucas Mangope. In sharp contrast, traditional leaders in the Northern Province seem supportive of its ANC administration and play a significant role in rural development[102]; in the Eastern Cape, chiefs support the ANC but adopt attitudes not dissimilar to those of their IFP-supporting counterparts in KwaZulu-Natal. In all these provinces, however, traditional leaders are significant actors.

Local Actors

At the local level, political parties remain dominant. As noted above, in the first elections, local leaders who had enjoyed a grassroots support base as either civic or shack dweller leaders failed to win election unless they secured an ANC nomination. In the second elections, attempts to foster independent representation in the ANC camp ranged from the formation of a loose alliance of former ANC councilors opposed to municipal privatization or cuts in services to households who did not pay for them to a slate of candidates sponsored by former ANC guerrillas. They failed to make an impression, winning only a couple of seats. This is particularly significant given evidence that a tendency within the ANC to expel activists who challenge the leadership is most pronounced at the local level.[103]

Party politics, as implied earlier, also tends to centralize decision making at national party caucuses. Recent illustrations of this are evident in the choice of mayoral candidates for metropolitan centers. Johannesburg's new mayor was the choice of party bosses rather than grassroots party members. The town of Middleburg, Mpumalanga, perhaps best illustrates attempts by the party to ensure that local structures toe the party line. With the support of opposition parties, eighteen ANC councilors voted against the National Executive Council (NEC) candidate for mayor, preferring to support their own candidate. Their decision was reversed by the NEC, which sent a senior delegation to the town to ensure that its mayor of choice was elected. The dominance of national party structures is illustrated by the speech made by the Minister for safety and security, Steve Tshwete in Middleburg, defending the NEC's decision: "[O]ur focus was to try to ensure that the decisions of the NEC are respected by the membership of the organization."[104] The strength of national structures not only undermines local autonomy, but could also impact negatively on the functioning of local structures. The effect of party interference is the appointment of councilors or local leaders unable to make their own decisions or adequately represent their constituencies—particularly when this requires going against the party—for fear of the repercussions. Although local government has a dual system that accommodates both proportional representation and constituency-based candidates, recent elections show that it may take a while before independent candidates garner enough support to become entrenched.

A key trend, analogous to that at the national level, is for cities to rely on technical support rather than citizens' participation. This coincides with a more general trend in which local government is increasingly reduced to a purely technical or managerial task and the quality of representation is reduced to a marginal position. And this in turn is influenced by a propensity to embrace fashionable notions, such as the "world class" or "competitive" city that imply (at least in the versions embraced by city managers) the need for technical and managerial competence rather than popular legitimacy.[105]

A key additional actor at this level is the South African National Civic Organization (SANCO), the successor to the civic movement that played a prominent role in domestic resistance to apartheid. While SANCO initially proclaimed itself a civil society "watchdog" on local government, its activists attempted in both elections to secure as many seats as possible on the ANC slate of local government candidates. In both, this attempt triggered conflict between it and the ANC; in the Eastern Cape, it was severe enough to prompt SANCO to nominate a slate of candidates who contested the election against ANC nominees. There are suggestions that the ANC hopes to ensure Sanco's demise by providing channels for its supporters to take up civic issues directly.[106] While the civic organization may have demonstrated its independence by contesting the Eastern Cape, it demonstrated too that it is no match for ANC dominance; its slate was defeated. But, for the moment at least, SANCO remains a local government actor despite the fact that it is clearly no match for the ANC in a contest for public support.

One key difference between local and provincial governments is that the former is not subject to national wage bargaining. Local government workers are not seen, for labor relations purposes, as part of the public service; their wages and work conditions are set by collective bargaining between municipal workers' unions and either individual municipalities or several local governments who unite to form a single bargaining unit. This creates a rationale for the establishment of municipal unions who are actors at this level, in particular the SA Municipal Workers Union, which is, in principle, opposed both to municipal privatization but also to public–private partnerships.[107] Despite this, service delivery partnerships are increasingly winning favor with local governments and are encouraged by national government. The effect, of course, is that private businesses—including a French-based multinational company that specializes in water management on behalf of public entities—have also become local actors.

Traditional leaders are actors in some regions' local governments as well. However, until 2000, as noted above, the chiefs' authority was not challenged by local governments. Now that municipalities will be operating in traditional areas, they can be expected to play a more prominent role at this level, if only as sources of resistance. How powerful this resistance will be if it materializes is a moot point: the chiefs' muscle has not been tested in a confrontation with the government. It also seems likely that resistance would be far more influential in some parts of the country—notably KwaZulu-Natal, where traditional leaders are overwhelmingly allies of the largest party in the province, the IFP—than in others. Traditional leaders have shown that they command enough influence to force the national executive to negotiate with them on local government. But it is not yet clear whether this holds at all times. The attempt to accommodate the chiefs prior to the last elections came amid central government apprehensions that they would disrupt the local elections. Now that this danger is past, national government may feel little incentive to address the chiefs' demands. Certainly, there has been little sign of urgency on this issue—the government began a white paper process on traditional leadership two years ago, and there is no sign yet of a policy emerging from it.

More generally, local government in particular is constrained by the continued existence of pre- or non-democratic forms of authority and service provision that compete with it to extract resources from and supply services to citizens. First, in addition to the points made above about traditional leadership, there is evidence of local forms of traditional authority in, for example, migrant worker hostels in urban areas extracting rents that are meant to accrue to local government.[108] Second, local patronage networks are often able to compete effectively with municipal governments for citizen loyalties.[109] Third, there is tentative evidence to suggest that in the inner cities of major urban areas, alternative forms of power and legitimacy exist that are still beyond the reach of decentralized government.[110] Fourth, informal methods of service delivery that reward entrepreneurs able to tap into public infrastructure to supply services to citizens denied them in the late apartheid period have proved difficult to dismantle.[111] Fifth, since 1994 municipalities have on occasion faced organized resistance from white businesses and individuals who resist the payment of fees and service charges to institutions they consider insufficiently responsive to their concerns. Local governments cannot therefore assume that they command the loyalties of citizens—particularly in the face of continued nonpayment of service charges. One of their key challenges is to extend their reach over these alternative forms of authority, whether by recourse to persuasion or—within the rules of the democratic polity—coercion.

In sum, decentralized governance may provide some opportunities for opposition parties and interest groups that do not exit at the national level. But it is not a forum for the creation of new coalitions, as regional and local politics in large measure reflects national patterns. Strong party loyalties, and the continued capacity of national leaderships to use these to ensure that provincial and local governments do not become sites of independent initiative, means that the potential for decentralized government to break the mold of national politics remains unrealized.

Critical Issues

Does South Africa need decentralized government institutions? In a society whose policy debate is currently dominated by the search for delivery, effectiveness, and international competitiveness, questions of this sort are generally answered by recourse to claims about the extent to which subnational government enhances or obstructs these goals. Elected governments are reduced to administrative vehicles.[112]

We would argue that the rationale for *elected* government at these levels (devolved administrative units would be needed in a country of South Africa's size regardless of the choice of political options) with significant powers must stand or fall by the degree to which they offer citizens an avenue for enhanced representation and participation. At present, if survey evidence is to be credited, most South Africans see no need to enhance subnational government powers and, perhaps, some cause to diminish them.

Consistent with a hallowed local tradition it is possible to argue—with considerable empirical justification[113]—that provincial and local governments create considerable scope for patronage and nepotism, and that they can provide unaccountable local elites with opportunities to use public institutions to entrench private power. Far from providing citizens with representative vehicles, decentralization, it is suggested, diminishes democratic possibilities by entrenching local elites. In the South African case, a similar debate, as implied above, revolves around racial and ethnic identities. Decentralization, particularly to provinces, either provides racial minorities with opportunities to escape majority rule or, as Mbeki complained in 1995, allows the divisive mobilization of ethnic identities.

The appropriate response, however, would need to focus less on what is than on what might be. As implied earlier, the inadequacies of national government are not seen as a rationale for closing it down but for improving it. Similarly, if decentralization in South Africa has potential to enhance democratic possibilities and to defuse—or at least not to escalate—identity conflicts, then current failings would suggest the need to strengthen it.

On the first score, the argument for elected regional and local government with strong powers seems unassailable. National identities—race in particular—are the key determinants of party loyalties. While this is not, as some commentators would have it, "irrational,"[114] it also ensures that there is much that remains unrepresented, in particular interest differences within the parties. In principle, subnational governments provide an important opportunity to express some of these differences in democratic politics. And, as our discussion on the NCOP suggested, this has considerable potential for introducing new dynamics and alliances into politics, thereby strengthening democracy. The salience of identities makes it unlikely that these would, as they have in other societies, prompt the emergence of fundamentally different alliances, at least for a time, and this is in theory an incentive to political elites to relax party discipline sufficiently to allow local distinctiveness to emerge. If we accept that a key feature of a viable democracy is countervailing power, the existence of forms of power within the democratic system able to balance that of the state, then provincial and local government provide a means of consolidating that power in a manner which will not threaten the ANC's continued hold over government. An analogy here is India where considerable regional distinctiveness in the Congress Party leadership did not threaten its lengthy monopoly of government and may conceivably have strengthened it by reducing incentives to break with the party.

It is worth noting here that, while recent South African experience has provided salutary warnings against the automatic equation of decentralization with deeper democracy and more accessible government—the oft-recited cliché that local government is "close to the people" ignores the fact that this is so only if municipalities devote considerable effort to creating this closeness—it remains difficult to imagine how grassroots citizens who often lack the literacy to write to representatives or the telephones to call them and, in some cases, the resources to travel long distances to them, are to gain access to representative government if they can rely only on the national. It is perhaps relevant here that one of the great ironies of the South African decentralization debate is that it is often the left that is most vociferous in its support for strong central government. Yet experience in societies such as India and Brazil suggest that subnational government is the most likely site for social innovation—far from foreclosing leftwing experimentation, decentralization may be its only plausible vehicle. As national government focuses firmly on fiscal discipline and international competitiveness, the prospects for effective action against poverty and inequality may lie chiefly at the local level.

The argument for decentralization as a response to racial tensions is far more dubious. In a society in which racial power has traditionally brought with it considerable privilege that has yet to disappear and to which its beneficiaries tenaciously cling, and in which the racial attitudes that created apartheid often survive in slightly disguised form, it may prove either very difficult or impossible to devise a form of decentralization that would both provide racial minorities with a sufficient sense of efficacy to defuse tensions and allay majority concerns that this is a means of evading the racial egalitarianism that the postapartheid order is meant to install. Similarly, while in many provinces the fear that regional powers are a disguised form of tribal assertiveness is contradicted by the ethnic heterogeneity of most provinces, it remains true that the most vociferous calls for decentralization to regions is made in provinces that are fairly ethnically homogenous such as KwaZulu Natal and Eastern Cape. Nevertheless, since it is axiomatic that decentralized powers would be exercised within the parameters of the national constitution and legislation explicitly allowing discrimination, the threat that they would become a vehicle for evading the consequences of nonracial democracy is illusory. While this might limit the degree to which decentralization can reduce minority alienation, there may still be important possibilities for decentralized governance to address some identity issues.

An important example is language. The lingua franca of the post-apartheid order is English. But, because the vast majority of citizens do not speak it at home, this closes off avenues for political participation by people able to discuss public affairs articulately in their own language but not in English.[115] Strengthened regional governance would create further opportunities for recognizing regional languages, thereby extending participation and reducing alienation of non-English speakers.

In sum, the dangers imputed to decentralization by its opponents may vastly exaggerate the dangers and greatly undervalue the potential advantages, provided that it is seen primarily as a means of deepening and strengthening democracy rather than as a managerial device. While current evidence confirms that the obstacles to vigorous decentralized representation are severe, the possibilities are further constrained by a pervasive failure to see local and regional discretion and initiative as sources of strength rather than threats. The greatest obstacle to enhanced local democracy is, therefore, failure to see its potential and possibilities. In this sense, decentralization in South Africa is trapped in a vicious circle in which its weaknesses reduce elite willingness to recognize its potential and so ensure that the weaknesses will persist.

These considerations seem far more important than a discussion of the specific issues that decentralized government might effectively address. The point here is not to exalt democratic quality above a crass Philistine concern with meeting citizens' material needs. It is, rather, to insist that the ability of decentralized government to make a valuable contribution to goals ranging from greater public safety through improved health and education to a more effective fight against HIV/AIDS will depend largely on the extent to which it becomes an effective vehicle for citizen participation, for only this will determine whether it is able accurately to identify priorities and citizen needs and to win the cooperation of citizens, which successful responses to these challenges will require.

This point is illustrated with reference to an area in which the case for decentralization is made particularly forcefully and persuasively—policing. At present, and consistent with tradition, the police service is highly centralized. While provinces, for example, appoint MECs of safety and security, they have little power to determine the shape and effectiveness of policing in their regions. And Durban is the only city that has a city police force, the result of a quirk that led to its establishing one relatively early in the twentieth century; even this force has relatively modest functions and powers, acting largely as an auxiliary to the national police.[116] A growing consensus among policing specialists holds that centralized policing is remote from needs on the ground and inflexible to local circumstances; provincial or national decisions which sabotage or end innovative local experiments are often cited. So, too, are cases in which citizens, despairing of finding a responsive ear in the police, resort to vigilante justice to combat crime. Decentralized policing, particularly the creation of metropolitan and municipal police forces responsible to local governments, would, it is argued, introduce the required degree of political oversight to guarantee a responsive police force. This view has been influential enough to ensure passage of legislation allowing cities to create these forces, although cost constraints and lack of enthusiasm from the national police are likely to sharply to limit their powers.

And yet, compelling as the arguments for decentralized policing are, so are the warnings that it can, in particular contexts, become a recipe for corruption (already perhaps the single most debilitating problem in the national police), cronyism, and arbitrariness, as local political elites cooperate with police chiefs to turn the force into a source of elite power rather than a service to citizens. Logically, whether local policing becomes a source of safety or of further predations on an already insecure public will depend on the quality of decentralized democracy. Unless local representatives are given enough leeway to represent citizens effectively—and, equally importantly, citizens are afforded sufficient opportunities to hold decentralized government to account—the effect will be not to solve the problem but to transfer it to another level of government.

In sum, the potential of decentralized governance to contribute solutions to the society's social challenges depends not on some sort of "technical" assessment of the functions that could most appropriately be performed by subnational governments, but on a new approach by the national elite (and by donor governments whose approaches so often reinforce those of domestic power holders) that begins by seeing decentralized government primarily as a form of democratic opportunity rather than an implementing agency for national decisions.

Notes

1. Constitution of the Republic of South Africa, as adopted on 8 May 1996 and amended on 11 October 1996 by the Constitutional Assembly Act 108 of 1996, Section 118(1).

2. Constitution, Section 140(3).

3. Ibid., Schedule 5.

4. Ibid., Schedule 4.

5. Constitution, Section 146.

6. This was a demand of the Inkatha Freedom Party, which represented traditionalist Zulu-speaking interests. Constitution, Section 143.

7. Constitution, Section 143(2).

8. Constitution, Section 100.

9. Constitution, Section 76.

10. Constitution, Section 68.

11. Centre for Policy Studies (CPS)/Canadian International Development Agency (CIDA), *South Africa Update* (Johannesburg: Centre for Policy Studies, June 2000).

12. Constitution, Section 41(1).

13. Constitution, Section 151(2).

14. Constitution, Section 152,153.

15. Constitution, Section 154.

16. Constitution, Section 163.

17. Constitution, Section 160(7).

18. Constitution Section 155.

19. Constitution Section 156.

20. Constitution, Schedules 4 and 5, and Section 156.

21. The stipulation is qualified by procedural requirements and the action must be reviewed regularly. But the local government would have no recourse if the procedures were followed. Constitution, Section 139.

22. Michael Sutcliffe, *Democracy and Demarcation,* Summary of seminar held at the Centre for Policy Studies, with the support of the Friedrich Ebert Stiftung Foundation (Johannesburg: Centre for Policy Studies, 2000).

23. CPS/CIDA, *South Africa Update,* January 2000.

24. In the *White Paper for Local Government,* local government functions range from providing basic services, instigating growth in the local economy, creating an environment conducive to the creation of employment, empowering marginalized groups, promoting local democracy, and fostering community participation, to creating livable integrated spaces. See Department of Constitutional Development, *The White Paper for Local Government* (Pretoria: Department of Constitutional Development, 1998).

25. Some sections of the Act were later repealed.

26. Republic of South Africa, *Municipal Structures Act,* Vol. 402, No. 19614 (1998). Category A municipalities are large urban metropolitan councils, category B municipalities are nonmetropolitan councils, and category C are district councils that compose a number of category B municipalities.

27. Ibid.

28. Republic of South Africa, *Municipal Systems Bill* (Government Gazette No. 21071, 2000), 10.

29. "Compact cities" is a planning concept used to denote a movement to "densify" and reduce urban sprawl. "Mixed land use" refers to multifunctional spaces that are a mix of land uses (e.g., an area that is both residential and industrial). Both these concepts are attempts to increase the efficiency of land use in urban areas.

30. See Department of Constitutional Development, *White Paper for Local Government.*

31. See David Savage et al., *A Review of Integrated Development Planning in the Western Cape* (Cape Town: Foundation for Contemporary Research, n.d.).

32. Ibid.

33. Each party selects a list of candidates in order of preference. Seats are allocated to it in proportion to the percentage of the vote that it wins, and these are then filled from the list. Voters have no say over the composition of the list and may not indicate support for any individuals on a list.

34. Constitution, Section 212.

35. Ministry for Provincial and Local Government, *Local Government: Municipal Structures Second Amendment Bill, 2000,* Notice 4481 of 2000 (Government Gazette, Vol. 425, No. 21782, 20 November 2000).

36. Mcebisi Ndletyana, *Draft Report on the Public Hearing on Municipal Structures, Second Amendment Bill Hosted by the Portfolio Committee on Provincial and Local Government and the Select Committee on Local Government and Administration* (Johannesburg: Friedrich-Ebert-Shiftung, 2000).

37. Caroline Kihato, with Mogudi Maaba and Paul Thulare, *Building in Power: Problems of Community Empowerment in a Gauteng Development Project* (Johannesburg: Centre for Policy Studies, 1998).

38. The other is the Northern Cape, whose population is minuscule compared to that of any other province, and in which the ANC won a plurality in 1994.

39. Ivor Chipkin, *City and Community: Local Government and the Legacy of the "One City" Slogan* (Johannesburg: Centre for Policy Studies, 1996).

40. For an analysis of the negotiations (with approval) as a process of minority surrender, see Patti Waldmeir, *Anatomy of a Miracle* (Harmondsworth: Penguin, 1997).

41. See Chris Landsberg, "Directing from the Stalls," in *The Small Miracle: South Africa's Negotiated Settlement,* edited by Steven Friedman and Doreen Atkinson, 276–300 (Johannesburg: Ravan, 1995).

42. Herman J Cohen, "The Current Situation," statement before the Sub-committee on Africa of the House Foreign Affairs Committee, Washington D.C., 23 July 1992, *U.S. Department of State Dispatch,* 3, no. 30, 27 July 1992.

43. Richard Humphries, Thabo Rapoo, and Steven Friedman, "The Shape of the Country: Negotiating Regional Government," in *The Small Miracle: South Africa's Negotiated Settlement,* edited by Steven Friedman and Doreen Atkinson (Johannesburg: Ravan, 1995), 153.

44. Centre for Policy Studies, *CPS Socio-Political Monitor,* prepared for the Development Strategy and Policy Unit, Urban Foundation 45 (Johannesburg: Centre for Policy Studies, August 1994).

45. See Centre for Policy Studies/National Business Initiative, *Quarterly Trends* (Johannesburg: CPS/NBI, April 1995).

46. For example, intervention by Mario Ambrosini, advisor to the Inkatha Freedom Party, at Commission on Provincial Government discussion of local powers (Pretoria, 1995).

47. National Party, *Constitutional Rule in a Participatory Democracy* (Pretoria: National Party, 1992). For a critique, see Kader Asmal, "Neighbourhood Laager: The Devolution of White Power," *Indicator South Africa* (Durban, University of Natal) 10, no. 3 (Winter 1993): 55ff.

48. Hermann Giliomee and Lawrence Schlemmer, *From Apartheid to Nation-Building* (Cape Town: Oxford University Press, 1989).

49. The most important was a stipulation giving racial minorities half the 60 percent of the seats that were elected on a "ward" or constituency system and requiring a two-third majority for passage of municipal budgets. This arrangement was an interim measure and applied only to the first (1995/1996) elections.

50. Steven Friedman and Richard Humphries, eds., *Federalism and Its Foes,* proceedings of a joint Institute for Multi-Party Democracy/CPS workshop entitled "The Politics and Economics of Federalism: A South African Debate," August 1992 (Johannesburg: Centre for Policy Studies, May 1993).

51. At the height of government disenchantment with the provincial system's management difficulties, a senior government official told a seminar that "constitutional constraints" made it inevitable that provinces would continue. This implies that the government feared negative reactions if it sought to amend the Constitution to abolish provinces. (Remarks by President's Office official, seminar on democracy and economic development, University of Cape Town, January 1998.) Since June 1999, the ANC has commanded enough votes in Parliament to muster, with the help of an opposition party opposed to the provinces, the two-thirds majority needed to abolish provinces. Despite speculation before the election that it would use such a majority to at least revise provincial powers, it has not done so.

52. CPS/CIDA, *SA Update,* June 2000.

53. An abbreviation of Minister-MEC. Thabo Rapoo, *Concealed Contest: Minmecs and the Provincial Debate,* Policy Brief 18 (Johannesburg: Centre for Policy Studies, 1999).

54. See discussant's contribution by Thabo Rapoo in Riaan de Villiers, ed., *Comparing Brazil and South Africa: Transitional States in Political and Economic Perspective* (Johannesburg: Centre for Policy Studies/Foundation for Global Dialogue/Instituto de Estudos Econômicos, Sociais e Políticos de São Paulo, 1996), 97ff.

55. Steven Friedman, "No Easy Stroll to Dominance: Party Dominance, Opposition and Civil Society in South Africa," in *The Awkward Embrace: One-Party Domination and Democracy,* edited by Hermann Giliomee and Charles Simkins, 97–126 (Amsterdam: Harwood Academic Publishers, 1999).

56. CPS/NBI, *Quarterly Trends* (Johannesburg: CPS/NBI, April 1999).

57. Thabo Rapoo, *Room to Manoeuvre? Premiers' Keynote Speeches in 1994 and 1999,* Issues and Actors 13.1 (Johannesburg: Centre for Policy Studies, 2000).

58. Institute for Democracy in South Africa (IDASA), *A Submission to the White Paper Secretariat by the Idasa Public Opinion Service* (Cape Town: IDASA, December 1997); IDASA, *Public Evaluations of and Demands on Local Government* (Cape Town: IDASA, February 1998).

59. Steven Friedman, *The Elusive 'Community': The Dynamics of Negotiated Urban Development* (Johannesburg: Centre for Policy Studies, 1993).

60. This analysis is impressionistic and is not based on a thorough analysis. It is disputed by the committee's founding chair, now speaker of the provincial legislature, Firoz Cachalia. *Mail and Guardian,* 11 February 2000.

61. Department of Constitutional Development, *White Paper for Local Government.*

62. Simon Stacey, *New Capacities for Old? Public–Private Partnerships and Universal Service Delivery in South Africa, Angola and Mozambique* (Johannesburg: Centre for Policy Studies, 1997).

63. Robert Mattes, *Public Evaluations of and Demands on Local Government* (Cape Town: Institute for Democracy in South Africa, 1998).

64. Caroline Kihato and Thabo Rapoo, *An Independent Voice? A Survey of Civil Society Organisations in South Africa, Their Funding, and Their Influence over the Policy Process* (Johannesburg: Centre for Policy Studies, 1999).

65. See, for example, interviews in Mary R. Tomlinson with Sivuyile Bam and Thomas Mathole, *More than Mealies and Marigolds: From Homeseekers to Citizens in Ivory Park* (Johannesburg: Centre for Policy Studies, Interfaith Community Development Association, 1995).

66. Ivor Chipkin, "East Rand Shows Why 'Regional Development' May Rob Local Democracy of its Meaning," *Synopsis* (Johannesburg: Centre for Policy Studies) 1, no. 2 (December 1996): 12.

67. CPS/NBI, *Quarterly Trends* (Johannesburg: CPS/NBI, January 1998).

68. Caroline Kihato, "'Megacity' Model Is Not the Route Greater Johannesburg Should Adopt," *Synopsis*, 1, no. 4 (September 1997): 5.

69. Steven Friedman, "Who We Are: Voter Participation, Rationality and the 1999 Election," *Politikon* (Johannesburg) 26, no. 2 (1999).

70. Institute for Democracy in South Africa, *A Submission to the White Paper Secretariat.*

71. Khetso Gordhan, Johannesburg city manager, radio interview.

72. Peter Cranko and Edgar Pieterse, *Integrated Development Planning Pilot Projects* (Cape Town: Isandla Institute, 1998).

73. A. Thomas, "What Makes Good Development Management?" *Development in Practice* 9, nos. 1–2 (1998): 9–17.

74. Ibid.

75. Policy analyst, Public and Development Management Programme, University of the Witwatersrand, interview by authors, 13 May 1999.

76. D. Porter and M. Onyach-Olaa, "Inclusive Planning and Allocation for Rural Services," *Development in Practice* 9, no. 1–2 (1999).

77. The term consultant driven is used to refer to the contracting of "experts" by government. The contracting of consultants has become commonplace in South Africa, as the government increasingly outsource expertise from the private sector. Ironically, in the case of IDPs, many of the consultants are former council officials who were responsible for implementing apartheid planning.

78. Republic of South Africa, *South African Schools Act,* Vol. 377, No. 175979 (1996).

79. Salim Valli, discussant at European Union Workshop, Johannesburg, 22 February 2000.

80. Continuing research at the Centre for Policy Studies, funded by the European Union.

81. See Kihato and Rapoo, *An Independent Voice?*

82. Ibid.

83. Ibid.

84. Steven Friedman, *Building Tomorrow Today: African Workers in Trade Unions, 1970–1984* (Johannesburg: Ravan, 1987).

85. CPS/NBI, *Quarterly Trends* (Johannesburg: CPS/NBI, January 1998).

86. See, for example, *Sunday Independent,* 4 February 2001.

87. In an apparent legacy of its partly military past, the ANC does not "transfer" or "appoint" members to posts; it "deploys" them.

88. CPS/CIDA, *South Africa Update,* January 2000.

89. For an overview of immigration policy debates, see, for example, Maxine Reitzes, *Divided on the "Demon": Immigration Policy Since the Election,* Policy, Issues and Actors (Johannesburg: Centre for Policy Studies, 1995).

90. See, for example, *Mail and Guardian,* 12 January 2001.

91. The Public Administration Amendment Act of 1999 gives the power to hire and fire DGs to the president nationally and to premiers in the provinces. The stated aim is to prevent ministers firing DGs at the slightest provocation. But observations after it was promulgated suggest that it has not prevented a continuing trend in which ministers insist on appointing senior public servants of their choice, and replacing those who served the previous minister. CPS/NBI, *Quarterly Trends,* November 1999.

92. Sean Jacobs, "An Imperial Presidency," *Siyaya* (Cape Town: Institute for Democracy in South Africa) 6 (Summer 1999): 4–9.

93. Steven Friedman and Maxine Reitzes, *Democratic Selections? State and Civil Society in Post-Settlement South Africa* (Midrand: Development Bank of Southern Africa, 1995).

94. Thami Ngqungwana and Zondi Masiza, "The Formulation and Implementation of GEAR Objectives," unpublished draft (Johannesburg: Centre for Policy Studies, 2001).

95. See Steven Friedman, "Terra Incognita: The Politics of Foreign Policy in Post-Apartheid South Africa," unpublished draft (Johannesburg: Centre for Policy Studies, 1998).

96. Steven Friedman, "An End in Itself: Democracy and the Building of Post-Apartheid South Africa," unpublished manuscript (Johannesburg: Centre for Policy Studies, 2000).

97. Khehla Shubane, *No Easy Walk to Civility: Civil Society Organisation and the South African Context* (Johannesburg: Centre for Policy Studies, 2000).

98. The National, Economic, Development and Labour Council, which brings together business, labor, the government, and "community organizations." It was created by legislation in 1995 and must discuss all socioeconomic legislation before it is tabled in Parliament.

99. Maxine Reitzes, "How Should Civil Society Formations Relate to Structures of Representative Government?" in *Civil Society After Apartheid,* edited by Richard Humphries and Maxine Reitzes, 110–115 (Johannesburg: Centre for Policy Studies/ Friedrich Ebert Foundation, 1995).

100. South African National NGO Coalition, "Progress Towards the Establishment of the National Development Agency (NDA)" (available at: www.sangoco.org.za).

101. Republic of South Africa, Government Gazette No. 19520.

102. For a discussion of these dynamics, see Thabo Rapoo, *Twist in the Tail? The ANC and the Appointment of Provincial Premiers,* Policy Brief (Johannesburg: Centre for Policy Studies, 1998).

103. Craig Charney, *Voices of a New Democracy: African Expectations in the New South Africa* (Johannesburg: Centre for Policy Studies, 1995).

104. Patrick Heller, "Civil Society: When the Going Gets Tough," in *Topical Trends: An Analysis of Current Political, Economic and Social Trends,* prepared by the Centre for Policy Studies with the support of the Friedrich Ebert Stiftung Foundation (Johannesburg: Centre for Policy Studies, September 2000).

105. SABC Online News, 5 February 2001 (available at: www.sabcnews.co.za).

106. Steven Friedman, "A Quest for Control: High Modernism and Its Discontents in Johannesburg, South Africa" (paper presented at Woodrow Wilson International Center for Scholars Workshop on Urban Governance in Major World Cities, Washington D.C., 6–7 December 2000).

107. CPS/CIDA, *South Africa Update,* April 2000.

108. Stacey, *New Capacities for Old?*

109. Ivor Chipkin, with Paul Thulare, *The Limits of Governance: Prospects for Local Government After the Katorus War* (Johannesburg: Centre for Policy Studies, 1997).

110. Graeme Gotz, "The Limits of Community: The Dynamics of Rural Water Provision," report for Rand Water (Johannesburg: Centre for Policy Studies, 1997).

111. Abdou Maliq Simone, "Urban Societies in Africa," in *Civil Society After Apartheid,* edited by Richard Humphries and Maxine Reitzes (Johannesburg: Centre for Policy Studies/Friedrich Ebert Foundation, 1995).

112. Centre for Policy Studies, "Illegal Electricity Connections: Local Partnerships Mooted," *Synopsis* 1, no. 1 (September 1996): 10.

113. Steven Friedman, "Power to the Provinces," *Siyaya!* (Cape Town) no. 4 (Autumn 1999): 44–46.

114. Gotz, "The Limits of Community"; Caroline White, *Makhulu Padroni? Patron–Clientelism in Shack Areas and Some Italian lessons for South Africa,* Policy, Issues and Actors (Johannesburg: Centre for Policy Studies, 1993).

115. Friedman, "Who We Are."

116. Charney, *Voices of a New Democracy.* See also article by Neville Alexander, *Mail and Guardian,* February 2001.

Chapter 7

Kenya's Decentralization through the Devolution of Power: Advances and Limits

Gilbert M. Khadiagala and Winnie V. Mitullah

Widespread recognition of the failure of the centralized state dominated in Africa at the turn of the 1990s. In its stead, decentralization became the organizational framework for a wide array of practices and policies prescribed by foreign agencies and domestic constituencies seeking new approaches to the crisis of African governance. Linked to the legacy of authoritarianism, centralization was perceived as the source of the debilitating economic and social crisis that engulfed most of Africa. Yet despite the remarkable experiments in decentralization and devolution of power, there are thus far few successful models of effective decentralization in Africa.[1]

Kenya is typical of African countries that are struggling with the legacy of centralization amidst pressures to embark on decentralization programs that would improve economic efficiency and restore a semblance of accountability and transparency in the management of public affairs. Although economic pressures have whittled the central government's capacity to provide effective public services, there has been a sporadic and lukewarm commitment to decentralization. The Kenyan case reveals that meaningful decentralization cannot occur with first creating broad-based participatory strategies for national governance. For this reason, decentralization in Kenya for most of the postindependence era has remained hostage to fundamental issues of political and constitutional change. Functioning local participatory self-governance institutions are inconceivable outside similar institutions at the national level.

In this chapter we weave these themes into an analysis of Kenya's attempts at decentralization since independence. We situate these efforts in larger contests and contexts about the constitutional framework in Kenya and elite strategies of ethnic management. In delineating the actors and issues in decentralization, we show that although decentralization has been the most frequently attempted politico-administrative reform, there has been very little tangible achievement in affording local authorities the resources and political latitude for self-governance.

Development of Institutional Framework

Decentralization takes various forms to facilitate the transfer and dispersal of authority in planning, management, and decision making from national to subnational levels. Rondinelli's classic distinctions among deconcentration, delegation, and devolution inform much of the debate about decentralization. Distinguished both by their legal status and degrees of autonomy, they speak to different forms of power relationships between the center and periphery. Under deconcentration, central governments disperse some administrative responsibilities to lower levels of government to rationalize services without a real transfer of authority to either local officials or the people. Common in unitary states, deconcentration has been the "easy" option for decentralization in most of Africa. In delegation, central government transfer responsibilities for decision making and administration of public functions to local governments or semi-autonomous organizations that are not wholly controlled by the center but are ultimately accountable to it. Devolution occurs where central governments transfer some authority for decision making, finance, and management to quasi-autonomous units of local government through a statutory provision. This allows local units to elect their representatives, raise their own revenues, and have independent authority to make investment decisions. Devolution strengthens subnational levels that are substantially independent of the national level with regard to defined functions.[2]

Except for a brief period when a federal constitution promised devolution of power, the dominant pattern in Kenya's experience has been deconcentration. This stems largely from the legacy of the colonial unitary state. The colonial state made no pretenses to democracy toward its African subjects, governing them through segregated institutions under control of the Provincial Administration. In the mid-1920s, the colonial state established Local Native Councils (LNCs), which became African District Councils (ADCs), seeking to grant some measure of local self-governance to Africans. In the European areas, it established the District Councils, Municipal Boards (urban), and County Councils to cater mainly to the white settler farmers. African institutions were intended to deflect African demands for participation in the political mainstream of the colony. For this reason, the Provincial Administration controlled the election and nomination of council members, set the agenda of their meetings, and controlled the scope of their revenue base.[3]

Nowhere was colonial emasculation of local self-government more evident than in treatment of traditional chiefs. Although the institution of chiefs was recognized by the colonial powers, it was transformed from representative of a community into a direct representative of the government through which the colonial authorities could give orders and pass information to the people. As a result, the chief was not answerable to the people but to the District Commissioner (DC). The latter also chose chiefs and councilors and determined resource allocation and use by the local councils.[4]

The nationalist yearning for self-rule and African participation culminated in Kenya's independence in 1963. In the immediate independence period, Kenya adopted a federal constitution that offered legislative powers, financial capacity, and executive authority to local governments in an attempt to undo the legacy of colonial paternalism and centralization. At the national level, the Constitution created a bicameral legislature (Senate and House of Representatives), an executive, headed by the prime minister, and a civil service. At the subnational level, the Constitution created eight semi-autonomous regions, each with a regional assembly, an executive led by the regional president, and a regional civil service.[5]

Under the federal constitution, the federal government at the center and the semi-autonomous authorities in the regions shared responsibilities of government. In matters of legislation, regional assemblies had absolute power to make legislation in all aspects of public life except those that had national consequences, which was the legislative responsibility of the federal parliament. Policy was formulated and implemented in the regions through their executive branches. The regions covered education, health care, public works, forestry, and archives and museums, while federal government had responsibility for the police force, national security, and foreign affairs.

Since the wide-ranging responsibilities allotted to regional governments imposed a severe financial burden, the Constitution made provisions for raising revenues for recurrent and development expenditures. As part of the goal of endowing regions with some measure of financial autonomy that would realize the goal of decentralization, the Constitution created a Regional Fund in each region. In addition, the Constitution specified measures for regional assemblies to levy certain categories of taxes while sharing revenues in other areas with the central government. More critical, the central government made direct grants to the regions.

Central to the decentralization efforts were the constitutional provisions for a two-tiered local government system within each region: municipalities and counties. Municipalities were further divided into local councils and counties were divided into townships, local council areas, and urban councils. Each of these authorities was composed of elected Councilors and a few nominated representatives. Each local government area was entitled to recruit administrative and technical staff managed by the Local Government Staff Commission (LGSC).[6]

These elaborate structures of regionalism and local governments that aimed to establish the basis for decentralization were, however, brittle from the outset, hostage to the uncertain ethnic cleavages and alliances that characterized Kenyan politics. On the eve of independence, minority ethnic communities, apprehensive of the postindependence political dominance of the two major ethnic groups, the Kikuyu and Luo, coalesced around the federal and decentralization constitutional order. The British settler community found common cause with these minorities in a political alliance, the Kenya Democratic African Union (KADU) against the Kenya African National Union (KANU) dominated by the Kikuyu and Luo.[7]

While KADU felt compelled to press for federalism and decentralization, KANU favored a strong centralized government and opposed federalism. KANU critics charged that federalism was too complex a system for the young nation and was bound to accentuate ethnic differences. Furthermore, for KANU, decentralization would limit the ability of the central government to control the population in the manner that the colonial government had done.[8] Without a unanimous vision of all the political interests about decentralization, its future was destined to be very bleak. At the

British-led constitutional conference in 1962, KANU grudgingly accepted the federal constitution, and after independence, it formed the majority party in government under Jomo Kenyatta.

Decline of Decentralization and Democracy, 1963–1991

The 1963–1991 period is significant in the history of decentralization and democratization because it witnessed the rapid and systematic dismantling of the decentralization structures of regionalism and local government enshrined in the Independence Constitution. Two events spelled contributed to the decline of these structures. First, in May 1963, KANU, the antifederalist party won the independence elections against the federalist KADU rival. Second, in November 1964, KADU disbanded and amalgamated with KANU resulting essentially in a de facto single-party state. Buoyed by these changes, KANU abandoned the federal structures and established a unitary constitution in which it would assert its hegemonic control.[9]

Within three years of independence, the Kenyatta administration dismantled the national and regional structures of federalism. Regions reverted to provinces under the tight control of the central government. Each province had several districts, divisions, locations, and sublocations, all equally controlled by the center. In addition, the technical departments became local units of central government ministries. At the center, the two chambers of the legislature were merged to form the National Assembly. The responsibilities of head of state and prime minister were combined to create a strong presidency with unhampered powers. These changes were enshrined in the Republican Constitution, promulgated in May 1968.

The reversals in federalism also mirrored the weakening of local government. Although KANU was not against the idea of local government as much as it was against regionalism, centralization of power in Nairobi affected the role of local governments. From the tentative experiment with power devolution envisaged under federalism, the political pendulum swung toward deconcentration starting in the mid-1960s. The main institutional structures for deconcentration were the District Development Committees (DDCs) and District Development Advisory Committees (DDACs), complemented by their provincial equivalents. Even though district local authorities and local members of parliament were represented on these bodies, they were dominated largely by central government administrators, notably the provincial and district commissioners. Given this dominance, these institutions served in an advisory role instead of being avenues for local participation.[10]

In an effort to correct the institutional decline of local government, the government appointed a commission in 1966 to examine how to "improve the capacity of local authorities to contribute toward the implementation of the National Development Plan." Concerned about the lack of provision for local authority participation in development planning, the commission noted that "the local authorities either individually or in suitable groups ought to be consulted at the drafting stage of implementation on any matters affecting local government." Further, it proposed the replacement of DDACs with committees of the county councils that would have representation on the Development Committees; the latter also would need to have wide-ranging powers to "collect and examine schemes to put forward to the appropriate Ministry and also give advice as to any relevant priority and control the implementation process."[11]

The government response to these recommendations foreshadowed its broader approach to questions of decentralization. Although accepting in principle the centrality of local government participation in the planning process, the government rejected these recommendations and instead launched a process in which local structures became entirely subordinate to the central administration through its local agents. The first step in this subordination was the 1969 transfer of responsibility for the provision of the three major services from county councils to the central government: primary education, health care and roads. The county councils retained responsibility for only the minor services, notably feeder roads, markets, and slaughterhouses.[12] Following this transfer, county councils as the essential units of local government lost their significance and standing in the eyes of the local population. Alongside this transfer, the central government abolished the graduated personal tax (GPT) levied by local government authorities, in effect transferring to the center the councils' main source of revenue. As Wallis notes:

> As far as involvement in development activities was concerned, these two changes had extremely damaging effects on all County Councils regardless of how well or badly they had been performing. The more efficient councils which had provided services whilst managing their finances fairly well suffered the same fate as those which had been rather profligate. . . . The new policy was not well received in local government; councilors often felt that that there was little left for them to do and re-

sented what they saw as financial redistribution to the benefit of the center and to their own disadvantage. In this process, an important form of local participation became significantly weaker.[13]

Second, the central government bestowed upon itself tremendous supervisory powers over local authorities, transforming them into appendages of the central government. Under these arrangements, the minister responsible for local government had the power to upgrade existing local government authorities and create new ones; establish local government electoral areas without necessarily consulting local residents; nominate members to local government councils without consulting the local people; dissolve local government councils including the elected membership, replacing them with central government–appointed commissions, and approve local government budget and development plan proposals. The policies cumulatively deprived local governments of independent sources of revenue and enhanced the extrajuridical supremacy of the provincial administration over local governments.[14]

A parallel movement launched in the 1960s, the Harambee (self-help movement) became the only avenue of local initiatives. Encouraged by the government to foster development and participation, this movement generated lots of enthusiasm from rural communities seeking to pool local resources to meet the basic needs that the central government could not provide.[15] With the decay of local government, the Harambee movement became the only avenue of political mobilization for development, particularly in areas that had resources and organizational structures. But, as this movement seemed to threaten central control over rural areas, local government agents moved to assert control over it. Over the years, this movement declined, becoming captive to the patronage politics of the central government.

To meet the challenges of declining state resources that dependence on the center had fostered, the government experimented with other forms of deconcentration. In the 1970s, for instance, the government initiated an experimental Special Rural Development Program (SDRP) in six divisions in the country whose goal was to involve local and communities in development planning. But, reflective of the low status accorded to local government, the main agents of the SDRP became the field offices of various government departments. From 1971 until its termination in 1976, local authorities made minimal contributions to this program despite representation by elected councilors.[16]

The trend of marginalizing local institutions in both participation and planning continued throughout the 1980s. But unlike previous decades, the government faced severe financial pressures to provide support for local authorities. With the virtual disappearance of government grants to local authorities and the latter having no meaningful alternative sources of revenue, the government faced a legitimacy crisis at the local level. Compounding its fiscal woes was donor pressure for local initiatives that would reduce the burdens of the central government in development and service delivery. It was against this background that the government of Daniel Arap Moi launched a new deconcentration program in 1983, the District Focus for Rural Development (DFRD). Under this system, a hierarchy of development committees was established at the district, divisional, location and sublocation level as forums for tapping local participation in preparing the five-year district development plans, the three-year forward budget, and the annual budget proposals.[17] However, the DFRD was not a showcase of decentralization, but rather shifted substantial planning responsibilities to field administrators, especially the district commissioners who were expected to play more critical roles in policy formulation and implementation. Incapable of making decisions that were not in conformity with the central government, the local committees did not enhance participation at the grassroots. In essence, the DFRD reinforced the strategy of deconcentration of administrative roles rather than devolution through locally representative councils.[18]

A similar program, the Rural Trade and Production Center (RPTC) that the government initiated in 1986, suffered the same fate as the DFRD. Promoted to reduce rural–urban differences, the RPTC sought to concentrate scarce resources for infrastructure development in selected small towns to boost investment in these towns and rural areas by improving agricultural productivity and removing constraints on small-scale enterprises. Although conceived from the center, the government intended the actual planning and execution to devolve to decentralized subnational units of government.[19] By 1989, however, the RPTC had fallen prey to central control, having been captured by government bureaucrats and implemented haphazardly. As Smoke and Evans argue,

In spite of their perceived economic benefits, decentralized development programs are not a sustained high priority for most senior officials of government widely perceived to be consolidating political control over the districts. Although they continue to refer to the RPTC in speeches and to support the idea in official forums, the fundamental conflicts inherent in Kenya's official decentralization policy hinder efforts to ensure progress and the availability of additional funding for subsequent rounds.[20]

At the beginning of the 1990s, Kenya's record of deconcentration was one of failure. Tenuous government commitment to decentralization coupled with bureaucratic mistrust of local initiatives had helped to create a situation where local structures existed without meaningful roles, responsibilities, or resources. As the economy further deteriorated, the government consolidated central power as a way to manage the centrifugal forces at the local level. Wallis summarizes the gloomy picture of Kenya's decentralization as follows:

> There is a sense in which central government policy toward local authorities has been a consistent one over the past twenty years. Two key points stand out: one is the incremental emphasis on centralized power, requiring increasing integration of local government into the general machinery of the state; the other has been the clear desire to ensure that local councils survive. Thus, the approach has combined gradual erosion of powers, functions, and resources with occasional radical change. Greater central government control has also been exerted through the District Focus approach which has brought about the integration of local government into the District Development Committee machinery in a way which, in effect, subordinates councils to the field administrators, notably the district commissioners. . . . All indications point to less autonomy, not more, whilst the resource base is very unlikely to improve other than marginally.[21]

Reemergence of Democracy, 1991–2001

The clamor that engulfed most of Africa for pluralism, democracy, and decentralization occurred against the backdrop of the failure of the centralized state. Kenya found itself in a classic dilemma of the lame leviathan[22]: a state that was sufficiently strong to counter domestic pressures for power devolution and constitutional change, but increasingly unable to be an effective provider of goods and services. Years of authoritarianism and economic mismanagement resulted in the diminishing capacity of the state to mediate conflicts and furnish an environment of economic growth, but its declining resource base had emboldened ruling elites to hang on to centralized power.

At the heart of the lame leviathan is the precarious legacy of ethnic bargaining that has characterized the political process since 1963. Ethnic conflict management under the rubric of a one-party centralized state seemed for a long time to be the ideal formula for national cohesion, invariably placing severe limits to participation at all levels of society. In the Kenyatta era (1963–1978), state institutions and practices coalesced around the hegemonic interests of the Kikuyu elite. Kenyatta neutralized the deleterious consequences of Kikuyu hegemony by constructing an elaborate system of patron–client relationships built around important regional and ethnic elites. The Kenyatta state was also relatively successful in containing ethnic conflicts because of a growing economy. Economic growth concealed the draconian side of Kenyatta's patronage politics and froze ethnic conflicts through the promise of prosperity.[23]

Moi sustained the spirit of Kenyatta institutions to broaden his legitimacy. Over time, however, he fundamentally put his own ethnic stamp on them, gradually whittling down Kikuyu power in an attempt to shore up a weak and tentative Kalenjin one. The Moi era reveals additional notable trends. Patron–client relations in place of open participation as a system of ethnic management presuppose a modicum of leadership confidence, stable alliances, and economic growth. Although Kenyatta's confidence emanated from his nationalist credentials and the numerical strength of the Kikuyu, Moi was continually haunted by membership in a marginal ethnic group, with tangential links to nationalism. Consequently, under Moi, the stability of alliance building essentially collapsed as ethnic insecurity colored state practices, and economic collapse followed.[24]

As the democratization movements of the 1990s generated new competitive forces that challenged the centralized state, elite attempts to remake the lethargic institutional structures of a weak state overshadowed debates about decentralization. Thus, just like in previous years, decentralization remained doubly difficult, hostage to the national dialogue about the nature of democratization and ethnic management and the imperatives of national rejuvenation. Moreover, moves toward strengthening the capacity of local institutions are still tentative because of the ingrained legacy of authoritarianism; hence the even weaker Kenyan state has increasingly become wary of devolving power to local authorities because of the implications of loosening the reins of central power.[25]

The other themes that Kenya's experience in the 1990s reveals is that without the ability to sustain a meaningful level of economic engagement with most critical sectors of the population, the state found itself ceding considerable power to nongovernmental organizations (NGOs) and civic groups. Energized by donor funding that deliberately deflected resources from the corrupt Moi machinery, NGOs and civic groups tried to recreate local organizational capacity founded on the tradition of self-help.[26] For this reason, decentralization has proceeded largely by default, thriving uneasily at the point of vulnerability where the weak state cannot deliver services and where alternative actors emerge to shame its incapacity. Yet decentralization by default is a precarious enterprise: these alternative avenues and initiatives to strengthen local governance will remain tentative, subject to legal and resource uncertainties, unless a national project emerges to capture them in solid debates about power sharing. Thus, the unresolved issues about political power at the center continue to impede significant debates about decentralization and nullify opportunities for local governance.

In 1991, Kenya repealed the single-party legislation, setting in motion constitutional changes from an authoritarian unitary state to a democratic society. From the outset, the democratization process focused mostly on reforming the structure, institutions, and political processes of the central government—the presidency, parliament, electoral rules, and the civil service. Very little attention was paid to reforming the structures, institutions, and processes of governance at the local level, notably in local government. Nearly all actors in the democratization endeavor assumed that the micro-level issues of governance were subordinate to those at the macro level. As a result, the constitutional changes that inaugurated the first multiparty elections since independence held in 1992 made little mention of local governance.[27]

With respect to the party system, the democratic crusaders in Kenya achieved the repeal of the single-party constitutional legislation, paving the way for the formation of a multiplicity of political parties. Although the party system is a function of democratization at all levels, the multiparty crusaders perceived it more as a means to replace the presidency and gain seats in parliament with little consideration for local governance. In the struggle for changes in the presidency, the agents of democratization focused on undoing its unlimited tenure because holders of the office have, through authoritarian tendencies, deprived society of the talents of other aspiring presidential candidates. Thus, in the constitutional amendments, the presidency was limited to two five-year terms. In addition, there was a new requirement in the electoral law that provided that the president had to obtain a minimum of 25 percent of the votes cast in at least five of the eight provinces.

The democratization effort also resulted in the transfer of responsibility for managing presidential and parliamentary elections (excluding local government elections) from the civil service, notably the provincial administration to a newly appointed Electoral Commission of Kenya. Given the history of the provincial administration's partiality to the ruling party, this change promised to create conditions for free and fair elections. Although the constitutional changes brought about a competitive environment of local elections, undemocratic practices of the past have persisted. For instance, the central government managed local government elections through the Ministry of Local Government, rather than the Electoral Commission. In addition, the minister of local government unilaterally filled all positions for nominated councilors almost exclusively from KANU ranks.[28]

Despite the 1992 and 1997 multiparty elections, the centralized state under KANU control remains very much in place. Throughout the 1990s, most of the democratic crusaders realized that electoral reforms without fundamental constitutional change still tilted effective power toward the Moi government. It is for this reason that since the onset of pluralism, leading opposition groups and members of civil society have demanded a radical revision of the Independence Constitution, which stacks the deck against emerging parties.[29] But the debates about constitutional change have further fragmented the national elite. On the one hand, some factions have proposed power devolution reminiscent of the immediate postindependence era of federalism (Majimbo). The proponents of federalism emanate from the KANU strongholds in the Rift Valley and coastal provinces. They prefer federalism not because of its potential to devolve power to regions, but as a guarantee against central loss of power by the incumbent president. Thus, their argument is that either KANU maintains control of a unitary Kenyan state or a federal system is established providing for the coast and the Rift Valley to exercise semi-autonomous authority and to control the presumably enormous natural resources within their respective territories. More radical voices of this faction have called for a federal arrangement that would lead to the eviction of "nonindigenous" ethnic communities from KANU strongholds, amounting essentially to ethnic balkanization. In the run-up to the 1992 and 1997 elections, this faction, with the connivance of the state, resorted to ethnic cleansing in the Rift Valley as a prelude to ethnic federalism.[30]

Most of the opposition has opposed federalism in favor of the continuance of the unitary state. But because of divisions along ethnic and sectarian lines, the opposition has thus far been unable to present a consistent voice in debates about constitutional change. Moreover, KANU has been adept at mobilizing the structures of the state to preempt serious discussion about fundamental political change. On decentralization, some opposition parties prefer the continuation of deconcentration and restoration of the autonomy of local governments. Their party manifestos make vague promises of devolution of excessive power and influence from the central government, replacement of the Provincial Administration with elected local authorities, and the decentralization of healthcare management and social services.[31]

Since the mid-1990s, the government, wary of the opposition's appropriation of the decentralization agenda, embarked on a review process under the framework of public sector reforms. At the core of these reforms was to the goal of enhancing citizen participation in governance, boosting the accountability and transparency of local authorities, and improving the delivery of local services.[32] Toward this end, the government appointed a commission on local authorities in 1995 to recommend the way forward. The commission began from the premise that "since independence, the number of local authorities has grown, but this growth has not been matched by the enhancement of the Ministry of Local Government's capacity to administer them."[33] But, although it recognized that the "the resource base for local government is inadequate as there is fairly little tax revenue sharing with the central government and there are hardly any grants from central to local government in support of general services," the commission nonetheless recommended that local authorities should assume the following "mandatory" functions: pre-primary and primary education, public health and sanitation, environmental protection and management, roads and drainage, water supply, urban planning and development control, and traffic and transport management.[34] At the end of the review process in May 2000, the commission concluded as follows:

> Decentralization policy is necessary to rationalize on sharing powers, responsibilities, and resources between central government ministries, parastatals, District Development committees, Local Authorities, and the private sector. This will depend on the best way functions can be carried out in order to provide services in the most effective and efficient way to the public. Decentralization policy is therefore a very critical element in the Local Government Sector Reform. . . . The policy will spell out which

functions, responsibilities and resources will be provided centrally, deconcentrated to line Ministries/Departments, delegated, commercialized, privatized or devolved to Local Authorities.[35]

In the late 1990s, domestic and international pressures for constitutional revisions overshadowed local government reforms. As street protests mounted and international financial institutions continued to withhold foreign aid, a beleaguered Moi consented to a Constitutional Review Commission in May 2001. After almost five years of procedural wrangles, the Commission began the task of collecting nationwide ideas and suggestions about the Constitution. At the end of this process, the Commission would submit a draft of the Constitution to the parliament and the president for approval. But the Commission had hardly begun its work when Moi induced one of the major opposition parties, the National Development Party, to join KANU in a new formidable ethnic alliance that sought to roll back the limited gains from pluralism Kenya achieved in the 1990s. In August 2001, the KANU–NDP unveiled a draft federal constitution with a three-tiered system of local, provincial, and national governments. Reminiscent of the 1963 Constitution with a bicameral parliament and decentralized regional governments, the proposal promised more equitable resource distribution and efficient local governments.[36]

Critics of the government's draft constitution point to the motives driving the initiative, notably the draconian efforts by the KANU–NDP alliance to preempt a review process in its infancy. Moreover, like the 1963 constitution, the authors of federalism seemed to be concerned more about consolidating ethnic economic gains than genuine commitments to the devolution of power. This view was strengthened by a provision in the draft constitution that replaced the president's two-term limit by an indefinite tenure, a move that would guarantee Moi's hold on power.

As the vicious inter-elite battle over the constitution of central power gained momentum, Kenya's periphery spawned local initiatives responding to the felt need for services such as education, health, and security. Far from the reach of the central government, the population seemed bent on carving out a new model of livelihood, effectively taking over activities abandoned by the state for lack of funds or interest. As a result of the collapse of social, economic, and physical infrastructure, the peasantry has turned increasingly from cultivation of export crops such as coffee and tea toward produce designed for the domestic market. But even as they strive to construct new local institutions to raise revenue and deliver collective goods, these efforts will remain halfway measures as long as reforms at the center are stalled.

Conclusion

The fate of decentralization in Kenya is tied intimately with democratization and the promotion of pluralism. The postindependence experience reveals that narrow-based regimes showed reluctance to countenance local institutions because such measures would deprive them of resources and unleash new countervailing leaderships and centers of power. Without the emergence of more broad-based and confident elites at the center, serious efforts toward decentralization as power devolution are unlikely. The fundamental reforms that democratization entails at the center would then be the preliminary step toward decentralization across the political spectrum.

The link between democratization and decentralization also explains why the larger questions of constitutional reforms and political change have overshadowed Kenya's decentralization efforts. Preoccupied with restoring competition at the center, elites have had less time to focus on the equally pertinent questions of democratizing local structures, which, since the 1990s, began to find their own leaders and institutions. The discordant voices between the elites and masses can only be harmonized in reforms that, in the long term, capture democratization at the center and the periphery.

Notes

1. For comprehensive debates about decentralization in the African context, see James S. Wunsch, "Refounding the African State and Local Self-Governance: The Neglected Foundation," in *Journal of Modern African Studies* 38, no. 3 (2000): 487–509; Jennie Litvak, Junaid Ahmad, and Richard Bird, *Rethinking Decentralization in Developing Countries,* Sector Studies Series (Washington, D.C.: World Bank, 1998); W. Dillinger, "Decentralization, Politics and Public Services," *Economic Notes,* no. 2, Country Department I, Latin American Region (Washington, D.C., World Bank, 1995); James S. Wunsch and Dele Olowu, eds., "The Failure of the Centralized African State," in *The Failure of the Centralized State: Institutions and Self-Governance in Africa,* edited by Wunsch and Olowu, 1–23 (Boulder, Colo.: Westview Press, 1990); Olowu, "The Failure of Current Decentralization Programs in Africa," in *The Failure of the Centralized State,* 74–99; and James Manor, *The Political Economy of Democratic Decentralization* (Washington, D.C.: World Bank, 1999).

2. Dennis Rondinelli, "Government Decentralization in Comparative Perspectives: Theory and Practice in Developing Countries," *International Review of Administrative Sciences* 47, no. 2 (1981): 133–45.

3. For analyses of colonial policies, see Bruce J. Berman, *Control and Crisis in Colonial Kenya* (Nairobi: East African Educational Publishers, 1990); and Berman and John M. Lonsdale, "Crisis of Accumulation, Coercion and the Colonial State: The Development of the Labor Control System in Kenya, 1919–1929," *Canadian Journal of African Studies* 14, no. 1 (1980): 55–81.

4. Berman and Lonsdale, "Crisis of Accumulation, Coercion and the Colonial State," 55–81.

5. For a review of an account of the provisions of the 1963 constitution, see Walter Oyugi, "Local Government in Kenya: The Case of Institutional Decline," in *Local Government in the Third World: The Experience of Tropical Africa,* edited by Philip Mawhood, 107–40 (Chichester: John Wiley, 1983); Oyugi, "Kenya: Two Decades of Decentralization Effort," *Cahiers Africaines d'Administration Publique* 26 (1986): 133–61.

6. Oyugi, "Local Government in Kenya." See also Cherry Gertzel, "The Provincial Administration in Kenya," *Journal of Commonwealth Political Studies* 4, no. 3 (1966): 201–15.

7. For excellent analyses of postindependence ethnic bargaining, see Colin Leys, *Underdevelopment in Kenya: The Political Economy of Neo-Colonialism, 1964–1971* (Berkeley: University of California Press, 1975) and Gavin Kitching, *Class and Economic Change in Kenya: The Making of an African Petty-Bourgeoisie* (New Haven, Conn.: Yale University Press, 1980).

8. Tom Mboya, *Freedom and After* (New York: Andre Deutsch, 1963).

9. Peter Anyan'g Nyong'o, "State and Society in Kenya: The Disintegration of the Nationalist Coalitions and the Rise of Presidential Authoritarianism, 1963–1978," *African Affairs* 88, no. 351 (1982): 229–51.

10. Oyugi, "Local Government in Kenya," and Malcom Wallis, "District Planning and Local Government in Kenya," *Public Administration and Development* 10 (1990): 438–40.

11. Republic of Kenya, *Report of the Local Government Commission: The Hardcare Report* (Nairobi: Government Printer, 1966).

12. Republic of Kenya, *Proposed Action by the Government of Kenya on the Report of Local Government Commission for Inquiry* (Nairobi: Government Printer, 1967).

13. Wallis, "District Planning and Local Government," 439.

14. C. K. Murumba, "Sharing Responsibility and Resources for Effective Central-Local Relations," *Planning and Administration* 14, no. 1 (1987): 100–109; John M. Cohen and R. M. Hook, "Decentralized Planning in Kenya," *Public Administration and Development* 7 (1987): 77–93; and Chweya Ludeki, "Regional Development in Kenya: An Assessment of Performance," in *Regional Development Policy in Africa: Problems and Prospects Towards the 21st Century,* edited by Ayele Tirfie et al., 153–64 (Nairobi: U.N. Center for Regional Development, 1998).

15. Philip M. Mbithi and R. Rasmusson, *Self-Reliance in Kenya: The Case of Harambee* (Uppsala: The Scandinavian Institute of African Studies, 1977); Barbara Thomas, "In Search of Effectiveness: Reflections on Comparative Lessons in Resource Management," in *International Review of Administrative Sciences* 53 (1987): 555–79.

16. Wallis, "District Planning and Local Government," 440–41.

17. Republic of Kenya, *District Focus for Rural Development* (Nairobi: Government Printer, 1987).

18. Joseph Makokha, *The District Focus: Conceptual and Management Problems* (Nairobi: Institute of Development Studies, 1985); Preston Chitere and Joshua Monya,

"Decentralization of Rural Development: The Case of the Kenya District Focus Approach," *Cahiers Africaines d'Administration Publique* 32 (1989): 33–46; and Wallis, "District Planning and Local Government," 442–49.

19. Republic of Kenya, *Economic Management for Renewed Growth* (Nairobi: Government Printer, 1986). See also Gary Gaile, "Improving Rural-Urban Linkages Through Small Town Market-Based Development," *Third World Planning Review* 14, no. 2 (1992): 131–48.

20. Paul Smoke and Hugh Emrys Evans, "Institutionalizing Decentralized Project Planning Under Kenya's Program for Rural Trade and Production Centers," *Third World Planning Review* 15, no. 3 (1993): 231.

21. Wallis, "District Planning and Local Government," 449.

22. We derive this concept from Thomas M. Callaghy, "Africa and the World Economy: More Caught Between a Rock and Hard Place," in *Africa in World Politics: The African State System in Flux,* edited by John Harbeson and Donald Rothchild, 43–82 (Boulder, Colo.: Westview Press, 2000).

23. For a comparative analysis of the Kenyatta and Moi regimes, see David Throup, "The Construction and Destruction of the Kenyatta State," in *The Political Economy of Kenya,* edited by Michael G. Schatzberg, 33–74 (New York: Praeger, 1987).

24. Ibid.

25. For current trends and obstacles, see Peter Wanyande, "Decentralizing the State in Kenya" (paper presented at the African Association of Political Science, Kenya Chapter, on "Democracy and Constitutional Politics, Nairobi, 6 June 1996); Pascaliah J. Omiya, "Citizen Participation for Good Governance and Development at the Local Level in Kenya," *Regional Development Dialogue* 21, no. 1 (2000); and Walter Oyugi, "Decentralization for Good Governance and Development Concepts and Issues," *Regional Development Dialogue* 21, no. 1 (2000); and Ludeki, "Regional Development in Kenya."

26. Stephen Ndegwa, *Civil Society in Kenya* (Hartford, Conn.: Kumarian Press, 1994); and Ndegwa, "Civil Society and Political Change in Africa: The Case of NGOs in Kenya," *International Journal of Comparative Sociology* 35, nos. 1–2 (1994): 19–36.

27. These trends are captured in David Throup and Charles Hornsby, *Multiparty Politics in Kenya: The Kenyatta and Moi States and the Triumph of the System in the 1992 Elections* (London: James Currey, 1998); and Barbara Grosh and Stephen Orvis, "Democracy, Confusion or Chaos: Political Conditionality in Kenya," *Studies in Comparative International Development* 31, no. 4 (1996–1997): 46–65.

28. Roger Southall and G. Wood, "Local Government and the Return to Multipartyism in Kenya," *African Affairs* 95, no. 381 (1996): 501–27.

29. James Kariuki, "'Paramoia': Anatomy of a Dictatorship in Kenya," *Journal of Contemporary African Studies* 14, no. 1 (1996): 69–86.

30. Gilbert M. Khadiagala, "Kenya: Intractable Authoritarianism," *SAIS Review* 15, no. 2 (1995): 53–73.

31. See, for instance, the opposition constitutional platform, "Kenya Tuitakayo (The Kenya We Want): Proposal for a Model Constitution" (Nairobi: CLARION, 1995).

32. Republic of Kenya, *Bringing Government Closer to the People: The Experience of Decentralization and Local Government Reform in Kenya,* Discussion Paper (Nairobi: Ministry of Local Government, 1999).

33. Republic of Kenya, *Report of the Commission of Inquiry on Local Authorities in Kenya: A Strategy for Local Government Reform in Kenya* (Nairobi: Government Printer, 1995).

34. Republic of Kenya, *Report of the Commission of Inquiry on Local Authorities.*

35. Republic of Kenya, *Kenya Local Government Reform Program Concept Paper* (Nairobi: Government Printer, January 2000).

36. "Plan to Remove Term Limit," *Sunday Nation,* 2 September 2001.

Part III

Asia

Chapter 8

The Philippines: Decentralization, Local Governments, and Citizen Action

Leonora C. Angeles and Francisco A. Magno

Domestic and international pressures for democratization have led to a new emphasis on local forms of governance below the nation-state level. Decentralization may be viewed as a form of "resurgence of the local,"[1] a trend taking place since the breakup of empires into nation-states. The most recent example of this trend is the break-up of the former Soviet Union due to the spread of democratic ideas and the emergence of a global political economic system that provides localities with an alternative to national capitals. By "decentralizing power, reducing hierarchy, improving democracy through better social communication, and promoting citizen service control via self-government,"[2] social institutions and governance can be improved by the pluralization of state authority and increased use of voluntary associations. The advantage of decentralization also lies is its provision of local space in which public awareness can be transformed into local political action that may lead to changes at the national and global levels.[3]

Proponents of decentralization emphasize the disillusionment of people around the world over the capacity of centralized systems to effectively implement necessary reforms and the perceived advantages of decentralization in revitalizing civil society.[4] Decentralization is often considered as one of the key elements necessary for successful governance in North America and Europe to meet the challenges of global and regional integration. It is considered essential to redefining the purpose of leaders and institutions, restructuring old ideologies, and redirecting the focus of responsibilities for governments and citizens. It is invariably seen as a necessary condition in the call for "a new democracy," "a new federalism," "a new moral infrastructure," "strategic cooperation," and "collaborative partnerships."[5] In African nations, the acceptance of diversity and decentralization has been considered necessary for efficient government, economic growth, and the establishment of civil society.[6] In countries rocked by religious and ethnonationalist conflicts, decentralization and democratic governance, along with alternative socioeconomic development, have been considered as the most effective ways to combat the excesses of economic liberalization and religious movements that propagate nationalist identities and negate the principles of equality and democracy.[7]

Similar hopes and perceived advantages of decentralization in bringing about democratic governance and social development have been raised in the Philippines. This Philippine study hopes to contribute to this volume's overall emphasis on cross-national and cross-cultural comparative analysis to illuminate the differences in the impact of decentralization on local governance across time and space. The study of decentralization, however, must be locally grounded and contextualized, as decentralization takes many different forms in different countries at different times.[8] Due to space and time constraints, we are unable in this chapter to present detailed local-level dynamics of decentralization processes, save for reference to a few community case studies by others. Our principal objective is to analyze the domestic and international pressures that led to democratization moves in the Philippines in the context of past and present institutional frameworks for governance, and the current problems faced by both government and civil society in the course of decentralization.

What is particularly interesting about the Philippines as a case study is the strong demand from civil society for decentralization, particularly the reorganization of local–national government relations and increased public participation in local governance. The desire to bring the government closer to the people is the oft-cited argument for decentralization. While there is no guarantee that decentralization will automatically result in democratization,[9] there is a strong expectation in the Philippines that strengthening local decision-making structures will significantly increase the impact of popular participation in politics and governance. The Philippines is an interesting case study in assessing the potentials of decentralization, and its limits, in bringing about democratization and new forms of participatory governance and in promoting economic development and greater social equity.

The chapter is organized as follows. The first part examines the legacy of centralization in the national government that served as an incubator of initiatives and reforms leading to decentralization in the post-Marcos period, focusing on the 1991 Local Government Code and related legislation. The second part looks at the various legal frameworks and institutional structures that have evolved as a result of recent attempts at decentralization. The third part analyzes some problems in intergovernmental and state–civil society relations that have emerged in light of decentralization moves. Critical issues that decentralization has attempted to address, such as environmental management, poverty alleviation, health care, and education are analyzed to support insights in the previous section. The last part provides some conclusions and direction for future research on decentralization in the Philippines.

Legacy of Centralization and the Impetus for Decentralization

Government decentralization has been an established national policy in the Philippines and may be considered one of the most important moves in the long-term post-Marcos adjustment and stabilization, which include the peace process, deregulation, and social reforms.[10] The government's decentralization policy is enshrined in the passage of the 1991 Local Government Code (LGC), the national legal framework that provides mechanisms for substantiating the democratization philosophy of the 1986 Philippine Constitution. Valdellon argues that decentralization in the Philippine context comes in two forms.[11] One form is political decentralization or devolution, that is, the transfer of national government powers and authority to local government units (LGUs). The other is deconcentration, also known as administrative decentralization, which involves the delegation of authority by the central government agencies to their regional or field offices. The process of political decentralization or devolution involves determining what functions of the central government are to be transferred to LGUs, and to what level. One could argue that decentralization below the state level involves choosing between bureaucracy and democracy, in the sense that it can mean either the delegation of administrative powers to local officials or the devolution of political authority to local governments.[12] To better understand the impetus and events leading to decentralization moves in the Philippines, it is important to analyze the legacy of centralization on governance problems in the country.

Centralization of powers in the national government has been a key feature of the Philippine political system. The persistence of a strong central government since the colonial era has been noted in several studies.[13] Spanish colonial rule for more than three centuries was characterized by an excessive concentration of power in Manila, the country's capital. The relative autonomy of local and provincial elites since the early 1900s kept the nation-state weak, as they used state resources to reinforce their position. A new elite of mercantile entrepreneurs emerged in the 1950s, joining the landed oligarchs in their dependence on state credit and political protection. The centralist tendencies of intergovernmental relations in the decades between the American colonial period and the Aquino administration have been determined by a number of factors. Among them were (1) perceived threats to national security; (2) personalities of the presidents of the Philippines; (3) demands of national integration in a multiethnic, multilingual, and multireligious country; (4) the push for national development goals; and (5) the central government's perception of the competence of local governments to assume more responsibilities.[14] The centralist tendencies in government were still evident in the 1986 Constitution, which states: "The President of the Philippine shall exercise general supervision over local government."[15] This provision for the general supervision of local government by the president stems from the provisions in the 1935 Constitution that concentrate power in the president.[16] These centralist provisions were later reinforced in the 1973 Constitution and subsequent amendments passed under martial law.[17]

Since the 1930s, several arguments in support of centralization, particularly the supervision of local governments by the president and national government, were often put forth. Centralization was deemed justified in view of the need to maintain minimum standards in local government services and to maintain administrative standards between and among various government levels. It was also viewed as necessary to control central expenditures as part of national economic planning and management, to protect citizens from abusive local government authorities, and to promote nation building in light of the ethnic, linguistic, and religious diversity of the population.[18]

As early as the American occupation in the early 1900s, the Philippines had started embarking on some decentralization initiatives, or more specifically, on establishing local autonomy. From the short-lived government established by the Malolos Constitution to the Instructions and Acts created during the American Rule period, the granting of administrative autonomy and the use of decentralization became popular. The Commonwealth period had laws for local government under the supervision of the president. After independence in 1946, Republic Act (RA) 2264 was passed in 1959, which amended the legislation governing LGUs. This was the beginning of local autonomy for the LGUs, as it vested greater fiscal, planning, and regulatory powers to these units.[19]

Government overcentralization was seen as effective in times when the national population was small and land was abundant, but it has become ineffective since the rapid Philippine population growth in the 1960s.[20] Despite overall concentration, a few government functions have relative success in being decentralized, such as irrigation administration. It has been noted, for example, that irrigation effectiveness in the Philippines was best enhanced not by the type (national or communal) and size of irrigation system, but by decentralization of decision making through increasing the number of work units horizontally or the level of authority vertically.[21]

In 1967, President Marcos enacted RA 5185 or the Decentralization Act of 1967 increasing the fiscal and decision-making powers of local governments. Consequently, with the declaration of martial rule in 1972, and consequent abolition of local elections, the local governments were directly under the control of the authoritarian government. But the government continued its advocacy for decentralization with the promulgation of the Local Government Code of 1983 (Batasang Pambansa 337).[22] This advocacy was in accordance with the 1973 Constitution which explicitly states that the autonomy of LGUs, especially the *barangays* (village units), will be guaranteed and promoted "to ensure their fullest development as self-reliant communities."[23]

Despite these early attempts at decentralization, the administrative structures remain heavily centralized. Centralization had been a major factor behind a number of governance problems that continued to persist in the local and national political culture. First, the postwar emergence of the state patronage system has been facilitated by the *overconcentration of powers in the national government and increased state intervention in the economy*.[24] The emergence of the state as the biggest dispenser of patronage necessitated the creation of new tax sources, acquisition of public debt, expansion of the state bureaucracy, and increase in state expenditures, especially for electoral spending, the "pork barrel" system, salaries of government personnel, provision of employment in the public sector, and creation of new state corporations.[25] A devastating consequence of centralized patronage dispensation is the heavy politicization of the government's delivery of services to local areas.[26] The national budget process, for example, has become a tool for patronage by providing Congress ease in appropriating items outside the budget. It also gives arbitrary powers to Congress and the president to facilitate fund transfers and utilize public savings to cover budget deficits.[27]

Second, the centralization of legislative and fiscal powers in the national government had created patronage-based interactions among the national executive, Congress, provincial governors, and local officials.[28] Provincial governors and mayors have to curry the favor of congressional representatives, national party officials, and executive heads in exchange for pork barrel funding. The overconcentration of power at the national level required provincial officials, especially those from remote areas, to spend much of their time dealing with the national government, traveling to Manila to facilitate release of funds, project approval, and other paperwork.[29]

Third, the overcentralized government and administrative structures have *exacerbated the extreme regional inequalities* in economic growth and industrial development in the Philippines.[30] The tourism industry, for example, was observed since the 1970s to have been overconcentrated in Manila, thus contributing to inequitable distribution of income and wealth and uneven regional development.[31]

President Marcos had in fact used the overconcentration of powers in the national legislature as a justification in declaring martial law, citing legislative impasse and political stalemate in Congress as major problems that hindered his national development vision. Ironically, he abolished Congress only to concentrate even more power in himself and his coterie of followers. President Aquino herself could not avoid the climate that necessitated political centralization in the post-Marcos transition. She governed in the earlier period of her presidency on the basis of the so-called Freedom Constitution that gave her control over local governments. President Aquino instituted a "sweeping purge of regional and local governments" to replace local authorities who were considered allies of the deposed Marcos regime.[32] Some observers would argue that this move was a strategy to consolidate support at local levels to the new regime and that granting local autonomy was only incidental to this purpose. The 1987 Constitution, however, guaranteed the creation of LGUs, namely provincial, municipal, and *barangay* units. Consequently, the Constitution mandates the creation of the code for local government that would institutionalize decentralization in the country.

The enactment of the LGC in 1991 has brought about significant changes in central–local government relations. The transformation of the country's governance structure that resulted from this legislation should be viewed within the broader context of a dual transition—a simultaneous process of democratic consolidation and economic liberalization that the country has undertaken after fourteen years of authoritarian rule. The democratic transition in 1986 provided an impetus to decentralization by encouraging people to participate in making decisions that affect their lives[33] and increasing collaboration between government and nongovernmental organizations (NGOs). The increased involvement of NGOs and popular organizations (POs) in local government structures is one means by which to decentralize and diffuse the power of a centralized politico-administrative machinery.[34] The potential for increased working relationships between NGOs and government organizations has been enshrined in the 1987 Constitution, the 1991 Local Government Code and the government's 1993–1998 Medium-Term Development Plan (MTDP). Taken together, these documents aimed to achieve people empowerment and international competitiveness through decentralization, democratic consultation, full cost recovery, and social equity.[35] The LGC in particular allows LGUs to discharge functions and responsibilities devolved to them by national government agencies. To assist LGUs in assuming their new financial roles in raising revenue and budget allocations, major tax innovations such as new tax rates, tax sharing schemes, and widening (or narrowing) of taxing policies were introduced.

Decentralization may be seen as a response of the state to the demand of progressive forces in civil society to open up political spaces for state–society engagement. The increased role of civil society organizations in the Philippines may be traced back to the period of massive opposition to authoritarian rule and cycles of deep economic crises, such as the severe 1984–1985 crisis, manifested in famine and malnutrition in the sugar-producing island of Negros. Many NGOs, often funded by international donor agencies, trace their origins to the mid-1980s when they provided much of the functions that the state had failed to do. As voluntary organizations driven by a commitment to people-centered development, these NGOs played a critical role not only in the peaceful overthrow of the Marcos government but also in opening discourse around alternative development paths and political institutions for better state–civil society relations. However, progressive groups that played a major role in bringing Aquino into power increasingly found themselves marginalized under the new regime, which began to bolster the power of old elites under the previous regime. In the absence of any real improvement in economic conditions and inability to implement radical political reforms (e.g., agrarian reform), the only way of quelling increasing dissatisfaction among competing political groups was to accommodate their demands for political liberalization. This was done by making the local levels the locus of decision making and by bringing decision-making institutions closer to the citizenry and integrating them into these institutions.

The push for decentralization in the postauthoritarian transition comes strongly from the provincial and local government officials themselves. They are the main beneficiaries of decentralization efforts by the national government, which have come to mean a greater share in the central government's income, more authority in running local affairs, and increased capability to solve local problems. Provincial governors who traditionally resented centralization, clamored for political decentralization in the forms of fiscal autonomy and more participation in the appointment of provincial administrative and military personnel.[36]

The change toward decentralization seems to be inevitable in light of population growth and the proliferation of politico-administrative units. As of 1999, there are already 78 provinces, 83 cities, and over 40,000 barangays or village units in 1,526 municipalities or towns. The barangay is the basic and smallest politico-administrative unit headed by a *kapitan* (captain) and *kagawad* (councilors). Both municipal and city governments are headed by a mayor assisted by a vice mayor and several councilors that are elected for a limited term, with possible reelection. Together, they compose the local government's legislative body, the *Sangguniang Bayan* (Municipal Council) or Sangguniang Panlungsod (City Council). Likewise, officials at the provincial level are all elected. The provincial government is also called the Sanggunian Panlalawigan (Provincial Council or Board).

In October 1989, the "Declaration of Common Accord" was signed by the presidents of the League of Provinces, League of Cities, League of Vice Governors and Vice Mayors, Municipal Mayors League, Provincial Board Members Association of the Philippines, and the League of Barangay Councilmen. It was signed during the first National Congress on Local Autonomy, urging the enactment of the Local Government Code. These Leagues were a mix of pro-Marcos local officials and Aquino supporters—some of whom came from the NGO and cause-oriented groups—as well as turncoats (former Marcos supporters who switched sides) who ran for office in the 1987 local and national elections. The varied composition of these Leagues suggests broad support for decentralization from both the opposition and the supporters of the incumbent government. Some 2,500 elected officials attended this national conference and passed resolutions outlining proposed changes to existing local government arrangements and legislation under debate in Congress. These various Leagues have joined forces to form the Union of Local Authorities of the Philippines (ULAP). The strong influence and corporatist bent of these Leagues is manifested in the Department of Interior and Local Government's (DILG) policy that no policy measure pertaining to the LGUs will be released without review by the ULAP.[37]

The impetus for decentralization in the Philippines was thus intensified by the confluence of international and national developments that came from various sources: national actors such as local government officials and leagues of provincial governors, municipal officials and village leaders, the national government and academy, and civil society organizations. International economic trends such as the global debt crisis, and international development agencies, including financial institutions such as the World Bank and the International Monetary Fund (IMF), as well as bilateral donor countries, also played an important role in pushing for decentralization.

The support of influential international organizations for public sector reform coincided with the country's postauthoritarian search for a political framework that could address issues of participation and legitimacy. It became clear to donor agencies that growth and development could be secured only if an effective institutional environment is established. Along with the notion that there is no substitute for market-based economic arrangements is the consensus that the state should be reduced in size but should be strong enough to create an institutional environment that sets the right policies[38] and institutes public sector reform and good governance.[39] In the area of central–local government relations, decentralization is promoted as an important element of the prescribed public sector reform program.[40]

The World Bank and the IMF are perhaps the best-known international development agencies pushing for decentralization as part of their emphasis on "good governance,"[41] and public sector reforms to improve project or program efficiency. This interest of the World Bank and the IMF in using decentralization as a centerpiece for economic restructuring and structural adjustment policies has often hampered the democratization process.[42]

In the Philippine case, both institutions have likewise pushed for administrative decentralization in the form of privatization of state corporations, most notably public utility companies, as part of its structural adjustment program loans. Decentralization in the form of fiscal autonomy of local units seems to be the logical consequence of massive cuts in national public investment programs and operations and maintenance expenditures since the adoption of the Fiscal Austerity Measures in response to the 1983–1985 crisis.[43]

Multilateral institutions were therefore in a very influential position to push for decentralization and other public sector reforms under the Aquino administration. The Aquino government was unable to resist these pressures because of the country's dependence on foreign capital to finance public sector investment and the ballooning balance of payments deficit.[44] The 1994–1996 IMF "Exit Program" in the Philippines included withdrawal of funds under the Extended Fund Facility to support "reengineering of the bureaucracy" aimed at privatization, merger or abolition of government units, and devolution of powers to LGUs. The IMF saw this as necessary for budgetary savings and the focusing of budgetary allocations on priority programs and functions of the government, such as poverty reduction through the Social Reform Agenda (see below).

International funding agencies have also supported efforts to improve the capabilities of national government agencies, LGUs, and local officials to adjust to the requirements of self-government and the decentralization process. They developed programs to strengthen the Department of Interior and Local Government as the primary government line agency tasked to develop LGU capacity and capability in local governance. The DILG's LGU Capability Program comprises the bulk of its activities, followed by LGU supervision, which includes assessment and awards and incentives programs. Other national government departments also directly affect decentralization in the country, especially the Departments of Finance, Budget and Management, Public Works and Highways, Environment and Natural Resources, and Education Culture and Sports. The National Economic and Development Authority likewise has a role in the planning of LGU projects.

As a result of the decentralization policy, many of these national government agencies have entered into partnerships with national academic institutions and foreign donors to assist LGUs in their new functions. The Local Government Academy under the DILG and the Local Government Center[45] under the National College of Public Administration and Governance at the University of the Philippines serve as training grounds for local elected officials in local governance and sources of information on decentralization. Both institutions have direct linkages with foreign funding institutions and international organizations in advancing the study and practice of local governance and are the source of information for the creation, articulation, and critique of laws, programs, and other government efforts in decentralization that led to the LGC of 1991. The national government's line agency efforts in advancing decentralization are reflected in the willingness of these agencies to devolve their powers and functions, and the promotion of the concept by academic public institutions like the University of the Philippines and the Local Government Academy. Aside from the line agencies, the national government's participation in international organizations (United Nations, Association of Southeast Asia Nations, etc.) and international conventions and treaties is apparent in prevailing notions of development and decentralization.

Among the foreign-funded programs to aid decentralization are several projects financed by the Canadian International Development Agency (CIDA), which had allocated a portion of its bilateral assistance program resources to capacity building of LGUs, POs, and NGOs to meet demands created by the new decentralization policy. CIDA has an ongoing project with the Philippine government called the Local Government Support Project (LGSP).[46] The goal of the first phase of the project is to aid the Philippine government in the process of decentralization in the Visayas and Mindanao provinces, by enhancing the structures and mechanisms of local government to increase their policymaking and administrative capabilities. The goal of the project's second phase is to assist the Philippine government in achieving its poverty alleviation goals through local government empowerment and increased grassroots participation.

Other foreign-funded projects that involved both NGOs and academic institutions include the U.S. Agency for International Development's (USAID) Local Development Assistance Program NGO Support Grants Component (LDAP-PBSP), the government of the Philippines-USAID's Decentralized Shelter and Urban Development (DSUD) tapped by the League of Cities for its Cities Sharing Program in 1992–1993. The Konrad Adenauer Foundation has been the main funding agency supporting the Local Government Development Foundation (LOGODEF) in its effort to promote decentralization. The Ford Foundation likewise provided financial support for the initial articulation and realization of the constitutional provision on autonomous regions, which led to the Organic Act of 1989 and the formation of the Cordillera Autonomous Region. The Galing Pook (Best

Place) Awards managed by the Galing Pook Foundation have been a significant motivation in improving local governance. These awards were organized in 1993 with the help of the Ford Foundation, the Local Government Academy, and the Asian Institute of Management, to recognize best practices and make a statement that decentralization and local governance works. A goal of the awards is for other LGUs to adopt the best practices.

Current Legal and Institutional Frameworks for Decentralization

The 1987 constitutional mandate to create LGUs[47] was given flesh in 1991 when President Aquino signed the Local Government Code (RA 7160) into law. In remarkable detail, the Code laid down the framework of central–local government relations. This is the primary legislation that propels the decentralization of powers and responsibility from the central or national government to the local government. Its provisions are aimed at promoting more responsive and accountable governance through the LGUs, and to improve technical efficiency and "subsidiarity" in governance. Subsidiarity emphasizes that management functions and responsibilities should be kept at the level where they could be most effectively addressed. This element of the LGC responds to the call for government to be more responsive to the needs of constituents by placing the responsibility for delivering government services in the hands of local institutions. Growing budget deficits also pushed the national government to divest itself of functions that could already be done at the local level.

There are at least three areas in which the 1991 LGC drastically differs from previous attempts at decentralization. The first is the extent and depth of devolution of functions that used to be enjoyed by national government agencies, particularly in the areas of health care, social services, infrastructure, and environmental and natural resources management. The second is in the area of fiscal autonomy granted to the LGUs. The third is the extent of popular participation in local governance. These three areas are discussed in more detail below.

Devolving National Government Functions

The 1991 LGC established the jurisdiction of the LGUs with respect to the national government.[48] Having decentralization in mind, the LGUs— provinces, cities, municipalities, and *barangays*—have been given authority and responsibility for institutions formerly controlled by the national government.[49] The LGC mandated that the provision of basic services and facilities such as agricultural extension services, healthcare and social welfare services, fisheries and aquatic resources, community-based forestry projects, and local infrastructure facilities such as roads, bridges, and school buildings have been devolved from national line agencies to local governments.

Starting with primary healthcare and social welfare services, the maintenance of healthcare and day-care centers is delegated to local governments. But the degree of responsibility delegated depends on the level of LGU. For instance, a municipal government has more responsibilities compared to barangays with regard to healthcare services. Municipal governments are mandated by the Code to implement programs and projects in the areas of primary health care, maternal and child care, and communicable and noncommunicable disease control (public health) services; in contrast, barangays are only mandated to maintain barangay healthcare and day-care centers. On the other hand, provinces are mandated to supervise healthcare services such as hospitals. Cities are mandated the same functions as the provincial and municipal governments.

Regarding social welfare, municipal governments are mandated to implement programs and projects in the areas of child and youth welfare, family and community welfare, women's welfare, welfare of the elderly and disabled persons, and community-based rehabilitation programs, beggars, street children, victims of drug abuse, and family planning services. Provincial-level services include projects for rebel returnees and evacuees, relief operations, and population development services (i.e., family planning).[50]

Agricultural facilities and activities, which include fisheries and aquatic resources, have also been devolved to the LGUs. Services such as distribution of planting materials and operation of farm produce collection and buying stations have been delegated to the barangays. Municipal governments have control over implementing on-site research services related to agriculture and fisheries, including distribution of breeder livestock and poultry and fingerlings, as well as distribution of rice, corn, and vegetables to seed farms and seedlings to fruit tree nurseries. Provinces assume agricultural services such as the prevention and control of plant and animal pests and diseases, dairy farms and livestock markets, and artificial insemination centers. They are also mandated to assist in the organization of farmer and fisher-folk cooperatives and other collective organizations, as well as the transfer of appropriate technology. The Agricultural and Fisheries Modernization Act of 1997 and the Fisheries Code of 1998 have strengthened the provision of the Code regarding fisheries and agriculture. For instance, the municipalities have been given the exclusive authority to grant fishery privileges in municipal waters and to impose rentals, fees, or other charges and penalize those who violate applicable fishery laws.[51]

Many functions of the Department of Environment and Natural Resources have also devolved to the LGUs. One is the implementation of community-based forestry projects, including the management and control of communal forests at the municipal level. Provincial responsibilities would include implementing pollution control laws, small-scale mining laws, and other laws pertaining to environmental protection. For instance, the Mining Act of 1995 (RA 7942) grants to LGUs the authority and responsibility, together with the Department of Environment and Natural Resources (DENR), to approve the issue of quarry permits in their jurisdiction. In the Clean Air Act of 1999 (RA 8749), the LGUs are given share responsibility for management and maintenance of air quality within their territorial jurisdiction.[52] Provisions in the Solid Waste Management Act (RA 9003) mandate the LGUs to sort, recycle, compost, and re-use waste.

Infrastructure facilities primarily intended to service the needs of LGU residents have also devolved, such as construction of roads and bridges, school buildings, clinics and healthcare centers, irrigation services and water supply systems, and drainage and sewage system for the municipalities. Provinces have similar functions with additional responsibilities such as implementing reclamation projects and low-cost housing and other multifamily residence construction projects.

Fiscal Autonomy

What distinguishes the post-Marcos decentralization initiatives from earlier initiatives is the degree of fiscal autonomy given to the LGUs. As will be demonstrated below, the decentralization initiatives of the 1990s attempted to grant fiscal autonomy to local governments commensurate to the level of responsibilities and functions devolved to them.

As mandated by the 1987 Constitution, the LGUs have the power to create their own revenues and to levy taxes, fees, and other charges, which accrue exclusively to the local governments.[53] A more interesting provision that was included in the Constitution and the LGC was institutionalization of the internal revenue allotment (IRA) for LGUs at the same time.[54] This has been a major source of revenue for most LGUs, many of which are completely dependent on the IRA. The IRA poses severe financial constraints for many LGUs, doubly so in light of decreasing allotments due to ballooning budget deficits.

IRA entitlements for LGUs were equivalent to 30 percent of taxes collected by the national government in 1992; this percentage increased to 35 percent in 1993, and rose to 40 percent in 1994 and thereafter.[55] IRA funds to the LGUs under Section 285 are distributed as follows: provinces, 23 percent; cities, 23 percent; municipalities, 34 percent; and barangays, 20 percent. The share of each province, city, and municipality is determined via a calculation that takes into consideration the following weighted variables: population, 50 percent; land area, 25 percent; and the extent of equal sharing of resources, 25 percent.

An important point here is that regardless of the available IRA amount, its release is *automatic*. The amount can only be changed upon the fulfillment of very stringent requirements. Therefore, unless the Local Government Code is amended, the LGUs' share in the IRA will be 40 percent indefinitely. Thus, the LGUs will have a 40-percent share in gross revenue collected by the national government from the preceding fiscal year from mining taxes, royalties, forestry and fishery charges, and so on. The Code also contains a scheme for computing the share in national wealth of each subnational government level. For instance, provinces' share in the national wealth is 20 percent; cities and municipalities, 45 percent; and barangays, 35 percent. In cases where natural resources are located in two or more provinces or municipalities or barangays, the computation is based on the population and land area of the LGU. Seventy percent is computed against the population and 30 percent against the land area. Another remarkable thing about the Code is the provision that LGUs should appropriate in their annual budget no less than 20 percent of the IRA to local development projects.

The power to tax has been devolved to the LGUs as well.[56] The taxation procedure should be uniform and more importantly, "equitable and based as far as practicable on the taxpayer's ability to pay."[57] But there are limitations to the taxation power of the LGUs, as it does not extend to taxes under the Cooperative Code of the Philippines and taxes of any kind levied by the national government, nor the levy of taxes on income, estate or inheritance, gifts, legacies, and other acquisitions *mortis causa;* customs duties; agricultural and aquatic products; business enterprises; and registration of motor vehicles and the like.

There is a formula allotted for computing the tax on each item that is taxable by the LGUs. For instance, a province may levy a tax on the transfer of real property ownership, provided that it is not more than 0.05 percent of the total consideration involved in such transaction. The province may also impose licensing fees and sales taxes on persons engaged in professions (professional tax), quarry resources, and on "amusements" (theater, sports, cinema, etc.).

There are many interesting provisions in the taxation powers of LGUs, especially with regard to exemptions. For example, take the case of the amusement tax. Operators and owners of venues such as theaters, sports arenas, cinemas, and concert halls are definitely not exempted from taxes, but may or may not be required to pay taxes depending on the nature of entertainment that takes place in such venues. The Code specifies that tax exemptions apply to owners of such venues when they host operas, classical concerts, dramas, recitals, painting and art exhibitions, musical programs, and literary and oratorical presentations are tax exempt. But owners of venues hosting pop, rock, and similar concerts are not tax exempt.[58]

Credit financing is another source of funding to which LGUs are entitled.[59] LGUs may contract loans, credit lines, and other forms of indebtedness with government and private banks as well as other lending institutions to finance the construction, improvement, or maintenance of public facilities, infrastructures, and even housing projects. They are also authorized to issue bonds, debentures, securities, collateral, notes and other obligations to finance self-liquidating, income-generating long-term projects. These bonds are still subject to the rules and regulations of the Central Bank and the Securities and Exchange Commission.

Camaraderie between and among LGUs is promoted with the provision that a local government that has a budget surplus may, with the approval of the majority of all *Sanggunian* members, extend grants, loans, or subsidies to other LGUs. Thus, situations in which LGUs might engage in unproductive competition may be minimized.

LGUs can also access foreign loans through multilateral and bilateral institutions. The World Bank, IMF, Ford Foundation, USAID, and CIDA are just some of the institutions that have disbursed loans and grants to finance local government projects such as infrastructure developments, leader training, and assistance in healthcare and social services projects. In 2000, the World Bank and the Philippines signed a US$100 million loan agreement for the Local Government Development and Finance Project. The project was expected to strengthen fiscal decentralization and self-reliance among LGUs, especially among lower-income LGUs.[60]

LGUs are also capacitated to enter into build-operate-transfer agreements (BOTs) to finance and construct infrastructure projects.[61] The LGUs are instructed to disclose all transactions involving BOTs to the public for transparency and accountability in case such projects fail. Under this mechanism, the project is given to the "lowest complying bidder"[62] whose offer is seen as an advantage to the local government. The LGU concerned would automatically grant the winning contractor the franchise to operate and maintain the facility, including the collection of tolls, fees, rentals, and charges. These tolls, fees, and charges must be approved by the local government and the levy and collection of such fees must be for a fixed period not to exceed 50 years. The contractor is liable for the maintenance and repair of the facilities included in the contract.

As discussed further in the next section, decentralization under the Local Government Code has created fiscal autonomy for LGUs, but has also opened a Pandora's box of problems over resource allocation and revenue generation. This could potentially aggravate the gap between the "have" and "have-not" municipalities, cities, and provinces, and pose serious obstacles to improved intergovernmental relations.

People's Participation in Governance

The LGC of 1991 institutionalized the participation of civil society organizations in the affairs of local governance, particularly its monitoring function on local government projects and programs to provide greater accountability. Accredited NGOs are tapped to participate in various councils in the LGUs. These bodies include the local development councils, prequalification bids and awards councils (PBACs), school boards, health boards, and peace and order councils. The LGC also provides for the direct involvement of civil society groups in the delivery of social services and facilities. Civil society organizations may also be involved in joint ventures and cooperative programs, financial and other forms of assistance; preferential treatment for marginal fisher-folk organizations and cooperatives; and financing, construction, maintenance operation, and management of infrastructure projects.[63]

The LGC also enables various civil society organizations to forge linkages with other institutions such as the Local Government Council, Local Government Academy, the various Leagues, and foreign funding agencies to advocate for decentralization and to enhance the capability of the local governments for self-governance. They may also engage in various forms of local participatory governance, including mandatory consultation and participation in hearings; recall of elected officials with unsatisfactory performance; local initiatives and referenda; sectoral representation in local legislative bodies; lobbying by petition signing, signature campaigns, and submission of position papers; forums, dialogues, and consultations with officials and candidates; bill drafting and sponsorship; filing, prosecution, and monitoring of complaints and cases before monitoring bodies; networking; and protest actions.[64] As will be seen below and in the next section, these provisions are laudable, but in practice, many of them open up possibilities for abuse or exploitation by local political elites, or are simply not used.

Increasing popular participation in governmental structures and enhancing the accountability of institutions have become important ingredients of political discourse in the Philippines. All local government officials in the Philippines are elected. Moreover, the LGC has bestowed on the citizenry the power to recall elected local officials for loss of confidence. A petition containing at least 25 percent of registered voters (of the LGU to which the elected local official subject to such recall belongs) or a resolution of a recall assembly (which consists of the LGU officials to which the elected local official subject to such recall belongs) constitutes valid grounds for a recall process to be acted upon by the Commission on Elections. The LGC provides that a recall election shall be set by the COMELEC not later than thirty to forty-five days after filing the recall petition or resolution.[65]

The decentralization process has the potential to unleash pent-up frustration with local leaders and the absence of any meaningful needs assessment monitoring and evaluation processes to ensure that local community needs are addressed. One example in terms of improving accountability is the effort of local watchdog groups, such as the Concerned Citizens of Abra, which has been engaged in monitoring road projects in Abra province.

In order to ensure transparency and hence deter shady dealings from taking place in government projects and procurements, two seats in the PBACs are reserved for NGOs in the local special body concerned. The task of this body is to oversee the prequalification of contractors, bidding, evaluation of bids, and recommendation of awards (Article 183). The PBAC's authority, however, is not all encompassing as "its scope of authority and jurisdiction applies only to local infrastructure projects and does not include procurement of supplies, purchase of office equipment, renovations and other disbursements by LGUs."[66]

In terms of putting the power of policymaking in the hands of the people, the LGC also provided for local initiative and referendum. As defined by the Code, "[L]ocal initiative is the legal process whereby the registered voters of an LGU may directly propose, enact, or amend any ordinance through an election called for the purpose." The local initiative could be resorted to should the legislative body of a particular LGU (*sanggunian*) fail to act favorably on a petition concerning the adoption, enactment, repeal, or amendment of an ordinance.[67]

Institutional arrangements at the local level are geared toward harnessing local expertise in local development planning and at the same time fostering citizens' ownership of development initiatives. The 1987 Philippine Constitution provides for representation of NGOs in regional development councils that were created specifically for administrative decentralization, acceleration of economic and social development, and to generally enhance the autonomy of local units (Article X, Section 14). The 1991 LGC has spelled out possible working arrangements and governing operational guidelines between LGUs and civil society organizations. Despite the apprehension of some sectors that decentralization will merely transfer power from national to self-aggrandizing local elites, the present institutional arrangement has presented NGOs and POs with an immense opportunity to increase the scale and impact of their participation in politics.

The Code states that civil society organizations should constitute not less than 25 percent of the total membership of fully organized local special bodies, namely the local development councils; prequalification, bids, and awards committees; health boards; health boards; peace and order councils; and people's law enforcement boards. In general, the functions of these local boards include proposing annual budgetary allocations for respective sectors; serving as an advisory committee; and creating committees that advise local agencies on matters such as the selection and promotion of personnel, budget review, and operations review.

The representation of fisher folk and their organizations in municipal/city fisheries and aquatic resources management councils (M/CFARMCs) is guaranteed by the 1998 Fisheries Code. The Fisheries Code mandates that an NGO representative, along with at least eleven fisher-folk representatives should be a member of these councils. Subject to the discretion of LGUs, barangay fisheries and aquatic resources management councils (BFARMCs) may also be created. When necessary, lakewide fisheries and aquatic resources management councils (LFARMCs) may also be created. In bays, gulfs, lakes, rivers, and dams bounded by two or more municipalities, integrated fisheries and aquatic resources management councils (IFARMCs), which consist of LGU representatives, one NGO representative, and at least nine from the fisher-folk sectors will also be created. These councils are tasked to "assist in the formulation of policies for the protection, sustainable development and management of fishery and aquatic resources" and assist in the formulation of national and municipal fisheries and industry development plans.[68] Membership in these councils enables civil society organizations to influence decisions by LGUs and/or the Department of Agriculture relating to the utilization of fisheries and aquatic resources. Such decisions include, but are not limited to the setting and/or establishment of the following: fees and other fishery charges[69]; catch ceiling limitations[70]; declaration of a closed season; designation of zones within which the construction of fish cages, fish traps, and other structures for the culture of fish and other fishery products are constructed[71]; declaration of fishery reserves[72]; and establishment of fishery refuges and sanctuaries.[73]

These institutional arrangements increase the possibility of local-level action. But responses to the availability of these opportunities have been varied. While some have eagerly sought accreditation in order to participate in local special bodies, others remain apprehensive that these bodies would be used by the government to co-opt civil society. The latter are also afraid that the government will use NGO council members to serve as part of the government's machinery. Since these bodies, such as the FARMCs, are not endowed with legislative or executive powers, some groups have raised the possibility that guarantees for NGO participation will be used only to legitimize unpopular local government decisions.[74] Some of these fears may be founded on past dealings with previous national and local governments that have demonstrated the desire to whitewash unpopular policies by courting the support of experts and NGOs. In other cases, fears on the part of civil society organizations may not be justified in the face of new leadership, but may be traced to previous experiences in dealing with insincere and uncooperative politicians who view NGOs with some disdain.

Despite these apprehensions, the participation of NGOs and POs in local special bodies is observable in many LGUs. Another significant trend is the creation of special bodies other than those explicitly provided for by the LGC, such as local environmental councils that have "localized jurisdictional mandates" (e.g., Palawan Council for Sustainable Development).[75] The most popular and innovative of such initiatives is the Naga City People's Council, a body that consists of NGOs and POs, which is empowered to participate in various levels of policy making.[76] Some LGUs such as General Santos and Baguio have gone as far as providing representation for new sectors such as tourism, business, sports, environment, and higher education, to sit in as sectoral representatives in their respective sanggunians.[77]

Civil society representation is also institutionalized by the Code in local legislative bodies. The Code mandates that there should be three sectoral representatives in local legislative bodies or *sanggunian* at all levels—municipal, city, and provincial. Three sectoral representatives are provided from (1) either the agricultural or industrial workers' group; (2) the women's sector; and (3) either the disabled and elderly sector, the indigenous communities, fisher folk, or any other sector.[78] The scope of participation by civil society organizations in local legislative bodies was institutionalized by a Supreme Court decision ruling which in essence provides that "the effectiveness of peoples' initiative as mandated by the 1987 Philippine Constitution should not be trivialized by limiting the process to resolutions and excluding ordinances from its coverage."[79] However, the enabling laws for the election of sectoral representatives in local legislative bodies are not yet enacted.

A DILG Opinion mandates that before national projects can be implemented, prior mandatory consultations are required, not only with the relevant *sanggunian* (as mandated by the LGC) but also with NGOs and POs.[80] However, the initial experience relating to this shows that the governing procedures on mandatory consultations are vulnerable to manipulation.

With the aim of institutionalizing a "comprehensive and decentralized project monitoring and evaluation system,"[81] then President Aquino mandated the establishment and adoption of the Regional Project Monitoring and Evaluation System (RPMES) through Executive Order No. 376. The executive order stipulated the two ways by which the role of NGOs as "project monitors" at both regional and subregional levels (provincial, city, and municipal) will be upheld: first, the RPMES is to be implemented by the development councils at the various local levels, and second, by their membership in project monitoring committees (PMCs). The NGO-authorized monitors have the responsibility of assisting the PMC or development council in monitoring and evaluation of projects by identifying implementation problems or outstanding performance through project reports, ensuring the effective and efficient implementation of projects through vigilance, and acting as government partners in ensuring transparency in project implementation.[82] "Subsequent funding requirements of the RPMES such as granting of financial incentives to NGOs monitors . . ." is provided in the General Appropriations Act.

President Ramos[83] broadened the types of projects that could be subjected to PMC monitoring,[84] provided for PO participation as "project monitors," and specified the number of seats allocated for NGOs and POs in

PMCs at all levels.[85] At the regional level, there should be three NGO/PO representatives (at least one shall come from the regional development council) and it is mandatory that two NGO/PO representatives in the provincial, city, and municipal PMCs are appointed as members.

In the area of environmental projects, there is a move to enhance transparency and social acceptability through the provisions for public participation in the environmental impact assessment (EIA) system. DENR Administrative Order No. 37, Series of 1996, enhanced the EIA system by broadening its scope, strengthening its implementation rules, making requirements more stringent, and subjecting the whole process to public scrutiny and acceptability. Article IV, Section I of the above order requires that the acceptability of a proposed project or undertaking could only be confidently determined through "meaningful public participation." Section 2 requires that proponents submit supporting documents showing efforts to convey to the public sufficient and easily discernible information about the project or undertaking. Section 3 requires that proponents initiate public consultations, and if necessary,[86] Section 4 requires the holding of public hearings.

In July 1995, President Ramos issued Executive Order No. 263, which provides for the adoption of community-based forest management (CBFM) as "the national strategy to achieve sustainable development and social justice." The CBFM represents a policy shift insofar as the decentralization of authority for forest resource management is concerned. Rather than employing external enforcement of regulatory mechanism, the communities themselves are entrusted with the responsibility for forest rehabilitation, protection, and conservation. Upon complying with prerequisites relating to ensuring sustainable forest resource utilization, organized communities may also be granted access to forest resources through long-term tenurial agreements with the government.

On the whole, the active participation of NGOs and POs in governance and policymaking may be considered as a manifestation or key indicator of the trend toward democratization in the country. Some of the more important cases that resulted from civil society's influence in policymaking are the Philippine Agenda 21 for "sustainable development," the Peace Agenda, and the Social Reform Agenda.[87]

Despite these laudable spin-offs and attempts at participatory governance under the LGC, there are a number of serious obstacles that impede popular participation in local decision making and governance. While many of the LGC provisions that attempt to introduce participatory governance in the political culture may be considered progressive, many of them remain underutilized. This is largely due to the lack of information dissemination and public awareness of such mechanisms. For example, the referendum initiative and recall provisions have been among the most underutilized mechanisms for increased government accountability.[88] These progressive provisions require a well-informed and well-organized citizenry to succeed. It is also feared that the recall process has been unscrupulously used by disgruntled rivals of local incumbents to harass or intimidate them. As will be pointed out in the next section, some of these obstacles arise not only from poor public awareness, but also from the gap between what the laws provide and what the local political culture allows.

Challenges in Decentralization: Issues in Public Administration and Government–Civil Society Interactions

A comparative analysis of why earlier phases of decentralization have failed in Asian countries will help to frame some contemporary challenges in public administration, especially budget allocation, and government–civil society interactions in the process of decentralization. The earlier phases of Asian countries' decentralization in the late 1970s and early 1980s failed due to a number of factors that relate to the mindset of national governments and their preference for strong, centralized states. Despite the variation in different patterns of decentralization found in Asian countries (India, Pakistan, Bangladesh, Thailand, Malaysia, Philippines, and China), in almost all cases, decentralization has been seen as a means of implementing national government policies, rather than facilitating local social and political development.[89] Likewise, attempts at decentralizing administration and planning in Thailand, the Philippines, Sri Lanka, Indonesia, Malaysia, and India often end up in failures because the political and administrative system refuses to relinquish central control and suffers from limited popular participation.[90]

In many Asian countries, there is still little conceptual clarity about the meaning of decentralization and devolution, and there are obvious gaps between policy and rhetoric on the one hand and implementation on the other.[91] Reyes, for example, notes that several decades of attempts to reform public-service delivery systems have faced obstacles posed by government bureaucracies.[92] A dysfunctional administrative system, budgetary deficits, declining resources, population growth, and rising public expectations impeded public sector organizational reform.

Despite some considerable gains of decentralization in enabling more public participation in local governance, it has also created a number of problems and unintended consequences. Regime politics and interrelated vested interests of rural elites, bureaucrats, politicians, and NGOs frustrate the extent to which decentralization promotes democratizing activities.[93] These governance problems related to decentralization are due to persistent features of Philippine political culture, which is dominated by strong local bosses and political families, patronage, and corruption.[94] As feared by many, the strength of local power wielders could be unwittingly strengthened by decentralization. There was the perennial problem of patronage and political appointments of civil servants to replace qualified personnel disliked by local political leaders, particularly in the transition and reorganization of LGUs in the first two years of the Aquino administration.[95] While some degree of decentralization had taken place under the Aquino administration, provincial politicians interested in occupying the central state apparatus had frustrated such attempts.[96]

In the early phase of LGC implementation, problems were noted in the delineation of new roles and responsibilities between municipalities and provinces due to the lack of clarity in the roles of devolved workers due to inadequate guidelines and overall lack of knowledge of LGU policies. New demands were placed on the devolved staff already performing multiple roles due to the need to interface with local leaders and NGOs. There was a lack of supervision and poor program implementation, especially due to the low priority given to social services by local leaders and their political opposition to programs, which affect their relationship with devolved staff.[97] In their analysis of the CIDA-funded LGSP, Angeles and Gurstein[98] noted the gender-specific difficulties of newly devolved staff in adjusting to "the innumerable pressures and demands in their work, as they need[ed] to exhibit greater flexibility and ability to assume new roles and responsibilities."

In one province where the LGSP was implemented, municipal staff members, mostly women, who were given scholarships to finish their master's degree in a local university in the capital city, were unable to finish their studies. In fact, about 80 percent of government employees who have enrolled in graduate programs in this university have not been able to graduate or finish their theses. Those at the stage of thesis writing did not feel that they had adequate support from both their government bosses and faculty supervisors, in terms of time off from work, and advice in research and writing. The women students particularly fall through the cracks because they are increasingly relied upon by their bosses in understanding the requirements of the new devolution regime, and yet, rarely get help from their husbands and other family members in their domestic duties.[99]

Decentralization processes have also led to a number of problems in the cooperation between LGUs, POs, and NGOs. In the first place, there is a lack of a common definition of NGOs, and thus the criteria for their accreditation for program participation, given their diversity, multiple roles, and objectives are unclear. There is also confusion between NGOs (i.e., nonprofit organizations) and private sector (profit-oriented companies), which are given equal space in LGU representation. Many so-called NGOs accredited by local governments are close to local officials or economic elites who saw new political opportunities under the LGC to penetrate local state institutions. Many smaller NGOs and grassroots organizations could not compete with the bigger or elite-controlled NGOs in this uneven political playing field. Due to the lack of understanding and appreciation of NGO roles and approaches to development issues, and the lack of common understanding of rationales behind PO–NGO cooperation, there is often an adversarial attitude toward NGOs by local officials, especially those who do not share their political orientation. This exacerbates the low levels of participation and representation of NGOs and POs in various special bodies, as well as the marginalization of NGOs in critical special bodies such as local development councils that deliberate on highly controversial land use, farmland conversion, and agrarian reform issues.[100] In most cases, local government officials fail to demonstrate enough trust, sincerity, and cooperation in dealing with NGOs, POs, and other groups that could be their potential partners in local governance. Decentralization programs and projects that rely on local elites often encounter difficulties and lead to poor outcomes, especially when popular organizing efforts are not supported and when capacities of alternative nonelite organizations are weak.[101]

The various legal mechanisms and organizational venues for active civil society participation are hampered by a number of procedural problems and structural obstacles that limit participation and utilization by the public. In the first place, some of the local laws passed by local governments work against the interests of some civil society groups, such as the continued eviction of slum dwellers, and criminalization of street vending and squatting on private and public lands.[102] The effectiveness of avenues for citizen participation is limited by lack of transparency, poor dissemination of information on new policies and participation guidelines, lack of consultation, lack of financial resources, and overcentralization of decision making on the part of the state. These problems occur at both policymaking and implementation levels. On the part of civil society, weaknesses seem to be underutilization of existing avenues, lack of technical expertise, poor organizational capacities, fear of cooptation by the state and general distrust of state initiatives, and ideological differences that limit people's ability to take a united position toward government and coordinate efforts and work together.[103]

Mutual distrust between state and civil society, and their ambivalence toward each other, influence much of government–civil society interactions. Civil society organizations' cynicism toward the state is the result of past experiences in dealing with national and local governments that are largely seen as corrupt, inefficient, and lacking in autonomy to mediate conflicting elite interests and uphold the public good. This negative perception of the state had deepened under the Marcos regime and the short-lived Estrada administration. Although the Aquino and Ramos administrations were largely seen to have been more open to the democratization process, they had also attempted to use civil society organizations to create their own base of political support and marginalize those critical of their policies. The Estrada government had done the same, but ironically, its bad policies have brought a considerable degree of unity and cooperation among various opposition groups that eventually led to a peaceful transition to the new Macapagal–Arroyo administration in January 2001.

Provisions on fiscal autonomy under the LGC have created problems surrounding resource generation and allocation. The biggest issue is the manner by which the IRA is distributed. Some LGUs argue that IRA distribution is not equitable, as some units receive more than necessary while others do not receive enough to sustain even minimum levels of specified functions. The system of computing for the IRA is cited as reason for this. There is inequitable sharing in the distribution of the allotment among the provinces and cities/municipalities. One argument is that provinces should be receiving more than the cities/municipalities due to the cost, for instance, of maintaining hospitals, which have devolved to them.[104] LGUs that could not raise local revenues to pay devolved staff face severe financial constraints. Hence, a situation where a number of local governments, especially municipalities and provinces, could not afford the cost of devolution in spite of their increased IRA share is not uncommon.[105]

Another issue is the dependence of LGUs on the IRA that they are receiving. In a 1999 study, the National Statistics Coordination Board found that the IRA represented two-thirds of LGU resources. For every 100 pisos received by the LGUs, an average of 67.50 came from the IRA, 18.70 from tax revenues, and 13.80 from nontax revenues. The study also revealed the disparity in IRA distribution. The five provinces with the highest IRAs in 1999 were Negros Occidental, Pangasinan, Cebu, Quezon, and Isabela, the more urbanized provinces. Provinces that could barely keep pace with economic developments in the country such as Biliran, Guimaras, Siquijor, Camiguin, and Batanes received the lowest IRAs.[106]

An example of the loss of fiscal independence when the LGC was implemented is Quezon City. A study conducted by the Local Government Center of the College of Public Administration at the University of the Philippines in Diliman for the 1990–1995 period shows that the city government revenue structure had shifted. Before implementation of the Code, the city's revenue structure consisted primarily of locally generated revenues. Almost 85 percent of its revenue came from its own sources. But the outcome changed in 1992 when local revenues decreased to 68 percent, and in the succeeding year, more than 55 percent of its revenues came from external revenues because of the substantial increase in the IRA and loans from government and private financial institutions.[107]

In addition to the inequitable distribution of the IRA is the continuing dominance of national government institutions in the allocation of financial resources in the administrative system. Given the extreme levels of minutiae involved in regulations emanating from the central government, it is not surprising that it is still extensively involved in the micromanagement of local government. Paradoxically, the budgets of national agencies such as the Departments of Health, Agriculture, and Environment and Natural Resources continue to increase in spite of the devolution and transfer of the delivery of services and personnel to local governments.[108] This paradoxical situation demonstrates that the national government has much to lose in completely giving up its control of national line agencies such as health, environment, and agriculture, where political benefits could be gained.

The technical knowledge of the LGUs of credit financing is also questionable. Not all LGU executives know how to engage in credit financing, which is a viable source of funding as provided for by the Code. There were no institutional agencies to inform the local governments of the available credit facilities during the early stages of Code implementation. Hence, not all have used that resource to add to their revenues, and until 1996, only a few really managed to negotiate loans and issue bonds through credit financing.[109]

The above problems in government–civil society interactions and public administration in the course of devolution and decentralization are discussed in greater detail, while focusing on environment and natural resource management, poverty alleviation, healthcare policy, and education reform.

These issues or areas of concern are most affected by decentralization and devolution under the LGC. These also happen to be the research topics most familiar to academic researchers. There are other issues or areas affected by decentralization, such as regional development planning, urban housing and management, interethnic relations and religious tensions, tourism, family planning, disaster preparedness, and industrial policy development. However, very little research has focused on these topics.

Decentralization in Environmental Management Sector

Faced with the continuing decline of environmental quality and ecological sustainability, there has been ongoing discussion on the extent of these problems and what went wrong with the environmental agenda of past and present governments. One of the major issues in this discussion is the question of decentralizing the environment sector. Proponents of the Green Agenda have pointed out that the big-brother approach of the state characterized by a highly centralized and police-like administration of the environment was highly ineffective in protecting and managing the country's ecological systems. The private sector, led by Philippine Business for the Environment and Philippine Business for Social Progress have meanwhile advocated voluntary action as part of their environmental and social responsibility. On the other hand, proponents of a centralized approach have argued that environmental problems transcend political borders by definition and cannot be confined to a particular area or sector. Aside from the question of whether to decentralize the environment sector, other big questions to be resolved are: What kind of decentralization? How to decentralize? In order to resolve these two questions, we must first identify the critical decentralization issues in the environment sector, which will serve as points of clarification for further discussion.

National policy now encourages marine resource co-management between the national government and local communities, with a strong emphasis on decentralization of decision making and recognition of local territorial use rights in fisheries. Decentralization plays a critical role in the strategy of fisheries co-management in a number of countries throughout the world, including the Philippines.[110] These cases point to the planning and implementation of community-based management and co-management systems that require new legal, administrative, and institutional arrangements at both national and community levels to complement contemporary political, economic, social, and cultural structures.[111] In the Philippines, the importance of strong community support for the success of decentralized decision making in marine co-management has been well documented. For example, the great success of management at Apo marine reserve was largely due to community support for the reserve concept, which has been actively maintained for the past sixteen years. In contrast, the level of community support for the Sumilon reserve waned over this period due to sociopolitical factors. These case histories have had a profound effect on marine resource management in the Philippines, particularly on the design of the National Integrated Protected Area System.[112] Decentralization is also critical in the success of community-based forest resource management. The experiences and issues surrounding the implementation of decentralization and devolution approaches in the Asia-Pacific region have been explored in the International Seminar on Decentralization and Devolution of Forest Management, held in Davao, the Philippines, on 30 November–4 December 1998.[113]

In discussing decentralization of the environment sector, it should be clarified that "devolution" does not mean the same as "decentralization" as provided for in Republic Act 7160, popularly known as the Local Government Code of 1991. Devolution of functions and powers of the DENR to LGUs, although important, is only one aspect of the decentralization process. Other aspects include "people's empowerment" through community participation, the Green Agenda, and corporate environmental and social responsibility or the "greening of business." A number of critical decentralization issues affecting the environment sector may be seen in the following areas: (1) devolution of the DENR as provided in the LGC of 1991; (2) participation of local communities; (3) civil society participation; and (4) the role of the private business sector.

Pursuant to the LGC of 1991, the DENR devolved some of its functions and powers to local governments. The rules and regulations implementing the devolution process are covered by Executive Orders 192 and 503, DENR Administrative Order 30, and the DENR-DILG Joint Memorandum Circular No. 98-01. Based on Section 17 of the LGC of 1991 and Section 3 of DENR Administrative Order 30, five areas of devolution were defined: (1) forest management; (2) protected areas and wildlife; (3) environmental management; (4) mines and geoscience development; and (5) land management. In general, the role of the LGUs (in coordination with the DENR) is to adopt adequate measures to protect the environment and conserve land, mineral, marine, forest, and other resources within their territorial jurisdiction. On the other hand, the DENR is mandated by RA 7160 to transfer to the concerned LGUs, the personnel and assets including pertinent records and equipment corresponding to the devolved functions. The devolution of the DENR did not diminish its centrality and importance in the environment sector. In fact, Section 1.1 of DENR Administrative Order No. 30 stated that: "The DENR shall remain as the primary government agency responsible for the conservation, management, protection, development and proper use of the country's environment and natural resources and the promotion of sustainable development." What the LGC hopes to achieve is not to diminish the role of the DENR but to institutionalize the LGUs as active partners in the sustainable management and development of the country's environment and natural resources. By doing so, it is hoped that devolution will lead to the empowerment of the LGUs, thus decentralizing the environmental management sector.

Although RA 7160 and its implementation rules and regulations appear to have "all bases covered" in terms of the devolution of DENR to the LGUs, practical experience in devolution has shown potential areas of difficulty. In a study Ramon J. P. Paje of DENR in 1992 involving a conceptual dissection of RA 7160, attention was focused on perceived issues and problems that give rise to legislative dysfunction. According to Paje, Code loopholes and areas of conflict were rooted in "broadly encompassing and expansive statements of functions and duties ascribed to the differing legislative and executive LGU bodies." Devolution of environmental management functions is adversely affected by the overlap, encroachment, duplication, confusion, and conflict in functions stemming from so-called "gray areas" in implementation, especially where the Code is silent or does not have clearcut provisions.

First, in particular, there is the issue of technical capacity and competency of LGUs, especially in the areas of mining, environmental protection, forest management, and the like. Considering the relatively low number of technical personnel and equipment transferred by the DENR to LGUs, it is expected that a shortage of technical expertise will remain a limiting factor in the effective implementation of the devolution process.

Second is the issue of financial support to local units. Considering the limited internal revenue allotment (IRA), devolved environment and natural resources programs and activities such as the Integrated Social Forestry Program and forest protection face the danger of inadequate or nonexistent financial support from concerned LGUs. This situation can be aggravated by the population bias of the mandated allocation formula (i.e., population,

50 percent; land area, 25 percent; equal sharing of resources, 25 percent), which leaves the upland programs (mostly located in remote and sparsely populated municipalities) with low levels of funding.

Third are administrative intricacies that, taken together, can become a major obstacle to the actual transfer of the devolved functions and personnel to LGUs. Among such administrative intricacies are (1) lack of office space; (2) increased overhead costs; (3) high salaries of national government agency staff devolved to LGUs; (4) nonacceptance by LGUs of devolved personnel; (5) displacement of devolved personnel; and (6) local politics (e.g., local chief executives may wish to accept only prospective supporters/voters).

Lastly, there is the issue of parallel organizations and duplication of functions. Although optional, RA 7160 under Section 484 mandates the appointment of a Provincial Environment and Natural Resources Officer (PENRO), a Municipal Environment and Natural Resources Officer (MENRO), and a City Environment and Natural Resources Officer (CENRO). Despite the clear definition of their functions through the issuance of Direct Administrative Order 30, duplications and conflicts are likely to occur given the broad functions of local chief executives and the relatively encompassing duties and responsibilities of the ENROs. These include, among others, the formulation of measures, development of plans and strategies, and coordination with government and NGOs pertaining to the delivery of services and provision of adequate facilities relative to environment and natural resource functions as provided for under Section 17 of the Code. Similarly, the DENR, being one of the agencies whose major functions were not devolved to LGUs, is mandated under Section 28 of the Code to further deconcentrate its retained functions and thereby strengthen its regional and field offices, specifically the PENRO and CENRO. This situation can cause the creation of parallel organizations at the field level, particularly in the provinces, whereby a DENR PENRO and a provincial ENRO may possibly be created.

Environment and natural resources functions devolved to municipal LGUs were different from those devolved to the provincial LGUs. For the municipalities, program implementation and management dealt with community-based projects and communal forests. Functions devolved to the provinces pertained to law enforcement, such as enforcement of forestry, mining, and environmental laws. Without clear-cut policies, a possible problem that can arise is whether municipalities that implement community-based projects can apprehend illegal loggers in their respective areas of jurisdiction when the Code did not stipulate law enforcement functions to municipal LGUs. What policies and/or administrative arrangements, therefore, should be instituted to address such potential legal conflicts?

Decentralizing the environmental sector has always been the avowed goal of civil society organizations. The long history of environmental advocacy by POs and NGOs worldwide has led to development of the Green Agenda, a comprehensive program of environmental protection and sustainable development. In the Philippines, where there is a strong civil society, the Green Agenda has been pioneered by environmental organizations such as Haribon Foundation Inc., Balik Kalikasan, World Wildlife Fund, and Green Peace Philippines, among others. Philippine POs and NGOs have even taken the lead in voter education by initiating the so-called Green Vote campaign during the 1992 and 1998 national and presidential elections. Overall, the situation in civil society with regard to the environment sector is quite positive. In terms of critical decentralization issues involving civil society and the environment sector, there are two issues that crop up. First is the increasing "politicization" of civil society along ideological lines, and the second is the issue of strategic positioning of the Green Agenda vis-à-vis the national government's environmental agenda. There is a need to address the "politicization" of civil society because the line that traditionally separates science and politics is getting blurred and sometimes a political agenda is the primary reason for environmental advocacy. What is the true state of the Philippine environment? Are incinerators really that bad? These are some of the questions that need objective answers based on scientific facts and not on political convictions alone. The question of strategic positioning of the Green Agenda vis-à-vis the state's environmental agenda should also be addressed since the Green Agenda can form the basis of a political party's government platform. Again, the critical issue here is whether or not to separate science and politics. Can the Green Agenda be the basis of a genuine decentralization of the environmental sector? Is civil society the appropriate vehicle to launch the decentralization process in the environmental sector?

For its part, the main issues affecting the local community in terms of environmental protection and management relate to issues of power and the decision-making role of the local community. Power is considered an important issue because as the primary stakeholders and/or beneficiaries, the local communities from the barangay (village) to the *purok* (ward) level have direct access or interaction with the environment. As the environmental maxim "think globally act locally" illustrates, decentralizing the environment sector can only be achieved by genuine people empowerment at the local level since everyone must first deal with their immediate environment. Since environmental advocacy involves political decision making, the issue of what role the local community will play in any environmental planning or undertaking by either local or national government must be taken into consideration. There must be a dynamic interaction between the national government, the LGUs and the local community in order to prevent the NIMBY, or "not in my backyard," and NIMEY, "not in my election year" syndromes, which often characterize the mindset of the local community and the LGUs.

Decentralization and Poverty Alleviation

Postwar governments in the Philippines considered poverty alleviation as a priority goal. In the post-Marcos transition, the Aquino government specifically mentioned poverty alleviation in its Medium-Term Development Plan, which launched the Low Income Municipalities program that focused on social services delivery to some fifth- and sixth-class municipalities. Under the Ramos administration, a comprehensive and coherent poverty reduction framework, the Social Reform Agenda (SRA), was formulated. The program was developed alongside multisectoral national summits, including the Anti-Poverty Summit, which created the Social Reform Council, the Presidential Council on Countryside Development, and Presidential Commission to Fight Poverty. It was launched during a "People Empowerment Caucus" in September 1994 as a package of poverty alleviation programs and an exercise in participatory governance. It was the first attempt by the bureaucracy to coordinate the functions of various government agencies that agreed on a minimum basic needs approach.[114] The SRA was institutionalized through the enactment in 1997 of RA 8425, the Social Reform and Poverty Alleviation Act, which led to the creation of the Social Reform Council, the mother organization for the antipoverty programs.

The SRA is a package of interventions organized around nine flagship programs under a lead government agency. Each program aimed at meeting the critical needs of farmers, fisher folk, indigenous peoples, and the urban poor ("basic sectors"). It highlighted social, economic, and environmental structural reforms, as well as governance-related reform. The SRA differed from previous poverty alleviation efforts in its shift in focus from income to socioeconomic governance and the cultural dimensions of poverty; use of decentralized, participatory approaches; emphasis on setting the agenda and poverty targets at the local level; and the integration of the efforts of various agencies through a convergence strategy.[115]

SRA implementation involved the creation of technical groups at all government levels, including the Legislative and Executive Development Advisory Committee (LEDAC) and of basic-sector counterpart councils in all regions of the country. SRA's institutionalization facilitated the passage of the Fisheries Code and the Indigenous Peoples' Rights Act, among other legislation affecting the four population groups, and the establishment of a consultative group among donor agencies focused on poverty. SRA implementation also included, albeit with uneven success, minimum basic needs (MBN) monitoring at the municipal level as the core strategy of the SRA convergence policy.[116] In accordance with the 1991 Local Government Code, the LGUs have the primary responsibility for the antipoverty campaign, including adoption at the municipal level of the Comprehensive and Integrated Delivery of Social Services (CIDSS) and Community-Based Poverty Indicators and Monitoring System (CBPIMS), both based on the MBN approach.

There are a number of issues critical to the success of this poverty alleviation program within a decentralized framework. First is the issue of financial resources. Three special funds totaling 6 billion pesos were created to augment regular resources to attain the objectives of the SRA: the 1996 Poverty Alleviation Fund, 1996 Local Government Empowerment Fund, and 1997 Poverty Alleviation Fund. Solita and Toby Monsod provided an excellent analysis of the SRA's financial difficulties. The lack of funds was not immediately obvious because the government's budget for the program increased by 53.6 billion pesos in 1996, a 253-percent rise from 20 billion pesos in the previous year, to which Congress added a 4-billion-peso Poverty Alleviation Fund for a total of 78 billion pesos. The figure seemed to have increased even more to 85.6 pesos in 1997. However, upon closer examination, Monsod and Monsod concluded that the 1996 SRA did not represent new money, and the actual increase was only 4.5 billion pesos. The additional amount was the result of re-labeling, that is, 82 percent of the increase in the SRA budget was actually the budget increase for the Philippine National Police. Other funding-related problems included diversion of scarce resources, misallocation, low actual utilization of funds, and the unconsolidated SRA-related budget.[117]

The second issue relates to the problem of leadership and continuity of poverty-related programs, that is, how the success of poverty alleviation programs depends a lot on the desires of national leaders to continue such programs within a decentralized framework. This is tied to the issue of institutionalization and sustainability of programs, particularly how decentralization could help prevent the overpoliticization of the poverty agenda, and the perpetuation of patronage politics.

These issues became very clear when the Estrada administration came to power. The fate of the SRA components became uncertain as President Estrada launched the Kilusan Kontra Kahirapan or Movement Against Poverty, and replaced the SRA nomenclature with the Poverty Eradication Program bearing his name. The Estrada administration had insisted on pursuing, mainly in rhetoric, a poverty eradication program rather than a poverty alleviation program, and popularized the president's campaign slogan "Erap Para Sa Mahirap" (Erap for the Poor). It aimed to reduce the incidence of poverty from 32.2 percent to 20 percent by the end of 2004, a 2 percent average reduction for each term Estrada is in office. This administration's antipoverty program refocused SRA on food security, modernization of agriculture and fisheries within the context of sustainable development, low-cost multifamily housing, active participation of the LGUs, and protection of the poor against crime and violence, all components that address the minimum basic needs of survival, security, and enabling services. The program's centerpiece is the attainment of food security and poverty alleviation through agricultural modernization, as embodied in the Agriculture and Fisheries Modernization Act. The Act intends to transform agriculture and fisheries into a technology-driven sector spurred by agribusiness by operationalizing the "Strategic Agriculture and Fisheries Development Zones" or "Food Baskets" approach. Another strategy was the consolidation of agricultural loan programs to make rural credit more accessible and affordable to small farmers and fisherfolk.[118]

This leads us now to the third issue of using expert and local knowledge and participatory governance strategies to support popular participation, as well as social learning to improve plans and program implementation. Concretely, this is concerned with how decentralization could be harnessed to combine the technical knowledge of experts and the local knowledge of poor communities, and the cooperation or partnership among government, policy researchers, academics, and local communities to attack poverty. For example, the Estrada administration's handling of its antipoverty agenda points to lessons to be learned from a flawed program and failed implementation due to lack of broad-based consultation and public input. The Estrada program targets the 100 poorest families in each province and in each city; the government is expected to deliver integrated and comprehensive services to enable them to get out of poverty by 2004. The Lingap Para Sa Mahihirap Program Fund was established as an antipoverty fund to be administered by the National Anti-Poverty Commission.[119] Critics point to specific weaknesses, such as insufficient budget allocations for the program and unrealistic eligibility requirements of the Economic Recovery through Agricultural Productivity (ERAP) bonds, which were effectively limited to large-scale businesses and large landowners. The most significant problem with the program is its lack of coherence due to the Estrada administration's deliberate revisions or departures from the concepts imbedded in the SRA, which were informed by development discourse beyond the Philippines. Estrada's alternative plan did not include more generic reforms (e.g., redistribution efforts, including agrarian reform); the role of basic-sector organizations and nongovernmental organizations; and the synchronization of antipoverty efforts by the National Anti-Poverty Commission. By abandoning the spirit of the SRA, mainly because of its association with the Ramos administration, the Estrada antipoverty program's reach and coverage have been considerably reduced. Targeting the poorest 100 families in every municipality would not meet the government's goal of reducing poverty by 20 percent in five years.[120] While the Estrada administration decided to delegate the task of ensuring food security for the poor to the LGUs, it had no clear system of prioritizing the LGUs in antipoverty programming, including providing direction on which vulnerable populations should be targeted at the various local levels, determining the availability of adequate funds, and providing the organizational infrastructure for local governments to mobilize various sectors within the community. Hence, the potential positive impact of poverty alleviation programs has not been maximized.

The fourth issue concerns the need to develop a comprehensive, area-based poverty alleviation program and community-based monitoring and service-delivery component that build on the experience of SRA implementation and its community-based CIDSS component. The current devolution process had provided the democratic space for some LGUs, progressive local leaders, and NGOs to create social safety nets to address the needs of poor communities in response to particular crises, especially in 1997.

In their analysis, Bautista, Angeles, and Dionisio accurately predicted the dim prospects for elevating the Estrada antipoverty slogan into a comprehensive and consistent program that could eventually conceptualize, nurture, and take responsibility for future social safety net programs. However, they also noted more optimistically some concrete indications that the more effective components of the SRA would continue, such as the CIDSS of the Department of Social Welfare and Development, which facilitated the interface between government and civil society groups. Despite some weaknesses of the SRA, particular components such as the CIDSS and the related CBPIMS, particularly the UNDP-funded programs for pilot sites in fifth- and sixth-class municipalities, have received favorable assessments. By December 1999, the 1,290 *barangays* in the fifty-six pilot municipalities in six provinces had successfully installed respective enhanced MBN-CBPIMS. Interagency province and municipality technical working groups had been established as institutional mechanisms for the convergence of poverty alleviation efforts that would strengthen regional-, provincial-, and municipal-level delivery systems. The working groups coordinated and integrated the efforts of various agencies, such as the National Statistics Office, the local planning and development office, local agricultural extension and social workers, and the local government operations officer.[121]

There were other documented cases of successful interventions that benefited from devolution. One such case is in San Carlos City, where the municipal government used its IRA to purchase private lots for housing construction and created an innovative payment scheme for indigent families to build their own houses. Another is in San Miguel, Bohol, where an outbreak of severe diarrhea in 1994 prompted the mayor to mobilize local residents to set up an infirmary and healthcare assistance program for poor communities, relying primarily on ninety-seven healthcare workers. In Surigao City, the LGU utilized its 20 percent development fund to purchase construction materials and employ poor residents displaced from their jobs to build public works that benefited 104,909 residents.[122]

Some LGUs in the poorest municipalities (designated as fourth and fifth class based on revenue levels) were also successful in instituting comprehensive municipal development programs to address livelihood and other concerns in their communities. For example, the Comprehensive Agricultural Development of Zamboangita, Negros Oriental, and the Accelerated Agriculture and Fisheries Productivity Program are cases in point. One particularly impressive case in instituting antipoverty programs that benefited from the climate of decentralization is the Municipality of Valencia, Negros Oriental. A participatory and comprehensive development plan for the municipality was developed by town officials, with the help of community organizers who mobilized the local folk to serve in several municipality-wide committees. These committees focus on specific issues such as agricultural development and subsistence, education and adult literacy, infrastructure and water supply, and health. They reached a level of organization that enabled them to develop an integrated system for purposes of delivering social services to residents, particularly the poor, and obtaining taxes from a surprisingly willing group of poor clients to sustain the services they received. The townwide cooperation helped the local government prepare for an outbreak of dengue fever by determining the blood type of its residents and establishing a network of blood donors from among relatives in the event they contracted the disease or other future health problems. In the short span of three years, Valencia succeeded in upgrading its status from a fifth-class to a third-class municipality.

LGUs could learn from these experiences in San Carlos City and Valencia in the areas of poverty monitoring, implementing antipoverty programs in their communities, and activating social safety nets to mitigate the effects of various crises. It is worthwhile to ask why such community-based programs succeeded in these two places and not elsewhere. Indeed, we need to identify the conditions under which decentralization and local-level cooperation between government and civil society could bring about economic prosperity through democratic governance. It is obvious in the case of San Carlos and Valencia, as well as Naga City, another showcase in successful local-level partnerships, that these places have progressive and visionary leaders who are able to transcend the perils of factional politics and obtain the cooperation of diverse social and political groups within their constituencies. They were also able to take advantage of new opportunities opened up by decentralization by generating new sources of revenue, coordinating government programs and agencies, and linking up with various outside institutions such as academics and international donors.

Community-based schemes to monitor poverty and identify the populations most vulnerable to shocks are quite limited. However, implementation of the CIDSS has been relatively successful as an experiment in cooperation among government agencies and between government and civil society that employed targeting, community organizing, and a total family approach. Poor barangays under the CIDSS experienced greater reductions in unmet basic needs compared to those that were not under this program. Despite the usual problems with multiagency cooperation efforts, it would be regrettable if government does not build on the groundwork of LGUs, academics, NGOs, and community workers in pilot areas in the interest of fast-tracking poverty alleviation efforts and activating social safety nets when future crises occur.

Decentralization in Healthcare Sector

Decentralization has been touted as a desirable organizational reform in the international healthcare literature.[123] Lessons from the management experience of large-scale district-level projects in Ghana, India, Iran, Korea, Philippines, Thailand, and Zaire point to the need to strengthen district-level management and for greater decentralization.[124] Decentralization requires a review of existing organizational structures and the strengthening of national-level planning and management capacities. However, there has been a lack of practical considerations worldwide on how to implement such reforms, particularly in determining the role of national and local government levels and the general public in policy formulation, planning, and implementation of policies and plans in the absence of formal controls.[125]

Prior to implementation of the LGC in 1991, there had already been some attempts to decentralize health education programs in the Philippines. In the early 1980s, for example, adolescent fertility information was regionalized in response to a national decentralization program and the need for a regional service-oriented approach to the problem of adolescent fertility.[126] The introduction of the 1991 LGC radically changed the structure of the public health system. The World Bank, in a document analyzing the risks and opportunities of the devolution of healthcare services in the Philippines, argues that the public health system is "the most affected sector within the national government."[127] The most contentious issue relating to the devolution of healthcare services is the disparity between resource allocation and responsibilities devolved to the LGUs under the decentralization program. This argument has two components: One, while healthcare service delivery is devolved to the LGUs, the budget of the national-level agency, the Department of Health (DOH) has steadily increased. Second, there has been an "inequitable burden of devolved functions across categories of local governments."[128]

The DOH is one of the four government agencies in the Philippines mandated to devolve its functions to LGUs in compliance with the LGC of 1991 (RA 7160). For instance, responsibility for hospitals and other tertiary healthcare centers has been devolved to the provinces, while the responsibility for the provision of primary health care and the purchase of medical supplies has been devolved to the municipalities.[129] Based on interviews with local government officials, health officers, and fieldworkers, Borlagdan, Gabronino, and Tracena[130] noted that strengthening the LGUs is expected to narrow the gap between health officers and fieldworkers, leading to a speedier decision-making process and program implementation. They predict further deterioration of the healthcare delivery system due to the questionable financial capability of the LGUs to absorb these devolved functions.

The USAID-funded Governance and Local Democracy Project found that 86 percent of the national budget is still under the control of and spent by national government agencies and offices.[131] Specifically, the budget of the DOH increased from 7.5 billion pisos in 1991 to 12.8 billion pisos in 1997. This occurred in spite of the fact that a large chunk of healthcare expenses in that period were assumed by the local governments, including salaries of 54,945 DOH personnel who had been "devolved" to local governments.[132]

There are also indications that unless apprehensions relating to security of tenure and compensation can be successfully resolved, devolved healthcare personnel themselves could pose as powerful stumbling blocks to decentralization initiatives. During the Ramos administration, the legislature approved a bill to re-centralize the public health system in response to a series of nationwide protests staged by devolved healthcare workers.[133] Many of these workers were protesting low salaries resulting from low IRA shares and lack of job security in the face of unfriendly local governments who had to approve the hiring and retention of healthcare personnel.

The seriousness of these problems obliges us to ask whether they could be adequately addressed within the existing institutional framework. In the study, *Seven Years of Devolution: Challenges and Strategies,* Juan Perez III, director of the Local Government Assistance and Monitoring Service argues that the existing framework for Philippine decentralization does not sufficiently address the requisite technical elements necessary for proper functioning of the healthcare system. He stated that contrary to what was envisioned by the LGC, local health boards are not in a position to handle problems relating to the transition of health service delivery from the national to the local governments. The resolution of most of these problems remains outside the ambit of local health board authorities.[134]

While the country's healthcare decentralization experience is replete with failures, nonetheless there is a consensus among the relevant stakeholders that re-centralization is not the appropriate solution. Former President Ramos, with the advice of the DOH and the LGUs themselves, vetoed the bill proposing the re-centralization of healthcare services.

Decentralization in Education Sector

Prior to passage of the LGC, the Philippine government had already initiated some decentralized programs, such as the Dropout Intervention Program that began in 1990–1992 as part of its effort to address high dropout rates and poor student performance in primary education. Pre- and post-intervention data were collected from twenty schools in selected low-income areas, as well as ten control schools, in order to evaluate the program's impact on dropout behavior and student performance. Interventions that provided teachers with learning materials, helped them to pace lessons according to students' differing abilities, and initiated parent–teacher partnerships, and involved parents in the schooling of their children were more successful, easily replicated, and economically sound, compared to a school nutrition intervention. A study that analyzed the program demonstrated the feasibility and relevance of decentralized monitoring and evaluating interventions in the education sector not only in the Philippines but also in other developing countries.[135]

Further decentralization of the educational system occurred with passage of the LGC. Under Section 98, a local school board is created in provincial, city, and municipal governments. The school board has several functions, including to "determine the annual supplementary budgeting needs for the operation and maintenance of public schools" within its area.[136] But the most important task of the school board is to serve as an advisory committee for educational matters within its jurisdiction.[137] The top officials of each government unit—provincial governors and city and municipality mayors, together with members of the Sanggunian—join forces with officials of the Department of Education, Culture and Sports in tackling education issues.

In the first eight years of Code implementation, the school boards had not been greatly impacted. Local officials can more efficiently deliver proper education services to their constituents, but this advantage has been overshadowed by various problems that arose from decentralization of the education sector. One point of concern is that not everyone is aware that the education sector has already devolved to the local government through these school boards.

It is interesting to note that in spite of decentralization, corruption in the education system is still alive and well. In 1999, the Philippine Center for Investigative Journalism reported massive corruption in the Department of

Education, which is very much propelled by corruption at the local level. One issue that hit the news was a textbook scam: school board officials were found to have accepted bribes from suppliers and textbook publishers. If decentralization increased the efficiency of textbook distribution to the public schools, so too has it increased corruption.[138] It is plausible that decentralization has facilitated corruption in other sectors as well.

Another concern about the decentralization of education is the increase in teacher allowances, especially in the provinces. Some teachers sought to augment their income through the Special Education Fund (SEF) that was created by law. Teachers' salaries are very low, about half of the required minimum cost of living, especially in urban areas.[139] While the SEF may provide temporary relief to poorly paid public school teachers, it only offers a palliative to the perennial problem of low pay and delayed disbursement of salaries to teachers. Creation of the SEF may even help deflect government and public attention from the need to pay teachers decent salaries that do not depend on the ability of their local governments to raise additional revenue beyond their IRAs.

As of this writing, bills to amend the existing Code have been filed in both houses of Congress by Representative Romeo Candazo[140] and Senate President Aquilino Pimentel.[141] The Senate bill contains several details for education decentralization, specifically in the school boards. Additional functions of the school boards were included, such as granting nontaxable monthly augmentation allowances to employees and a provision on funds for scholarships and allowances, with priority for poor and deserving students. There is also an amendment on the establishment and maintenance of classes not only in formal education, but in nonformal and training programs as well.

Eight years after the devolution of functions from the Department of Education, the system had not changed. Moreover, the quality of education was still dismal. The proportion of students who complete their education at all levels has declined, particularly at the primary level. The argument that not all functions have been devolved is not a reason for failing to properly implement those already mandated by law. Much remains to be done in the education sector for the general public actually experiences the stated objectives of decentralization. More research also needs to be done to determine whether centralization is a factor in declining educational standards. It is also important to determine the conditions under which decentralization objectives to improve the quality of Philippine public schools could be attained. Would direct democratic control over schools work in the

Philippine context, where the general public has limited experience in democratic governance in education and minimal exposure to parallel experiments in other places? Would centralized control, promotion of uniformity in curriculum, and delegation of educational policy choices to experts work better in this context?

Conclusions and Future Research Directions

Decentralization in the Philippine context has been taking place in the aftermath of a postauthoritarian transition toward political democratization and economic liberalization. It evolved from a combination of local, national, and international pressures to initiate public sector reforms and address problems arising from the overcentralization of functions and decision-making powers in the national government. By giving a voice, decision-making powers, and participatory initiatives to local governments and civil society representatives, decentralization is expected to bring about more effective results in public administration, trim the bureaucracy, reduce budgetary benefits, and empower communities in local governance.

More than ten years after the enactment of the Local Government Code, the most important document outlining the country's decentralization policy, the full benefits of decentralization in promoting democratization, participatory governance, and economic prosperity have yet to be realized. The implementation of the Code has on the one hand, opened up a number of new possibilities for local communities who have been fortunate to elect sincere, cooperative, and civic-minded politicians. Local governments with such leaders have been able to take advantage of new opportunities to develop locally designed social programs, generate tax revenues to support social service provision, create subsidized housing and recreational facilities, access foreign funds, and revitalize government–civil society partnerships. On the other hand, there are communities that seemed worst off in the aftermath of decentralization due to their dependence on revenue allotments from the central government, lack of entrepreneurship of their local governments, and many obstacles to harnessing the potentials of decentralization. In most cases, these are the places where there is an overall lack of initiative, cooperation, and sincerity on the part of the local government to fully harness local residents' participation as their partners in local governance.

Like the globalization game, there are people and communities who stand to gain and lose in the process of decentralization. One cannot simply be a disinterested player in situations where even those sitting on the sidelines get mud on their sleeves. We need to take into account not just the role of local government institutions, but also coalitions of various social actors, the private sector, and other national and international governmental bodies and institutions that stand to lose and gain from decentralization. We need to understand who the players are who ultimately share in the distribution of costs and benefits. What types of local communities and governments are the likely losers and winners in the decentralization process?

This realization has led various stakeholders, such as LGUs, national agencies, and civil society groups affected by the decentralization, as well as international donor agencies to take a keen interest in reviewing the effects and prospects of decentralization. To this end, there is a mandatory Congressional review of the LGC implementation every five years. There are also several bills filed in the Lower House and the Senate to amend some provisions of the Code. A Joint Working Group of NGOs and POs has also been formed to review the LGC to parallel the Congressional mandatory review of the Code every five years. The NGO–PO Working Group's advocacy led to their substantive inputs into the joint House and Senate "Empowerment Bill" sponsored by Senator Flavier and Congressman Abad. It also developed a framework for maximizing the LGC through faithful and mature implementation, capacity building, defense of devolution gains, improvement of empowerment components, and harmonization with other laws, programs, and agendas of sectoral groups. The legislators would like to promote progressive state initiatives and lobby for new laws such as the Fisheries Code, National Land Use Code, and Ancestral Domain and Forestry Laws, among others. They view these initiatives and laws to be essential in promoting a kind of decentralization that would cushion basic sectors from the harsh effects of global restructuring (e.g., GATT/WTO negotiations). They also emphasized some of the principal obstacles to effective implementation of the LGC, including local officials' lack of skills and knowledge to maximize the Code's participatory mechanisms, and the abuse by politicians of some of these mechanisms, especially the recall process, to harass their opponents.

We have already mentioned some critical areas that need more research in terms of filling in basic knowledge gaps, utilizing participatory action research in monitoring implementation and analyzing policy impacts, and providing substantive inputs to policy-making. Regarding basic knowledge gaps, there is a need to track down local and national cases of referenda, plebiscites, and recalls of unaccountable and incompetent politicians that involve civil society initiatives. In other words, are LGC provisions for participatory governance underutilized? How are these provisions being utilized and why? We need more systematic studies to understand the processes and conditions of success, as well as failure, over the course of decentralization. What are the characteristics of communities and their local governments that stand to lose or gain from decentralization? Why do some communities succeed in maximizing the LGC provisions for civil society representation in local government councils, while others do not? What are the conditions under which government–civil society interactions happen, and what are the conditions under which they are likely to fail? How can these conditions that guarantee relative success be scaled-up and replicated in other places? Participatory forms of research and community initiatives could be undertaken to address some of the research questions that have applied or practical implications.

Thus far, there has been little documentation of how decentralization efforts have affected shifts in local political alliances, and even less on how such shifts have influenced national political coalitions and electoral outcomes.[142] It would be also be interesting, for example, to examine how decentralization has paved the way for the formation of several parties and groups that run for Congressional seats under the new party list system in the last two national elections. There is a great need for progressive national political coalitions to organize barangay and municipal leaders who have shown enthusiasm and leadership skills under the decentralized setup, and to organize them to challenge traditional leaders. Since decentralization may also help strengthen local and provincial politicians with large local constituencies,[143] what prospects are there for new political centers and parties to develop locally and nationally as a result of political decentralization?

Regarding planning-related and policy research, there is a need for systematic studies on the outcomes, successes, and limitations of many foreign-funded projects (e.g., CIDA's LGSP and USAID's LDAP). The same holds true for government-sponsored programs (e.g., DILG's LGU Capacity-Building Program) to assist LGUs in their efforts to adjust to the new demands of decentralization. There is a great need to determine the appropriate mechanisms for participatory governance in areas that are not affected by the Local Government Code, such as local budgeting, revenue generation, improving accountability, and public inputs in policy setting and electoral reform. Government decentralization policy must be shaped to support antipoverty and rural development objectives, particularly through training in farm and nonfarm skills, social preparation of rural ar-

eas for community organizations and cooperatives, and community participation in the delivery of basic services and in building rural infrastructures.[144] It has been noted that antipoverty and rural development programs
have not been effectively integrated with population and family planning,
and this lack of integration had been exacerbated by the contradiction between decentralization and national control, passive community participation, organizational management weaknesses, and weak sectoral and environmental linkages.[145] There is also a great need for studies on how regime
change under President Estrada, for example, has led to the centralization
of regional development planning, particularly in armed conflict areas of
Mindanao. Recommendations emerging from these types of research could
feed into the new government-sponsored bills, social programs, and advocacy of civil society organizations.

More research also needs to be done on the role of civil society in decentralization efforts. While "the weakness of the Philippine state is
reflected in the relative strength of Philippine civil society,"[146] civil society
organizations are also quite weak in terms of affecting substantive policy
changes. This happens not so much because civil society organizations have
no alternative programs but because of lack of state and social support, as
well as the absence of any meaningful social learning within government,
civil society, and in the course of state–civil society interactions. How can
civil society organizations improve themselves, and be supported by the
government, in their move beyond advocacy politics and into the arenas of
policymaking and program implementation?

Related to this issue of social learning and discussion of democratic governance is the question of which social forces will lead the state to greater
democracy and who will benefit most from this transformation.[147] Decentralization, to be effective, must be accompanied by a framework for the political representation of excluded communities to effectively channel resources to local needs.[148] Decentralization moves toward democracy need
to incorporate more than political representation and rights.[149] They must
include the transformation of economic inequalities and the forms of participation of people in the governmental and programmatic decisions affecting their lives. This expanded notion of democratic decentralization emphasizes that processes of structural inequalities, which perpetuate poverty
and all forms of domination, destroy the means by which consensus and
noncoercive forms of governance can be built and maintained. Decentralization should ensure that it becomes a meaningful instrument for uphold-

ing the public good by bringing about greater democratization and economic prosperity for the most marginalized and powerless groups.

Notes

1. Henry Teune, "Local Government and Democratic Political Development," *Annals of the American Academy of Political and Social Science* 540 (July 1995): 11–23.

2. Paul Hirst, "Associative Democracy, A Comment on David Morgan," *Australian and New Zealand Journal of Sociology* 32, no. 1 (March 1996): 20–26.

3. Ladislau Dowbor, "Response to Critics," *Latin American Perspectives* 25, no. 1 (January 1998): 49–52.

4. Allan Rosenbaum, "Gouvernance et Decentralisation—Lecons de l'Experience," *Revue Francaise d'Administration Publique* 88 (October–December 1998): 507–16.

5. Jan M. Grell and Gary Gappert, "The Future of Governance in the United States: 1992–2002," *Annals of the American Academy of Political and Social Science* 522 (July 1992): 67–78.

6. Steven Friedman, "Agreeing to Differ: African Democracy, Its Obstacles and Prospects," *Social Research* 66, no. 3 (Fall 1999): 825–58.

7. Kiran Saxena and Pradeep K. Sharma, "Hindutva and Economic Liberalization," *International Review of Sociology* 8, no. 2 (July 1998): 239–51.

8. S. Schiavo-Campo, "Government Employment and Pay: The Global and Regional Evidence," *Public Administration and Development* 18, no. 5 (1998): 457–478.

9. Richard C. Crook and James Manor, *Democracy and Decentralization in South Asia and West Africa: Participation, Accountability and Performance* (Cambridge: Cambridge University Press, 1998), 2.

10. Segundo E. Romero, "The Philippines in 1997: Weathering Political and Economic Turmoil," *Asian Survey* 38, no. 2 (1998): 196–202.

11. I.B. Valdellon, "Decentralization of Planning and Financing for Local Development: The Case of the Philippines," *Regional Development Dialogue* 20, no. 2 (1999): 61–73.

12. Nirmal Mukarji, "Decentralization Below the State Level: Need for a New System of Governance," *Economic and Political Weekly* 24, no. 9 (March 1989): 467–72.

13. Ruby R. Paredes, ed., *Philippine Colonial Democracy* (Quezon City: Ateneo de Manila Press, 1989); David Wurfel, *Filipino Politics: Development and Decay* (Ithaca, N.Y.: Cornell University Press, 1988); Vicente T. Paterno, "Perspectives on Rural Development," *Philippine Journal of Public Administration* 33, no. 4 (October 1989): 327–40; and Gaudioso C. Sosmena, "Local Autonomy and Intergovernmental Relations," *Philippine Journal of Public Administration* 21, no. 3 (July 1987): 231–56.

14. Sosmena, "Local Autonomy and Intergovernmental Relations," 232–33.

15. Section 4, Article X, 1986 Constitution, cited in Sosmena, "Local Autonomy and Intergovernmental Relations," 231.

16. Section 10, Article VII, 1935 Constitution states: "The President shall exercise general supervision over all local governments as may be provided by law." Cited in Sosmena, "Local Autonomy and Intergovernmental Relations," 237.

17. See Amendment to the 1973 Constitution ratified in the national referendum plebiscite on 16 October 1976, and Section 16, Article VII amending Section 16, Article IX of the 1973 Constitution, amended 30 June 1981. See Sosmena, "Local Autonomy and Intergovernmental Relations," 237.

18. Raul P. de Guzman and Proserpina D. Tapales, eds., *Philippine Local Government: Issues, Problems and Prospects* (Manila: Local Government Center, College of Public Administration, University of the Philippines, 1973), 146–47, cited in Sosmena, "Local Autonomy and Intergovernmental Relations," 239–40.

19. Alex B. Brillantes, *Decentralization, Devolution and Development in the Philippines,* Asia Occasional Paper 44 (Manila: U.N. Urban Management Program, March 1999).

20. Paterno, "Perspectives on Rural Development," 327.

21. Nenita E. Tapay, Alan C. Early, and Dennis S. Mileti, "Irrigation Organization in the Philippines: Structure and Effectiveness of National and Communal Types," in *Research in Rural Sociology and Development* 3 (1987): 209–21.

22. Brillantes, *Decentralization, Devolution and Development in the Philippines.*

23. Section 10, Article XI, 1973 Constitution, cited in Sosmena, "Local Autonomy and Intergovernmental Relations," 237.

24. See Leonora Angeles, "The Survival of Privilege: Strategies of Political Resilience of Oligarchies in the Philippines, 1946–1992" (Ph.D. diss., Queen's University, 1995), 99.

25. Ibid., 103–108.

26. Ibid., 109.

27. Ibid., 110–11.

28. Ibid., 111–12.

29. Thomas P. Walsh, "Executive Time Utilization in the Philippine Provincial Governorship," *Philippine Journal of Public Administration* 20, no. 2 (1976): 153.

30. This regional inequality due to centralization had been observed not in the Philippines but also in Indonesia, Malaysia, and Thailand. See Kamal Salih, Phisit Pakkasem, E.B. Prantilla, and Sugijanto Soegijoko, "Decentralization Policy, Growth Pole Approach and Resource Frontier Development: A Synthesis of the Response in Four Southeast Asian Countries," in *Growth Pole Strategy and Regional Development Policy: Asian Experience and Alternative Approaches,* edited by F.C. Lo and K. Salih, 79–120 (Oxford; New York: Published for the United Nations Centre for Regional Development by Pergamon Press, 1978).

31. William L. Thomas, "Progressive Rather than Centralized Tourism: A Recommendation for Improving International Tourism in the Philippines," *Philippine Geographical Journal* 22, no. 2 (1978): 55–82.

32. G. Luis Igaya, "The Political Economy of the Philippine Democratic Transition," in *Transitions to Democracy in East and Southeast Asia,* edited by Kristina Garlan (Quezon City: Institute for Popular Democracy, 1999), 34.

33. Mark Turner, Introduction to *Central–Local Relations in Asia-Pacific: Convergence of Divergence?* edited by Mark Turner (New York: St. Martin's Press, 1999), 2.

34. Alex B. Brillantes, Jr., "Re-democratization and Decentralization in the Philippines: The Increasing Leadership Role of NGOs," *International Review of Administrative Sciences* 60 (1994): 575–86.

35. Victor E. Tan and Rose Marie-R. Nierras, "NGO–GO Relationships: Prospects and Experience," *Philippine Sociological Review* 41, no. 1–4 (January–December 1993): 37–39.

36. Thomas P. Walsh, "Perceptions of Gubernatorial Authority: Aspects of the 'Reality World' of the Philippine Governor," *Philippine Journal of Public Administration* 20, no. 1 (1976): 68–103.

37. ULAP's president Laguna Governor Joey Lina was named the new secretary of the DILG in the Macapagal–Arroyo administration. The ULAP's former name is League of Leagues; membership includes all leagues of local officials in the country.

38. David Williams, "Constructing the Economic Space: The World Bank and the Making of the *Homo Oeconomicus,*" *Millennium Journal for International Studies* 28, no. 1 (1999): 79–99.

39. Turner, Introduction, 2.

40. Ibid.

41. The World Bank defined governance as "the manner in which power is exercised in the management of the country's economic and social resources for development." Good governance therefore is "epitomized by predictable, open, and enlightened policy-making (that is, transparent processes); a bureaucracy imbued with professional ethos; an executive arm of government accountable for its actions; and a strong civil society participating in public affairs; and all behaving under the rule of law." World Bank, *Development in Practice: Governance, The World Bank's Experience* (Washington, D.C.: World Bank, 1994), vii.

42. Florence McCarthy, "Dilemmas of Decentralization and the Contradictions of Democratic Process" (paper presented at annual meetings of the American Sociological Association, Miami, August 1994).

43. The fiscal austerity measures entailed reduction of the public investment program by almost 50 percent in real terms between 1983 and 1985, or from 7.4 percent of the GNP to about 3.5 percent. There were considerable delays on completion of existing projects and severe reductions, especially in transport and communications (–80 percent), manufacturing (–83 percent), and energy (–54 percent). Operations and maintenance expenditures were cut by 50 percent in real terms compared to 1982 levels. These measures were done to cover budgetary deficits and public borrowing requirements. See International Monetary Fund Staff Report for the 1986 Article IV Consultation and Request for Standby Arrangement—Supplementary Information, 17 October 1986, cited in Nerissa Tungol-Esguerra, "Background Research on SAP and Budget" (Freedom from Debt Coalition, Quezon City, Philippines, 2 July 1999).

44. G. Luis Igaya, "The Political Economy of the Philippine Democratic Transition," in *Transitions to Democracy in East and Southeast Asia,* edited by Kristina Gaerlan (Quezon City: Institute for Popular Democracy, 1999), 38.

45. Now the Center for Local and Regional Governance under the National College of Public and Governance.

46. CIDA has allocated $5 million to LSGP I (1991–1998), and $9.5 million for LGSP II (1998–2004). In its first phase, LGSP provides technical assistance to the Regional Development Councils for the purpose of planning and programming development projects in their areas of influence. In the second phase, the project hopes to build on the accomplishments of the first phase, that is, trained personnel from local and private institutions; implementation of community-based projects that demonstrate local capabilities; stronger local governments with community support and involvement; a feedback mechanism for policy dialogue; an environment more conducive to effective local government action; trained management, and technical and professional staff for local governments; and public-private sector projects based on linkages between Filipino and Canadian partners.

47. Article X, 1987 Constitution of the Philippines.

48. Local Government Code, Section 2, RA 7160 states: "Towards this end, the State shall provide for a more responsive and accountable local government structure instituted through a system of decentralization whereby local government units shall be given more powers, authority, responsibilities, and resources."

49. Local Government Code, Section 17, states: "Local government units shall endeavor to be self-reliant and shall continue exercising the powers and discharging the duties and functions currently vested upon them. They shall also discharge the functions and responsibilities of national agencies and offices devolved to them pursuant to this Code."

50. Ibid., Section 17.

51. Ibid., Section 149.

52. Ibid., Section 36.

53. Section 5, 1987 Constitution of the Philippines.

54. Ibid., Section 6.

55. Local Government Code, Section 284.

56. Ibid., Section 129 states: "Each local government unit shall exercise its power to create its own sources of revenue and levy taxes, fees and charges subject to the provision herein, consistent with the basic policy of local autonomy."

57. Ibid., Section 130.

58. Ibid., Section 140.

59. Ibid., Section 296 states: "General Policy.—It shall be the basic policy that any local government unit may create indebtedness, and avail of credit facilities to finance local infrastructure and other socio-economic development projects in accordance with the approved local development plan and public investment program."

60. Released through the website of the World Bank Group, available at www.worldbank.org.

61. Ibid., Section 302.

62. Ibid.

63. Trinidad Osteria, "Implementation of the Local Government Code in the Philippines: Problems and Challenges," in *Social Sector Decentralization: Lessons from the Asian Experience,* edited by Osteria, 17–64 (Ottawa: International Development Research Center, 1996).

64. Marlon A. Wui and Ma. Glenda S. Lopez, eds., *State–Civil Society Relations in Policy-Making,* Philippine Democracy Agenda 2 (Quezon City: Third World Studies Centre, 1997), 7–8.

65. Rule XXI, 1991 Local Government Code.

66. Tomas Villarin, *People Empowerment: A Guide to NGO–PO Partnership with Local Governments* (Quezon City: Kaisahan Foundation, 1996), 103.

67. Rule XX, 1991 Local Government Code.

68. 1991 Local Government Code, Section 79.

69. Ibid., Section 6.

70. Ibid., Section 8.

71. Ibid., Section 51.

72. Ibid., Section 80.

73. Ibid., Section 81.

74. Rudy Sambajon, national chair of PAMALAKAYA, interview by Cresmar Yparraguirre and Kareff May Rafisura, Quezon City, 4 January 2001.

75. Alex Brillantes, Jr., and Jorge V. Tigno, "GO–NGO–PO Partnerships in the Philippines and the 1991 Local Government Code: An Anatomy of the Empowerment Process," *GO–NGO Watch* (Institute of Strategic and Development Studies, Quezon City) (September 1993): 37.

76. Myrna J. Alejo, "Political Decentralization in Naga City" (Civil Society and Governance Project, Social Development Research Center De La Salle University, Manila, forthcoming).

77. Alex Brillantes, "The GO–NGO Watch Project: Reexamining Dominant Paradigms of Local Governance," *GO–NGO Watch* (Institute of Strategic and Development Studies, Quezon City, no. 5 (September 1994): 7.

78. Department of Interior and Local Government, *Rules and Regulations Implementing the Local Government Code of 1991* (Manila: Department of Interior and Local Government, 1991), 75.

79. SC Decision En Banc Garcia vs. Commission on Elections, G.R. No. 11 1230, 30 September 1994, cited in Alberto C. Agra, *Compendium of Decisions, Rulings, Resolutions, and Opinions on Local Autonomy and Local Government* (Manila: Rex Bookstore, 1996), 273.

80. DILG Opinion No. 5-1996, cited in Agra, *Compendium,* 276.

81. "Establishing the Regional Project Monitoring and Evaluation System (RPHES)," Executive Order no. 376, 2 November 1989, par. 5.

82. Executive Order 376, Section 4.

83. Executive Order 93, 1993.

84. Ibid., Section 1, par. 3 and 4.

85. Ibid., Section 3.

86. A public hearing is required when (1) the magnitude of the project is such that a great number of people are affected; (2) there is mounting public opposition against the proposed project; or (3) there is a written request for the conduct of such public hearing from any of the stakeholders.

87. See Alex Brillantes, "State–Civil Society Relations in Policy-Making; Civil Society and the Executive," in *State–Civil Society Relations in Policy-Making,* edited by Marlon A. Wui and Ma. Glenda S. Lopez, 21–31 (Quezon City: Third World Studies Centre, 1997).

88. The only recent case reported in the papers was the initiative of local Caloocan City residents to petition the recall of Mayor Rey Malonzo, a former action movie star turned politician, who was accused of incompetence by his political opponents and segments of his constituency.

89. H. J. Friedman, "Decentralized Development in Asia: Local Political Alternatives," in *Decentralization and Development,* edited by G. S. Cheema and D. A. Rondinelli, 35–57 (Beverly Hills, Calif.: Sage, 1983).

90. K. Mathur, "Administrative Decentralization in Asia," in *Decentralization and Development,* edited by G. S. Cheema and D. A. Rondinelli, 59–76 (Beverly Hills, Calif.: Sage, 1983).

91. R.J. Fisher, "Devolution and Decentralization of Forest Management in Asia and the Pacific," *Unasylva* 50 (1999): 3–5.

92. Danilo R. Reyes, "Tensions in the Troubled Bureaucracy: Reform Initiatives in Public Organizations and Service Delivery Systems," in *Philippine Journal of Public Administration* 37, no. 3 (July 1993): 239–64.

93. McCarthy, "Dilemmas of Decentralization."

94. Alfred W. McCoy, ed., *Anarchy of Families: State and Family in the Philippines* (Madison: University of Wisconsin Press; Quezon City: Ateneo de Manila Press, 1993).

95. Osteria, "Implementation of the Local Government Code in the Philippines."

96. Wilhelm G. Wolters, "Rise and Fall of Provincial Elites in the Philippines: Nueva Ecija from the 1880s to the Present Day," *Sojourn* 4, no. 1 (February 1989): 54–74.

97. Osteria, "Implementation of the Local Government Code in the Philippines," 61–63.

98. Leonora C. Angeles and Penny Gurstein, "Planning for Participatory Capacity Development: The Challenges of Participation and North–South Partnerships in Capacity-Building Projects," *Canadian Journal of Development Studies* 21 (October–December 2000): 454 (special issue on "Participatory Development," edited by William Cowie).

99. Ibid.

100. See for example, Osteria, "Implementation of the Local Government Code in the Philippines; Soliman Santos, ed., *Working Group, Working Papers: NGO–PO Perspectives for the Local Government Code Review* (Quezon City: Institute of Politics and Governance, 1997).

101. See, for example, assessment of foreign-funded healthcare projects in relation to local politics, in Colette St. Hilaire, "Canadian Aid, Women and Development: Rebaptizing the Filipina," *The Ecologist* 23, no. 2 (1993): 57–60. Also printed in *Philippine Development Briefing* 3 (December 1992): 2–15.

102. See Jocelyn Vicente Angeles, "The Role of the Naga City Urban Poor Federation in the Passage of Pro-Poor Ordinances and Policies," and Juan Climaco Elago II, "The Role of Local Governments in the Eviction and Demolition Cases of Urban Poor Residents," in *State–Civil Society Relations in Policy-Making,* edited by Marlon A. Wui and Ma. Glenda S. Lopez, 107–110 and 113–124, respectively (Quezon City: Third World Studies Centre, 1997).

103. Wui and Lopez, *State–Civil Society Relations in Policy-Making,* 5–18.

104. Perla E. Legaspi and Eden V. Santiago, "The State of the Devolution Process: The Implementation of the 1991 Local Government Code in Selected LGUs," *Local Government Bulletin* 32, no. 2–4 (April–December 1997).

105. Brillantes, *Decentralization, Devolution and Development in the Philippines,* 8.

106. National Statistics Coordination Board, "The Internal Revenue Allotment (IRA) as a Source of Funds for Local Governance" (Manila: National Statistics Coordination Board, 1999).

107. Alicia B. Celestino, "Fiscal Decentralization in Quezon City: An Initial Assessment," *Local Government Bulletin* 30, no. 2–4 (April–December 1996).

108. Ibid.

109. Jocelyn Cuaresma and Simeon Ilago, *Local Fiscal Administration in the Philippines* (Quezon City: UP Local Government Center and the German Foundation for International Development, 1996).

110. Robert S. Pomeroy and F. Berkes, "Two to Tango: The Role of Government in Fisheries Co-Management," *Marine Policy* 21, no. 5 (1997): 465–80.

111. Robert S. Pomeroy, "Community-Based and Co-Management Institutions For Sustainable Coastal Fisheries Management In Southeast Asia," *Ocean and Coastal Management* 27, no. 3 (1995): 143–62.

112. G. R. Russ and A. C. Alcala, "Management Histories of Sumilon and Apo Marine Reserves, Philippines, and Their Influence on National Marine Resource Policy," *Coral Reefs* 18, no. 4 (1999): 307–19.

113. R. J. Fisher, "Devolution and Decentralization of Forest Management in Asia and the Pacific," *Unasylva* 50 (1999): 3–5.

114. Solita Monsod and Toby Monsod, "International and Intranational Comparisons of Philippine Poverty," in *Causes of Poverty: Myths, Facts and Policies,* edited by Arsenio Balisacan and Shiegeaki Fujisaki (Quezon City: University of the Philippines Press, 1999), 89, citing Victoria Bautista, "Indigenization of HDN Index: The Case of the Minimum Basic Needs Approach" (paper prepared for the Human Development Network, Quezon City, 1999).

115. Transcripts of the Roundtable Discussion on the Ramos Administration's Social Reform Agenda with Emmanuel Buendia, former head of the Social Reform Council Secretariat, Center for Integrative and Development Studies, Quezon City, 28 July 1999.

116. MBN involves the integration of nonincome indicators in the formula for poverty incidence as an offshoot of putting greater emphasis on "quality of life" indicators in measuring development. The indicators are divided into three groups that are arranged in a hierarchical manner, that is, (1) survival needs indicators (health, nutrition, water, and sanitation); (2) security needs indicators (income, shelter, peace, and order); and (3) enabling needs indicators (basic education and political participation). See Maria Cynthia Rose Banzon Bautista, Leonora Angeles, and Josephine Dionisio, "Asian Responses to the 1997 Financial Crisis: Social Safety Net Programs in the Philippines," in *The Poor at Risk: Social Safety Net Programs in Southeast Asia,* edited by Terry McGee, et al. (Vancouver: Centre for Southeast Asian Studies, University of British Columbia, 2001).

117. Solita Monsod and Toby Monsod, "International and Intranational Comparisons of Philippine Poverty," in *Causes of Poverty: Myths, Facts and Policies: Myths, Facts and Policies,* edited by Arsenio Balisacan and Shiegeaki Fujisaki (Quezon City: University of the Philippines Press, 1999), 90–92. Cited also in Bautista, Angeles, and Dionisio, "Asian Responses to the 1997 Financial Crisis."

118. About PHP 6.7 billion in credit for farmers and fisher folk would have been available under this new lending scheme, using funds from cooperative banks, rural banks, and financially viable nongovernmental rural organizations identified by the Agricultural Credit Policy Council. See Bautista, Angeles, and Dionisio, "Asian Responses to the 1997 Financial Crisis."

119. Under the 1999 General Appropriations Act, PHP 2.5 billion were allocated for this fund: PHP 500 million for food, nutrition, and medical assistance through the Department of Health; PHP 500 million for enterprise and job skill livelihood development through the Cooperative Development Authority; PHP 500 million for multifamily housing through the National Housing Authority; PHP 300 million for protective services for children and youth through the Department of Social Welfare and Development; and PHP 400 million for price supports for rice and corn through the National Food Authority. See Bautista, Angeles, and Dionisio, "Asian Responses to the 1997 Financial Crisis."

120. Emmanuel S. De Dios, "The Philippine Anti-Poverty Plan: A Rapid Assessment" (Manila U.N. Development Programme, 1999), 5–6, criticized the administration's strategy in meeting its target of enabling 2 million families to cross the poverty

line by 2004. Instead of area-based localities, the targeting approach of reaching 100 of the poorest families in each province and city, regardless of the level of development of the areas will involve only 16,100 families, which would not translate to 2 million families by 2004.

121. Draft Midterm Evaluation Report of Component 2 of the U.N. Development Programme (UNDP) project, cited in Bautista, Angeles, and Dionisio, "Asian Responses to the 1997 Financial Crisis."

122. These cases are retold in Bautista, Angeles, and Dionisio, "The Poor At Risk: Surviving the Economic Crisis in Southeast Asia," final report of the project Social Safety Net Programs in Selected Southeast Asian Countries, 1997–2000 (Vancouver: Centre for Southeast Asian Research, University of British Columbia, 2000). See also documents on the activities of the UNDP-funded project that include the installation of the enhanced Community Based Poverty Indicators Monitoring System (CBPIMS); establishment of Institutional Mechanisms for Convergence of Regional, Provincial and Municipal Levels; formulation of Local Poverty Alleviation Plans; and design and pilot testing of a monitoring system for poverty alleviation.

123. Jane A. Thomason and Stephen G. Karel, "Integrating National and District Health Planning in a Decentralized Setting," *Evaluation and Program Planning* 17, no. 1 (January–March 1994): 13–18.

124. J. P. Vaughan and D. Smith, "The District and Support for Primary Health Care: The Management Experience from Large-Scale Projects," *Public Administration and Development* 6, no. 3 (1986): 255–66.

125. Thomason and Karel, "Integrating National and District Health Planning," 13–18.

126. Corazon M. Raymundo and Cecilia M. Ruiz, "Adolescent Fertility in the Regions," *Philippine Population Journal* 1, no. 4 (December 1985): 1–29.

127. World Bank, *Philippines Devolution and Health Services: Managing Risks and Opportunities,* Report No. 12343-PH (Washington, D.C.: World Bank, 23 May 1994).

128. Juan A. Perez III, "Seven Years of Health Devolution: An Assessment," *Health-Beat Supplement* (Manila: Department of Health, 9 October 1998), 8.

129. I. B. Valdellon, "Decentralization of Planning and Financing for Local Development: The Case of the Philippines," *Regional Development Dialogue* 20, no. 2 (1999): 61–73.

130. Salve B. Borlagdan, Gloria Gabronino, and Apollo C. Tracena, "Health Service Delivery: Issues, Problems, and Prospects of Devolution," *Philippine Journal of Public Administration* 37, no. 1 (January 1993).

131. "Devolution: Is It Curse or Blessing?" *Manila Bulletin,* 2 November 1999, p. 17.

132. Alex B. Brillantes, Jr., "Five-Year Assessment of the Implementation of Devolution in the Local Government Code," in *Local Government in the Philippines: A Book of Readings,* vol. 3, edited by Proserpina Domingo Tapales, Jocelyn C. Cuaresma, and Wilhemina L. Cabo (Quezon City: Center for Local and Regional Governance/National College of Public Administration and Governance, University of the Philippines, 1998), 526–27.

133. Ibid., 526.

134. Perez, "Seven Years of Health Devolution," 9.

135. J. P. Tan, J. Lane, and G. Lassibille, Student Outcomes in Philippine Elementary Schools: An Evaluation of Four Experiments, *World Bank Economic Review* 13, no. 3 (1999): 493–508.

136. Section 99, Local Government Code, RA 7160.

137. Ibid.

138. Yvonne T. Chua, "Up to 65% of Textbook Funds Goes to Bribes," Report from the Philippine Center for Investigative Journalism, 3–6 March 1999, available at: www.pcij.org/stories/1999/textbooks.

139. Tonette Orejas, "Pampanga Educators ask for P500 More," *Philippine Daily Inquirer,* 8 October 2000.

140. Filed HB No. 7845 amending certain provisions of Local Government Code, RA 7160.

141. Filed SB No. 2064 amending certain provisions of Local Government Code, RA 7160.

142. The few works that are available—such as Soliman Santos, *Working Group, Working Papers: NGO–PO Perspectives for the Local Government Code Review* (Quezon City: Institute of Politics and Governance, 1997)—tend to focus on how decentralization and devolution of powers under the Local Government Code have improved local governance and democratization, and the related question of how NGOs and POs could fully participate in implementation.

143. For example, Cebu governor Lito Osmena exercised efficient local management skills as provincial governor in using decentralized authority to bring economic growth to Cebu. He formed a Cebu-based party, the Probinsya Muna Development Initiative (PROMDI), which enabled him to garner fourth place in the 1998 presidential elections. PROMDI is now part of the ruling People's Power Coalition. Civil society participation is not prominent in the politics of PROMDI.

144. Paterno, "Perspectives on Rural Development," 327–29.

145. Amelia P. Varela, "Policy Issues in Integration for Rural Development: The Case of the Population/Family Planning Program," *Philippine Journal of Public Administration* 28, no. 3 (July 1984): 173–202.

146. Felipe Miranda, "Political Economy in a Democratizing Philippines: A People's Perspective," in *Democratization: Philippine Perspectives,* edited by Felipe Miranda (Quezon City: University of the Philippines Press, 1997), 165.

147. Ladislau Dowbor, "Response to Critics," in *Latin American Perspectives* 25, no. 1 (January 1998): 49–52.

148. Mike Geddes, "Poverty, Excluded Communities and Local Democracy," in *Transforming Cities: Contested Governance and New Spatial Divisions,* Nick Jewson and Susanne MacGregor, 205–18 (London: Routledge, 1997).

149. McCarthy, "Dilemmas of Decentralization."

Chapter 9

Decentralization and Regional Autonomy in Indonesia

Syarif Hidayat and Hans Antlöv

On January 1, 2001, Indonesia set in motion perhaps the most radical decentralization policies anywhere in the world during the last fifty years. Authority over all government services but religious affairs and the "federal four" (finances, foreign affairs, defense, and justice) was transferred to cities and districts (bypassing provinces), providing far-reaching regional autonomy to some 380 local governments. This was done just two years after the first democratic president for forty years was elected and after more than three decades of highly centralized and authoritarian rule. It was done in a period of deep economic crisis (the rupiah had devalued by 400 percent); political uncertainties (the first president Abdurrahman Wahid was forced to resign after less than two years, replaced by present president Megawati Soekarnoputri); widespread corruption (according to several recent studies, Indonesia is the most corrupt country in Asia); and ethnic and religious vi-

The views expressed in this chapter are our own and do not reflect those of the institutions with which we are affiliated.

olence (East Timor, Maluku, Papua, and Aceh, to name but the most well known). It is a huge ongoing experiment like few others. In this chapter, we will try to put the decentralization process in its political and legal context, discuss some of the problems of implementing such massive policies, and describe some of the opportunities and hopes for the future, from the perspectives of both local governments and civil society.

Indonesia is the world's fourth largest country with 220 million people, more than 17,000 islands, and 300 ethnic communities, with a broad range of social and economic standards of living and ways of life. For half a century, a nationalist vision of cultural unity remained the prime integrative force. Under President Suharto's so-called "New Order" (1965–1998), economic growth further integrated the diverse regions in Indonesia, managed through a regulated and centralized system of plans and programs emanating from Jakarta down through provinces to districts, subdistricts, and villages. Government offices, from central agencies in Jakarta to village branches, were in control of this process and its policy blueprints.

Indonesia's degree of centralization (prior to regional autonomy in 2001) cannot be overemphasized. There were few comparable countries in the world. In 1995, the central government in Jakarta collected 93 percent of total fiscal resources and spent more than 90 percent, through its intricate web of line ministry agencies.[1] Indonesia was (and remains) an extremely resource-rich country (in oil, gas, timber, minerals—GDP in the mid-1990s rivaled that of Canada) and the bulk of revenues was raised outside of the urban areas. But the resource-rich provinces (e.g., Riau, East Kalimantan, Papua) saw very little of this wealth. The central government collected taxes and revenues from the provinces and distributed them in very opaque ways. A massive patronage system was created in which the central government awarded local governments with budget allocations in exchange for loyalty. If not loyal, they would not get funds. Budget allocations were not based on performance or need, but rather on how close local governments were to the central government, and how well local elites could lobby decision makers in Jakarta. The resulting rent-seeking system was effective in rapidly building the economy, but was not sustainable and created great regional disparities, and thus dissatisfactions.

The planning process was also centralized. Priorities and initiatives were determined from on top and were seldom in line with local demands. There was on paper a very impressive budget and policy planning procedure, with meetings held first in each and every village. In reality, on each level of the planning process upward and on the implementation process downward, there were mark-ups and deviations, so that the funds and projects that after some nine to eighteen months (after the meetings) actually reached the community were very different from those originally proposed. The diversity of socioeconomic conditions, cultures, customary rights, and modes of decision making were effectively ignored.

For more than three decades, an administrative system was in place based on hierarchy, centralization, and an upward-oriented civil service. The national bureaucracy was divided into five layers: a national government with 27 provinces, 280 (rural) districts, 80 (urban) municipalities, 3,300 subdistricts, 61,000 (rural) villages, and 8,000 (urban) neighborhoods (figures from 1997). In addition, villages and neighborhood were further divided into wards (*rukun warga*) and quarters (*rukun tetangga*), with unpaid administrative staff.

The hierarchical relationship between the administration and civil society was characterized by paternalism, rent seeking, and a centralization of power. The implementation of policies and regulations was determined from above and took place without questions and without participation of the people targeted. Local government officials were accountable to central government authorities rather than local constituencies, and thus had very little grassroots liability and support. There were few participatory mechanisms in deciding community priorities, and the diversity of socioeconomic conditions, cultures, customary rights, and modes of decision making were often effectively ignored. Afraid of repression, citizens could not demand changes from their government. State actors determined public policies, and the voice of citizens was limited to the occasional letter to the editor and participation in forced labor parties or the controlled elections process every five years.

Suharto's authoritarian New Order was designed to minimize the resurgence of regional movements that troubled Indonesia during the early postcolonial period of the late 1940s and 1950s, and to guarantee the achievement of the "political stability" required to facilitate the New Order's commitment to economic development. As a result, it is not surprising that, in the beginning, the New Order government system was highly centralistic, with virtually no independent decision making by local governments. However, after consolidating political and economic stability, in the 1970s reforms took place to deconcentrate a number of central government services to the local governments.[2]

Importantly, it was *deconcentration,* not *decentralization.* The distinction is crucial. Decentralization involves a degree of autonomy, whereas deconcentration does not. Decentralization is usually defined as the transfer of authority from central government to a local government. Deconcentration is the delegation of administrative tasks and functions from the central government to its agencies at the local level, or the delegation of tasks from the top level to a lower level of the hierarchy within central government offices, with authority and decision making retained at higher levels. The New Order restrained the implementation of meaningful decentralization through redefining the principle of autonomous local government. This was codified in Law 5 of 1974. Even though the words "decentralization" and "regional autonomy" were used, it was a highly centralized structure. If a local government was considered incapable (or disloyal), the central government could reduce or withdraw the delegated function. With deconcentration, local governments received the mandate to provide certain functions, but they remained under the control of higher authorities. In fact, the degree of centralization and central government interference in Indonesia *increased* with deconcentration, since it meant that central government agencies had local branches all over the country. One of the most notable characteristics of the New Order was its presence in almost all aspects of everyday life in Indonesia, from the forest of government signs in front of offices and censured TV programs, to forced family-planning programs. There were few opportunities to escape the hegemony of the New Order.

It is thus important to remember that effective governance in Suharto's Indonesia was not absent, and that government was close to the people. In fact, it could be argued that the government was too close to people and too effective, intervening in almost all aspects of public and private life. Indonesia has had economic growth, rising social indicators, representative bodies, and a trained civil service. But there has been no accountability or transparency, along with paralyzing paternalism and discouragement of local initiatives.

Regional Autonomy—Finally

The authoritarian New Order government lasted for 32 years, with a single president. Suharto was forced to resign in May 1998, after a year of severe political and economic turbulence, intense regional conflicts, and demands for a revised balance of power between the center and regions. With the new government, Indonesia was set on a path toward democratization. Four interlinked processes created the new framework for democratic decentralization. First, a process toward genuine devolution of public services and power to local governments was set in motion with the design of the laws to be described below. Second, the new democratic government was searching for innovations in providing services to the public. Citizens and politicians alike increasingly considered the centralized system as inept, prone to corruption, and not sustainable in the long term. Wide-ranging reforms were necessary. Third, popular demands for fundamental governance reforms moved rapidly outside of Jakarta. In 1998–1999, hundreds of village heads and subdistrict and district chairs were forced to resign, replaced by more responsive leaders. Fourth, social activists and creative citizens developed new approaches to directly engage with local bureaucracies that have been used to encourage more transparent and accountable local government, such as monitoring development projects and local budgets.

All of this came together in the legal framework for decentralization and fiscal balance, as set out in two laws passed by the transitional Habibie government in May 1999. Law No. 22 of 1999 on local governance gives authority to districts and municipalities to manage a number of services and duties. Similar to a federal system, finances, the legal system, foreign affairs, defense, and religion are retained at the national level, while authority over roads, harbors, and other "areas of strategic national interest" is transferred to the provincial level, an administrative arm of the central government. Districts and municipalities are given authority over the remaining functions, including health care, education, public works, arts, and natural resources management.

Authority is given to the district and municipalities, effectively bypassing the province. It seems that this decision was not primarily based on a prior analysis of the optimal level of service provision, but rather that the central government was worried that if too much authority and power were given to provinces, they might be strong enough to challenge the central government. Numerous districts and municipalities (out of approximately 380), however, would not individually be able to face up to the central government. It is a classic divide-and-rule policy. The subdistrict (*kecamatan*) is mentioned only once in the law as the extended arm of the district/municipal government, without any autonomy or self-government. Villages, finally, are given a degree of autonomy, with the right to raise their own revenues and manage their own affairs (see below for more details).

Law No. 25 of 1999 outlines the new fiscal relations between center and regions and provides new formulas for dividing revenues. Districts retain 90 percent of the residential property tax, 80 percent of land tax, 80 percent of forest and fishery revenues, 15 percent of oil, and 20 percent of gas revenues. In the previous law (No. 5 of 1974), the fiscal relations were not outlined in detail, leading to a situation in which for many years existing instruments of intergovernmental fiscal relations were not based on a consistent legal framework.[3] The revenues that previously could be retained by districts and provinces were based on lobbying with senior officials in Jakarta, with built-in kickbacks and mark-ups for all parties. The new legislation attempts to stop this rent-seeking behavior through preestablished resource-sharing formulas.

There are several reasons why a national government may decide to provide more authority to local governments. One is to promote democratization, recognizing that national democratization cannot be sustained very long without recognizing a similar need at the local level. Another is to make service delivery more efficient, by de-bureaucratizing and giving direct authority to agencies that actually interact with citizens on a day-to-day and eye-to-eye basis. There is also the hope that decentralization in a period of transition from one form of government to another will build trust in government, making it more direct, immediate, and productive by encouraging people to become involved in the political issues that matter most to them, which in turn stimulates greater accountability and demands for more efficient public service. All of these commitments are mentioned in the preface to Law 22, and are at work in Indonesia, especially local democracy (through the empowered parliaments). But another crucial reason—some would say the most important—was the need to "save the nation." In the aftermath of the transition in 1998, many regional actors made demands for revised relationships between the center and regions. Several provinces threatened to break away; there were separatist movements in East Timor, Aceh, Papua, and Maluku, and vocal demands for more autonomy were common in resource-rich provinces such as East Kalimantan and Riau. The Ministry of Home Affairs recognized that the only way to address these issues—that is, to prevent national disintegration—was to provide for a radically revised balance of power between Jakarta and the provinces.

The attempt to prevent disintegration is related to another crucial factor. The central government's financial capacity had declined dramatically following the economic crisis of 1997–1999. During the New Order, budget allocation to local governments was a tactic employed to reduce tension (resulting from regional disillusion in the central government) and to avoid the reemergence of the regional secession movements of the late 1950s. The financial crisis shrunk the central government's coffers, which meant that the new government could no longer employ funding as a political tool to silence regional dissatisfactions. The central government had little choice but to revise the revenue-sharing formula, which carries with it a hidden agenda of transferring financial burdens from the center to the regions. We return to this later.

The role of donors and multilateral financial institutions should also be mentioned. From the very beginning, the World Bank and International Monetary Fund (IMF) were especially supportive of the new policies. De-centralization policies were mentioned as conditionality in several letters of intent between the government and the IMF. The World Bank has in many other countries pushed for decentralization measures as a step toward cre-ating more responsive local governments.[4] The final implementation of the policies, in legislation to go into effect after two years of preparation, was pushed back to eighteen months in a letter of intent in 2000, as a sign of the government's willingness to reform its public administration.

We return to the content of these laws in the next section. Here, let us note only that there was much public criticism of the laws during the prepa-ration phase. Much of the early criticism was directed toward the highly un-democratic drafting process. Unlike the consultative drafting processes in countries such as South Africa and India, there were no open consultations or public deliberations. It was a state-driven process, without any mecha-nism for formal input from the public. There was lobbying from various ministries and interest groups to make sure that their particular function would be maintained at the center (but only the minister for religion was successful). During the deliberation process in the House of Representative (the Indonesian parliament), many government agencies were called to tes-tify or otherwise participate. Civil society input was confined to seminars and op-ed pieces, which were largely ignored. The law was seen by some as a kind of political rhetoric created by the transitional government to cool down or distract the wave of regional movements after Suharto's departure. Even if the law in a way is "better" than could have been expected of the Suharto-appointed parliament (the law was passed in May 1999, one month before democratic elections), commentators saw only defects, because the process was undemocratic.[5]

The Legal Framework for Decentralization

So, what kind of decentralization and regional autonomy does this legisla-tion actually allow for? Perhaps the first thing to observe is the different names of the new and old laws: Law 5 of 1974 was "Governance in the Regions" (Pemerintahan di Daerah) while the new Law 22 of 1999 is "Regional [or Local] Governance" (Pemerintahan Daerah). This small difference carries an important distinction: while the previous law detailed how the state governed in the districts, the new law emphasizes the autonomy of regional governments. It outlines the future structure of local governments and provides them with far-reaching self-government through a process of decentralization and regional autonomy.

The desire to swing the pendulum toward more decentralization is clearly indicated by the definition of decentralization itself, which says that decentralization is the transfer of central government authority to autonomous local governments (Paragraph 1e). This can be compared with the former law, No. 5 of 1974, which states that decentralization is the transfer of certain governmental affairs from central to local governments (Paragraph 1b).

The definition of decentralization is further detailed in the crucial paragraph 7, which deals with the power relationship between the central and local governments. Here, it is stated that local governments' authorities cover all governmental authorities, except those of foreign affairs, defense, justice, finances, religious affairs, and other authorities. The point to be emphasized here is that at a conceptual level, Law 22 manages to limit the central government's power to that of the above five authorities. However, the central government still assumes "other authorities" as stated at the end of paragraph 7, and this has engendered much controversy among scholars. The debate here is not questioning the existence of the central government's "other authorities," but rather the ways in which these authorities are to be determined. Ideally, the "other authorities" should be decided on the basis of bargaining and negotiation between the central and local governments. In other words, it must not be unilaterally decided by central government.

The question here is what is meant by "other authorities" in Law 22. The answer is outlined in Government Regulation No. 25 of 2000, which details the functions of the central and provincial levels of government.[6] Here, other authorities have been translated into 218 functions for the central government (besides the five authorities stated in Paragraph 7) and 111 functions for provincial governments. The 218 are mainly functions of standardization, regulation, and oversight, which are tasks that central governments tend to perform in most federal and/or decentralized polities. For instance, the Department of National Education will be responsible for development of the single national curriculum. Provinces have the authority to monitor implementation of this curriculum and ensure compliance. The authority to provide the educational services, however, has been devolved to districts and cities, who can decide on funding for school buildings, teachers' salaries (even though there is separate national legislation regulating civil servant salaries—a contentious issue!), and how the national curriculum is to be enacted in their district or city.

Interestingly, province- and central-government authorities are to be regulated. The government functions carried out at the district/municipal level are defined as those that will *not* be carried out at the central and provincial level. As we discuss later, this has led to problems, since local governments for decades were accustomed to being the implementers of central government agencies and ministries, and thus only carried out what they were told. Now, they are free to do whatever is not mentioned in Government Regulation 25 of 2000, but many are still waiting for and dependent on instructions from the center.

By reading the law this closely, we start to see a certain ambivalence between the need to decentralize and provide regional autonomy and thus keep the nation together, on the one hand, while powerful actors want to retain as much power as possible in the center, on the other hand. Thus, what we have is state-driven regional autonomy, almost decentralization by default. And this ambivalence is creating tensions, as we shall discuss shortly.

Another distinctive feature of Law 22 of 1999 is that it attempts to create a more balanced power relationship between the executive and legislative branches of government. While in Law 5 of 1974, the local parliament was given the status of inseparable part of the local government, in Law 22 of 1999 the parliament has been separated from the executive branch of government. There is thus a separation of power. To clarify the functions of the local parliament, Law 22 outlines the tasks and authorities assigned to the parliament. Among other things, the parliament is to elect local government heads (governor and vice governor; district head and vice district head; mayor and vice mayor—there are no direct elections of heads of government in Indonesia, although this is being discussed for the 2004 elections); initiate the drafting of by-laws and local regulations, and to approve this legislation; assess and approve the local budget proposed by the executive branch of government; and to provide day-to-day supervision of local government. This is very different from the Suharto era, when local parliaments simply rubberstamping agencies for executive decision making. As we will see, however, this newfound power has also in many cases led to excesses and abuses.

Significantly, Law 22 bypasses the provincial government to give authority and autonomy to district and municipal governments. To strengthen the position of district and municipal governments vis-à-vis the province, it is stated in Paragraph 4 of Law 22 that the provincial government, on the one hand, and district and municipality governments, on the other hand, are self-governments that are not in a hierarchical relationship to each other. As we will see, however, this has caused problems in practical implementation since some local governments have argued that they are no longer under the authority of a provincial government, and therefore need not heed its authority.

While Law 22 outlines the power relationship between central and local government, Law 25 provides the framework for a new financial and fiscal relationship between the two. Paragraph 3 of Law 25 states that the sources of local government revenue are (1) local government's own incomes; (2) central–local balance funds; (3) local loans; and (4) other legal revenues. Local income consists of local taxes, user fees, and revenue from local government–owned companies. Central–local balance funds consist of revenues from real estate and construction taxes, revenue sharing from natural resources, and various forms of funding allocations from the central government.

The most important part of Law 25 is the new revenue-sharing formulas. In the past, almost all local revenues were transferred to Jakarta before they were handed back in the form of projects or funds to local governments, without any clearly defined basis. As mentioned above, Law 25 allows local governments to retain 90 percent of the residential property tax, 80 percent of the land tax, 80 percent of forest and fishery revenues, 15 percent of oil revenues, and 20 percent of gas revenues. These revenues are further divided between province- and district-level governments, as defined specifically in the law.

Notably, important revenues such as income and corporate taxes remain the prerogative of the central government. This has meant that one of the incentives for local government innovation has yet to emerge: in line with neo-liberal thinking, local governments would compete over investments and thus provide "better" public services in order to attract companies and investors. But since corporate taxes go to Jakarta, there is no strong incentive at present to provide improved governance for this purpose.

Implementation of Laws 22 and 25

The decentralization policies were enacted on 1 January 2001, after eighteen months of planning and preparation. The two laws were passed in May

1999 and had initially a two-year preparation period, but as discussed above, the IMF and international donors pressed hard to move the implementation date forward, as a step toward institutional reforms. At the time of this writing, Laws 22 and 25 had been in force for a little more than eighteen months. There are problems inherent in such a radical and rapid decentralization. Law 22 assigns the provision of virtually all public services to district administration, without establishing the appropriateness of devolving these functions to this particular tier of government, how this might be achieved, the required sequence of measures, and how funding is to be secured. This devolution initially led to deterioration in the provision of services, as government expenditure for social services such as public hospitals and schools were reduced. It also meant an exacerbation of inequalities between districts, as localities are asked to pay for more and more of their own services. Regional autonomy has allowed resource-rich localities to keep their riches for themselves, and has thus augmented existing interregional disparities. A few resource-rich provinces have become richer (notably Riau and East Kalimantan) while others have become poorer.

There are no comprehensive studies yet, but most commentators seem to agree that the economic benefits of regional autonomy have to date largely been captured by local elites. It has also reinforced existing unequal relations, and led to a deterioration of natural resources. The fact that a larger share of revenues must be raised by the local government has acted as an incentive for districts to make ultimate use of their resources—in some provinces this has led to a rapid exploitation of minerals and forests. Funds have generally not been used to provide better public service or democratize local politics by pushing decision making closer to residents of the district or region, but to rather to support the local parliament and government. Large portions of local budgets are used for routine spending, such as salaries for civil servants and elected councilors (who get free housing and generous allotments for line items such as per diem and study tours).

One of the risks in the present quest for regional autonomy is that the former centralized pattern of decision making will be devolved downward. With more and more resources to be managed at the local level, the decision-making capacity of the local administration will automatically be reinforced, since the central government will have less authority. In other words, rather than having one strongman in the center (the president), many local strongmen may emerge. The central government has foreseen this, and therefore empowered local parliaments. But many members of parliament are neophytes. They do not have great skill in, for instance, applied budgetary analysis or policy planning. The existing public administration, on the other hand, has functioned for decades with well-greased machinery. Before local political accountability takes hold, devolved authority and resources are being used for less-than-laudable goals, leading to an increase in corruption and the possible rise of local strongmen.

One should perhaps not be surprised by this phenomenon, since the carrying out of Indonesian public administration on a day-to-day basis involves much bargaining and coalition building among government elites on various levels.[7] The key to understanding this phenomenon, we would argue, lies in the relative capacity of local government elites to make autonomous choices. Crucial here is the capacity to interpret central government policies, knowledge of local problems, alliances with particular social groups, and individual connections with high-level state officials. We would argue that autonomous decision making by local elites has been strengthened since 1999. In other words, enactment of Laws 22 and 25 has created more space for local state elites to pursue their own individual goals. The implementation of decentralization, then, is characterized by bargaining and coalition building among local elites, and the decision-making process tends to be concentrated in the hands of a few people, especially those who have assumed power in local governments and parliaments.

Local elites are more independent than in the past to carry out policies of their choice. While it was hoped that autonomy from the central government would be balanced by increased dependence up and responsiveness toward local constituencies, this has not necessarily happened. The reason is the absence of a clear mechanism for public accountability. Parties and politicians do not have clear-cut constituencies, and feel accountable primarily toward their party. But since most political parties are shallow, without any membership basis, there is a missing link in the accountability dimension. As we argue at the end of this chapter, this is one of the weaknesses of decentralization in Indonesia, and indeed demonstrates that decentralization without democracy will not necessarily be effective in shaping better public policies.

Therefore, it seems safe to say that the major obstacle to democratic decentralization in Indonesia is the resilience of state elites, including both civil servants and politicians. Most state officials have not embraced the idea of new procedures and standards accompanying decentralization and democratic reforms. Civil servants maintain old work patterns and attitudes, with a resulting paternalistic and hierarchical bureaucracy. Indeed, patterns of thinking and behavior rooted in the New Order remain strong. Indonesia is today one of the most corrupt countries in the world, reinforced by its list-ing as number 122 out of 133 countries in Transparency International's 2003 Corruption Perception Index.[8] Corruption prevails not only at the upper lev-els of government, but has trickled down to bureaucrats in local offices and even elected officials. Many, if not most, civil servants and local politicians lived very comfortably—and gained considerable power and wealth—un-der the Suharto administration, with privileged access to resources and power. They are today deeply worried about their future. These people, who are crucial for the implementation of decentralization, might initially be very reluctant to support democratic decentralization. It is ironic and greatly problematic that the people who should implement anticorruption and other good governance reforms are those who have the most to lose from these reforms: access to and control of the administration. We can thus not expect them to play an active role in reforming themselves.

We must immediately note here that local governments have no monop-oly on corruption and power abuse. The contrary is probably true: central government agencies in the past broke ground for rent seeking and patron-age, and local government elites had little choice but to abide by these prac-tices. While the character of corruption has changed somewhat since *refor-masi* (it has become less ordered and more difficult to control), central government agencies remain principal players. Patronage ties and rent-seeking relations are still in place. Thus, decentralization has not caused corruption. But neither has regional autonomy managed to eradicate the old practices.[9]

There are, therefore, no strong champions for decentralization policies in the central government. The law was initially drafted by a team in the Home Affairs Ministry that eventually became the core of a short-lived Min-istry of Regional Autonomy. Because of strong resistance from line min-istries, this ministry was discarded after a year. Since then, there have been no influential figures in Jakarta championing regional autonomy. In other countries, ministries of home affairs are often allies of local governments, speaking on their behalf and supporting their autonomy. In Indonesia, the Home Affairs Ministry has for decades played the opposite role, being the central government's extended arm and watchdog in the regions, and gain-ing both power and privileged access to funds through that centralized con-trol. In other words, the people who are to implement regional autonomy (Home Affairs) have the most to lose from implementing the regulations. One should perhaps not be terribly surprised if the central government sometimes is seen as stalling the process.

In fact, many observers talk about the half-hearted manner in which the central government is implementing the decentralization policies.[10] This is seen for instance in recent laws and regulations by line ministries such as Forestry and Mining. The authority over these functions, in Law 22, is devolved to local governments. But the national parliament has passed laws that allow line ministries to retain much of their authority. The ministries argue that these functions are covered by the "other authorities" of Law 22, which allow them to retain whatever authority they wish at the ministerial level, and they have been able to convince the parliament to support them. Critics and local governments argue that this only goes to show that the government is not taking decentralization seriously: they take back with their left hand what they have given with the right. Another sign of the hesitant manner in which the central government is implementing Laws 22 and 25 is the slowness by which implementing regulations are produced by the minister of Home Affairs. To date, only a limited number of the many governmental regulations mentioned in the two laws have been produced. And when they are produced, they are often counterproductive, in that they introduce new concepts and notions that do not appear in the two original laws. One case in point is Implementing Regulation No. 76 of 2001 on village governance, which in several key areas distorts, if not corrupts, the meaning and spirit of Law 22.[11] In short, the result is hesitation from the central government to fully implement regional autonomy. While the central government often states that "regions are not ready yet" (*daerah belum siap*) as one reason for the hesitation, in reality it is more likely that the central government is not quite ready yet for regional autonomy!

While various critics have accused the central government of stalling the process, there are signs that some local governments are excessively implementing their decentralized authorities—referred to by the elite in Jakarta as *otonomi kebablasan* ("over-acting autonomy"). Those who subscribe to this proposition, including powerful people in the Home Affairs Ministry who want to return power to central government authorities, usually point to the fact that local autonomy has, in many cases, been translated by local governments as a freedom to do whatever they wish to do (*sekali merdeka, merdeka sekali* [once independent, independence is all]).

Among the evidence to prove this position is the overwhelming manner in which local parliaments perform their supervisory authority. Law 22 introduces the notion of separation of powers by giving the local parliament three major functions: legislative, budgetary, and supervisory. In resource-rich provinces such as Riau, the local parliament has employed these new authorities as "weapons" for pushing through its annual budget vis-à-vis the local executive body. Law 22 only provides very basic outlines of relations between the parliament and local government executive. Assignment of the three functions to local parliaments has not been supported by clear-cut regulations on the specific forms and scope of each function. This situation has been exacerbated by the fact that many members of local parliaments are neophytes who lack governance skills.

Among other evidence quoted to show the practice of *otonomi kebablasan* by officials in Jakarta is the mushrooming of local regulations introduced by local governments for revenue raising, either in the form of local taxes or in the form of user fees. A recent study by Susanto,[12] for instance, argues that a majority of local officials interviewed in the province of East Kalimantan felt that local autonomy meant that they were free to make and implement decisions as they wished, without interference, including the freedom to define and enforce local regulations for revenue raising. As a result, we should not be surprised to learn that in the resource-rich district of Tenggarong, East Kalimantan, the government has introduced a large number of regulations to generate local revenue, such as user fees for and taxes on roads, non-timber forests, boats, fisheries development, timber production, and vehicles.

The argument stated by local elites to justify their behavior is quite intriguing. Local government elites rationalize their discretion in exercising authority through pointing to the unclear features of the decentralization policies and the delay in promulgation of central government regulations. The point that needs to be made here is that the conflicting features of the regulatory framework, delays in central government regulations, and the lack of clear mechanisms of citizen participation have allowed government elites (on all levels) to justify their practice of independent decision making.

In a survey by Hidayat and Firdausy,[13] many local government officials confirmed that a major objective of decentralization and local autonomy is to provide for and enhance social welfare. However, when they were asked why social welfare policies were not policy priorities in their districts, they emphasized the need to raise local revenues before social welfare improvements could be achieved. We should not be surprised to hear this argument, since it was used for decades by the Suharto regime: social equity and poverty alleviation could only be achieved after a measure of financial autonomy had been achieved. Moreover, many civil servants, as discussed above, have yet to change their basic orientation.

Let us now turn to some positive achievements of regional autonomy and decentralization. First, we need to qualify our previous remarks about the civil service: we are obviously not talking about all local governments and all local government officials here. What we have noted here is a tendency, and one that the Jakarta elite has been quick to respond to. Differences in governance styles and practices will become more common in the future. In the province of East Kalimantan, as an example, the different styles of the three neighboring governments in West, East, and Kertanegara Kutai have led to political tensions among them. Most international donors prefer the more participatory style of the West Kutai government and are providing technical assistance and funds to this government. Kertanegara Kutai is extremely resource rich and local officials have been able to mobilize their own resources. Meanwhile, not much is happening in East Kutai. We can thus expect that ten years hence, these three districts will be quite different. Hopefully, local governments will learn from each other's best practices, but this has not really started to happen yet.

Many encouraging developments are underway as a result of the new legislation. The positive sides of the decentralization policies are striking, and need to be appreciated. There is much innovation and new energy in local governments, with the new authority and trust instilled in them. Importantly, regional autonomy and democratization have opened up political space for citizens to become active in governing their communities. The momentum was initially provided by reformasi in 1998, with freedom of the press and of speech. With Law 22, policymaking has been pushed down to cities and districts, where people's voices are more easily heard than on the national level. In general, decentralization promises that decision making would become more transparent and accountable, as it is pushed downward, closer to the citizenry. Indeed, decentralization policies are often cited as prerequisites for the growth of local democracy.

In spite of the many problems outlined above, the legislation has provided the impetus for the growth of a public sphere at the local level. Even though the laws were drafted mainly to consolidate the nation, civil society has quickly seized the new opportunities. Primary among the new opportunities is that decisions are now taken at the level where they are carried out (the "subsidiarity principle"). In the past, with deconcentration, decisions were taken by higher authorities and local governments implemented whatever was decided for them. Even if democratic opportunities had existed for people to question public decisions, they would have had to go to distant high-level authorities to lobby in the corridors of power. Today, with decentralization, public decision making is done in the city or district where people live. It is much easier for citizens to access information and question decisions that affect their lives. We can see this in the rapid growth during the past few years of various local government watchdog nongovernmental organizations, such as budget-watch, parliament-watch, and media-watch groups, among others. By being members of the same larger community as decision makers, civil society organizations have been successful in questioning the government and upholding their democratic authority over public matters.

Local government elites are very excited about their new authority and power. This tendency is easy to understand, since the enactment of regional autonomy has resulted in the increased capacity of local bureaucrats and political leaders in local government to put pressure on central government policies, and to obtain a larger slice of national wealth for local governments. Efforts to bring local governments' concerns to the attention of the national government have been channeled not only through the formal government structure, but also through associations established by both local officials and political leaders, such as the Association of Provincial Governments, Association of District Governments, Association of District Parliaments, and Association of Municipal Parliaments. The point to be emphasized here is that the emergence of these associations is a positive result of regional autonomy policies. These associations have become useful instruments to increase local governments' bargaining power vis-à-vis the central government.

The separation of powers between the executive and legislative branches of local government holds many promises. As discussed above, this has not always occurred in practice, but there is much excitement. When nongovernmental organizations hold seminars today, and invite government officials or local councilors, they will come. There is a shift in mind-set, in which elected officials in many districts and cities are more responsive and responsible. According to a recent appraisal of decentralization by the Asia Foundation, the separation of powers and the growth of local democracy is clearly a major achievement.[14] Citizens feel that their voices are stronger, and that local governments have become more responsive. This varies across regions, but in spite of the slowness of change in public administration, much positive change has occurred thus far.

But again, this does not automatically mean that public decisions and service delivery will improve. Indeed, for an individual peasant, it does not really matter if a regulation or project is designed in Jakarta, the provincial capital, or the district: what matters is how good, efficient, and desirable the project is. Although decentralization promises to move decision making closer to the citizenry and thus make government more direct and responsive, this must be proved in practice. In fact, an authoritarian local government could be even *more* oppressive than its national counterpart, since it has direct access to subordinate levels of government.

Village Governance and Autonomy

One very important and positive impact of Law 22 is the democratization of village governments. There are nineteen paragraphs in Law 22 on village governments, replacing the unpopular Law 5 of 1979 on village governments. The 1979 law was very undemocratic and narrow, as it did not allow for any variations in organizational structure—all 61,000 village governments had to have the same uniform organization. The village was under the authority of the subdistrict, and the village government could not make any independent decisions. In exchange for their loyalty, though, headmen were given unlimited powers in the village. Separation of powers and autonomy did not exist under the old law.[15] There was some basic democracy, since the headman was elected, but these elections were tightly controlled by higher authorities, who could ensure that only loyal New Order candidates were elected.

There is a sense of real change in at the village level today as a result of Law 22. The law states (General Clarification, 9.1) that the basis for village government is "diversity, participation, real autonomy, democratization and people's empowerment." The law provides ample room for diversity, local aspirations, and responsiveness. The village is to be "based on origins and local customs," and it has the right to reject projects from outside if they are not accompanied by funding, personnel, and infrastructure. No longer is there a uniform pattern in which villages had no independent decision-making power. Today, villages have a certain degree of autonomy (although the term is not used in Law 22).

There is also considerable democratic renewal of the village government. Similar to the district and municipal levels, Law 22 provides for separation of powers in villages: the reformed village government consists of the headman and his staff, and the Village Councils (Badan Perwakilan Desa, literally "Village Representative Board"). The headman is primarily responsible to the village population through the Village Council. The headman is no longer oriented upwards; instead, he is accountable to the village population, and must answer questions at council meetings.

The introduction of the Village Council has been greeted with enthusiasm by everybody but perhaps some old-style village headmen. It is basically a miniature parliament, a legislative body elected every five years by and among villagers. The Village Council has the right to draft village regulations and the village budget, and it has the right to monitor village government. It even has the right to propose to the district chairman that the headman be removed from his post (but this decision is taken by the district government). The council has revolutionalized village governance, not only because it provides a mechanism for checks and balances of village government, but also because it revises the old paradigm of villagers as objects of development projects, to one in which villagers feel that they have the right to exercise their democratic authority over public matters in their home communities. The authority and autonomy of the Village Council is far greater than of the former Village Assembly (the Lembaga Musyawarah Desa). Candidates to the headmanship or Village Council are no longer subjected to political screening, although candidates must still fulfill certain criteria, including minimum education and maximum age.

After the reinvention of local autonomy and village democracy, there is in Indonesian villages a new sense of self-esteem and pride. It is a revival of an everyday form of democratic spirit that for decades was corrupted by the New Order. After having been the lowest rung in the Indonesian bureaucracy and firmly under the control of higher authorities for decades, villages are finally managed by the local population through the Village Council. There is a strong sense of local ownership, which of course is a crucial precondition for building trust with higher levels of government. People can accept that villages remain at the bottom rung of the Indonesian bureaucracy, as long as they have the right to decide over what is important for them in their everyday lives. With this sense of ownership has also come a new willingness to work together. In 2002, for example, it became much easier to mobilize people for various village-based labor parties, such as renovating irrigation channels or cleaning roadsides. With the new village-level autonomy, people feel that the community in which they live belongs to them, and they themselves have the right to manage the village. There are thus very strong and positive feelings among village residents toward their newfound autonomy and democracy.

However, this village autonomy is not clearly inscribed in legislation; Law 22 and 25 do not contain any clearly defined relationship or fiscal balance between the district and village. Villages are thus still dependent on funding from the district. In order for village autonomy to be meaningful and lasting, there is a need for improved legislation that provides decentralization of functions and funds from district governments to villages.

Revising the Law?

Because of the abovementioned ambiguities and abuses of Law 22, in mid-2001 President Megawati asked the Ministry of Home Affairs to revise the law. The central government has been worried over abuses of the law, especially as they relate to the separation of powers between the local government and parliament, and relations between district and provincial governments.

The first draft revision was officially released in November 2001. Since the revision has been inspired by the central government's desire to thwart the distortions discussed above, it should not come as a surprise that the substance of the revision itself seemed to bring back the previous New Order's concept of decentralization and regional autonomy as exercised through Law No. 5 of 1974 (see Table 9.1). Many observers are thus worried that the revisions will mean a return to the New Order paradigm of uniformity and centralism, which is another sign of the half-heartedness by which the central government has tended to implement regional autonomy.

Just to mention a few examples, it is stated in the Paragraph 1(a) of the revision draft that "the local government is the caretaker for the autonomous local government which consists of the local government head and the local parliament." This seems to imply that the local parliament is no longer separated from the local executive body (as stated in Law 22), but rather has been assigned the status of a part of local government. Another example is revision of the definition for decentralization itself. Paragraph 1 (f) of the revision draft states: "[D]ecentralization is the transfer of governmental matters [*urusan pemerintah*] from the central government to autonomous local governments." Meanwhile, according to the Law No. 22 of 1999, "decentralization is the transfer of government authorities to autonomous local governments." No longer is its authority and power to be devolved, but only the right to carry out certain matters. This revised definition for decentralization is similar to the definition of decentralization stated in the Law No. 5 of 1974. A final example pertains to the form and scope of central and local government authorities. According to Paragraphs 6 (2) and 7 (2) of the revision draft, "local governments have to execute compulsory governmental affairs and other governmental affairs which concerns the interest of lo-

Table 9.1

Issue Comparison of 1974 and 1999 Laws

	Law No. 22 of 1999	Draft Revision of Law 22 of 1999	Law 5 of 1974
Status of local representative body (regional assembly; Dewan Perwakilan Rakyat Daerah)	Local government consists of local government head and apparatus for autonomous region, which assumes function as local executive body Paragraph 1.b). Local parliament is local house of representatives (Paragraph 1.e).	Local government is caretaker for autonomous local government, which consists of local government head and local parliament (Paragraph 1.a).	Local government is local government head and local parliament (Paragraph 13.1).
Definition of decentralization	Decentralization is transfer of central government authorities to autonomous local governments (regions) within frame of unitary state of Indonesia (Paragraph 1.e).	Decentralization is transfer of governmental matters from central government to autonomous local governments (Paragraph 1.f).	Decentralization is transfer of governmental matters from central government to local governments or from upper- to lower-level local governments (Paragraph 1.b).
Form and scope of central and local government authority	Local governments' authority covers all governmental authorities, except those of foreign affairs, defense, justice, finances, and religious affairs (Paragraph 7.1).	Local governments must execute mandatory governmental affairs and other governmental affairs that concern local community interests (Paragraph 6.2). The central government's authority covers all authorities concerning foreign affairs, defense, security, immigration, finances, and religious affairs (Paragraph 7.2).	Local governments have right, authority, and responsibility to manage their own affairs (Paragraph 7). Assignment of certain governmental affairs to local government is determined by central government regulations (Paragraph 8.1).

cal communities . . . central government's authorities cover all of authority concerning foreign affairs, defense, security, immigration, finances, religious affairs, and other particular authorities." By comparison, as stated in Law No. 22 of 1999, "local governments' authorities cover all of the governmental authorities, except those of foreign affairs, defense, justice, finances, religious affairs, and other authorities." In the revision, the central government is clearly increasing authority to ministry-level agencies in Jakarta. Table 1 summarizes the above examples, highlighting the differences between the revision draft and Law No. 22 of 1999, on the one hand, and similarities with Law No. 5 of 1974, on the other.

Soon after completion of the revision draft, the Ministry of Home Affairs decided to sponsor a series of workshops in the regions to gather further input for improving the draft. However, many scholars and observers across the country have expressed their concerns that the central government is trying to "re-centralize" and return to the center some of the authorities and tasks that had been devolved to local governments. The main reason for the strong resistance to the draft is not that the law does not need to be revised (given the distortions discussed above), but rather a fear that the end result will be legislation that is even less conducive to local democracy. Consequently, observers have argued that it would be much better if central government ministries put their energy into producing implementation regulations, many of which have not yet been completed, rather than revision of the legislation.

In May 2002, the home affairs minister and President Megawati stated in public that although they still wanted Law 22 to be revised, the process had momentarily been halted. There were also strong lobbying from regional interest groups, such as the Association of District Governments (APKASI) and the Association of Municipal Governments (APPEKSI), and notably, from the former government party Golkar, which has its power base outside of Jakarta. Consequently, it seems that decentralization, with all of its good and bad features, will be given a chance in Indonesia.

Conclusions

Decentralization is a necessary but not sufficient precondition for the growth of meaningful local democracy. As the stories in Indonesia about mismanagement and power abuse attest to, decentralization policies in themselves do not necessarily promote good governance. Effective and

more democratic state management requires improved governance practices at the local level, practices that encourage everyday involvement of citizens in public affairs. According to Pimbert,[16] "the democratic potential of
decentralization is usually greatest when it is linked with the institutionali-
sation of local level popular participation and community participation."
There is no direct relationship between decentralization and democracy.
Decentralization must simultaneously strengthen local capacity *and* build
responsive governance systems.

Decentralization is less than two years old in Indonesia (after four
decades of authoritarian rule and extreme centralization), and we should not
expect long-held attitudes and practices to change overnight. The top layer
of government elites may have changed (legislators and executive and ministry heads), but in recent decades the abuse of power has become such an
ingrained praxis of bureaucratic behavior (i.e., it has become *systemic*), that
even the new democratically elected government has great problems in
eradicating abuse. In many cases, officials committed to ending such abuses
are well-meaning and responsive people, but they are forced to deal with a
long-established system—and it will take much longer than a few years to
change attitudes and behaviors.

To make things even a bit more difficult, the central government is only
half-hearted in its support for decentralization. Line ministries in Jakarta are
issuing laws and regulations that retract authorities devolved with Law 22. In
some instances, they have not created implementation agencies. In others,
such agencies have been created but some contradict Law 22. Studies in various countries—and this is also confirmed by some of the chapters in the current volume—highlight the central government's role in the success of decentralization. Indeed, this is a principal argument in Tendler's well-known
book on decentralization in Brazil.[17] Her point of view, and we think that the
experience of Indonesia supports this argument, is that decentralization will
only be effective and produce better public policies if the central government
(in addition to local governments and civil society) is clearly in favor of devolution. If high-ranking officials are, as is the case in Indonesia, still interested in maintaining the old system, it will be difficult to achieve meaningful
and effective autonomy. Instead, local governments are always pushing for
autonomy, sometimes overstepping legal boundaries (which critics then immediately label *otonomi kebablasan*), while the central government stalls the
process, and is criticized by both provincial and civil society actors, who want
to see a revised balance of power. This situation leads to tension, suspicion,
and distrust, all of which Indonesia cannot afford at present.

The solution to the dilemmas and problems of decentralization in Indonesia, in our view, is to deepen democratic processes, and there are great opportunities for this, with democratization and regional autonomy. One way is to move beyond political participation in elections to what has been called citizen participation.[18] Citizen participation involves systematic participation in decision formulation and decision making by groups of citizens, and of linking those who have developed participatory methods for consultation, planning, and monitoring to the new governance agenda. Citizen participation is usually driven by innovative and committed citizens demanding that their voices be heard. But the modus operandi can also be provided by state agencies as ways to overcome distrust in government and to empower local communities. In Indonesia, both of these ways to achieve citizen participation are needed, if the decentralization process is to be saved from excesses and abuses.

The "democratic" in democratic decentralization must be meaningful. It should mean that persons in authority in local councils or institutions are elected by secret ballot.[19] There are problems with this in Indonesia, with an election system based on party-list and proportional representation and no direct elections of heads of government. Mayors and governors are elected by the local parliament, and members of local parliaments are appointed by parties, in accordance with how many seats they won in the election. Since most political parties are not based on membership, ordinary people cannot influence this selection. Thus, voters in Indonesia do not know who represents them in parliament.

Has regional autonomy managed to "save the nation" as it was designed to do? It is really too early to say, but previously "restive" resource-rich provinces in Sumatra and Kalimantan are less vocal today. They are rather busy implementing regional autonomy. The risk is that the half-hearted attitude of the central government might lead to further demands from the regions. Regional autonomy has thus, to some extent, reduced regional dissatisfaction with the center. The ongoing democratic decentralization process must, however, be insulated from the central government's desire to "bring power back" to the center again.

What is our overall verdict for decentralization in Indonesia? Well, the jury is still out. There are many positive results of regional autonomy, including increased opportunities for popular participation, more responsive local governments, and the fact that local governments have by and large coped well with the massive transfer of authority and staff. A new balance of power and funding structure between center and regions is emerging. On the negative side of the equation is the continued misuse of public monies. However, this is not directly related to decentralization, since it has existed for decades. Perhaps we should not even expect decentralization policies to address corruption and abuse of power. These efforts need to be complemented by policies promoting the deepening of democracy, such as public consultations, citizen forums, and other deliberative mechanisms. Only through democracy and citizen participation will the full potential of decentralization and regional autonomy be achieved in Indonesia.

Notes

1. Claudia Buentjen, *Fiscal Decentralization in Indonesia,* Report P4D 1998-11 (Jakarta: German Technical Cooperation, 1998), 15.
2. C. MacAndrews and Amal Ichlasul, eds., *Hubungan Pusat-Daerah Dalam Pembangunan* (Jakarta: Raja Grafindo Persada, 1993), 48.
3. Buentjen, *Fiscal Decentralization in Indonesia,* 8.
4. For the arguments, see James Manor, *The Political Economy of Democratic Decentralization* (Washington, D.C.: World Bank, 1999).
5. This goes to show that a flawed law but a good process can be more acceptable to the public than a good law but a flawed process. Curiously, when the law was set to be revised by the Minister of Home Affairs in mid-2001 (see below), most public commentators defended the law and described it as fairly decent.
6. This governmental regulation, as well as the laws and other relevant legislation, is available in English at www.gtzsfdm.or.id.
7. Syarif Hidayat, "Decentralised Politics in a Centralised Political System" (Ph.D. diss., Flinders University, 1999).
8. Transparency International, Transparency International Corruption Perceptions Index 2003, press release, 7 October 2003 (available at: www.transparency.org/pressreleases_archive/2003/2003.10.07.cpi.en.html).
9. The fact that over the past five years, Indonesia has declined in Transparency International's corruption ranking has to do with the fact that this is a *perception* index. What counts is how corruption is perceived, and thus how visible it is. Rent-seeking behavior under Suharto was seldom in the censured media. Today, with freedoms of press and speech, the media is full of corruption stories. Consequently, corruption is more visible, which does not mean that it has increased in absolute terms.
10. See, for instance, the headlines in *Jakarta Post,* 2 July 2002.
11. For details, see Hans Antlöv, "Village Governance and Local Politics in Indonesia," in *Decentralization and Democracy in Southeast Asia,* edited by Anne Booth and Jonathan Riggs (London: Routledge/Curzon Press, forthcoming).
12. Hari Susanto, "Pengelolaan Sumber Daya Ekonomi Dalam Perspective Penguasa, Akademisi, dan Pengusaha Lokal" [Managing Economic Resources in the Perspective of Local State Elites, Academicians, and Local Business People], in *Otonomi Daerah dalam Perspektif Lokal* [The Regional Autonomy in Local Perspective], edited by Syarif Hidayat (Jakarta: Pusat Penelitian Ekonomi, 2001).

13. Syarif Hidayat and Carunia Firdausy, *Exploring Indonesian Local State-Elites' Orientation Towards Local Autonomy* (Jakarta: Japan International Cooperation Agency, 2002).

14. The Indonesia Rapid Decentralization Appraisal was initiated by the Asia Foundation and the U.S. Agency for International Development in December 2001. A synopsis of findings was released in July 2002.

15. See Hans Antlöv, *Exemplary Center, Authoritarian Periphery: Rural Leadership and the New Order in Java* (London: Curzon Press, 1995) for the old paradigm, and Antlöv, "Village Governance and Local Politics in Indonesia," for how this is changing today.

16. Michael Pimbert and Krishna Ghimire, *Social Change and Conservation* (London: Earthscan Publications, 2000), 81.

17. Judith Tendler, *Good Government in the Tropics* (Baltimore, Md.: Johns Hopkins University Press, 1997).

18. Hans Antlöv, "The Making of Democratic Local Governance in Indonesia," in *Democracy, Globalization and Decentralization in Southeast Asia,* edited by Francis Loh and Joakim Öjendal (Copenhagen: NIAS Press, forthcoming).

19. James Manor and Richard C. Crook, *Democracy and Decentralization in South Asia and West Africa* (New York: Cambridge University Press, 1998), 9.

Conclusion

Chapter 10

Decentralization and Democratic Governance: Lessons and Challenges

Andrew D. Selee and Joseph S. Tulchin

Over the past twenty years, most countries around the world have undergone significant processes of decentralization. Numerous factors have driven these processes, including the need to shore up the legitimacy of the state during economic crises, the desire to streamline the state, and the hope for improving democracy. This volume looks comparatively at the way decentralization processes have shaped democratic governance in six countries that have undergone or are negotiating transitions to democracy.[1] These six countries—Mexico, Chile, South Africa, Kenya, the Philippines, and Indonesia—have different political systems and histories of state–society relations and have followed diverse paths toward democratization. Nonetheless, all have undergone decentralization processes since the 1980s that political leaders, civic associations, international organizations, and scholars have argued would improve democratic governance.

We are grateful to Jonathan Fox, Philip Oxhorn, Gary Bland, Jim Manor, and Aprodicio Laquian for helpful comments on an earlier draft. Any errors, omissions, or imprecision remain our responsibility.

Decentralization is widely thought to improve democratic governance by bringing government closer to the people and thereby increasing state responsiveness and accountability. With authorities, functions, and resources redistributed among the various levels of government, the central government then coordinates and regulates the activity of the various levels.[2] This approach suggests that a strong state and strong civil society can and should be mutually reinforcing, and that decentralization can strengthen the state by making it more responsive and accountable to citizens.[3] This also suggests that decentralization could play an important role in what Oxhorn in the introduction terms the "social construction of citizenship" in new democracies by making the subnational arena a space for vibrant democratic participation.

The studies in this book lend support to the argument that decentralization can, under the right conditions, contribute to better democratic governance. The authors find important evidence of advances in democratic innovation at the local and regional level, and highlight a resurgence of public interest in political processes at the subnational level. However, these studies also underline that actual decentralization processes have often produced mixed results for democratic governance as well as for equity. Regions of improved government performance and heightened democratic participation co-exist with regions of authoritarian retrenchment and diminished state capacity.

Three factors appear to account for the variance in outcomes. First, there is often a significant gap between the rhetoric of decentralization and the actual policies implemented. The *motivations* of key actors in decentralizations processes, therefore, shed light on the kinds of decentralized regimes that are negotiated and their consequences for democratic governance. Second, the kinds of *institutional arrangements* employed often limit the capacity and autonomy of subnational governments to implement the functions that they are supposed to perform, which, in turn, undermine their relevance in the democratic process. In addition, institutional arrangements sometimes exacerbate existing inequalities, strengthening the capacity of some subnational governments at the expense of others. Finally, the uneven *texture of state-society relations* conditions the effects of decentralization on democratic governance within countries. The same process may simultaneously unleash democratic dynamism in one region or locality while reinforcing authoritarian enclaves in another. Only by understanding the historical patterns of state–society relations across regions and localities can we understand the ways that decentralization alters power relationships among local and regional actors.

Roots of Centralization

Decentralization is not a new phenomenon. Most of the countries in this volume have long histories of negotiating center–periphery relations and have experienced previous waves of decentralization.[4] In many countries, colonial regimes left a legacy of highly centralized government institutions but these co-existed with the existence of significant regional elites that competed for power and influence. After independence, postcolonial governments fought ongoing battles to rein in regional elites, going through cycles of centralization and decentralization. Ultimately, national elites were able, in all the countries in this study, to subject regional elites to a substantial degree of centralized power, although usually by negotiating informal channels for their continued influence.[5] In many countries, the fear of ethnic fragmentation further encouraged the centralization of power, as did the belief in state-driven development processes prevalent in the post–World War II period. As we argue elsewhere, the centralization of power was by no means an unattractive goal, since in many cases it allowed the state to avoid fragmentation and promote development.[6] However, in most countries in this volume, centralized authority was also used by authoritarian governments to limit citizenship rights and ensure the permanence of nondemocratic political systems. This has contributed to the current wave of decentralization as newly democratic governments seek to throw off the shackles of an old and oppressive order.

The patterns of centralization varied considerably from country to country. In Africa, colonial and postcolonial governments imported centralized European institutions of governance but applied them differentially in urban and rural areas. Mamdani has argued that rural governance was maintained through alliances with tribal leaders. The most extreme example of this system is postcolonial South Africa, where apartheid divided peoples into citizens (whites) and tribal members (blacks) with residual categories for people of mixed race and Indian descent. However, the colonial powers throughout the continent applied a somewhat similar system elsewhere, maintaining bifurcated systems of citizenship through pacts with tribal leaders in rural areas and citizenship relations with people in the cities. Post-colonial governments generally replicated these systems of "indirect governance" through tribal leaders.[7]

The countries of Latin America and Asia in this study also followed a similar pattern of national elite–regional elite bargaining in order to maintain governability. The governments of Mexico, Chile, the Philippines, and Indonesia succeeded in centralizing formal powers extensively into the hands of the national government, but maintained *de facto* pacts with regional elites who continued to have substantial informal powers in local affairs and shared the spoils of the political system with national political elites.[8] The Philippines and Latin America complemented strongly centralized government institutions imported originally from Spain with substantial informal rules that allowed regional bosses to govern some day-to-day affairs of citizens in their areas of influence.[9] In Indonesia, the fear of ethnic division played an extensive role in the centripetal tendencies of the state, as it did in Kenya.[10]

During the period after World War II, the predominant theories of development emphasized a preeminent role for the state as a motor of growth and industrial innovation.[11] This provided an additional motivation to centralize power and authority in the capital and in many cases helped generate new elites with loyalty to the central government rather than to regional interests. State-led development produced important achievements in growth for most developing countries and helped spawn national industrial capacity in many of them. However, the results of these achievements were often poorly distributed and often primarily concentrated in the capital and a few major cities.[12]

Although centralization sometimes helped eliminate competing regional elites, prevent ethnic fragmentation, and achieve a measure of development, it also helped sustain nondemocratic and exclusive political systems. In South Africa, the centralization of power and indirect rule were the bases for upholding apartheid. In Kenya and Mexico, single-party governments maintained themselves in power by reaching accommodations with regional leaders, intimidating opposition, and recycling political leaders through the party. Suharto's and Ferdinand Marcos's highly personalized regimes maintained strong central control on developments in Indonesia and the Philippines, respectively, by sharing spoils with local autocrats. And Chile, which had a long-standing history of democratic centralism, fell under almost two decades of centralized dictatorship under the military regime of Augusto Pinochet. Whatever gains centralization may have achieved for development and national unity, by the time these countries transitioned to democracy in the 1980s and 1990s, citizens largely identified centralization with the anti-democratic legacies of these regimes, the regional inequalities they spawned, and the absence of horizontal accountability in the political system.

Motivations for Decentralization

Great economic and political upheaval characterized the last two decades of the twentieth century. Most of the countries discussed here experienced economic slowdowns and a series of financial crises, which in turn led to significant changes in economic policy and the level of indebtedness. Trade and communications technology increased dramatically within this period, changing the nature of global markets. At the same time, the economic crises of the 1980s and 1990s undermined existing patronage networks and generated widespread disillusionment among citizens with their leaders. This contributed to the growth of citizen and civic organizations demanding greater political openness and accountability that helped undermine nondemocratic regimes.[13]

These factors combined to influence the decisions by governments around the world to decentralize. The case studies in this volume suggest that international institutions, although enthusiastic about decentralization, played minor or nonexistent roles in large-scale decisions to decentralize.[14] Rather, as Steven Friedman and Caroline Kihato observe (Chapter 6), domestic political elites seized on the internationally popular idea of decentralization to accomplish their own particular ends within the context of rapid political and economic changes.[15] These processes received the support of a broad range of political and social actors of diverse ideologies, although often for quite distinct reasons.

In most countries in this volume, decentralization has been, in part, linked to the desire of state elites to shore up their legitimacy in the eyes of citizens during processes of democratic transition. This is particularly true in the Philippines, where a strong civic movement helped remove the Marcos dictatorship and influenced the writing of a new constitution. The constitution presaged the writing of the Local Government Code, which granted subnational governments unprecedented authority. The active role of then President Corazón Aquino, who was concerned about her legacy, also helped expedite this process.[16] Similarly, in South Africa, the debate over decentralization began as part of the writing of a new constitution for the post-apartheid era and has continued within the context of negotiations among national elites, local elites, and civil society organizations to reform the constitution.[17] In Chile, political negotiations over municipal autonomy took place within the first few years of the restoration of democracy, as the elected government searched for a means of extending democratic governance to the local sphere.[18] In Indonesia, Hidayat and Antlöv (Chapter 9) argue that decentralization has been pursued largely as an emergency measure to keep the country together after the collapse of the Suharto regime and the chaotic return to democracy. National leaders in these countries saw decentralization as a means of restoring legitimacy to the state and, in some cases, themselves during the first few years of democratic rule.

In other cases, political leaders have used decentralization as a means of shoring up their legitimacy while simultaneously trying to forestall greater democratic openness. In Mexico and Kenya, for example, local political groups excluded from power in the central government pushed for greater decentralization to open up spaces at the margins of the political system; at the same time, central government elites saw decentralization as a means of redirecting attention away from the need for further democratic reforms at a national level. In Mexico, this succeeded in containing some of the conflict over national democracy for a few years and helped the governing party maintain itself in power, as Mizrahi argues (Chapter 2). Ultimately, however, opposition parties were able to use the political openings at the subnational level to increase their leverage and credibility and to negotiate changes in national electoral laws that ultimately led to a regime change.[19]

At the same time, decentralization has also been pushed as a response to particular conceptions of state reform, especially the desire to create a more efficient and globally competitive state. In Chile, for example, subnational governments were strengthened during the authoritarian regime of Augusto Pinochet as a means to achieve efficient administration. The elected governments of the 1990s further strengthened regional governments, but kept them as unelected bodies that serve primarily as "transmission belts" for national policies, according to Serrano (Chapter 4), even while municipal governments had been granted greater autonomy.[20] Friedman and Kihato (Chapter 6) argue that South Africa's provincial governments have been seen largely as administrative implementers, as their almost complete dependence on fiscal transfers indicates. Similarly, in Mexico national leaders saw decentralization to state governments also as a strategy to reduce central state expenditures and achieve a more efficient delivery of services (particularly in health care and education), according to Mizrahi (Chapter 2). In the case of

Mexico and Chile, initial efforts at decentralization in the 1980s were even seen as a means for the state to reduce its overall expenditures. Similarly, the Indonesian decentralization laws of 1999 were driven in part by a severe national government fiscal crisis (Hidayat and Antlöv, Chapter 9).

Motivations do not always determine outcomes, but the multiple and contradictory motivations for decentralization shed light on the complexity of the process and suggest that we should not be surprised to find multiple and contradictory outcomes as well (Table 10.1). At the outset, decentralization in these countries almost always has been pursued by national elites for a mixture of reasons, including strengthening democracy, directing attention away from national demands for democracy, making government more efficient, and reducing state expenditures. National leaders have often held several of these motivations simultaneously and pursued decentralization as a favorite strategy to address a series of highly distinct objectives.

Table 10.1
Initial Motivations for Decentralization

Country	Major Motivations in Initial Decisions to Decentralize
Mexico	Democratic transition: desire to deflect democratic demands; increasing influence of opposition parties in subnational governments
	State reform: desire to make the state more efficient
Chile	Democratic transition: return to democracy; desire to grant greater authority to municipal governments
	State reform: interest in efficiency; decentralization of responsibilities to regional governments
South Africa	Democratic transition: negotiation of a new constitution with the end of apartheid and beginning of majority rule
	State reform: decentralization of some functions to provinces with limited authority for policy in the postapartheid era
Kenya	Democratic transition: desire to deflect demands for greater democratic openness by constraining some of the local influence of central government authorities and allowing limited new powers to local officials
Philippines	Democratic transition: negotiation of new constitution after the fall of the Marcos regime; passing of the Local Government Code; influenced by President Aquino's interest in a democratic legacy
Indonesia	Democratic transition: decentralization to municipalities used under Suharto to undercut regional influences; major decentralization in 1999–2001 after democratization to forestall secessionist interests, restore legitimacy to political system, and respond to state fiscal crisis

While most initial negotiations on decentralization have primarily involved national leaders (often from both the executive and the legislative
branches), the strengthening of subnational governments gives new actors a
stake in the process of decentralization. Therefore, subsequent negotiations
on decentralization often involve new rounds of bargaining among national
leaders, local elites, and civil society actors over the future of decentralization.[21] Subnational governments have become increasingly important actors
in decentralization negotiations in some countries, but in others subnational
political leaders remain subordinate to national leaders. The Philippines is
perhaps the strongest example among the countries studied of an association
of mayors and governors that has become a successful interlocutor on decentralization reforms. In Mexico, each of the three main parties has created
its own association of mayors, as Santín notes (Chapter 3), which shows the
beginnings of common concerns among mayors, but still subordinate to par-
tisan concerns. In South Africa, Friedman and Kihato (Chapter 6) note that
subnational leaders remain largely subordinate to national officials, in large
part because of the vertical structure of the African National Congress, which
controls most subnational governments. In some countries, civil society organizations have gradually begun to see local government structures as essential for improving democratic governance and become more involved in
decentralization debates, as Santín observes for Mexico (Chapter 3) and Angeles and Magno for the Philippines (Chapter 8). This suggests that while
we need to look primarily at the motivations of national elites to understand
initial decisions to decentralize, we may need to look at a broader spectrum
of actors who become involved in the process, as well as their motivations
and interests as decentralization processes are renegotiated and reformed.

The Impact of Institutional Arrangements

Institutional arrangements determine the legal status of subnational governments, their degree of autonomy, capacity to assume particular responsibilities, channels of accountability, and resources.[22] Decentralization processes
have political, administrative, and fiscal dimensions.[23] Decentralization involves the redistribution of authority between national and subnational units
and between subnational governments and citizens (political); the assignment of specific functions among levels of government (administrative); and
determinations on the collection of revenues and the exercise of expenditures
at different levels (fiscal). It is particularly important, as Oxhorn notes in the

introduction, to look at both the democratization of subnational governments as well as the extent to which they have sufficient autonomy and capacity to function as relevant governance structures.

The political dimension of decentralization has first and foremost involved the clearer delineation of the status of regional and local governments vis-à-vis national governments. In most countries in this volume, the status of subnational governments was often unclear or contained overlapping authority with the national government. Decentralization processes generally defined the authority of the various levels of government and distinguished separate spheres of authority more clearly. As summarized in Table 10.2, in some cases, these changes were enshrined in new constitutions (South Africa, Philippines); constitutional amendments (Mexico, Kenya); or major pieces of legislation (Philippines, Indonesia, and Chile). In all cases, these reforms clarified roles for different levels of government and altered the balance of power among them to a greater or lesser extent.

The second political dimension has involved the implementation of democratically elected governments in all the countries. All six countries had some form of subnational government historically, although these tended to be quite weak as structures of democratic governance. In some cases, subnational governments had important functions but were not elected and therefore acted as implementation arms of central authorities. In other cases, subnational governments were chosen in regular elections but these elections were far from free and the subnational governments had few relevant functions. In these cases, subnational governments served primarily as proving grounds for aspiring politicians and key links in elaborate patronage networks. Significant decentralization reforms helped ensure competitive elections in all local governments in the six countries, although the degree of competitiveness and openness of these elections varies considerable *within* some of these countries. At a regional level, directly elected governments exist in three of the countries (Mexico, Philippines, and Indonesia) with indirectly elected regional governments in Chile and South Africa and appointed regional (provincial) governments in Kenya.

At the same time, administrative and fiscal decentralization has given subnational governments additional functions and resources in recent years, making them much more relevant actors in the policymaking process. As Table 10.3 indicates, in less than a decade subnational expenditures in Mexico rose from just over 18 percent to more than 28 percent; in the Philippines from under 8 percent to over 18 percent; and in South Africa from 18 to 34 percent. However, in other countries, such as Kenya and Chile, the

Table 10.2

Institutional Structure of Decentralization Reforms

Country	Legal Basis of Decentralization Reforms	Subnational Divisions
Mexico	Various constitutional changes, especially to article 115 in 1983, 1984, and 1999; repeated changes in fiscal formulas; several decentralization laws giving additional functions for health care and education to state governments	31 states and 1 federal district; 2,412 municipalities
Chile	1980 municipal law under military dictatorship transferred health care and education responsibilities to municipalities; 1992 Organic Municipal Law introduced the direct election of municipal officials; regional governments given legal status in 1993 with Organic Constitutional Law on Governance and Administration within the State	13 regions, 342 municipalities
South Africa	1996 Constitution created the current structure of provinces and municipalities and outlined their functions; the Municipal Structures Act (1998), Municipal Systems Bill (2000), and other laws have subsequently shaped the relationship among the "spheres" of government	9 provinces; 284 municipalities
Kenya	A few constitutional and legal changes as a result of the 1997 Inter-Parties Parliamentary Group limited the authority of the presidentially appointed provincial administrator, allowing district governments to have greater authority in policymaking	7 provinces plus Nairobi Area; 63 districts; further administrative divisions within districts
Philippines	Constitution set framework in 1987; the Local Government Code of 1991 defined the authority of different levels of government	78 provinces; 83 cities; 1,526 municipalities and towns; and 40,000 *barangays*
Indonesia	Law No. 22 on Local Governance (passed 1999, enacted 2001) granted authority to districts and municipalities to manage most services; Law No. 25 restructured fiscal relations	30 provinces; 380 districts and municipalities; 61,000+ village governments

Sources: Chapters in this volume; Richard Stren et al., "Decentralization in Global Perspective: A Review of Twenty-Eight Country Experiences" (report prepared for UN-Habitat, Nairobi, Kenya, October 2002).[24]

Table 10.3

Percent of State Expenditures by Subnational Governments

Country	1990	1998
Mexico	18.43%	28.97% (1997)
Chile	7.22% (1992)	8.52%
South Africa	18.40%	34.22%
Kenya	4.34%	No data
Philippines	7.78%[a]	18.26%[a]
Indonesia	11.19%	10.08%[b]

Source: World Bank, "Fiscal Decentralization Indicators," World Bank Decentralization Database (available at: www1.worldbank.org/publicsector/decentralization). These figures are based on the International Monetary Fund's government finance statistics.

Note: Statistics on subnational expenditures are notoriously unreliable, but these show general trends that are useful for comparison.

[a] The International Monetary Fund's government finance statistics do not have updated information on the Philippines; therefore, the data for the Philippines are drawn from Rosario G. Manasan, "Fiscal Decentralization: The Case of the Philippines" (paper presented at World Bank course, Decentralization and Intergovernmental Fiscal Reform in East Asia, Bangkok, Thailand, 6–7 June 2002), 13.

[b] As of 2001, revenue sharing by the Indonesian central government was 25% of national revenues.[25]

percentage of expenditures by subnational governments remained quite minimal and showed little change throughout the 1990s. This was also true of Indonesia throughout the 1990s; however, the 2001 reforms appear to have dramatically increased the revenues of subnational governments.

The increased share of state expenditures that subnational governments are responsible for reflects new functions that they have taken over from the central government in each of the countries. In the Philippines, subnational governments are responsible for a range of functions, from education to natural resource management to infrastructure development. In Mexico and South Africa, state and provincial governments, respectively, have taken over most aspects of education and health care, while municipal governments have new responsibilities for most local services and some secondary healthcare functions. In Indonesia, perhaps the most extensive decentralization process of the six countries, subnational governments have been given responsibility since 2001 for everything but religious affairs and what Hidayat and Antlöv (Chapter 9) call the "federal four": finances, foreign policy, defense, and justice.[26]

These extensive responsibilities and level of expenditure hide real limitations in the autonomy and capacity of subnational governments in all six countries, however. Since the responsiveness of the state to citizens is partially a function of whether the subnational units have the autonomy and capacity to perform their functions effectively and responsively to citizens, the functions attributed to subnational governments and their ability to undertake new responsibilities are central to democratic governance. In Mexico, Chile, and South Africa, regional governments have been assigned ever-increasing functions for health care, education, and social services from the national governments (Mizrahi, Chapter 2; Serrano, Chapter 4; Ducci, Chapter 5; and Friedman and Kihato, Chapter 6). Nonetheless, these are primarily transfers of existing responsibilities and staff from the national government, and these transfers sharply limit the autonomy of subnational governments to set policy in these areas. In addition, the regional level of government in these three countries depends almost entirely on national government resource transfers, which come with very specific conditions for expenditure. In South Africa, the decision-making capacity of the provincial governments is further limited by the constitutional figure of concurrency, which assigns joint responsibility for most functions to both the national and provincial governments. In the case of Kenya (Khadiagala and Mitullah, Chapter 7) and, until recently, Indonesia (Hidayat and Antlöv, Chapter 9), transfers of responsibilities have often been in the form of deconcentration, through which the national government assigns responsibilities to its regional offices in coordination with subnational governments but without any significant policymaking responsibilities for the subnational governments. Ironically, deconcentration often strengthens the central government by giving it direct control over local affairs at the expense of local governments.[27]

Of the cases studied, only in the Philippines do provincial governments have clearly defined responsibilities separate from those of the national government with their own major revenue sources, supplemented by national government resource transfers. It is perhaps no surprise that national leaders have been skeptical about strong regional authorities in many countries, preferring to grant local governments greater autonomy than regional governments as a means of avoiding potential challenges to national policy from strong regional leaders.

The case of local governments is substantially different in most of the countries studied since these tend to raise a larger percentage of their own revenue and to have wider latitude for setting policies. Local governments have assumed primary responsibility for a series of municipal services, often including water, waste disposal, local infrastructure, and some social development functions. Local governments thus appear to have been the more innovative structures of democratic governance in many countries, since they have a margin for decision making that regional governments do not. This is particularly noticeable in Chile, Mexico, South Africa, and Indonesia. On the other hand, local governments have significantly fewer resources than regional governments and are limited in the kinds of concerns they can address.

Local governments also have strikingly uneven capacities to assume their new responsibilities. Since local governments are more likely to depend on their own revenue sources, wealthier localities often have much more effective governments than their poorer counterparts. Friedman and Kihato (Chapter 6) note that fiscal autonomy has exacerbated disparities among municipalities in South Africa as more urban and historically wealthier municipalities have consolidated their tax base while others have been left behind. This problem holds true for both local and regional governments in the Philippines, Indonesia, and Mexico. Transfers to subnational governments in these countries follow formulas that fail to redistribute these resources adequately and often end up benefiting wealthier municipalities and regional governments.[28]

This points to one of the key difficulties in the institutional arrangements of fiscal policy: the need to balance self-generated resources with fiscal transfers that equalize the resources available to subnational governments. All of the countries studied have had to negotiate the tension between allowing subnational governments the ability to raise their own revenues, which allows them greater flexibility and responsiveness to citizen concerns in policy decisions, and the need to ensure equitable access to resources via equalizing national transfers. This is often compounded by transfer formulas that fail to ensure an equitable distribution of resources and are so arcane that it is difficult to figure out their real effects. In both the Philippines and Mexico, for example, transfer formulas try to balance several competing criteria for distribution, including population size, economic need, and capacity for local resource mobilization.

Decentralization, therefore, runs the risk of exacerbating existing disparities among wealthier and poorer regions and localities within countries. This can be addressed partially through institutional designs that target poorer regions with additional resource transfers. However, targeting poorer regions is no guarantee that the poor themselves will receive those resources, since even poorer areas often have great internal disparities as well.[29] Therefore, it is equally important to look at the institutional structures of local and regional governments and the ways that these influence intralocal resource distribution. In many cases, accountability mechanisms from the national government that require subnational governments to take into account normally excluded groups (e.g., farmers in a mixed urban–rural municipality) may play a key role in this process.

Implications: Democratic Innovation and Authoritarian Enclaves

As decentralization has produced uneven outcomes for the autonomy and capacity of subnational governments, it has also produced uneven outcomes with regards to their ability to serve as loci of democratic innovation. As Oxhorn notes in the introduction, decentralization processes cannot be viewed separately from the democratization of subnational governments. Although we generally view democratization as a national process, most countries show significant differences in state–society relations across regions and localities.[30] Democratization at a national level often leads to democratization at a subnational level. Democratization with decentralization can lead to very innovative experiences of local-level democracy. However, in some places authoritarian and clientelistic patterns of state–society relationships continue to persist even after the consolidation of a *polyarchical* regime at a national level, and decentralization may strengthen these.[31]

The authors in this volume give evidence that subnational governments have generated significant innovations in democratic governance in many of the countries studied. In the Philippines, Local Development Councils, Health Boards, Peace and Order Councils, School Boards, Project Monitoring Committees, and Prequalification Bids and Awards Councils, among others, give citizens an opportunity to participate actively in the implementation of local public policies and keep elected officials accountable (Angeles and Magno, Chapter 8).[32] Similarly, Integrated Development Plans in South Africa and School Governing Councils may provide new channels for citizen input in South Africa (Friedman and Kihato, Chapter 6). In Mexico, Municipal Planning and Development Councils and increased collaborations between nongovernmental organizations and municipal governments in Mexico also provide new opportunities for citizen engagement (Santín, Chapter 3).[33] These institutional innovations, under the right conditions, have the potential to give citizens added opportunities to engage with policymakers on key decisions and create a new ethos of public accountability. In addition, these participatory institutions may help create forums where citizens can participate in deliberative decision making by debating public policy with elected leaders and other citizens. This may allow people to construct new conceptions of their collective needs and interests, rather than merely expressing their choices retrospectively at the ballot box.[34]

Nonetheless, these participatory institutions are not very widespread, and even when they are employed, they often fall short of their stated goals of promoting greater accountability and civic engagement. In South Africa, Friedman and Kihato (Chapter 6) observe that Integrated Development Plans are in most case too technically cumbersome to serve as real instruments of public engagement. Similarly, in Chile and Mexico, legally mandated municipal planning boards have rarely functioned well except in cases where local officials and civil society organizations have adapted these to their own local needs.[35] In many cases, Angeles and Magno observe (Chapter 8), civil society organizations may be suspicious of government efforts to create participatory governance structures given real histories of manipulation and mistrust. Moreover, they note that regional elites often co-opt participatory boards or use them to penetrate the state by forming their own civil society organizations that can participate in these structures.

On balance, the use of participatory instruments to build new relations between citizens and the state appears to be one of the innovative outcomes of decentralization that deserves further scrutiny because of its potential to strengthen democratic governance. At the same time, it is unclear to what extent most of these structures have succeeded in living up to their potential. The case studies suggest three tentative lessons about participatory approaches to local governance. First, participatory approaches to democratic governance appear to work well when they are locally initiated rather than mandated from above. Second, participatory instruments appear to function well only where strong representative democracy with "downward accountability" to citizens already exists.[36] Where representative democracy is weak, participatory approaches to governance may instead strengthen authoritarian local leaders.[37] Third, municipal governments have become a much more important site of democratic innovation than regional governments in the countries discussed. This is partially a result of the limitations placed on regional governments, but also of the potential for smaller units that are spatially closer to citizens to experiment with innovative strategies for deepening democracy.

Although decentralization has produced important examples of democratic innovation, it has also reinforced some local and provincial governments as bastions of authoritarian control and helped them to resist democratizing tendencies at the center.[38] Local strongmen in the Philippines,

Indonesia, Mexico, and Kenya have also been able to strengthen their hold on their particular power bases, especially in rural areas, with the legitimacy conferred by the resources and responsibilities of decentralization reforms. These enclaves of authoritarian rule are often the product of national authoritarian regimes that maintained power through agreements with local and regional elites. Elected regimes have often kept these relationships of accommodation with subnational authoritarian regimes in order to ensure governability.[39] As a result, civil and political rights tend to be unevenly distributed within societies.[40] These findings suggest that in some cases national government efforts to increase the capacity of civil society organizations, preserve associational autonomy, strengthen the judicial system, and hold subnational governments accountable for resource expenditures may be necessary to undermine the control of local elites and help strengthen civil society.[41]

The research summarized in this volume does not enable us to draw firm conclusions on the reasons why decentralization produces such different outcomes across the political landscape of the same country other than to suggest that the landscape of existing state–society relationships influences these outcomes significantly. One influential theory suggests that social capital, defined as norms of reciprocity and networks of civic engagement, helps determine the degree to which particular localities can take advantage of decentralized governance as a strategy for improved democratic governance.[42] Unfortunately, no similar national studies exist for developing countries, and a few empirical studies have cast doubts on whether civic engagement automatically leads to better democratic governance in countries with recent authoritarian histories.[43] Other approaches look at the micropolitics of state–society relations[44] and the way that civil society actors in specific contexts develop social capital and negotiate demands with the state.[45] These approaches suggest that we may need to pay greater attention to the historical patterns of state–society interactions over time and the way that organizations autonomous from the state develop internally and in relationship to state actors. One recent comparative study of several municipalities in Mexico finds that successful municipal innovations take place when there is a synergy among local government, civil society organizations, and the private sector, and that local leadership may be particularly relevant for achieving these outcomes.[46] Another study highlights the presence of strong civil society organizations with the ability to monitor and hold local governments accountable.[47]

Decentralization outcomes are also influenced by the nature of intra-local politics. Local power relations are often highly unequal with significant divisions between wealthier and poorer citizens or between more urbanized and rural areas. Although the evidence from the case studies is inconclusive on this subject, we suspect that the success of decentralization initiatives in improving democratic governance depends in part on the restructuring of local power relationships by empowering previously excluded sectors.[48] The presence of strong civil society organizations representing excluded groups can play an important role in this. Similarly, rules that require local government accountability for outcomes, such as requirements on how resources must be distributed, may also be able to play a role in this. In this sense, the role of central governments in decentralization regimes may be critical for achieving positive local outcomes.

Challenges for Policy and Research

The studies in this volume suggest that in countries emerging from long periods of authoritarian rule where power has been concentrated almost exclusively in the central government, decentralization can play an important role in building new linkages between the state and citizens based on accountability. At the same time, the studies make it clear that decentralization, in and of itself, does not improve democratic governance. Rather the motivations for decentralization, the patterns of state–society interaction, and the nature of institutional arrangements all influence the extent to which decentralization may contribute to a more dynamic and democratic relationship between the state and its citizens. Within this context, the study suggests several challenges for policymakers who would like to use decentralization as a tool for improving democratic governance and for researchers who can help us understand this relationship better.

One challenge is the need to respond to the varied and uneven nature of subnational democratic regimes. While there is no single approach to address this, decentralization needs to be viewed together with other measures that seek to democratize public life, ensure the transparency of institutions, promote the flow of information, safeguard citizens' rights, and undermine clientelistic relationships. In many cases, this may require specific attention to strengthening political and civil society organizations that may be able to help citizens articulate their participation more effectively in governance structures. In other cases, it may require developing structures of account-ability between subnational and national governments that restrict the mar-gin for action of authoritarian subnational elites. This also means giving ad-ditional attention to the judicial system, subnational electoral institutions, and laws that provide access to information.

One promising trend that several of the studies discuss is the growth of participatory planning and oversight institutions at the local level, which al-low citizens to engage in policymaking between elections, increase their in-teraction with the government, and suggest alternatives for policy. While these institutions do not always work as expected, in some cases they ap-pear to have had a positive effect on accountability, responsiveness, and civic engagement. Innovative institutions for giving citizens a voice in pub-lic affairs often function well when they are locally generated, complement strong representative institutions, and empower citizens who are often ex-cluded from the policy process.

A second challenge is to improve the design of institutional arrange-ments for decentralization. This includes defining clearly the responsibili-ties that can be implemented effectively at different levels, deciding on the sequencing of decentralization reforms, and determining the linkages be-tween national and subnational governments that can maximize efficiency and maintain accountability. Decentralization processes may need to ex-plore creative approaches to decentralization that allow subnational gov-ernments to assume different kinds of responsibilities depending on their interests and capacities. Several innovative strategies for addressing this have been tried in recent years and may serve as possible models to build on further. One of these is "asymmetrical decentralization," which allows subnational governments to choose from a menu of possible functions that they want to assume and, therefore, allows them to adapt their responsibil-ities to their capacities and the interests of citizens and policymakers.[49] The decentralization of healthcare services to the states in Mexico partially fol-lowed this approach, as Mizrahi (Chapter 2) notes. Another strategy is to al-low small- and medium-sized municipalities to associate themselves to take advantage of economic development opportunities as a collective, thus maximizing their comparative advantage. Although associated municipali-ties exist in some countries (including Guatemala and Argentina, countries not addressed in this volume), this is a relatively new and untested idea still.[50] A third strategy looks for ways of bringing together metropolitan ar-eas to plan and execute policy together. Large metropolitan cities are often fragmented politically among the principal city and other suburban municipalities, which makes coordinated policy planning difficult. Metropolitan-wide governance has been tried with limited success in Jakarta and Manila, as well as in cities outside of the countries discussed in this book, but has yet to become a generalized practice.[51] These innovative strategies for adapting decentralization to particular contexts suggest that current institutional arrangements need to be evaluated in the light of the particular needs and concerns of citizens in various subnational units and the capacities of subnational governments to assume new functions.

Within the design of institutional structures, one of the most important challenges is to find the right balance between fiscal autonomy and adequate financial transfers to ensure an equitable distribution of resources to subnational governments. A degree of fiscal autonomy is necessary in order to ensure some flexibility in policymaking at subnational levels. Nonetheless, transfer schemes that balance out economic inequalities must be central to any attempt to create an equitable process of decentralization, and they are equally vital for the degree of long-term confidence that citizens have in the democratic system itself.

A third and final challenge is to find inclusive strategies to debate and decide on future decentralization reforms. Institutional reforms that include input from citizens and a broad range of political, civil society, and private sector organizations are much more likely to have legitimacy and the support of citizens. Moreover, the process of debate and decision making is central to engaging political and social actors with the state in new ways and empowering them to be able to respond to reforms and take advantage of new opportunities for participation in democratic governance. Although initial decentralization reforms have usually been designed and decided by political elites, the deepening of this process will need more inclusive and pluralistic processes for future decision making.

The studies included in this volume shed light on a range of key issues in the relationship between decentralization processes and democratic governance, and they show the importance of cross-national and cross-regional studies for approaching this issue. The sharing of experience across countries and regions allows us to find both the commonalities among different countries' experience as well as vital differences that can help us understand the nuanced particularities of each country. These studies also open up questions for future research in order to better understand the complex relationship between decentralization and democratic governance. First, more research is needed to understand how decentralization reforms contribute to changes in the patterns of representation and participation at the subnational and national level. In particular, we know very little about the reasons why some subnational governments become successful innovators in democratic governance while others reinforce authoritarian patterns. The results do not appear to conform to the predictions of social capital theories, which leaves open questions of what factors contribute to innovation and successful democratic experimentation. At the same time, we need to know more about how decentralization is transforming party systems at subnational levels and under what conditions participatory governance institutions can effectively complement strong representative systems. In addition, we need to connect findings about local democratization to national-level analyses of democratic processes to understand whether gains in democratic governance at a local level actually contribute to improved national-level democracy as well. In short, we need to find ways of analyzing the conditions that promote improved governance and the relationship that this has to the overall political system.

Second, we need to understand better the way that decentralization affects state capacity and the ability of the state, seen as a whole, to be responsive and accountable to citizens. Has decentralization strengthened the state's capacity in the aggregate or undermined its ability to carry out its functions? How has this varied across regions and localities within countries and among various state sectors (e.g., health, education, social welfare, environment)? In particular, we need to understand better the variables that allow localities and regions to take advantage of decentralized arrangements and the kinds of fiscal, administrative, and political arrangements that create an equitable and effective devolution of responsibilities to subnational governments. The connections between state capacity at all levels and democratic governance provide a key arena to explore the overall impact of decentralization on the quality of democratic governance.

As the studies in this book show, decentralization does not always guarantee improved democratic governance. However, democratic governance requires new strategies for bringing the government closer to citizens and making it more accountable and responsive to them. We need to learn more about the conditions that facilitate successful decentralization outcomes and the institutional frameworks that help ensure its effectiveness and equity. This should be a central task for those who are concerned about the quality of democracy.

Notes

1. We define democratic governance as the set of interrelations and rules mutually agreed upon that hold the state and its citizens accountable to one another.

2. Patrick Heller, "Moving the State: The Politics of Democratic Decentralization in Kerala, South Africa, and Porto Alegre," *Politics and Society* 29, no. 1 (March 2001): 131–63.

3. Cf. the articles by Atul Kohli and Vivienne Shue, "State Power and Social Forces: On Political Contention and Accommodation in the Third World," in *State Power and Social Forces: Domination and Transformation in the Third World,* edited by Joel S. Migdal, Atul Kohli, and Vivienne Shue, 293–326 (Cambridge: Cambridge University Press, 1994), and Naomi Chazan, "Associational Life in Sub-Saharan Africa," in *State Power and Social Forces,* edited by Migdal, Kohli, and Shue, 255–89 (Cambridge: Cambridge University Press, 1994).

4. On previous waves of decentralization, see Kent Eaton, "Politics Beyond the Capital: The Design of Subnational Institutions in South America" (unpublished manuscript, Princeton University, n.d.); and Richard Stren, "The Newest Decentralization: Can We Sustain It?" (unpublished manuscript, University of Toronto, 2002); an abridged version is available in the newsletter of UN-Habitat *Habitat Debate* 8, no.1 (March 2002).

5. Cf. Joel S. Migdal, *Strong Societies and Weak States: State–Society Relations and State Capabilities in the Third World* (Princeton, N.J.: Princeton University Press, 1988).

6. Andrew Selee, "Decentralization and Democratic Governance in Latin America" (Washington, D.C.: Latin America Program, Woodrow Wilson International Center for Scholars, n.d.). The degree to which the central government promoted these goals differed among the different countries *and* among different time periods in each country. However, it is worth noting that the centralization of power often helped ensure goals of development and democracy at the expense of regional elite interests.

7. Mahoud Mamdani, *Citizen and Subject: Contemporary Africa and the Legacy of Late Colonialism* (Princeton, N.J.: Princeton University Press, 1996).

8. For Latin America, see Frances Hagopian, "Traditional Power Structures and Democratic Governance in Latin America," in *Constructing Democratic Governance: Latin America and the Caribbean in the 1990s,* edited by Jorge I. Domínguez and Abraham F. Lowenthal, 64–86 (Baltimore: Johns Hopkins University Press, 1996); and Selee, "Decentralization and Democratic Governance in Latin America." For Mexico, see Yemile Mizrahi (chapter 2, this volume) and Alberto Díaz Cayeros, *Desarrollo Económico e Inequidad Regional: Hacia un Nuevo Pacto Federal en México* (Mexico City: Miguel Angel Porrúa, 1995). For Chile, see Claudia Serrano (chapter 4, this volume). For the Philippines, see Leonora Angeles and Francisco Magno (chapter 8, this volume). For Indonesia, see Syarif Hidayat, "Decentralisation in Indonesia" (paper presented at the Woodrow Wilson International Center for Scholars Workshop on Decentralization, Washington, D.C., 20–21 February 2000).

9. Claudio Veliz, *The Centralist Tradition in Latin America* (Princeton, N.J.: Princeton University Press, 1980). In the case of Latin America, most countries in the postcolonial period modified these institutions to reflect French innovations, which were also highly centralized.

10. Anwar Shah, "Balance, Accountability, and Responsiveness: Lessons about Decentralization," World Bank Policy Research Working Paper No. 2021 (Washington, D.C.: World Bank, December 1998). A previous version of this paper was presented at the World Bank Conference on Evaluation and Development, Washington, D.C., 1–2 April 1997.

11. James Manor, *The Political Economy of Decentralization* (Washington, D.C.: World Bank, 1999). See also Philip Oxhorn's introduction to this volume.

12. Robert H. Bates, *Markets and States in Tropical Africa: The Political Bases of Agricultural Policies,* (Berkeley: University of California Press, 1981); Díaz Cayeros, *Desarrollo Económico e Inequidad Regional.*

13. Leonardo Avritzer, *Democracy and the Public Space in Latin America* (Princeton, N.J.: Princeton University Press, 2002); Naomi Chazan, "Engaging the State"; and Douglas A. Chalmers, Scott B. Martin, and Kerianne Piester, "Associative Networks: New Structures of Representation for the Popular Sectors," in *The New Politics of Inequality in Latin America: Rethinking Participation and Representation,* edited by Carlos Vilas Chalmers et al., 543–82 (New York: Oxford University Press, 1997).

14. There is some reason to believe that international institutions may have influenced sectoral decentralization programs, however. Kurt Weyland proposes a model for policy learning sectoral reform that combines the influence of recommendations by international financial institutions and the needs of policymakers in particular countries, which is similar to the findings of the studies in this volume. Weyland, Introduction to *Learning from Foreign Models in Latin American Policy Reform,* edited by Weyland (Washington, D.C.: Woodrow Wilson Center Press; Baltimore: Johns Hopkins University Press, 2004).

15. Cf. Manor, *Political Economy,* 36–37; and Anwar Shah and Theresa Thompson, "Implementing Decentralized Local Governance: A Treacherous Road with Potholes, Detours, and Road Closures" (Washington, D.C.: World Bank, 2002), 3–4.

16. Angeles and Magno, Chapter 8; and Kent Eaton, "Political Obstacles to Decentralization: Evidence from Argentina and the Philippines," *Development and Change* 32 (2001): 101–27.

17. Steven Friedman and Caroline Kihato, Chapter 6.

18. Serrano, Chapter 4; and Gary Bland, "Enclaves and Elections: The Decision to Decentralize in Chile," in *Decentralization and Democracy in Latin America,* edited by Alfred P. Montero and David J. Samuels (South Bend, Ind.: University of Notre Dame Press, forthcoming).

19. Mizrahi, Chapter 2; Joseph S. Tulchin and Andrew D. Selee, Introduction to *Mexico's Politics and Society in Transition,* edited by Tulchin and Selee, 5–28 (Boulder, Colo.: Lynne Rienner, 2003).

20. It should be noted, however, that regional governments are of relatively recent creation in Chile, whereas they have deeper historical roots in the other countries in this study.

21. Similarly, Manor observes that civil society actors were rarely involved in the initial decisions to negotiate but often became involved at later stages after subnational governments had been strengthened. *Political Economy of Decentralization,* 29–32.

22. Jennie Litvack, Junaid Ahmand, and Richard Bird, *Rethinking Decentralization in Developing Countries,* World Bank Sector Studies Series, Poverty Reduction and Economic Management (Washington, D.C.: World Bank, 1998), 8.

23. Dennis Rondinelli, "Government Decentralization in Comparative Perspective:

Theory and Practice in Developing Countries," *International Review of Administrative Science* 47, no. 2 (1981): 133–45.

24. Richard Stren, Alain Delcamp, Christopher Gore, Heinrich Hoffschulte, and Om Prakash Mathur, "Decentralization in Global Perspective: A Review of Twenty-eight Country Experiences" (Report prepared for UN-Habitat, Nairobi, Kenya, October 2002). We are grateful to Richard Stren for sharing this with us.

25. Bootes Esden, "Indonesia: Rising above Challenges," in *Decentralization and Power Shift: The Imperative of Good Governance (A Sourcebook on Decentralization Experiences in Asia),* Vol. 1, edited by Alex B. Brillantes, Jr., and Nora G. Cuachon (Manila: Asian Resource Center on Decentralization, 2002).

26. The most recent Indonesian decentralization process began in 2001, so it is as yet too early to evaluate fully its implementation, but it is by far the most extensive decentralization process on paper of the six countries discussed in this volume.

27. Siyarif Hidayat and Hans Antlöv (chapter 9) make this point for Indonesia's 1974 deconcentration reforms.

28. See Chapters 9 by Hidayat and Antlöv, 2 by Mizrahi, and 8 by Angeles and Magno. For Mexico, cf. Peter M. Ward and Victoria E. Rodríguez, with Enrique Cabrero Mendoza, *New Federalism and State Government in Mexico,* U.S.–Mexican Policy Report No. 9 (Austin: Lyndon B. Johnson School of Public Affairs, University of Texas at Austin, 1999), especially p. 102. There is some evidence that this has improved in recent years, although it continues to be a problem. John Scott, Decentralization, Focalización y Pobreza en México," in *Las Políticas Sociales de México al Fin del Milenio: Descentralización, Diseño y Gestión,* edited by Rolando Cordera and Alicia Ziccardi, 481–91 (Mexico City: Miguel Angel Porrúa, 2000).

29. Martin Ravallion, "Poverty Alleviation through Regional Targeting: A Case Study for Indonesia," *The Economics of Rural Organization: Theory, Practice, and Policy,* edited by Karla Hoff, Avishay Braveman, and Joseph E. Stiglitz (New York: Oxford University Press, 1993).

30. Jonathan Fox, "The Difficult Transition from Clientelism to Citizenship: Lessons from Mexico," *World Politics* 46, no. 2 (January 1994): 151–84.

31. Robert Dahl defines *polyarchy* as a regime with free and fair elections, elected officials, inclusive suffrage, the right to run for office, freedom of expression, alternative information sources, and associational autonomy. Dahl, *Democracy and Its Critics* (New Haven, Conn.: Yale University Press, 1989).

32. See also Proserpina Domingo Tapales, Jocelyn C. Cuaresma, and Wilhelmina L. Cabo, eds., *Local Government in the Philippines: A Book of Readings,* 2 vols. (Manila: Center for Local and Regional Governance and the University of the Philippines, 1998).

33. Additional experiences in innovative participatory approaches in municipal governance in Mexico have been documented in Enrique Cabrero, *La Nueva Gestión Municipal en México: Análisis de Experiencias Innovadoras en Gobiernos Locales* (Mexico City: Miguel Angel Porrúa, 1996); and Enrique Cabrero, ed., *Innovación en Gobiernos Locales: Un Panorama de Experiencias Municipales en México* (Mexico City: Centro de Investigación y Docencia Económicas, 2002), especially part three on innovations in democratic governance.

34. On deliberative democracy, see Amartya Sen, *Development as Freedom* (New York: Alfred P. Knopf, 1999), 153–54; Archon Fung and Erik Olin Wright, "Deepening Democracy: Innovations in Empowered Participatory Governance," *Politics & Society*

29, no. 1 (March 2001): 5–42; James Bohman and William Rehg, eds., *Deliberative Democracy: Essays on Reason and Politics* (Cambridge, Mass.: MIT Press, 1997); and David Crocker, "Participatory Development: The Capabilities Approach and Deliberative Democracy" (paper presented at workshop "Deliberative Democracy: Principles and Cases," University of Maryland, 13–14 May 2003).

35. See Serrano (Chapter 4) for Chile, and for Mexico, Mauricio Merino, "Descentralización, Democracia y Participación Ciudadana en Gobiernos Locales" (comments presented at Centro de Investigación y Docencia Económicas/Woodrow Wilson International Center for Scholars Conference on Decentralization, Democracy, and Regional Development, Mexico City, 20 May 2002.

36. Arun Agrawal and Jesse Ribot, "Accountability in Decentralization," *Journal of Developing Areas* 33 (Summer 1999): 473–502. Cf. Steven Friedman, "Democracy, Inequality, and the Reconstruction of Politics," in *Democratic Governance and Social Inequality,* edited by Joseph S. Tulchin, 13–40 (Boulder, Colo.: Lynne Rienner, 2002).

37. Cf. Litvack, Ahmand, and Bird, *Rethinking Decentralization in Developing Countries,* 26.

38. Cf. Richard Snyder, "After the State Withdraws: Neoliberalism and Subnational Authoritarian Regimes in Mexico," in *Subnational Politics and Democratization in Mexico,* edited by Wayne A. Cornelius, Todd A. Eisenstadt, and Jane Hindley (La Jolla: Center for U.S.–Mexican Studies, University of California–San Diego, 1999).

39. Mamdani, *Citizen and Subject;* Hagopian, "Traditional Power Structures and Democratic Governance in Latin America."

40. James Holston and Teresa Caldeira, "Democracy, Law, and Violence: Disjunctures of Brazilian Citizenship," in *Fault Lines of Democracy in Post-Transition Latin America,* edited by Felipe Aguero, Felipe and Jeffrey Stark, 263–98 (Boulder, Colo.: Lynne Rienner, 1998); and José Murilo de Carvalho, *Desarrollo de la Ciudadania en el Brasil* (Mexico City: Fondo de Cultura Económica, 1995).

41. Cf. Jonathan Fox and John Gershman, "The World Bank and Social Capital: Lessons from Ten Rural Development Projects in the Philippines and Mexico," *Policy Sciences* 33, nos. 3–4 (2000): 399–419.

42. Robert Putnam, *Making Democracy Work* (Princeton, N.J.: Princeton University Press, 1993); definition on p. 167.

43. Ariel C. Armony, *The Dubious Link: Civic Engagement and Democratization* (Stanford, Calif.: Stanford University Press, forthcoming); John A. Booth and Patricia Bayer Richard, "Social Capital and Electoral Participation: Early Post-Revolutionary Nicaragua in Comparative Context" (paper presented at the 2001 meeting of the Latin American Studies Association, Washington, D.C., 6–8 September 2001); Michael W. Foley, "Laying the Groundwork: The Struggle for Civil Society in El Salvador," *Journal of Interamerican Studies and World Affairs* 38, no. 1 (Spring 1996): 67–104; Michael W. Foley and Bob Edwards, "The Paradox of Civil Society," *Journal of Democracy* (July 1996): 38–52.

44. Shue and Kohli, "State Power and Social Forces."

45. Jonathan Fox, "How Does Civil Society Thicken? The Political Construction of Social Capital in Rural Mexico," *World Development* 24, no. 6 (June 1996): 1089–103; John Durston, "Building Social Capital in Rural Communities (Where It Doesn't Exist)" (paper presented at the 1998 meeting of the Latin American Studies Association, Chicago, 24–26 September 1998).

46. Enrique Cabrero, "Decentralización y Desarrollo Local: Procesos Paralelos o Convergentes?" (paper presented at Centro de Investigación y Docencia Económicas/ Woodrow Wilson International Center for Scholars conference, Decentralization, Democracia y Desarrollo Regional, Mexico City, 21 May 2002).

47. Jonathan Fox, "La Relación Reciproca entre la Participación Ciudadana y la Rendición de Cuentas: La Experiencia de los Fondos Municipales en el México Rural," *Política y Gobierno* 9, no. 2 (2002).

48. Giles Mohan and Kristian Stokke, "Participatory Development and Empowerment: The Dangers of Localism," *Third World Quarterly* 21, no. 2 (2001): 247–68.

49. Shah, "Balance, Accountability, and Responsiveness," 31; and Litvack, Ahmand, and Bird, *Rethinking Decentralization,* 23–24.

50. Stren, "The Newest Decentralization"; Selee, "Decentralization and Democratic Governance."

51. Aprodicio Laquian, "Urban Governance: Some Lessons Learned" (paper presented at the Working Group Meeting of the Comparative Urban Studies Project, Woodrow Wilson International Center for Scholars, Washington, D.C., 10–11 December 2001); Richard Stren, Introduction to *Urban Governance Around the World,* by Blair A. Ruble, Richard E. Stren, Joseph S. Tulchin, and Diana H. Varat, 1–12 (Washington, D.C.: Woodrow Wilson International Center for Scholars, 2001); Elena M. Panganiban, "Metropolitanization within a Decentralized System: The Philippines Dilemma," in *Local Government in the Philippines,* Vol. 1, edited by Proserpina Domingo Tapales, Jocelyn C. Cuaresma, and Wilhelmina L. Cabo (Manila: Center for Local and Regional Governance and the University of the Philippines, 1998).

Selected Bibliographies:
General and Regional

General Bibliography

Armony, Ariel C. *The Dubious Link: Civic Engagement and Democratization.* Stanford, Calif.: Stanford University Press. Forthcoming.

Avritzer, Leonardo. "Democratization and Changes in the Pattern of Association." *Journal of Interamerican Studies and World Affairs* 42 (Fall 2000): 59–76.

Bohman, James, and William Rehg, eds., *Deliberative Democracy: Essays on Reason and Politics.* Cambridge, Mass.: MIT Press, 1997.

Burki, Shahid J., and William Dillinger. *Beyond the Center: Decentralizing the State.* Washington, D.C.: World Bank, 1999.

Burki, Shahid J., and Guillermo Perry. *Beyond the Washington Consensus: Institutions Matter.* Washington, D.C.: World Bank, 1998.

Dahl, Robert. *Who Governs: Democracy and Power in an American City.* New Haven, Conn.: Yale University Press, 1961.

———. *Democracy and Its Critics.* New Haven, Conn.: Yale University Press, 1989.

Durston, John. "Building Social Capital in Rural Communities (Where It Doesn't Exist)." Paper presented at the Latin American Studies Association conference, Chicago, 24–26 September 1998.

Eaton, Kent. "Political Obstacles to Decentralization: Evidence from Argentina and the Philippines." *Development and Change* 32 (2001): 101–27.

321

————. "Politics Beyond the Capital: The Design of Subnational Institutions in South America." Princeton, N.J.: Princeton University Press, n.d.

Evans, P. *Embedded Autonomy: States and Industrial Transformation.* Princeton, N.J.: Princeton University Press, 1995.

Fox, Jonathan. "The Difficult Transition from Clientelism to Citizenship: Lessons from Mexico." *World Politics* 46, no. 2 (January 1994): 151–84.

————. "How Does Civil Society Thicken? The Political Construction of Social Capital in Rural Mexico." *World Development* 24, no. 6 (June 1996): 1089–103.

Fox, Jonathan, and John Gershman. "The World Bank and Social Capital: Lessons from Ten Rural Development Projects in the Philippines and Mexico." *Policy Sciences* 33, nos. 3–4 (2000): 399–419.

Friedman, Steven. "Democracy, Inequality, and the Reconstruction of Politics." In *Democratic Governance and Social Inequality,* edited by Joseph S. Tulchin, 13–40. Boulder, Colo.: Lynne Rienner, 2002.

Fung, Archon, and Erik Olin Wright. "Deepening Democracy: Innovations in Empowered Participatory Governance." *Politics & Society,* 29, no. 1 (March 2001): 5–42.

Gaventa, John, and Camilo Valderrama. "Participation, Citizenship and Local Governance." Background note and report, Strengthening Participation in Local Governance workshop, Institute of Development Studies, University of Sussex, 21–23 June 1999.

Grindle, Merilee S. *Audacious Reforms: Institutional Invention and Democracy in Latin America.* Baltimore: Johns Hopkins University Press, 2000.

Heller, Patrick. "Moving the State: The Politics of Democratic Decentralization in Kerala, South Africa, and Porto Alegre." *Politics and Society* 29, no. 1 (March 2001): 131–63.

Huntington, Samuel. *Political Order in Changing Societies.* New Haven, Conn.: Yale University Press, 1968.

————. *The Third Wave: Democratization in the Late Twentieth Century.* Norman: University of Oklahoma Press, 1991.

Laquian, Aprodicio. "Urban Governance: Some Lessons Learned." Paper presented at the Working Group Meeting of the Comparative Urban Studies Project, Woodrow Wilson International Center for Scholars, Washington, D.C., 10–11 December 2001.

Litvack, Jennie, Junaid Ahmand, and Richard Bird. *Rethinking Decentralization in Developing Countries,* World Bank Sector Studies Series, Poverty Reduction and Economic Management. Washington, D.C.: World Bank, 1998.

Mamdani, Mahmoud. *Citizen and Subject.* Princeton, N.J.: Princeton University Press, 1996.

Manor, James. *The Political Economy of Democratic Decentralization.* Washington, D.C.: World Bank, 1999.

Mansbridge, Jane. *Beyond Adversary Democracy.* New York: Basic Books, 1980.

Migdal, Joel S. *Strong Societies and Weak States: State-Society Relations and State Capabilities in the Third World.* Princeton, N.J.: Princeton University Press, 1988.

Migdal, Joel S., Atul Kohli, and Vivienne Shue, eds. *State Power and Social Forces: Domination and Transformation in the Third World.* Cambridge: Cambridge University Press, 1994.

Mohan, Giles, and Kristian Stokke. "Participatory Development and Empowerment: The Dangers of Localism." *Third World Quarterly* 21, no. 2 (2001): 247–68.

O'Donnell, Guillermo, and Philippe Schmitter. *Transitions from Authoritarian Rule: Tentative Conclusions about Uncertain Democracies.* Baltimore: Johns Hopkins University Press, 1986.

Parekh, B. "The Cultural Peculiarity of Liberal Democracy." *Political Studies* 40 (Special Issue 1990): 160–75.

Putnam, Robert. *Making Democracy Work.* Princeton, N.J.: Princeton University Press, 1993.

Rondinelli, Dennis. "Government Decentralization in Comparative Perspective: Theory and Practice in Developing Countries." *International Review of Administrative Science* 47, no. 2 (1981): 133–45.

———. "What Is Decentralization?" Jennie Litvack and Jessica Seddon, eds. *Decentralization Briefing Notes.* WBI Working Papers. Washington, D.C.: World Bank Institute/Poverty Reduction and Economic Management, n.d.

Rueschemeyer, Dietrich, Evelyne Stephens, and John Stephens. *Capitalist Development and Democracy.* Chicago: University of Chicago Press, 1992.

Schumpeter, Joseph. *Capitalism, Socialism and Democracy.* New York: Harper and Row, 1950.

Sen, Amartya. *Development as Freedom.* New York: Alfred P. Knopf, 1999.

Shah, Anwar. "Balance, Accountability, and Responsiveness: Lessons about Decentralization." Policy Research Working Paper No. 2021. Washington, D.C.: World Bank, December 1998. (A previous version of this paper was presented at the World Bank Conference on Evaluation and Development, Washington, D.C., 1–2 April 1997.)

Shah, Anwar, and Theresa Thompson. "Implementing Decentralized Local Governance: A Treacherous Road with Potholes, Detours, and Road Closures." Washington, D.C.: World Bank, 2002.

Stren, Richard. Introduction to *Urban Governance Around the World,* by Blair A. Ruble, Richard E. Stren, Joseph S. Tulchin, and Diana H. Varat, 1–12. Washington, D.C.: Woodrow Wilson International Center for Scholars, 2001.

———. "The Newest Decentralization: Can We Sustain It?" Toronto: University of Toronto, n.d.

Stren, Richard, Alain Delcamp, Christopher Gore, Heinrich Hoffschulte, and Om Prakash Mathur. "Decentralization in Global Perspective: A Review of Twenty-eight Country Experiences." Report prepared for UN-Habitat, Nairobi, Kenya, October 2002.

Tilly, Charles. "Citizenship, Identity and Social History." In *Citizenship, Identity and Social History, International Review of Social History Supplement 3,* edited by Charles Tilly, 1–17. Cambridge: Press Syndicate of University of Cambridge, 1996.

Walzer, Michael. "The Civil Society Argument." In *Dimensions of Radical Democracy,* edited by Chantal Mouffe, 89–107. London: Verso, 1992.

———. "Rescuing Civil Society." *Dissent* (Winter 1999): 62–67.

Selected Bibliography: Latin America

Aghón, Gabriel, and L. Letelier. "Local Urban Government Financing: A Comparison Between Countries." *Estudios de Economía* 23 (August 1996).

Agüero, Felipe, and Jeffrey Stark, eds. *Fault Lines of Democracy in Post-Transition Latin America.* Miami: North–South Center Press, University of Miami, 1998.

Arocena, José. *El Desarrollo Local: Un Desafío Contemporáneo.* Uruguay: Editorial Nueva Sociedad, 1995.

Artana, D., and R. Lopez Murphy. "Descentralización Fiscal y Aspectos Macroeconómicos: Una Perspectiva Latinoamericana." In *Descentralización Fiscal en América Latina: Nuevos Desafíos y Agenda de Trabajo.* Santiago: Comisión Económica para América Latina e el Caribe/Gesellschaft für Technische Zusammenarbeit, August 1997.

Bailey, John. "Centralism and Political Change in Mexico: The Case of National Solidarity." In *Transforming State-Society Relations in Mexico: The National Solidarity Strategy,* edited by Wayne A. Cornelius, Ann L. Craig, and Jonathan Fox. San Diego: University of California, 1994.

Banco Interamericano de Desarrollo. *Descentralización Fiscal: La Búsqueda de Equidad y Eficiencia.* Informe de Progreso Económico y Social en América Latina. Washington, D.C.: Banco Interamericano de Desarrollo, 1994.

———. *América Latina Tras Una Década de Reformas.* Informe de Progreso Económico y Social en América Latina. Washington, D.C.: Banco Interamericano de Desarrollo, 1997.

Bazdresch, Miguel, ed. *Congreso Gobiernos Locales El Futuro Político de México.* Mexico City: Centro de Investigación y Formación Social/Investigación en Gobiernos Locales Mexicanos, 2000.

Birdsall, Nancy, and Augusto de la Torre, with R. Menezes. *Washington Contentious: Economic Policies for Social Equity in Latin America.* Washington, D.C.: Carnegie Endowment for International Peace and Inter-American Dialogue, 2001.

Bland, Gary. "Enclaves and Elections: The Decision to Decentralize in Chile." In *Decentralization and Democracy in Latin America,* edited by Alfred P. Montero and David J. Samuels. South Bend, Ind.: University of Notre Dame Press. Forthcoming.

Boisier, Sergio. "Palimpesto de las Regiones como Espacios Socialmente Construidos." Santiago: Instituto Latinoamericano y del Caribe de Planificación Económica y Social, 1988.

———. *En Busca del Esquivo Desarrollo Regional: Entre la Caja Negra y el Proyecto Político.* Santiago: Instituto Latinoamericano y del Caribe de Planificación Económica y Social, 1995.

———. *Teorías y Metáforas sobre Desarrollo Territorial.* Santiago: United Nations/ Comisión Económica para América Latina e el Caribe, 1999.

Borges Mendez, R., and V. Vergara. "The Participation–Accountability Nexus and the Decentralization in Latin America." Paper presented at Decentralization and Accountability of the Public Sector, annual World Bank Conference on Development in Latin America and the Caribbean, Valdivia, Chile, 21–23 June 1999.

Borja, Jordi. "Dimensiones Teóricas, Problemas y Perspectivas de la Descentralización del Estado." In *Descentralización del Estado, Movimiento Social y Gestión Local,* edited by Jordi Borja, et al. Santiago: Facultad Latinoamericana de Ciencias Sociales, 1987.

———. *Descentralización y Participación Ciudadana.* Mexico City: Centro de Servicios Municipales "Heriberto Jara," 2000.

Cabrero, Enrique, ed. *La Nueva Gestión Municipal en México: Análisis de Experiencias Innovadoras en Gobiernos Locales.* Mexico City: Miguel Angel Porrúa, 1996.

———, ed. *Las Políticas Descentralizadoras en México (1983–1993): Logros y Desencantos.* Mexico City: Miguel Angel Porrúa/Centro de Investigación y Docencia Económicas, 1998.

————, ed. *Innovación en Gobiernos Locales: Un Panorama de Experiencias Municipales en México*. Mexico City: Centro de Investigación y Docencia Económicas, 2002.

Campbell, Tim. *The Quiet Revolution: Decentralization and the Rise of Political Participation in Latin American Cities*. Pittsburgh: University of Pittsburgh Press, 2003.

Chalmers, Douglas A., Scott B. Martin, and Kerianne Piester. "Associative Networks: New Structures of Representation for the Popular Sectors." In *The New Politics of Inequality in Latin America: Rethinking Participation and Representation*, edited by Chalmers, Carlos Vilas, Katherine Hite, Scott B. Martin, Kerianne Piester, and Monique Segarra, 543–82. New York: Oxford University Press, 1997.

Comisión Económica para América Latina e el Caribe. *Descentralización Fiscal en América Latina: Nuevos Desafíos y Agenda de Trabajo*. Proyecto Regional de Descentralización Fiscal. Comisión Económica para América Latina e el Caribe/ Gesellschaft für Technische Zusammenarbeit, August 1997.

Cordera, Rolando, and Alicia Ziccardi, eds. *Las Políticas Sociales de México a Fin del Milenio. Descentralización, Diseño y Gestión*. Mexico City: Miguel Angel Porrúa/ Universidad Nacional Autónoma de México, 2000.

Cornelius, Wayne A., Todd A. Eisenstadt, and Jane Hindley, eds. *Subnational Politics and Democratization in Mexico*. La Jolla: Center for U.S.–Mexican Studies, University of California-San Diego, 1999.

Curbelo, José Luis. "Economía Política de la Descentralización y Planificación del Desarrollo Regional." *Pensamiento Iberoamericano* 10 (July–December 1986).

Davis, Diane E. "The Power of Distance: Re-Theorizing Social Movements in Latin America." *Theory & Society* 28 (August 1999): 585–638.

Díaz Cayeros, Alberto. *Desarrollo Económico e Inequidad Regional: Hacia un Nuevo Pacto Federal en México*. Mexico City: Miguel Angel Porrúa, 1995.

————. "Diez Mitos Sobre el Federalismo Mexicano." In *La Ciencia Política en México*, Serie Biblioteca Mexicana, edited by Mauricio Merino. Mexico City: FCE-CONACULTA, 1999.

Di Gropello, E. *Descentralización de la Educación en América Latina*. Serie Reforma de Política Pública 57. Santiago: Comisión Económica para América Latina e el Caribe, 1997.

Di Gropello, E., and R. Cominetti, eds. *La Descentralización de la Educación y la Salud: Un Análisis Comparativo de la Experiencia Latinoamericana*. Santiago: Comisión Económica para América Latina e el Caribe, 1998.

Dornbusch, R., and S. Edwards, eds. 1991. *The Macroeconomics of Populism in Latin America*. Chicago: University of Chicago Press, 2000.

Finot, I. *Descentralización del Estado y Participación Ciudadana en América Latina: Un Enfoque Crítico*. Santiago: Comisión Económica para América Latina e el Caribe, 1998 (Documento CEPAL LC/IP/R.206).

Fox, Jonathan. "La Relación Reciproca entre la Participación Ciudadana y la Rendición de Cuentas: La Experiencia de los Fondos Municipales en el México Rural." *Política y Gobierno* 9, no. 2 (2002).

Friedrich, C. J. "Federalism and Opposition." *Government and Opposition* 1, no. 3 (1996): 286–96.

Giugale, Marcelo, and Steven Webb, eds. *Achievements and Challenges of Fiscal Descentralizations: Lessons from Mexico*. Washington, D.C.: World Bank, 2000.

Guerrero, Juan Pablo, and Tonatiuh Guillén, eds. *Reflexiones en Torno a la Reforma Municipal del Artículo 115.* Mexico City: Miguel Angel Porrúa/Centro de Investigación y Docencia Económicas, 2000.

Guillén, Tonatiuh. *Gobiernos Municipales en México: Entre la Modernización y la Tradición Política.* Tijuana: Colegio de la Frontera Norte/Miguel Angel Porrúa, 1996.

Hagopian, Frances. "Traditional Power Structures and Democratic Governance in Latin America." In *Constructing Democratic Governance: Latin America and the Caribbean in the 1990s,* edited by Jorge I. Dominguez and Abraham F. Lowenthal, 64–86. Baltimore: Johns Hopkins University, 1996.

Hernández Chávez, Alicia. "Federalismo y Gobernabilidad en México." In *Federalismos Latinoamericanos: México, Brasil, Argentina,* edited by Marcello Carmagnani. Mexico City: FCE/El Colegio de México, 1993.

Holston, James, and Teresa Caldeira. "Democracy, Law, and Violence: Disjunctures of Brazilian Citizenship." In *Fault Lines of Democracy in Post-Transition Latin America,* edited by Felipe Aguero, Felipe and Jeffrey Stark, 263–98. Boulder, Colo.: Lynne Rienner, 1998.

Koreniewicz, Roberto, and William Smith. "Poverty, Inequality, and Growth in Latin America: Searching for the High Road to Globalization." *Latin American Research Review* 35, no. 3 (2000): 7–54.

Larranaga, O. "Descentralización y Equidad: El Caso de los Servicios Sociales en Chile." *Cuadernos de Economía* 33, no. 100 (December 1996).

———. "Chile: A Hybrid Approach." In *The Public–Private Mix in Social Services: Health Care and Education in Chile, Costa Rica, and Venezuela,* edited by Elaine Zuckerman and Emanuel de Kadt. Washington, D.C.: Inter-American Development Bank, 1997.

Lira, Luís, and Fernando Marinovic. *Estructuras Participativas y Descentralización: El Caso de los Consejos Regionales en Chile.* Santiago: Comisión Económica para América Latina e el Caribe-Instituto Latinoamericano y del Caribe de Planificación Económica y Social, 1999.

Lustig, Nora. *La Superación de la Pobreza: Diálogos Nacionales.* Washington, D.C.: Banco Interamericano de Desarrollo, 1999.

Martelli, Giorgio, and Esteban Valenzuela. *Propuestas de Reformas a los Gobiernos Regionales para su Fortalecimiento y Democratización.* Santiago: Fundación Friedrich Ebert, 1999.

Marván, Ignacio. "Reflexiones sobre Federalismo y Sistema Político en México." *Política y Gobierno* 1 (1997).

de Mattos, Carlos. "La Descentralización: ¿Una Nueva Panacea para Enfrentar el Desarrollo Local?" *Revista Economía y Sociedad* 3 (March 1990): 165–78.

Mejía Lira, José. "La Participación Ciudadana en la Modernización y Gestión de los Municipios." In *Gaceta Mexicana de Administración Pública Estatal y Municipal,* vols. 45–47. Mexico City: Instituto Nacional de Administración Pública, 1994.

Merino, Mauricio. *Fuera del Centro.* Veracruz, Mexico: Universidad Veracruzana, 1992.

———, ed. *En Busca de la Democracia Municipal: La Participación Ciudadana en el Gobierno Local Mexicano.* Mexico City: El Colegio de México, 1994.

Molinar, Juan, and Jeffrey A. Weldon. "Electoral Determinants and Consequences of National Solidarity." In *Transforming State–Society Relations in Mexico: The National Solidarity Strategy,* edited by Wayne A. Cornelius, Ann L. Craig, and Jonathan

Fox, 123–41. La Jolla: Center for U.S.–Mexican Studies, University of California–San Diego, 1994.

Montero, Alfred P., and David J. Samuels, eds., *Decentralization and Democracy in Latin America.* Notre Dame, Ind.: University of Notre Dame Press, 2004.

Oxhorn, Philip. *Organizing Civil Society: The Popular Sectors and the Struggle for Democracy in Chile.* University Park: Pennsylvania State University Press, 1995.

———. *When Democracy Isn't All That Democratic: Social Exclusion and the Limits of the Public Sphere in Latin America.* North–South Agenda Paper 44. Coral Gables, Fla.: North–South Center, University of Miami, April 2001.

———. "Social Inequality, Civil Society and the Limits of Citizenship in Latin America." In *The Politics of Injustice in Latin America,* edited by Susan Eckstein and Timothy Wickham-Crowley. Berkeley: University of California Press. Forthcoming.

Oxhorn, Philip, and Graciela Ducatenzeiler, eds. *What Kind of Market? What Kind of Democracy? Latin America in the Age of Neoliberalism.* University Park: Pennsylvania State University Press, 1998.

Oxhorn, Philip, and Pamela K. Starr, eds. *Markets and Democracy in Latin America: Conflict or Convergence?* Boulder, Colo.: Lynne Rienner, 1999.

Pastor, Manuel, and Carol Wise. "From Poster Child to Basket Case." *Foreign Affairs* 80, no. 6 (November–December 2001): 61–72.

Raczynski, Dagmar, and Claudia Serrano, eds. *Descentralización: Nudos Críticos.* Santiago: Corporación de Investigaciones Económicas para Latinoamérica, 2001.

Ramírez, Juan Manuel. "Ciudadanía, Territorio y Poder Local." *Ciudades* 39 (July–September 1998).

Rivera, Liliana. "Organización y Participación Social en los Gobiernos Locales." *Ciudades* 39 (July–September 1998).

Roberts, Kenneth. "Beyond Romanticism: Social Movements and the Study of Political Change in Latin America." *Latin American Research Review* 32, no. 2 (1997): 137–51.

Rodríguez, Victoria. *Decentralization in México: From Reforma Municipal to Solidaridad to Nuevo Federalismo.* Boulder, Colo.: Westview Press, 1997.

Serrano, Claudia. "Gobierno Regional e Inversión Pública Descentralizada." *Colección de Estudios CIEPLAN* 42 (June 1996).

———. "Inversión Pública y Gestión Regional, Nudos Críticos." In *Descentralización: Nudos Críticos,* edited by Raczynski, Dagmar and Claudia Serrano. Santiago: Corporación de Investigaciones Económicas para Latinoamérica, 2001.

Serrano, Claudia, and Jorge Rodriguez. "Cómo Va el Proceso de Descentralización del Estado en Chile." In *Construyendo Opciones. Propuestas Económicas y Sociales para el Cambio de Siglo,* edited by R. Cortázar and J. Vial. Santiago: Corporación de Investigaciones Económicas para Latinoamérica/Editorial Dolmen, 1998.

Spahn, P. B. "El Gobierno Descentralizado y el Control Macroeconómico." *Descentralización Fiscal en América Latina: Nuevos Desafíos y Agenda de Trabajo. Proyecto Regional de Descentralización Fiscal.* Santiago: Comisión Económica para América Latina e el Caribe/Gesellschaft für Technische Zusammenarbeit, 1997.

Tulchin, Joseph S., and Andrew D. Selee, eds. *Mexico's Politics and Society in Transition.* Boulder, Colo.: Lynne Rienner, 2002.

Valenzuela, Esteban, and G. Martelli. "Regionalismo en Chile: La Reforma Pendiente para el Desarrollo." Santiago: Fundación F. Ebert, 2000.

Véliz, Claudio. *The Centralist Tradition of Latin America.* Princeton, N.J.: Princeton University Press, 1980.

Verdesoto, Luis. *El Control Social de la Gestión Pública: Lineamientos de una Política de Participación Social.* Quito, Ecuador: Ediciones Abya-Yala, 2000.

Von Haldenwang, Christian. "Hacia un Concepto Politológico de la Descentralización del Estado en América Latina." *Revista EURE* 16, no. 50 (1990): 61–77.

Ward, Peter M., and Victoria E. Rodríguez, with Enrique Cabrero Mendoza. *New Federalism and State Government in Mexico.* U.S.–Mexican Policy Report no. 9. Austin: Lyndon B. Johnson School of Public Affairs, University of Texas at Austin, 1999.

Weisner, Eduardo. *Descentralización Fiscal: La Búsqueda de Equidad y Eficiencia.* Informe de Progreso Económico y Social en América Latina. Washington, D.C.: Inter-American Development Bank, 1994.

Weyland, Kurt. Introduction to *Learning from Foreign Models in Latin American Policy Reform,* edited by Weyland. Washington, D.C.: Woodrow Wilson Center Press and Johns Hopkins University Press. 2004.

Williamson, John. "The Progress of Policy Reform in Latin America." In *Latin American Adjustment: How Much Has Happened?* edited by J. Williamson. Washington, D.C.: Institute for International Economics, 1990.

World Bank. World Bank Decentralization Database. Available at: www1.worldbank. org/publicsector/decentralization.

Ziccardi, Alicia, ed. *La Tarea de Gobernar: Gobiernos Locales y Demandas Ciudadanas.* Mexico City: Instituto de Investigaciones Sociales/Universidad Nacional Autónoma de México/Miguel Angel Porrúa, 1995.

Selected Bibliography: Africa

Agrawal, Arun, and Jesse Ribot. "Accountability in Decentralization." *Journal of Developing Areas* 33 (Summer 1999): 473–502.

Bates, Robert H. *Markets and States in Tropical Africa: The Political Bases of Agricultural Policies.* Berkeley: University of California Press, 1981.

Beukes, M. "Governing the Regions: Or Regional (and Local) Government in Terms of the Constitution of the Republic of South Africa." [Act 200 of 1993] *South African Public Law* 9, no. 2 (1994): 393.

Cameron, Robert. *The Democratisation of South African Local Government: A Tale of Three Cities.* Pretoria: J. L. van Schaik, 1999.

Chazan, Naomi. "Associational Life in Sub-Saharan Africa." In *State Power and Social Forces: Domination and Transformation in the Third World,* edited by Joel S. Migdal, Atul Kohli, and Vivienne Shue, 255–89. Cambridge: Cambridge University Press, 1994.

Chipkin, Ivor, and Paul Thulare. *The Limits of Governance: Prospects for Local Government after the Katorus War.* Johannesburg: Centre for Policy Studies, 1997.

Cloete, Fanie. *Local Government Transformation in South Africa.* Pretoria: Van Schaik, 1995.

Dillinger, W. "Decentralization, Politics and Public Services." In *Economic Notes,* no. 2. Washington, D.C.: World Bank, Country Department I, Latin American Region, 1995.

Erasmus, G. "The New Constitutional Dispensation: What Type of System?" *Politikon* 21, no. 1 (1994).

Friedman, Steven. "Agreeing to Differ: African Democracy, Its Obstacles and Prospects." *Social Research* 66,no. 3 (Fall 1999): 285–58.

Friedman, Steven. "Power to the Provinces." *Siyaya!* (Cape Town) no. 4 (Autumn 1999): 44–46.

Friedman, Steven, and Richard Humphries, eds. *Federalism and Its Foes.* Proceedings, Institute for Multi-Party Democracy/Centre for Policy Studies workshop, The Politics and Economics of Federalism: A South African Debate, August 1992. Johannesburg: Centre for Policy Studies, May 1993.

Gotz, Graeme. *The Limits of Community: the Dynamics of Rural Water Provision.* Johannesburg: Centre for Policy Studies, 1997.

Heymans, Chris. *Local Government Transition and Beyond: Observations and Suggestions.* Paper 21. Halfway House: Development Bank of Southern Africa, Corporate Affairs Division, March 1994.

Heymans, Chris, and Gerhard Totemeyer, eds. *Government by the People: The Politics of Local Government in South Africa.* Cape Town: Juta, 1988.

Humphries, Richard, Thabo Rapoo, and Steven Friedman. "The Shape of the Country: Negotiating Regional Government." In *The Small Miracle: South Africa's Negotiated Settlement,* edited by Steven Friedman and Doreen Atkinson, 148–81. Johannesburg: Ravan Press, 1995.

Institute for Democracy in South Africa (IDASA). *Public Evaluations of and Demands on Local Government.* Cape Town: IDASA, February 1998.

Ismail, Nazeem, and J. J. Mphaisha. *The Final Constitution of South Africa: Local Government Provisions and Their Implications.* Johannesburg: Konrad-Adenauer-Stiftung, 1997.

Kihato, Caroline, and Rapoo Thabo. *An Independent Voice? A Survey of Civil Society Organisations in South Africa, Their Funding, and Their Influence over the Policy Process.* Johannesburg: Centre for Policy Studies, 1999.

Ndegwa, Stephen. "Civil Society and Political Change in Africa: The Case of NGOs in Kenya." *International Journal of Comparative Sociology* 35, nos. 1–2 (1994): 19–36.

———. *Civil Society in Kenya.* Hartford, Conn.: Kumarian Press, 1994.

Olowu, Dele. "The Failure of Current Decentralization Programs in Africa." In *The Failure of the African Centralized State: Institutions and Self-Governance in Africa,* edited by James S. Wunsch and Dele Olowu, 74–99. Boulder, Colo.: Westview Press, 1990.

Oyugi, Walter. "Local Government in Kenya: The Case of Institutional Decline." *Local Government in the Third World: The Experience of Tropical Africa,* edited by Philip Mawhood, 107–40. Chichester, UK: John Wiley, 1983.

———. "Decentralization for Good Governance and Development Concepts and Issues." *Regional Development Dialogue* 21, no. 1 (2000).

Rapoo, Thabo. *Twist in the Tail? The ANC and the Appointment of Provincial Premiers.* Johannesburg: Centre for Policy Studies, 1998.

———. *Concealed Contest: Minmecs and the Provincial Debate.* Policy Brief 18. Johannesburg: Centre for Policy Studies, 1999.

Republic of Kenya. *Bringing Government Closer to the People: The Experience of Decentralization and Local Government Reform in Kenya.* Discussion Paper. Nairobi: Ministry of Local Government, 1999.

Southall, Roger, and G. Wood. "Local Government and the Return to Multipartyism in Kenya." *African Affairs* 95, no. 381 (1996): 501–27.

Swilling, Mark, Richard Humphries, and Khehla Shubane, eds. *Apartheid City in Transition.* Cape Town: Oxford University Press, 1991.

de Villiers, Bertus. *Birth of a Constitution.* Kenwyn: Juta, 1994.

———. *Local-Provincial Intergovernmental Relations: A Comparative Analysis.* Johannesburg: Konrad-Adenauer-Stiftung, 1997.

de Villiers, Riaan, ed. *Comparing Brazil and South Africa: Transitional States in Political and Economic Perspective.* Johannesburg: Center for Policy Studies/Foundation for Global Dialogue/Instituto de Estudos Econômicos, Sociais e Políticos de São Paulo, 1996.

Wanyande, Peter. "Decentralizing the State in Kenya." Paper presented at the African Association of Political Science (Kenya Chapter) conference, Kenya, Nairobi, 6 June 1996.

Wunsch, James. "Refounding the African State and Local Self-Governance: The Neglected Foundation." *Journal of Modern African Studies* 38, 3 (2000): 487–509.

Wunsch, James, and Dele Olowu. "The Failure of the Centralized African State." *The Failure of the Centralized State: Institutions and Self-Governance in Africa,* edited by Wunsch and Olowu, 1–23. Boulder, Colo.: Westview Press, 1990.

Selected Bibliography: Asia

Agra, Alberto C. *Compendium of Decisions, Rulings, Resolutions, and Opinions on Local Autonomy and Local Government.* Manila: Rex Bookstore, 1996.

Angeles, Leonora C. "The Survival of Privilege: Strategies of Political Resilience of Oligarchies in the Philippines, 1946–1992." Ph.D. diss., Queen's University, 1995.

———. "Grassroots Democracy and Community Empowerment: The Political and Policy Requirements of Sustainable Poverty Reduction in Asia." Paper presented at Democracy and Civil Society in Asia: The Emerging Challenges and Opportunities conference sponsored by Institute for Research on Public Policy and Center for the Study of Democracy, Queen's University, Kingston, Canada, 19–21 August 2000.

Angeles, Leonora C., and Penny Gurstein. "Planning for Participatory Capacity Development: The Challenges of Participation and North-South Partnerships in Capacity-Building Projects." *Canadian Journal of Development Studies* 21 (October–December 2000): 447–78.

Antlöv, Hans. *Exemplary Center, Authoritarian Periphery: Rural Leadership and the New Order in Java.* London: Curzon Press, 1995.

———. "The Making of Democratic Local Governance in Indonesia." In *Democracy, Globalization and Decentralization in Southeast Asia,* edited by Francis Loh and Joakim Öjendal. Copenhagen: NIAS Press. Forthcoming.

———. "Village Governance and Local Politics in Indonesia." In *Decentralization and Democracy in Southeast Asia,* edited by Anne Booth and Jonathan Riggs. London: Routledge/Curzon Press. Forthcoming.

Aquino, Belinda. "Political Structures and Processes: An Overview." *Journal of Asian Pacific and World Perspectives* 1, no. 2 (1977): 1–82.

Bird, R., and E.R. Rodriguez. "Decentralization and Poverty Alleviation. International Experience and the Case of the Philippines." *Public Administration and Development* 19, no. 3 (1999): 299–319.

Brillantes, Alex. "Re-democratization and Decentralization in the Philippines: The Increasing Leadership Role of NGOs." *International Review of Administrative Sciences* 60 (1994): 575–86.

———. "The GO-NGO Watch Project: Reexamining Dominant Paradigms of Local Governance." *GO-NGO Watch* (Institute of Strategic and Development Studies, Quezon City) 5 (September 1994).

Brillantes, Alex, and Jorge V. Tigno. "GO-NGO-PO Partnerships in the Philippines and the 1991 Local Government Code: An Anatomy of the Empowerment Process." *GO-NGO Watch* (Institute of Strategic and Development Studies, Quezon City) (September 1993).

Buentjen, Claudia. *Fiscal Decentralization in Indonesia.* Report P4D 1998–11. Jakarta: Gesellschaft für Technische Zusammenarbeit, 1998.

Crook, Richard C., and James Manor. *Democracy and Decentralization in South Asia and West Africa: Participation, Accountability and Performance.* Cambridge: Cambridge University Press, 1998.

Cuaresma, Jocelyn, and Simeon Ilago. *Local Fiscal Administration in the Philippines.* Quezon City: UP Local Government Center and German Foundation for International Development, 1996.

Davey, K. "Central-Local Financial Relations." In *Financing Local Government in Indonesia,* edited by N. Devas. Monographs in International Studies, Southeast Asian Series, no. 84. Athens, Ohio: Ohio University Center for International Studies, 1989.

Esden, Bootes. "Indonesia: Rising above Challenges." In *Decentralization and Power Shift: The Imperative of Good Governance (A Sourcebook on Decentralization Experiences in Asia),* Vol. 1, edited by Alex B. Brillantes, Jr., and Nora G. Cuachon. Manila: Asian Resource Center on Decentralization, 2002.

Friedman, H. J. "Decentralized Development in Asia: Local Political Alternatives." In *Decentralization and Development,* edited by G.S. Cheema and D.A. Rondinelli, 35–57. Beverly Hills, Calif.: Sage, 1983.

Gaerlan, Kristina, ed. *Transitions to Democracy in East and Southeast Asia.* Quezon City: Institute for Popular Democracy, 1999.

Geddes, Mike. "Poverty, Excluded Communities and Local Democracy." In *Transforming Cities: Contested Governance and New Spatial Divisions,* edited by Nick Jewson and Susanne MacGregor, 205–18. London: Routledge, 1997.

Hidayat, Syarif. "Decentralised Politics in a Centralised Political System." Ph.D. diss., Flinders University, 1999.

———. "Decentralisation in Indonesia." Paper presented at Woodrow Wilson International Center for Scholars Workshop on Decentralization, Washington, D.C., 20–21 February 2000.

Hidayat, Syarif, and Carunia Firdausy. *Exploring Indonesian Local State-Elites' Orientation Towards Local Autonomy.* Jakarta: Japan International Cooperation Agency, 2002.

Hirst, Paul. "Associative Democracy: A Comment on David Morgan." *Australian and New Zealand Journal of Sociology* 32, no. 1 (March 1996): 20–26.

Humplick, Frannie, and Azadeh MoiniAraghi. *Decentralized Structures for Providing Roads: A Cross-Country Comparison.* Washington, D.C.: International Bank for Reconstruction and Development, Policy Research Department Environment Infrastructure, and Agriculture Division, 1996.

Legaspi, Perla E., and Eden V. Santiago. "The State of the Devolution Process: The Implementation of the 1991 Local Government Code in Selected LGUs." *Local Government Bulletin* 32, nos. 2–4 (April–December 1997).

Legge, J. D. *Central Authority and Regional Autonomy in Indonesia: A Study in Local Administration 1950–60.* Ithaca, N.Y.: Cornell University Press, 1963.

Manasan, Rosario G. "Fiscal Decentralization: The Case of the Philippines." Paper presented at World Bank course on Decentralization and Intergovernmental Fiscal Reform in East Asia, Bangkok, Thailand, 6–7 June 2002.

Mathur, K. "Administrative Decentralization in Asia." In *Decentralization and Development,* edited by G. S. Cheema and D. A. Rondinelli, 59–76. Beverly Hills, Calif.: Sage, 1983.

Mukarji, Nirmal. "Decentralization Below the State Level: Need for a New System of Governance." *Economic and Political Weekly* 24, no. 9 (March 1989): 467–72.

Osteria, Trinidad. "Implementation of the Local Government Code in the Philippines: Problems and Challenges." In *Social Sector Decentralization: Lessons from the Asian Experience,* edited by Trinidad Osteria. Ottawa: International Development Research Center, 1996.

Paredes, Ruby R., ed. *Philippine Colonial Democracy.* Quezon City: Ateneo de Manila Press, 1989.

Polvorosa, Cesar G., Jr. "The Relevance of the Industrial Decentralization Policies of Japan to the Philippines." *CB Review* 39 (1987): 17–28.

Ravallion, Martin. "Poverty Alleviation through Regional Targeting: A Case Study for Indonesia." In *The Economics of Rural Organization: Theory, Practice, and Policy,* edited by Karla Hoff, Avishay Braveman, and Joseph E. Stiglitz. New York: Oxford University Press, 1993.

Rosenbaum, Allan. "Gouvernance et Decentralisation—Lecons de l'Experience." *Revue Francaise d'Administration Publique* 88 (October–December 1998): 507–16.

Sajo, Tomas A. "Local and Regional Public Management Education in the Context of Decentralization." *Philippine Journal of Public Administration* 34 (1990): 103–203.

Schneider, Hartmut. *Participatory Governance: The Missing Link for Poverty Reduction.* OECD Policy Brief no. 17. Paris: Organisation for Economic Cooperation and Development, 1999.

Sosmena, Gaudioso C. "Local Autonomy and Intergovernmental Relations." *Philippine Journal of Public Administration* 21, no. 3 (July 1987): 231–56.

Tapales, Proserpina Domingo, Jocelyn C. Cuaresma, and Wilhemina L. Cabo, eds. *Local Government in the Philippines: A Book of Readings.* Quezon City: Center for Local and Local Governance and National College of Public Administration and Governance, 1998.

Thomason, Jane A., and Stephen G. Karel. "Integrating National and District Health Planning in a Decentralized Setting." *Evaluation and Program Planning* 17, no. 1 (January–March 1994): 13–18.

Timberman, David G., ed. *The Philippines: New Directions in Domestic Policy and Foreign Relations.* Singapore: Institute of Southeast Asian Studies, 1998.

Turner, Mark, ed. *Central-Local Relations In Asia-Pacific: Convergence or Divergence?* Chippenham, Wiltshire, UK: Anthony Rowe Ltd., 1999.

Valdellon, I. B. "Decentralization of Planning and Financing for Local Development: The Case of the Philippines." *Regional Development Dialogue* 20, no. 2 (1999): 61–73.

Vaughan, J. P., and D. Smith. "The District and Support for Primary Health Care: The Management Experience from Large-Scale Projects." *Public Administration and Development* 6, no. 3 (July–September 1996): 255–66.

Villarin, Tomas. *People Empowerment: A Guide to NGO-PO Partnership with Local Governments.* Quezon City: Kaisahan Foundation, 1996.

Wolters, Wilhelm G. "Rise and Fall of Provincial Elites in the Philippines: Nueva Ecija from the 1880s to the Present Day." *Sojourn* 4, no. 1 (February 1989): 54–74.

Wui, Marlon A., and Ma. Glenda S. Lopez, eds. *State-Civil Society Relations in Policy-Making.* Quezon City: Third World Studies Center, 1997.

Wurfel, David. *Filipino Politics: Development and Decay.* Ithaca, N.Y.: Cornell University Press, 1988.

Contributors

Leonora C. Angeles is assistant professor of women's studies and community and regional planning at the University of British Columbia.

Hans Antlöv is the representative of the Ford Foundation in Jakarta.

María Elena Ducci is a professor at the Instituto de Estudios Urbanos of the Pontífica Universidad Católica de Chile.

Steven Friedman is director of the Centre for Policy Studies in Johannesburg.

Syarif Hidayat is a researcher at the Centre for Economic and Development Studies of the Indonesian Institute of Sciences in Jakarta.

Gilbert M. Khadiagala is associate professor of comparative politics and acting director of the African Studies Program at the Johns Hopkins University's School of Advanced International Studies and serves as consulting director of the Woodrow Wilson Center's Africa Project.

Caroline Kihato is a development consultant and a former research associate at the Centre for Policy Studies in Johannesburg.

Francisco A. Magno is director of the Social Development Research Center at De La Salle University in Manila.

Winnie V. Mitullah is professor at the Institute of Development Studies at the University of Nairobi.

Yemile Mizrahi is a public policy scholar at the Woodrow Wilson Center and former professor of political science at the Centro de Investigación y Docencia Económicas in Mexico City.

Philip Oxhorn is associate professor of political science and associate dean of graduate studies and research at McGill University.

Leticia Santín del Río is a researcher at the Facultad Latinoamericana para las Ciencias Sociales in Mexico City.

Andrew D. Selee is director of the Woodrow Wilson Center's Mexico Institute.

Claudia Serrano is a senior researcher at the Corporación Investigaciones Económicas para Latinoamerica in Santiago.

Joseph S. Tulchin is director of the Latin American Program at the Woodrow Wilson Center and previously taught history at Yale University and the University of North Carolina.

Index

337